RACING & FOOTBALL OUTLOOK

FOOTBALL
Guide 2004-2005

Edited by Sean Gollogly

Contributors: Paul Charlton, Chris Cook, Steve Cook, Alex Deacon, James Goldman, Chris Mann, Mirio Mella, Max Oram, Andy Smith, James Smith, Stuart Carruthers, Nigel Speight, Daniel Vano.

Published in 2004 by Raceform
Outlook Press is an imprint of Raceform Ltd
a wholly owned subsidiary of Trinity Mirror plc

A catalogue record for this book is available from the British Library.

ISBN 1-904317-54-5

Printed in Great Britain by William Clowes Ltd, Beccles, Suffolk

Cover photo: Chelsea's Frank Lampard in action against Spurs' Rohan Ricketts in the Blues' 4-2 win at Stamford Bridge last September

Sponsored by Stan James

RACING & FOOTBALL

Outlook

Contents

Sponsored by Stan James

Sponsored by Stan James

Outlook

Editor's introduction

/EVEN the most casual venturer into the forest of football betting cannot afford to be without the *Racing & Football Outlook*. It's the definitive guide to football betting; no other publication covers the myriad markets that are now available to football punters so well.

Whether your tastes run to Fixed Odds, Spreads, Asian Handicaps, Pools or exchange betting, RFO has all bases covered.

The phenomenal rise of the exchanges has revolutionised betting, not only in racing but also in football, and the *Outlook* is the first publication to have a dedicated trading column, *Match Trader*.

Match Trader true odds quote the optimum back or lay line on a selection of games, allowing direct comparison with the live prices on the exchanges.

We thought last year's annual was good but this edition is the proverbial dogs bo****ks.

Our unbeatable combination of analysis and data makes us, as ever, comprehensive. We give you the run-down on all 92 English clubs as well as the big 12 in Scotland.These pen portraits give you the clubs' unique high low *Outlook* form rating, as well as the all the key stats regarding each outfit. The *Outlook Index* rates each side in England and the Scotland, as well as the four major European Leagues, allowing objective cross-divisional and national league comparisons.

The fixture list has been beefed up and for the first time includes the Conference, and all re-arranged fixtures up to May 2005. Additionally there are six-season head-to-head scores as well as 15-year fixture histories. The stats section has been expanded and an overview of Europe and the non-league has been added.

Whatever your betting motivation, we will give you the necessary information to make it a profitable one.

Euro 2004 was a breath of fresh air. The Otto Rehhagel-inspired Greeks confounded everyone and put the so-called footballing superstars firmly in their place.

The success of that team, who are paid a fraction of their contemporaries, will have left many higher-profile players and coaches shuffling uncomfortably in their boots.

In betting terms, will this be the year of the underdog in the domestic leagues?

In terms of the Premiership the answer is a resounding "no". Only Arsenal, Chelsea and possibly Manchester United are in with a shout of landing the title.

How can Arsene Wenger improve on the Gunners' near-perfect season? There is little chance of the Gunners remaining unbeaten and, with the speculation surrounding the future of Vieira, it could be a tough season at Highbury with Chelsea and United snapping at their heels. In contrast to the Premiership, the Football League is in a parlous state with a frightening number of clubs staring into the financial abyss.

In a competitive sense, the equality of poverty has levelled up the playing field as was seen by the respective triumphs of Norwich, Plymouth and Doncaster last term.

Finally the re-branding of the Football League is a typical piece of media-driven candyfloss. Fans will not be clamouring to get through the turnstile or to bet on the outcome of a game just because of a new name.

What grass roots football needs is a good old bit of wealth redistribution. Football is part of the community. To let it wither and die while a select group of teams attempt to ring-fence their wealth should not be permitted. How much more money has to be stuffed down the throats of the Premiership? Anyone know a Robin Hood?

AUGUST

6 Start of the Bundesliga
7 Start of the Coca-Cola Football League
   Start of Bank Of Scotland Scottish Premier League
   Start of the Bell's Scottish League
   Start of Le Championnat
8 FA Community Shield
   Arsenal v Manchester United
10 CIS Insurance Cup First Round
10 UEFA Champions League Third qualifying round, first-legs
   UEFA Inter Toto Cup Final first-leg
11 UEFA Champions League Third qualifying round, first-legs
12 UEFA Cup Second Qualifying Round first-legs
14 Start of the FA Barclaycard Premier League
23 Carling Cup First Round dates TBC
24 CIS Insurance Cup Second Round
   UEFA Champions League Third qualifying round, second-legs
   UEFA Inter Toto Cup Final second-leg
25 UEFA Champions League Third qualifying round, second-legs
26 UEFA Cup Second Qualifying Round second-legs
27 Super Cup
   Porto v Valencia
28 FA Cup Extra Preliminary Round
31 Bell's Challenge Cup Second Round

SEPTEMBER

4 FA Cup Preliminary Round
   World Cup Qualifiers
   England v Austria
   Northern Ireland v Poland
   Republic of Ireland v Cyprus
   Wales v Azerbaijani
8 World Cup Qualifiers
   England v Poland
   Republic of Ireland v Switzerland
   Scotland v Slovenia
   Wales v Northern Ireland
14 Bell's Challenge Cup Third Round
   UEFA Champions League Group stage, match day one
15 UEFA Champions League Group stage, match day one
18 FA Cup First Round Qualifying
20 Carling Cup Second Round dates TBC
23 LDV Vans Trophy First Round dates TBC
24 CIS Insurance Cup Third Round
28 Bell's Challenge Cup Semi-Final
   UEFA Champions League Group stage, match day two
29 UEFA Champions League Group stage, match day two

OCTOBER

2 FA Cup Second Round Qualifying
9 World Cup Qualifiers
   Northern Ireland v Azerbaijan
   Republic of Ireland v France
   Scotland v Norway

Sponsored by Stan James

Wales v England
13 World Cup Qualifiers
England v Azerbaijan
Northern Ireland v Austria
Republic of Ireland v Faroe Islands
Scotland v Moldova
Wales v Poland
16 FA Cup Third Round Qualifying
19 UEFA Champions League Group stage, match day three
20 UEFA Champions League Group stage, match day three
21 Uefa Cup Group stage, match day one
25 Carling Cup Third Round dates TBC
30 FA Cup Fourth Round Qualifying
31 Bell's Challenge Cup Final

NOVEMBER
1 LDV Vans Trophy Second Round
2 UEFA Champions League Group stage, match day four
3 UEFA Champions League Group stage, match day four
4 CIS Insurance Cup Fourth Round
Uefa Cup Group stage, match day two
8 Carling Cup Fourth Round dates TBC
13 FA Cup First Round
20 Tennent's Scottish Cup First Round
23 UEFA Champions League Group stage, match day five
24 UEFA Champions League Group stage, match day five
25 Uefa Cup Group stage, match day three
29 Carling Cup Quarter-Finals dates TBC
LDV Vans Trophy Area Quarter-Finals dates TBC

DECEMBER
1 Uefa Cup Group stage, match day four
2 Uefa Cup Group stage, match day four
3 Carling Cup Fourth Round
CIS Insurance Cup Fourth Round
4 FA Cup Second Round
7 UEFA Champions League Group stage, match day six
8 UEFA Champions League Group stage, match day six
11 Tennent's Scottish Cup Second Round
15 Uefa Cup Group stage, match day five
16 Uefa Cup Group stage, match day five
22 UEFA Champions League First knockout round first-legs
23 UEFA Champions League First knockout round first-legs

JANUARY
4 FA Cup Third Round
8 Tennent's Scottish Cup Third Round
10 Carling Cup Semi-Final first-leg dates TBC
24 Carling Cup Semi-Final first-second dates TBC
29 FA Cup Fourth Round
LDV Vans Trophy Area Semi-Finals dates TBC

FEBRUARY

1 CIS Insurance Cup Semi-Final
3 CIS Insurance Cup Semi-Final
8 Tennent's Scottish Cup Fourth Round
14 LDV Vans Trophy Area Final first-legs
16 UEFA Cup First knockout round, first-legs
17 UEFA Cup First knockout round, first-legs
19 FA Cup Fifth Round
24 UEFA Cup First knockout round, second-legs
26 Tennent's Scottish Cup Fifth Round
27 Carling Cup Final

MARCH

7 LDV Vans Trophy Area Final second-legs
10 UEFA Cup Second knockout round first-legs
12 FA Cup Sixth Round
17 UEFA Cup Second knockout round second-legs
20 CIS Insurance Cup Final
26 World Cup Qualifiers
   England v Northern Ireland
   Republic of Ireland v Israel
   Scotland v Italy
   Wales v Austria
30 World Cup Qualifiers
   England v Azerbaijan
   Northern Ireland v Poland
   Wales v Austria

APRIL

4 UEFA Cup Quarter-Final first-legs
5 UEFA Champions League Quarter-Final first-legs
6 UEFA Champions League Quarter-Final first-legs
9 Tennent's Scottish Cup Semi-Final
10 LDV Vans Trophy Final
   Tennent's Scottish Cup Semi-Final
12 UEFA Champions League Quarter-Final second-legs
13 UEFA Champions League Quarter-Final second-legs
14 UEFA Cup Quarter-Final second-legs
16 FA Cup Semi-Finals
26 UEFA Champions League Semi-Final first-legs
27 UEFA Champions League Semi-Final first-legs
28 UEFA Cup Semi-Final first-legs

MAY

3 UEFA Champions League Semi-Final second-legs
4 UEFA Champions League Semi-Final second-legs
5 UEFA Cup Semi-Finals second-legs
18 UEFA Cup Final
21 FA Cup Final
25 Champions League Final
28 Coca-Cola League Division Two Play-Off Final
28 Tennent's Scottish Cup Final
29 Coca-Cola League Division One Play-Off Final
30 Coca-Cola League Championship Play-Off Final

Sponsored by Stan James

SCHEDULED LIVE MATCHES

LIVE ON SKY SPORTS

August		Competiton
Sat 7	Leeds United v Derby County	Championship
	Coventry City v Sunderland	Championship
Sun 8	Arsenal v Manchester United	Community Shield
	Stoke City v Wolves	Championship
Mon 9	Watford v QPR	Championship
Tue 10	West Ham v Reading	Championship
Fri 14	Cardiff City v Plymouth	Championship
Sat 14	Tottenham v Liverpool*	Premiership
	Middlesbrough v Newcastle*	Premiership
Sun 15	Everton v Arsenal	Premiership
	Chelsea v Man United	Premiership
Mon 16	Huddersfield v Hartlepool	League Division One
Wed 18	Scotland v Hungary	International
Wed 18	Latvia v Wales	International
Fri 20	Preston v Sheffield Utd	Championship
Sat 21	Southampton v Blackburn*	Premiership
Sun 22	West Brom v Aston Villa	Premiership
	Arsenal v Middlesbrough	Premiership
Mon 23	Rochdale v Wolverhampton Wanderers	Carling Cup
Tues 24	Crystal Palace v Chelsea	Premiership
Wed 25	Newcastle v Norwich	Premiership
Fri 27	Gillingham v QPR	Championship
Sat 28	Blackburn v Man United*	Premiership
	Norwich v Arsenal*	Premiership
Sun 29	Bolton v Liverpool	Premiership
Mon 30	Portsmouth v Fulham	Premiership
	Leicester City v Brighton	Championship
Tue 31	Hull City v Bradford	League Division One
September		
Fri 3	Wycombe v Oxford United	League Division One
Sat 4	Austria v England	World Cup Qualifier
Sat 4	Azerbaijan v Wales	World Cup Qualifier
Sat 4	Republic of Ireland v Cyprus	World Cup Qualifier
Wed 8	Poland v England	World Cup Qualifier
Wed 8	Wales v Northern Ireland	World Cup Qualifier
Wed 8	Scotland v Slovenia	World Cup Qualifier
Wed 8	Switzerland v Republic of Ireland	World Cup Qualifier
Wed 8	Austria v Azerbaijan	World Cup Qualifier
Wed 8	Israel v Cyprus	World Cup Qualifier
Sat 11	Aston Villa v Chelsea*	Premiership
	Portsmouth v Crystal Palace	Premiership
Sun 12	Tottenham v Norwich	Premiership
	Ipswich Town v Millwall	Championship
Mon 13	Charlton v Southampton	Premiership
Sat 18	Arsenal v Bolton*	Premiership
Sun 19	Southampton v Newcastle	Premiership
	Chelsea v Tottenham	Premiership
Mon 20	Man United v Liverpool	Premiership
Fri 24	Leeds Utd v Sunderland	Championship
Sat 25	Middlesbrough v Chelsea*	Premiership
Sun 26	Portsmouth v Everton	Premiership
	Nottm Forest v West Ham	Championship
Mon 27	Charlton v Blackburn	Premiership
October		
Sat 2	Southampton v Man City*	Premiership
	West Brom v Bolton*	Premiership
Sun 3	Chelsea v Liverpool	Premiership
	Coventry City v Ipswich Town	Championship
Mon 4	Crystal Palace v Fulham	Premiership
Sat 9	Scotland v Norway	World Cup Qualifier
Sat 9	Azerbaijan v Northern Ireland	World Cup Qualifier

Sat 9	Austria v Poland	World Cup Qualifier
Wed 13	Azerbaijan v England	World Cup Qualifier
	Republic of Ireland v Faroe Islands	World Cup Qualifier
	Wales v Poland	World Cup Qualifier
Fri 15	Nottm Forest v Wolves	Championship
Sat 16	Birmingham v Man United*	Premiership
Sun 17	Charlton v Newcastle	Premiership
	Gillingham v Sheffield United	Championship
Mon 18	Portsmouth v Tottenham	Premiership
Fri 22	Burnley v Derbu County	Championship
Sat 23	Norwich v Everton*	Premiership
	Liverpool v Charlton	Premiership
Sat 24	Southampton v Birmingham	Premiership
	Man United v Arsenal	Premiership
Fri 29	Crewe v Sheffield Utd	Championship
Sat 30	Birmingham v Crystal Palace*	Premiership
	Blackburn v Liverpool*	Premiership
Sun 31	Bolton v Newcastle	Premiership
	Leeds Utd v Wigan Athletic	Championship

November

Mon 1	Man City v Norwich	Premiership
Fri 5	Millwall v Sunderland	Championship
Sat 6	Aston Villa v Portsmouth*	Premiership
	Crystal Palace v Arsenal	Premiership
Sun 7	Middlesbrough v Bolton	Premiership
	Man United v Man City	Premiership
Sat 13	Tottenham v Arsenal	Premiership
	Birmingham v Everton*	Premiership
Sun 14	West Brom v Middlesbrough	Premiership
	Newcastle v Man United	Premiership
Wed 17	Scotland v Sweden	International
Fri 19	Cardiff City v Preston North End	Championship
Sat 20	Man United v Charlton*	Premiership
	Portsmouth v Man City	Premiership
Sun 21	Blackburn v Birmingham	Premiership
	Sunderland v Ipswich Town	Championship
Mon 22	Aston Villa v Tottenham	Premiership
Sat 27	Fulham v Blackburn*	Premiership
Sun 28	Newcastle v Everton	Premiership
	Liverpool v Arsenal	Premiership

December

Sat 4	Chelsea v Newcastle*	Premiership
	Blackburn v Tottenham	Premiership
Sun 5	Crystal Palace v Charlton	Premiership
Mon 6	Middlesbrough v Man City	Premiership
Fri 10	West Ham v Leeds Utd	Championship
Sat 11	Everton v Liverpool*	Premiership
	Rotherham v Sheffield Utd	Championship
Sun 12	Aston Villa v Birmingham	Premiership
	Arsenal v Chelsea	Premiership
Mon 13	Fulham v Man United	Premiership
Fri 17	Nottm Forest v Leicester City	Championship
Sat 18	Liverpool v Newcastle*	Premiership
Sun 19	Portsmouth v Arsenal	Premiership
	Reading v QPR	Championship
Mon 20	Charlton v Fulham	Premiership
Sun 26	Chelsea v Aston Villa*	Premiership
	Birmingham City v Middlesbrough	Premiership
	West Brom v Liverpool	Premiership
Tue 28	Liverpool v Southampton	Premiership
	Aston Villa v Man United	Premiership
Wed 29	Newcastle v Arsenal	Premiership

Games marked with * Sky Premier Plus (pay-per-view)

Sponsored by Stan James

Lower leagues offer us a profit

AT THIS time of year, that advice focuses on the new. What's changed from last season, and what remains the same?

Will Arsenal and Manchester United remain untouchable or will megabucks Chelsea buy their way to the title under the stewardship of Champions League winner Jose Mourinho?

Does the ever-growing gulf between the 'haves' and the 'have-nots' mean that it's all change in the somewhat murky waters of the lower leagues?

I'll leave others to discuss the relative merits of the Premiership contenders for now and focus on the fortunes of those who have just gained entry to the big league.

Assessing the chances of clubs that have changed divisions is one of the great joys of pre-season punting. Sides that have spent a year lording it over their rivals as big fish in small ponds are suddenly faced with a different challenge.

How they cope with those changing circumstances (and, more pertinently, how we cope) is crucial to a successful punting season.

So, what's in store for Norwich, West Brom and Crystal Palace as they try to make the grade in the top flight?

If common assumption and the bookmakers' prices are to be believed, a world of pain is the answer.

The three promoted clubs occupy the first three berths in the relegation market and a season of toil would appear to be on the cards.

But, while there appears little chance of any of the three sides making a title charge, recent history suggests it's not all doom and gloom for the new boys.

The table alongside summarises the performances of promoted clubs in their first season in a new division.

And it's worth noting that just seven of the 18 clubs to have gained access to the top flight in the last six years have immediately slipped back into what we are now obliged to call the Championship.

Whether any of this year's batch can achieve survival is a judgement call, but several teams that appeared to have no chance have gone on to surprise the layers.

Our three latest promotees have attracted labels that should toll the death bell for small teams taking a stab at the Premiership, labels like "unadventurous" (West Brom), "lacking depth" (Norwich) and "inexperienced" (Crystal Palace).

But these could also have been applied to Charlton (a team that, like the Baggies, refused to splash out following a year-long hiatus in the Nationwide), Bradford (who confounded the critics in 1999/2000, despite a team described by many as cannon fodder) and Ipswich (fifth in 2000/01, despite an almost total lack of top-flight experience).

Anyway, who wants to sit around all year and wait for a 2-5 shot to be relegated when there's better opportunities to be had elsewhere. Coca Cola League Two, to be precise.

It's long been said that there's little to choose between the Conference and the Football League's basement division and the past six seasons have supported that view.

The seven teams promoted from the Conference in that period have had an average finishing position of 8-9 and included last year's champions Doncaster.

That's not reason enough on it's own to lump on Chester and Shrewsbury, but good news for those of us who fancy some short-term profit.

In the course of the last six seasons, layers have consistently underestimated the chances of teams taking their or another stab at the Football League.

As you can see from the profit/loss summary tables alongside, backing such teams blindly over the course of each season would have returned £143.20 profit to £10 level stakes.

Confused layers don't yet seem to have caught on to the fact that these teams usually have no trouble competing at the 'higher' level.

And, as you would expect, this confusion pays greatest dividends at the start of each season. Taking the league to the end of October, with around a third of the season gone, we see a profit/loss figure of £93.80.

There is a commonly-held belief in football circles that newly-promoted teams enjoy a honeymoon period during the opening weeks of the season, gaining results through a combination of adrenaline and the element of surprise, and the results of teams promoted from the Conference suggests that this applies to the punting world too.

Layers, like everyone, need time to adjust each season and the evidence of recent history suggests it is to the unlikely realm of League Two that we should look to make this pay.

Promoted teams post 1998/99

Promoted to	sample	average finishing position	average points	champs	promoted	relegated	top 8	others
Premiership	18	14	41.8	0	n/a	7	2	9
Championship	18	12.5	62.6	0	2	5	7	6
League One	24	15.1	57.2	1	2	6	5	13
League Two	7	8.57	69.3	1	1	0	4	3

profit/loss record *(to level stakes of £1)*

	HW*	HD*	HL*	AW*	AD*	AL*
Premiership	-£2.87	£0.42	-£2.91	-£3.04	-£3.57	-£0.92
Championship	-£0.87	-£3.14	-£3.84	-£3.80	-£0.38	-£3.14
League One	-£2.68	-£0.52	-£0.52	-£1.78	-£0.09	-£2.03
League Two	**£9.20**	-£9.00	-£15.25	**£5.12**	**£0.55**	-£8.97
Overall	**£2.78**	-£12.24	-£22.51	-£3.50	-£3.49	-£15.05

profit/loss record *(level stakes of £1)* **for games prior to October 31**

	HW*	HD*	HL*	AW*	AD*	AL*
Premiership	**£0.13**	-£0.26	-£1.10	**£0.12**	-£0.35	-£0.28
Championship	-£0.19	-£0.07	-£1.98	-£0.31	-£1.31	-£1.07
League One	-£1.23	**£0.23**	-£0.16	**£1.20**	-£0.92	-£0.96
League Two	**£5.38**	-£1.20	-£5.25	**£4.00**	-£1.35	-£3.79
Overall	**£4.09**	-£1.31	-£8.49	**£5.00**	-£3.93	-£6.10

profit/loss summary

	full season			to end of October		
	back	back draw	back opponents	back	back draw	back opponents
Premiership	-£5.91	-£3.15	-£3.83	**£0.25**	-£0.22	-£1.38
Championship	-£4.67	-£3.52	-£6.97	-£0.50	-£1.48	-£3.05
League One	-£4.46	-£0.61	-£2.55	-£0.04	-£0.69	-£1.12
League Two	**£14.32**	-£9.55	-£24.22	**£9.38**	-£2.55	-£9.04
Overall	-£0.72	-£16.83	-£37.57	**£7.09**	-£4.94	-£14.59

*HW - profit/loss to £1 level stakes backing team to win each home game
HD - to draw each home game, and so on

ARSENAL

Nickname: The Gunners
Colours: Red and white
Ground: Highbury
Capacity: 38,500
Tel: 020 7704 4000
www.arsenal.com

THE Gunners face the unenviable task of following up a near perfect season. Whilst their attempt to lift a third consecutive FA Cup was foiled by Man United and European success continues to elude them, it is hard to imagine how Arsenal can match, let alone improve upon, their record breaking romp to the Premiership title.

The single perceived weak link in the squad is goalkeeper Jens Lehmann, who has proved an erratic replacement for David Seaman since joining from Borussia Dortmund last summer. It was on that position that the bulk of the summer transfer talk - at least concerning incoming players - was concentrated. The result was the signing of Celta Vigo cat Manuel Almunia. Otherwise, the talk was of players leaving the club, although it is fringe players such as Wiltord, Stepanovs and Kanu who are on their way.

The challenge for manager Arsene Wenger will be to maintain the momentum. For a week, when Arsenal went out of the FA Cup and Champions League to Man United and Chelsea in quick succession there was talk of a crisis at Highbury and no doubt, when the Gunners do eventually get beaten in the league, there will be a similar overreaction in the press.

With expectations now so high, the Highbury faithful are unlikely to settle for anything less than perfection. If they are to fill the new 60,000 seater stadium at Ashburton Grove, continued success is a prerequisite. With the possible departure of Vieira it promises to be a fascinating - and important - season in north London.

Longest run without loss: 27
Longest run without win: 1
High - low league position: 1-3
High - low Outlook form figure: 67-53
Final Outlook Index figure: 969

Key Stat: *They Gunners have now gone 40 league games unbeaten.*

2003/04 Premiership Stats

	Apps	Gls	YC	RC
J Aladiere	3 (7)	0	1	0
D Bentley	1 (0)	0	0	0
D Bergkamp	21 (7)	4	2	0
S Campbell	35 (0)	1	2	1
G Clichy	7 (5)	0	1	0
A Cole	32 (0)	0	5	1
P Cygan	10 (8)	0	1	0
Edu	13 (17)	2	4	0
T Henry	37 (0)	30	3	0
J Hoyte	0 (1)	0	0	0
N Kanu	3 (7)	1	0	0
M Keown	3 (7)	0	1	0
Lauren	30 (2)	0	5	0
J Lehmann	38 (0)	0	2	0
F Ljungberg	27 (3)	4	2	0
R Parlour	16 (9)	0	7	0
R Pires	33 (3)	14	0	0
J Reyes	7 (6)	2	0	0
G Silva	29 (3)	4	2	0
K Toure	36 (1)	1	4	0
P Vieira	29 (0)	3	9	1
S Wiltord	8 (4)	3	0	0

League Stats
Clean sheets 15
Yellow cards 52 Red cards 3
Players used 22
Leading scorer:
Thierry Henry 38 (30 league)

Outlook forecast: 1st

Your forecast:

ASTON VILLA

Nickname: The Villans
Colours: Claret and blue
Ground: Villa Park
Capacity: 42,584
Tel: 0121 327 2299
www.avfc.co.uk

VILLA reached the semi-finals of the League Cup, missed out on Uefa Cup football only on goal difference however despite the disappointment of no silverware and failing to reach Europe, they can reflect on a decent season.

It was certainly a vast improvement over their 2002-03 campaign where the Villans finished just two places and three points out of the relegation zone thanks to some woeful away form that saw them win just one match away from Villa Park all term. The arrival of David O'Leary in May 2003, saw Villa become a much tougher team on the road.

Whilst O'Leary has gone a long way towards proving his detractors wrong after a solid first season in charge, it is doubtful that he will be able to mastermind much more improvement without a major injection of cash. With chairman Doug Ellis still at the helm that seems unlikely.

Even so, Villa are active in the transfer market, and if the current plight of Leeds is anything to go by, perhaps it is better that O'Leary won't have tens of millions of pounds to spend.

Whilst their resurgence was a surprise, Villa will expect to be in the fight for a European place again. They boast a strong squad, recently bolstered by the arrival of Danish international defender Martin Laursen.

If Darius Vassell can regularly reproduce the best of his explosive England form in a claret and blue shirt, perhaps they are capable of going one better than last time.

Longest run without loss: 7
Longest run without win: 4
High - low league position: 5-18
High - low Outlook form figure: 67-37
Final Outlook Index figure: 894

Key Stat: *Wakey wakey – No Premiership team was off-side more often -159 times.*

2003/04 Premiership Stats

	Apps	Gls	YC	RC
M Allback	7 (8)	1	0	0
Alpay	4 (2)	1	0	0
J-P Angel	33 (0)	16	3	0
G Barry	36 (0)	3	3	1
P Crouch	6 (10)	4	1	0
U De La Cruz	20 (8)	0	2	0
M Delaney	23 (2)	0	4	0
D Dublin	12 (11)	3	1	0
M Hadji	0 (1)	0	0	0
L Hendrie	32 (0)	2	10	0
T Hitzlsperger	22 (10)	3	4	0
R Johnsen	21 (2)	1	3	0
M Kinsella	2 (0)	0	0	0
L Moore	0 (7)	0	1	0
S Moore	2 (6)	1	0	0
G McCann	28 (0)	2	4	1
O Mellberg	33 (0)	1	4	0
S Postma	0 (2)	0	0	0
L Ridgewell	5 (6)	0	0	0
J Samuel	38 (0)	2	6	0
N Solano	10 (0)	0	1	1
T Sorensen	38 (0)	0	1	0
D Vassell	26 (6)	9	0	0
P Whittingham	20 (12)	0	4	0

League Stats
Clean sheets 12
Yellow cards 52 Red cards 3
Players used 24
Leading scorer:
Juan Pablo Angel 23 (16 league)

Figaro's forecast: 6th
Your forecast:

BIRMINGHAM CITY

Nickname: The Blues
Colours: Blue
Ground: St Andrews
Capacity: 30,016
Tel: 0121 772 0101
www.bcfc.com

IT'S testament to how well Birmingham have adapted to life in the top flight that a tenth place finish should have been cause for disappointment at the end of last season.

After surviving their first season in the top flight, following their promotion via the play-offs in 2002, the Blues strengthened their squad with the signings of David Dunn, Mikael Forssell and Matthew Upson.

Last season saw Steve Bruce's men in the hunt for a European place for much of the campaign before going off the boil at towards the tail end.

The arrival of Muzzy Izzet on a free transfer in June, in the face of competition from other clubs, not only shows that Birmingham have established themselves in the Premiership firmament but also that they are an ambitious club.

Some decent results last season, including draws against both Chelsea and Arsenal, further bolster their claims to be considered as part of the establishment.

That is not to say however that survival will not be their first priority. Outside of the top three, there is little to separate most of the teams and it may be necessary for Forssell to repeat last season's excellent form.

His goals might prove the difference in ensuring Blues' survival. The Finn weighed in with 19 goals in all competitions last term - almost four times the total of the next nearest contributors, Bryan Hughes and Clinton Morrison who bagged five apiece. City will be relieved that his loan period at St Andrews has been extended for the coming season.

Longest run without loss: 5
Longest run without win: 8
High - low league position: 4-11
High - low Outlook form figure: 59-32
Final Outlook Index figure: 876

Key Stat: *Going places? Blues spent just one week outside the top ten last term.*

2003/04 Premiership Stats

	Apps	Gls	YC	RC
A Barrowman	0 (1)	0	0	0
I Bennett	4 (2)	0	0	0
D Carter	1 (4)	0	0	0
A Cisse	5 (10)	0	5	0
J Clapham	22 (3)	0	0	0
S Clemence	32 (3)	2	4	0
K Cunningham	36 (0)	0	2	1
P Devlin	0 (2)	0	0	0
C Dugarry	12 (2)	1	4	1
D Dunn	20 (1)	2	2	0
L Figueroa	0 (1)	0	0	0
M Forssell	32 (0)	17	1	0
M Grainger	3 (1)	1	0	0
G Horsfield	2 (1)	0	0	0
B Hughes	17 (9)	3	0	0
S John	7 (18)	4	0	0
D Johnson	31 (4)	1	6	0
J Kenna	14 (3)	2	1	0
J Kirovski	0 (6)	0	0	0
S Lazaridis	25 (5)	2	0	0
C Morrison	19 (13)	4	1	0
D Purse	9 (0)	0	0	1
R Savage	31 (0)	3	12	0
Maik Taylor	34 (0)	0	0	2
Martin Tayor	11 (1)	1	0	0
O Tebily	17 (10)	0	4	0
M Upson	30 (0)	0	2	0

League Stats
Clean sheets 15
Yellow cards 45 Red cards 5
Players used 27
Leading scorer:
Mikael Forssell 19 (17 league)

Outlook forecast: *11th*

Your forecast:

BLACKBURN ROVERS

Nickname: Rovers
Colours: Blue and white
Ground: Ewood Park
Capacity: 31,367
Tel: 08701 113 232
www.rovers.co.uk

ARTE ET LABORE

AFTER a sixth place finish in 2002-03, Rovers were brought back to earth with a bump last season as injuries decimated the squad.

They finished a lowly fifteenth after going out of the Uefa Cup at the first hurdle to Turkish side Genclerbirligi.

It is easy to blame their problems in scoring for their decline. Andrew Cole was top marksman with eleven goals, but with Dwight Yorke not pulling his weight - he netted just four times - and Damien Duff and David Dunn sold to Chelsea and Birmingham respectively, they were lacking firepower.

However Souness did unearth a jewel in the Nationwide. Since arriving from Huddersfield in February, Jonathan Stead has made the transition from Division Three to the Premiership with ease, scoring six times in thirteen appearances including a late winner against Man United.

The arrival of Paul Dickov from Leicester and transfer rumours linking Rovers with seemingly every wide player in Europe suggests that Graeme Souness is looking to boost Rovers anaemic attack.

However, it was also a bad season for the defence as only Leicester, Leeds and Wolves, all of whom were relegated, shipped more league goals than Rovers total of 59 conceded.

In the end they finished comfortably above the relegation places, eleven points clear of Leicester, but they will need to strengthen both attack and defence to be sure of another season in the top flight.

Longest run without loss: 4
Longest run without win: 6
High - low league position: 6-19
High - low Outlook form figure: 60-33
Final Outlook Index figure: 877

Key Stat: *Unpredictable: in three weeks they beat Man Utd after losing to Leeds.*

2003/04 Premiership Stats

	Apps	Gls	YC	RC
L Amoruso	11 (1)	3	3	0
M Andresen	11 (0)	0	3	0
M Babbel	23 (2)	3	2	0
D Baggio	0 (9)	1	1	0
A Cole	27 (7)	11	3	1
N Danns	0 (1)	0	0	0
J Douglas	14 (0)	1	3	0
B Emerton	31 (5)	2	4	0
P Enckelman	2 (0)	0	0	0
B Ferguson	14 (1)	1	3	0
G Flitcroft	29 (2)	3	9	0
B Friedel	36 (0)	1	0	0
P Gallagher	12 (13)	3	2	0
C Grabbi	0 (5)	0	0	0
M Gray	14 (0)	0	1	0
V Gresko	22 (2)	2	6	0
M Jansen	9 (10)	2	0	0
N Johansson	7 (7)	0	0	0
A Mahon	1 (2)	0	0	0
L Neill	30 (2)	2	6	1
S Reid	9 (7)	0	1	1
C Short	19 (0)	1	1	0
J Stead	13 (0)	6	0	0
M Taylor	10 (1)	0	0	0
D Thompson	10 (1)	1	5	0
A Todd	19 (0)	0	4	0
Tugay	30 (6)	2	4	0
D Yorke	15 (8)	4	0	0

League Stats
Clean sheets 8
Yellow cards 61 Red cards 3
Players used 28
Leading scorers:
Andrew Cole 11 (all league)

Outlook forecast: 14th
Your forecast:

BOLTON WANDERERS

Nickname: The Trotters
Colours: Blue and white
Ground: Reebok Stadium
Capacity: 28,723
Tel: 01204 673673
www.bwfc.co.uk

LAST season's eighth place was a great finish for Bolton, a club whose most realistic ambition was simply survival in the top flight.

Long serving boss Sam Allardyce is regularly lauded as one of the best in the business and yet routinely passed over when the bigger jobs become available. At the same time his team, made up as it is of a selection of misfits and ageing stars is regularly derided as a band of mercenaries.

The Trotters bounced back from a 4-0 defeat at Old Trafford on the opening day to finish as a top ten side and even made the League Cup Final, where two Middlesbrough goals in the first seven minutes were enough to end their challenge.

Since winning promotion in 2001, Wanderers have spent much of their Premiership life fighting for survival, finishing sixteenth in 2002 and seventeenth in 2003. But after such a dramatic improvement, on the back of much better away form, expectations will be higher at the Reebok Stadium.

Allardyce has continued his policy of making bargain basement signings with the likes of out-of-contract Michael Bridges joining from Leeds and out-of-favour Aliou Cisse on the way from Birmingham. There was even talk of Rivaldo heading to Lancashire, a move which would have doubled the number of World Cup winners in the Bolton squad at a stroke.

For all the optimism, survival will remain Bolton's priority and a mid-table finish will be regarded as a success.

Longest run without loss: 6
Longest run without win: 7
High - low league position: 7-19
High - low Outlook form figure: 67-35
Final Outlook Index figure: 892
Key Stat: *Yet another strong finish with five straight wins in four weeks.*

2003/04 Premiership Stats

	Apps	Gls	YC	RC
I Ba	0 (9)	0	0	0
A Barness	11 (4)	0	0	0
I Campo	37 (1)	4	9	0
S Charlton	28 (3)	0	1	0
K Davies	38 (0)	9	9	0
Y Djorkaeff	24 (3)	9	1	0
D Facey	0 (1)	0	0	0
P Frandsen	22 (11)	1	5	0
R Gardner	20 (2)	0	5	0
S Giannakopoulos	17 (14)	2	4	0
S Howey	2 (1)	0	2	0
N Hunt	28 (3)	1	6	0
J Jaaskelainen	38 (0)	0	1	0
M Jardel	0 (7)	0	1	0
Javi Moreno	1 (7)	0	0	0
F Laville	5 (0)	0	1	0
G Little	0 (4)	0	0	0
B N'Gotty	32 (1)	3	3	0
K Nolan	37 (0)	9	8	0
J Okocha	33 (2)	0	4	0
J Otsemobor	1 (0)	0	1	0
H Pedersen	19 (14)	7	1	0
E Thome	25 (1)	0	7	0
R Vaz Te	0 (1)	0	0	0

League Stats
Clean sheets 10
Yellow cards 66 Red cards 0
Players used 24
Leading scorer:
Kevin Nolan 12 (9 league)

Outlook forecast: 10th
Your forecast:

CHARLTON ATHLETIC

Nickname: Addicks
Colours: Red and white
Ground: The Valley
Capacity: 26,875
Tel: 020 8333 4000
www.cafc.co.uk

AFTER finishing seventh in the Premiership table and missing out in the Uefa Cup Fair Play League draw, the Addicks will be disappointed that Millwall will be south-east London's only representatives in Europe this season.

Over the past four seasons, they have re-established themselves in the Premiership after spending a year out of the top flight after being relegated on the final day of the 1998/99 campaign. Thanks to prudent management both on and off the pitch, the club did not suffer unduly and have since proved twice that a top ten finish is not beyond them.

After 13 years in the Charlton hotseat, Alan Curbishley finds himself in the unusual position of having some money to spend and was confident enough in the club's future to sign a new deal at the beginning of this year. He is rightly regarded as one of the best managers in the game - he certainly seems tailor made for the Charlton job - and his continued tenure will be a positive factor in their continued survival at the highest level.

Paulo Di Canio will spend another season - perhaps his last in the game - at The Valley and the talk from the Charlton camp is of a top six finish in their centenary season. However, without adding a first class goalscorer to the team that may prove to be over ambitious.

For the past three seasons, Jason Euell has been their only player to score double figures in the league and it will take more than that to make their dreams come true.

Longest run without loss: 5
Longest run without win: 5
High - low league position: 4-14
High - low Outlook form figure: 59-40
Final Outlook Index figure: 876

Key Stat: *Di Canio, re-signed for a year, topped the Premiership assists table.*

2003/04 Premiership Stats

	Apps	Gls	YC	RC
S Bartlett	13 (6)	5	1	0
J Campbell-Ryce	0 (2)	0	0	0
C Cole	8 (13)	4	0	0
P Di Canio	23 (8)	4	1	0
J Euell	24 (7)	10	3	1
M Fish	23 (0)	0	1	1
J Fortune	21 (7)	2	2	0
M Holland	38 (0)	6	0	0
H Hreidarsson	33 (0)	2	3	0
C Jensen	27 (4)	4	1	0
J Johansson	16 (10)	4	0	0
D Kiely	37 (0)	0	1	1
R Kishishev	30 (3)	0	4	0
P Konchesky	17 (4)	0	7	0
K Lisbie	5 (4)	4	0	0
S Parker	20 (0)	2	6	1
C Perry	25 (4)	1	6	0
C Powell	11 (5)	0	1	0
G Rowett	1 (0)	0	0	0
S Royce	1 (0)	0	0	0
G Stuart	23 (5)	3	0	0
M Svensson	1 (2)	0	0	0
J Thomas	0 (1)	0	0	0
L Young	21 (3)	0	5	0

League Stats
Clean sheets 10
Yellow cards 37 Red cards 3
Players used 24
Leading scorer:
Jason Euell 11 (10 league)

Outlook forecast: 8th

Your forecast:

CHELSEA

Nickname: The Blues
Colours: Blue and white
Ground: Stamford Bridge
Capacity: 42,449
Tel: 0870 300 1212
www.chelseafc.co.uk

NEW coach Jose Mourinho has his work cut out for him to improve on Claudio Ranieri's record last season.

Although part of chief executive Peter Kenyon's brief is to establish Chelsea as a global brand so that the Blues become self-sufficient, they are inevitably at the centre of myriad transfer rumours.

Abramovich doesn't seem to be able to restrain himself - it must be difficult for any billionaire with a football team - and perhaps the club's acquisitive nature will prove to be the hardest hurdle for Jose Mourinho to overcome in his bid to win their first title since 1955.

A handful of Porto players look set to follow their former boss to Stamford Bridge and if even a quarter of the other transfer rumours come true, Mourinho will be left with a massive squad to juggle with, even allowing for players leaving the club.

What Mourinho will bring is a proven track record in European competition, Porto won the Uefa Cup and Champions League in successive seasons under his direction, as well as domestic success. Portugal's Superliga is certainly a second tier competition in European terms, but in reality the Premiership is barely more competitive.

Arguably at Chelsea, Mourinho finds himself in a very similar situation to that in which he produced instant results at Porto.

It would be unwise to think that he could not follow suit, especially if injuries make Arsenal's much smaller squad look threadbare and Manchester United endure another annus horribilis.

Longest run without loss: 8
Longest run without win: 4
High - low league position: 1-5
High - low Outlook form figure: 68-44
Final Outlook Index figure: 933
Key Stat: *Lampard was the only player to start all 38 Premiership games.*

2003/04 Premiership Stats

	Apps	Gls	YC	RC
M Ambrosio	8 (0)	0	0	0
C Babayaro	5 (1)	1	0	0
W Bridge	33 (0)	1	0	0
J Cole	18 (17)	1	3	0
H Crespo	13 (6)	10	1	0
C Cudicini	26 (0)	0	0	0
M Desailly	15 (0)	0	0	0
D Duff	17 (6)	5	0	0
W Gallas	23 (6)	0	1	0
Geremi	19 (6)	1	0	1
J Gronkjaer	19 (12)	2	5	0
E Gudjohnsen	17 (9)	6	0	1
J-F Hasselbaink	22 (8)	13	5	0
R Huth	8 (8)	0	6	1
G Johnson	17 (2)	3	3	0
F Lampard	38 (0)	10	3	0
C Makelele	26 (4)	0	2	0
M Melchiot	20 (3)	2	1	0
A Mutu	21 (4)	6	5	0
A Nicolas	1 (1)	0	0	0
F Oliveira	0 (1)	0	0	0
S Parker	7 (4)	1	2	0
E Petit	3 (1)	0	0	0
M Stanic	0 (3)	0	0	0
N Sullivan	4 (0)	0	0	0
J Terry	33 (0)	2	5	0
J Veron	5 (2)	1	0	0

League Stats
Clean sheets 21
Yellow cards 45 Red cards 3
Players used 27
Leading scorer:
Jimmy Floyd Hasselbaink 17 (12 league)

Outlook forecast: 2nd
Your forecast:

CRYSTAL PALACE

Nickname: The Eagles
Colours: Blue and red
Ground: Selhurst Park
Capacity: 26,309
Telephone: 0208 768 6000
www.cpfc.co.uk

ALTHOUGH the Eagles won promotion to the Premiership via the play-offs, they were the form team in Division One in the second half of the season.

When Iain Dowie left Oldham to take over at Selhurst Park last December, Palace were languishing in the nether regions of the division close to the relegation places.

He made an inauspicious start, losing 1-0 at home to Millwall, his first game in charge, and crashing out of the FA Cup to Tottenham shortly afterwards. He soon had the Eagles winning though, and following a sixth place finish their momentum carried them through the play-offs. In the second half of the season with Dowie in charge, Palace won better than half-a-point a game more than before he took over.

Whether he can carry this through to the Premiership is another matter entirely but the presence of Birmingham and Bolton - both recent play-off final winners - in the top ten last time will inspire Palace.

Their biggest worry might be whether or not they can hold on to Dowie, arguably their biggest asset, after what happened with Steve Bruce who left the club to make his reputation at Birmingham in 2001 after just 18 games in charge.

On the pitch, it was a breakthrough season for Andrew Johnson, who netted 27 times in the league. His goals were a vital component of the Eagles promotion push and his transition to life in the top flight will have a significant bearing on their chances of survival. Make no mistake, survival will be their sole ambition.

Longest run without loss: 7
Longest run without win: 5
High - low league position: 1-22
High - low Outlook form figure: 72-38
Final Outlook Index figure: 827

Key Stat: *Palace were in the relegation zone last Xmas. It'll be the same this time!*

2003/04 Division One Stats

	Apps	Gls	YC	RC
C Berthelin	17 (0)	0	0	0
T Black	12 (13)	0	2	1
G Borrowdale	14 (9)	0	3	0
D Butterfield	45 (0)	4	3	0
M Clarke	4 (0)	0	0	0
S Derry	25 (12)	2	9	1
R Edwards	6 (1)	1	1	0
C Fleming	15 (2)	0	3	0
D Freedman	20 (15)	13	1	0
D Granville	21 (0)	3	3	0
J Gray	24 (0)	3	5	1
G Heeroo	0 (1)	0	0	0
M Hudson	14 (0)	0	0	1
M Hughes	34 (0)	3	13	1
A Johnson	40 (2)	27	5	0
M Leigertwood	7 (5)	0	1	0
H Mullins	10 (0)	0	5	0
T Myhre	15 (0)	0	0	0
T Popovic	34 (0)	1	11	0
D Powell	10 (0)	0	0	1
A Riihilahti	24 (7)	0	7	0
W Routledge	32 (12)	6	2	1
N Shipperley	40 (0)	8	6	0
J Smith	13 (2)	0	3	0
T Soares	0 (3)	0	0	0
C Symons	12 (3)	0	1	1
N Vaesen	10 (0)	0	1	0
B Watson	8 (8)	1	3	0

League Stats
Clean sheets 14
Yellow cards 79 Red cards 7
Players used 28
Leading scorer:
Andrew Johnson 31 (27 league)

Outlook forecast: 17th
Your forecast:

EVERTON

Nickname: The Toffees
Colours: Blue and white
Ground: Goodison Park
Capacity: 40,260
Tel: 0151 330 2200
www.evertonfc.com

THE good news for Everton is that they were not a one-man team last term. Wayne Rooney certainly didn't hit the dizzy heights of his breakthrough year and came nowhere near the form he produced for England in Portugal. The bad news for Everton is that he was still their top scorer with nine goals.

It was a bitterly disappointing season for the Goodison Park faithful after 2002/03 had promised so much. Under David Moyes, the Toffees had become one of the most consistent and hard to beat teams in the division. Expectation was high last season but, largely as a result of woeful away form - their only away win all season was against Portsmouth in December - Everton found themselves embroiled in a relegation battle instead.

The signs are there that all is not well within the camp. Rooney's fractious relationship with Moyes is well documented and Everton are surely resigned to losing him sooner or later despite his lifelong affinity with the club. Indeed, financially, Rooney could serve Everton better by going rather than staying.

Influential midfielder Thomas Gravesen is rumoured to want out of the club and Tomasz Radzinski - the club's most consistent striker - has had a transfer request turned down. Moyes is looking for new players, but inevitably these are competent rather than dazzling.

Everton are the longest serving club in the top flight, but have flirted with danger in recent years. Unless Moyes can lift them another dogfight looks inevitable.

Longest run without loss: 5
Longest run without win: 9
High - low league position: 8-18
High - low Outlook form figure: 58-42
Final Outlook Index figure: 855

Key Stat: *Troubled times? They won just one of their last ten games.*

2003/04 Premiership Stats

	Apps	Gls	YC	RC
K Campbell	8 (9)	1	1	0
L Carsley	15 (6)	1	3	0
N Chadwick	1 (2)	0	0	0
P Clarke	1 (0)	0	0	0
D Ferguson	13 (7)	5	4	1
T Gravesen	29 (1)	2	5	0
T Hibbert	24 (1)	0	1	0
F Jeffers	5 (13)	0	2	0
K Kilbane	26 (4)	3	1	0
Li Tie	4 (1)	0	0	1
T Linderoth	23 (4)	0	4	0
N Martyn	33 (1)	0	0	0
J McFadden	11 (12)	0	3	0
G Naysmith	27 (2)	2	2	1
A Nyarko	7 (4)	0	1	0
L Osman	3 (1)	1	0	0
M Pembridge	4 (0)	0	0	0
A Pistone	20 (1)	0	1	0
T Radzinski	28 (6)	8	2	0
W Rooney	26 (8)	9	11	0
S Simonsen	1 (0)	0	0	0
A Stubbs	25 (2)	0	2	0
D Unsworth	22 (4)	3	3	0
S Watson	22 (2)	5	4	0
D Weir	9 (1)	0	1	0
R Wright	4 (0)	0	0	0
J Yobo	27 (1)	2	0	0

League Stats
Clean sheets 10
Yellow cards 54 Red cards 3
Players used 27
Leading scorer:
W Rooney & D Ferguson 9 (9 & 5 league)

Outlook forecast: *18th*

Your forecast:

FULHAM

Nickname: The Cottagers
Colours: Black and white
Ground: Craven Cottage
Capacity: 22,000
Tel: 020 7893 8383
www.fulhamfc.com

THE Cottagers have confounded their critics since they won promotion to the top flight as Division One champions in 2001.

They are regularly tipped for the drop, but so far have managed to stay up and last season's top ten finish was their best so far in the Premiership.

Manager Chris Coleman has been a revelation since taking over from Jean Tigana last April and has quickly made a reputation for himself as one of the best young managers around. It will be fascinating to see if he can maintain the pace he has set.

As with many of the Premiership's middle ranking clubs, the lack of a grade A striker might hamper Fulham's ambitions.

Louis Saha was Fulham's top league scorer last season despite the fact that he left for Man United in early January. In his absence, wins turned into draws and their challenge for a European place trailed off.

Accordingly a striker was at the top of Coleman's shopping list. Andy Cole is an imminent arrival and the club hope that their return to a renovated Craven Cottage, after nearly two years at Loftus Road, will help in their quest to attract more fresh blood.

Whether the return home in itself will make much difference to their results is open to question. The Cottagers have performed consistently 'at home' in all three of their seasons in the top flight.

Their improved league position was due to a much better performance on the road. Last term, they won as many games away from home as they had in the previous two seasons put together.

Longest run without loss: 4
Longest run without win: 4
High - low league position: 4-10
High - low Outlook form figure: 59-44
Final Outlook Index figure: 881

Key Stat: *Six clean sheets in their last nine Premiership games.*

2003/04 Premiership Stats

	Apps	Gls	YC	RC
L Boa Morte	32 (1)	9	8	1
C Bocanegra	15 (0)	0	2	1
J Bonnissel	16 (0)	0	0	0
M Buari	1 (2)	0	0	0
L Clark	25 (0)	2	2	0
M Crossley	1 (0)	0	0	0
S Davis	22 (2)	5	5	0
M Djetou	19 (7)	0	3	0
A Goma	23 (0)	0	5	0
A Green	4 (0)	0	1	0
J Harley	3 (1)	0	0	0
B Hayles	10 (15)	4	2	0
J Inamoto	15 (7)	2	7	0
C John	3 (5)	4	1	0
Z Knight	30 (1)	0	4	0
D Leacock	3 (1)	0	2	0
S Legwinski	30 (2)	0	7	1
S Malbranque	38 (0)	6	3	0
S Marlet	1 (0)	1	0	0
B McBride	5 (10)	4	0	0
A Melville	9 (0)	0	0	0
I Pearce	12 (1)	0	0	0
M Pembridge	9 (3)	1	1	0
B Petta	3 (5)	0	0	0
D Pratley	0 (1)	0	0	0
Z Rehmen	0 (1)	0	0	0
L Saha	20 (1)	13	1	0
F Sava	0 (6)	1	0	0
E Van der Sar	37 (0)	0	0	0
M Volz	32 (1)	0	5	0

League Stats
Clean sheets 15
Yellow cards 63 Red cards 3
Players used 30
Leading scorer:
Louis Saha 15 (13 league)

Outlook forecast: 13th

Your forecast:

LIVERPOOL

Nickname: The Reds
Colours: Red
Ground: Anfield
Capacity: 45,362
Tel: 0151 263 2361
www.liverpoolfc.tv

LIVERPOOL supporters hope that the new season will herald the beginning of a new era at Anfield as former Valencia boss Rafael Benitez takes over the reigns from Gerard Houllier.

The Frenchman brought silverware to Anfield during his tenure, but the Cup treble of 2001 proved to be a false dawn and another season scrapping it out for a Champions League place was not enough to satisfy the Liverpool board.

Benitez has impressive credentials. After forgettable spells in charge at Extremadura, Real Valladolid and Osasuna, he took Tenerife into the Primera Liga in 2001 before joining Valencia that summer.

A Uefa Cup win, a Champions League quarter-final and two league championships quickly followed - the league title had not gone to the Mestalla since 1971.

The challenge at Liverpool, though, is perhaps even greater. Since their glory days in the 1970s and 1980s, the Reds have become also-rans and put the lie to the cliche about class being permanent.

Last season they finished 30 points behind champions Arsenal, and Benitez will be expected to bring about a significant improvement.

He has passed his challenge to keep the best of the Reds talent, Michael Owen and Steven Gerrard, at the club.

But Benitez has proved at Valencia that he can win trophies with a team that is not full of household names and it will be interesting to chart his progress over the coming campaign.

Longest run without loss: 6
Longest run without win: 4
High - low league position: 4-15
High - low Outlook form figure: 64-45
Final Outlook Index figure: 909

Key Stat: *They had the most corners (264) and the most shots (310) in the section.*

2003/04 Premiership Stats

	Apps	Gls	YC	RC
M Baros	6 (7)	1	2	0
L Bernardi	0 (1)	0	0	0
I Biscan	27 (2)	0	4	0
J Carragher	22 (0)	0	2	0
B Cheyrou	9 (3)	2	0	0
S Diao	2 (1)	0	1	0
E-H Diouf	20 (6)	0	9	1
J Dudek	30 (0)	0	0	0
S Finnan	19 (3)	0	4	0
S Gerrard	34 (0)	4	2	0
D Hamann	25 (0)	2	6	0
S Henchoz	15 (3)	0	2	0
E Heskey	25 (10)	7	1	0
S Hyypia	38 (0)	4	1	0
P Jones	2 (0)	0	0	0
H Kewell	36 (0)	7	6	0
C Kirkland	6 (0)	0	1	0
A Le Tallec	3 (10)	0	0	0
D Murphy	19 (12)	5	2	0
J Ostemobor	4 (0)	0	1	0
M Owen	29 (0)	16	0	0
J Riise	22 (6)	0	0	0
S-Pongolle	3(12)	2	0	0
V Smicer	15 (5)	3	1	0
D Traore	7 (0)	0	0	0
J Welsh	0 (1)	0	1	0

League Stats
Clean sheets 15
Yellow cards 50 Red cards 1
Players used 26
Leading scorer:
Michael Owen 19 (16 league)

Outlook forecast: 5th
Your forecast:

MANCHESTER CITY

Nickname: The Citizens
Colours: Blue and white
Ground: City of Manchester Stadium
Capacity: 48,000
Tel: 0161 231 3200
www.mcfc.co.uk

THE pressure is on Kevin Keegan to improve on last season's disastrous Premiership campaign.

After flirting with relegation and eventually finishing sixteenth, Keegan's target - set by the Man City board - is to finish eighth or better.

Typically for a Keegan side it all started so well, with promotion to the top flight as runaway Division One champions followed by a solid ninth place finish in 2003.

Equally typical was the inconsistency that undermined their aspirations to follow it up last season. The highlight of their season was the 4-1 win at home to Man United. The 2-1 defeat at Elland Road that followed it was the story of their season.

City's home form will worry their supporters. During their first season in the new City of Manchester Stadium, only fifteenth placed-Blackburn and relegated Leeds and Leicester scored fewer points in front of their own supporters. Luckily for City, their above average record away from home was enough to keep them up.

Keegan spent the season assuring us that his expensively assembled squad were capable of more. Collectively, City failed to deliver but, perhaps surprisingly, Nicolas Anelka was a notable exception with a respectable tally of 17 goals while Shaun Wright-Phillips and Joey Barton both earned rave reviews.

More of the same this term might easily result in a third relegation from the Premiership, regardless of the quality in Keegan's squad.

Longest run without loss: 4
Longest run without win: 12
High - low league position: 3-17
High - low Outlook form figure: 62-42
Final Outlook Index figure: 863

Key Stat: *Toughen up? They committed the fewest fouls (426) in the Premiership.*

2003/04 Premiership Stats

	Apps	Gls	YC	RC
N Anelka	31 (1)	17	1	1
J Barton	24 (4)	1	8	0
E Berkovic	1 (3)	0	2	0
P Bosvelt	22 (3)	0	3	0
S Distin	38 (0)	2	6	0
R Dunne	28 (1)	0	5	0
S Elliott	0 (2)	0	0	0
R Fowler	23 (8)	7	2	0
D James	17 (0)	0	0	0
S Jordan	0 (2)	0	0	0
J Macken	7 (8)	1	0	0
S McManaman	20 (2)	0	1	0
C Reyna	19 (4)	1	0	0
D Seaman	19 (0)	0	0	0
A Sibierski	18 (15)	5	1	0
T Sinclair	20 (9)	1	2	0
D Sommeil	18 (0)	1	3	0
K Stuhr-Ellegaard	2 (2)	0	0	0
Sun Jihai	29 (4)	1	7	0
M Tarnat	32 (0)	3	6	0
D Tiatto	1 (4)	0	1	0
D Van Buyten	5 (0)	0	0	1
P Wanchope	12 (10)	6	1	0
S Wright-Phillips	32 (2)	7	1	1

League Stats
Clean sheets 7
Yellow cards 49 Red cards 3
Players used 24
Leading scorer:
Nicolas Anelka 25 (17 league)

Outlook forecast: **15th**
Your forecast:

MANCHESTER UNITED

Nickname: The Red Devils
Colours: Red and white
Ground: Old Trafford
Capacity: 68,174
Tel: 0161 868 8000
www.manutd.com

HAVING endured a difficult season in 2003/04, it will be up to Sir Alex Ferguson to prove that we are not witnessing the end of an era at Old Trafford.

It is easy for United supporters to lay the blame elsewhere. Ferguson's public spat with John Magnier over Rock Of Gibraltar's stud rights, the subsequent enquiry into United's transfer dealings and Rio Ferdinand's suspension all distracted attention from an ageing team struggling to come to terms with competition from Arsenal and Chelsea.

The Red Devils remain the richest club in the world, but they have been supplanted in the transfer market by the Roman Abramovich fuelled Chelsea.

Ferdinand's suspension may have been the turning point in United's season. Without him in the side, United conceded almost half a goal per game more than with him and slipped from the top of the Premiership table in January to third on the final day.

Carlos Queiroz will resume his post as Ferguson's assistant after a season in charge at Real Madrid. Queiroz was responsible for reorganising United's defence in their last championship season and that bodes well.

Whether it will be enough is debatable. Arguably, United's last title victory in 2003 was as much a result of Arsenal's collapse than United's superb comeback. Their dominant performances in 2000 and 2001 seem a long time ago. A title this term would go down as Fergie's greatest victory.

Longest run without loss: 8
Longest run without win: 3
High - low league position: 1-3
High - low Outlook form figure: 62-42
Final Outlook Index figure: 936
Key Stat: *Stable or what? No club used fewer players last season.*

2003/04 Premiership Stats

	Apps	Gls	YC	RC
D Bellion	4 (10)	2	0	0
W Brown	15 (2)	0	1	0
N Butt	12 (9)	1	2	0
R Carroll	6 (0)	0	0	0
E Djemba-Djemba	10 (5)	0	1	0
R Ferdinand	20 (0)	0	0	0
D Fletcher	17 (5)	0	0	2
D Forlan	10 (14)	4	2	0
Q Fortune	18 (5)	0	2	0
R Giggs	29 (4)	7	3	0
T Howard	32 (0)	0	0	0
R Keane	25 (3)	3	2	0
Kleberson	10 (2)	1	1	0
G Neville	30 (0)	2	5	0
P Neville	29 (2)	0	4	0
J O'Shea	32 (1)	2	1	0
C Ronaldo	15 (14)	4	3	1
L Saha	9 (3)	7	1	0
P Scholes	24 (4)	9	5	0
M Silvestre	33 (1)	0	2	0
O Solskjaer	7 (6)	0	2	0
R van Nistelrooy	31 (1)	20	4	0

League Stats
Clean sheets 14
Yellow cards 41 Red cards 3
Players used 22
Leading scorer:
Ruud van Nistelrooy 28 (20 league)

Outlook forecast: **3rd**
Your forecast:

MIDDLESBROUGH

Nickname: Boro
Colours: Red
Ground: The Riverside Stadium
Capacity: 35,100
Tel: 01642 877700
www.mfc.co.uk

NEARLY ten years after Bryan Robson and Juninho arrived on Teeside, Boro finally have some silverware to show for their efforts after Steve McClaren's side beat Bolton to capture the League Cup.

Whilst the revolution may not quite have lived up to the hype, when the newly completed Riverside Stadium was decked out in green and gold, it has been a successful one. Boro are now firmly established in the Premiership having spent just one season out of the top flight since Robson took them up and the supporters have seen an impressive roster of players pass through the Riverside, albeit often players at the tail end of their careers.

Gibson now wants a top six finish and will look for McClaren to capitalise on the Cup win and attendant European place to take Boro to the next level.

A lack of goals was Boro's biggest concern last term and, accordingly, new strikers top the shopping list. However, even with the prospect of Uefa Cup football, it has been difficult to get the players they want. They have finally landed Mark Viduka but it was a long hard search.

McClaren had expressed an interest in Alan Smith, who went to Man United, Emile Heskey, who went to Birmingham and Patrick Kluivert who dismissed the move out of hand, saying he didn't want to go to a "small club".

Whilst Kluivert slipping through the net may turn out to be a blessing in disguise, it will take much more success to alter the perception that Boro are a mid-table team.

Longest run without loss: 11
Longest run without win: 6
High - low league position: 9-19
High - low Outlook form figure: 66-42
Final Outlook Index figure: 872
Key Stat: *Yawn. One run of nine games yielded just six goals.*

2003/04 Premiership Stats

	Apps	Gls	YC	RC
G Boateng	35 (0)	0	6	0
M Christie	7 (3)	1	1	0
C Cooper	17 (2)	0	3	0
A Davies	8 (2)	0	0	0
Doriva	19 (2)	0	6	0
S Downing	7 (13)	0	0	0
U Ehiogu	16 (0)	0	3	0
J Greening	17 (8)	1	5	0
J-D Job	19 (5)	6	1	0
B Jones	1 (0)	0	0	0
Juninho	26 (5)	8	2	0
M Maccarone	13 (10)	6	1	0
C Marinelli	1 (0)	1	0	0
G Mendieta	30 (1)	2	3	0
D Mills	28 (0)	0	8	0
J Morrison	0 (1)	0	0	0
C Nash	1 (0)	0	0	0
S Nemeth	17 (15)	9	2	0
S Parnaby	8 (5)	0	1	0
F Qeudrue	31 (0)	0	4	0
M Ricketts	7 (16)	2	2	0
C Riggott	14 (3)	0	2	0
M Schwarzer	36 (0)	0	0	0
G Southgate	27 (0)	1	1	0
R Stockdale	0 (2)	0	0	0
A Wright	2 (0)	0	0	0
B Zenden	31 (0)	4	3	1

League Stats
Clean sheets 14
Yellow cards 56 Red cards 1
Players used 27
Leading scorer:
Szilard Nemeth 9 (all league)

Outlook forecast: 7th

Your forecast:

NEWCASTLE UNITED

Nickname: The Magpies
Colours: Black and white
Ground: St James' Park
Capacity: 52,218
Tel: 0191 201 8425
www.nufc.co.uk

NEWCASTLE clinched fifth place and a Uefa Cup spot on goal difference on the final day of the season after they drew with Liverpool and Villa were beaten by Man United.

However slim the margin of success, Bobby Robson has delivered European football to Tyneside for a third season in succession and whilst they are not challenging for the title in the way they did during the Keegan years, it remains a notable achievement.

Last term's success was all the more remarkable when you consider that the Magpies won only twice away from home all season. Only Everton and Wolves won fewer games on the road.

But even if Newcastle weren't winning games away from St James', they weren't losing either. Draws were the predominant feature of the Geordies' season.

In total, they drew twelve times away from home and if some of these draws had been converted to wins, some excellent home form would have seen the Toon competing in the Champions League this season instead of Liverpool.

The highlight of the season, though, was United's Uefa Cup run. After failing to negotiate the Champions League qualifying rounds, somehow the Toon were able to reverse their poor away form to beat NAC Breda, Basle and Mallorca on their travels.

Crucially though, their only defeat was against Marseille in the second leg of the semi-final, where a brace from Didier Drogba ended the Magpies' hopes of winning their first major trophy since 1969.

Longest run without loss: 6
Longest run without win: 6
High - low league position: 4-19
High - low Outlook form figure: 63-42
Final Outlook Index figure: 902
Key Stat: *Their last league away win was in October.*

2003/04 Premiership Stats

	Apps	Gls	YC	RC
D Ambrose	10 (14)	2	3	0
S Ameobi	18 (8)	7	0	0
C Bellamy	13 (3)	4	3	0
O Bernard	35 (0)	1	4	0
L Bowyer	17 (7)	2	5	0
T Bramble	27 (2)	0	7	0
M Bridges	0 (6)	0	0	0
M Brittain	0 (1)	0	0	0
S Caldwell	3 (2)	0	1	0
M Chopra	1 (5)	0	0	0
K Dyer	25 (0)	1	1	0
S Given	38 (0)	0	1	0
A Griffin	5 (0)	0	2	0
A Hughes	34 (0)	0	0	0
J Jenas	26 (5)	2	3	0
L LuaLua	2 (5)	0	0	0
A O'Brien	27 (1)	1	2	2
L Robert	31 (4)	6	1	1
A Shearer	37 (0)	22	1	0
N Solano	8 (4)	0	0	0
G Speed	37 (1)	3	6	0
S Taylor	1 (0)	0	0	0
H Viana	5 (11)	0	2	0
J Woodgate	18 (0)	0	3	0

League Stats
Clean sheets 11
Yellow cards 47 Red cards 3
Players used 24
Leading scorer:
Alan Shearer 28 (22 league)

Outlook forecast: 4th
Your forecast:

NORWICH CITY

Nickname: The Canaries
Colours: Yellow and green
Ground: Carrow Road
Capacity: 24,349
Tel: 01603 760 760
www.canaries.co.uk

FOLLOWING Premiership relegation in 1995, Norwich resisted trying to buy their way back and began to rebuild within their budget.

Nigel Worthington finally took the club back into the Premiership last season and they are still playing it safe with few new arrivals expected, although the arrival of David Bentley on-loan from Arsenal is interesting.

Whilst this safety-first policy ensures the club's long-term future, it does little for their chances of avoiding the drop this season.

Although teams promoted as champions have a good record for consolidating in the Premiership, the last four champions Portsmouth, Man City, Fulham and Charlton - are all still there, their squads have been augmented significantly pre-season.

Defensively, Norwich are solid, they conceded less than a goal a game last term, with keeper Robert Green singled out for praise, but Premiership attacks are a different proposition and one would expect them to ship more in the top flight.

Darren Huckerby was top scorer with a relatively modest fourteen and in the past has blown more cold than hot in the Premiership. Whilst Pompey, Man City, Fulham and Charlton all had outstanding strikers during their promotion years in Todorov, Goater, Saha and Hunt respectively, only Saha has flourished in the Premiership.

Norwich differ in that their goals were spread throughout the squad, but without fresh blood, it is easy to worry for the Canaries Premiership future.

Longest run without loss: 8
Longest run without win: 3
High - low league position: 1-14
High - low Outlook form figure: 68-47
Final Outlook Index figure: 854

Key Stat: *Their record against the top four Div One sides was 1-3-2, scoring just 3.*

2003/04 Division One Stats

	Apps	Gls	YC	RC
Z Abbey	1 (2)	0	0	0
J Brennan	7 (8)	1	0	0
K Briggs	1 (2)	0	0	0
K Cooper	6 (4)	0	2	0
P Crouch	14 (1)	4	2	1
A Drury	42 (0)	0	3	0
C Easton	8 (2)	2	1	0
M Edworthy	42 (1)	0	5	0
C Fleming	46 (0)	3	3	0
D Francis	39 (2)	7	5	0
R Green	46 (0)	0	1	0
E Hammond	0 (4)	0	0	0
K Harper	9 (0)	0	2	1
I Henderson	14 (5)	4	4	0
G Holt	46 (0)	1	5	0
D Huckerby	36 (0)	14	5	0
R Jarvis	0 (12)	1	0	0
M Mackay	45 (0)	4	3	1
L McKenzie	12 (6)	9	2	0
P McVeigh	36 (8)	5	4	0
P Mulryne	14 (20)	3	4	0
D Nielsen	2 (0)	0	1	0
A Notman	0 (1)	0	0	0
M Rivers	7 (5)	4	2	0
I Roberts	13 (28)	8	3	0
J Shackell	4 (2)	0	0	0
M Svensson	16 (4)	7	3	0

League Stats
Clean sheets 18
Yellow cards 63 Red cards 3
Players used 27
Leading scorer:
Darren Huckerby 14 (all league)

Outlook forecast: 19th

Your forecast:

PORTSMOUTH

Nickname: Pompey
Colours: Blue
Ground: Fratton Park
Capacity: 20,101
Tel: 023 9273 1204
www.pompeyfc.co.uk

A SUPERB run of form resulting in 21 points from their last ten games saw Pompey confound the pundits who tipped them for the drop. They finished their first Premiership season in a very respectable thirteenth place - but frustratingly, one place behind their bitter rivals Southampton.

Although lacking the spending power of some of his Premiership rivals, Pompey boss Harry Redknapp has played the transfer market astutely, creating a blend of youth, experience and foreign talent at Fratton Park.

He has also made good use of the rule allowing loans between Premiership clubs. Redknapp managed to get the best out of his loan signings, with the likes of Chelsea's Russia captain Alexei Smertin becoming a Pompey regular and Lomano LuaLua rejecting the chance to return to Newcastle for the Uefa Cup semi-final to save his energy for Portsmouth's forthcoming clash with Leeds instead.

However, but for the late rally, Portsmouth would have been much closer to fulfilling the prophets of doom. The 21-point haul from March, April and May was almost half of their total for the entire season.

Away from Fratton Park they won just twice all season, less than either Leicester or Leeds, who were both relegated. Only Everton, who finished one place above the relegation zone, and bottom club Wolves scored fewer points on the road than Pompey. To survive, Redknapp must ensure his side is firing on all cylinders from day one and rectify their abysmal away form.

Longest run without loss: 8
Longest run without win: 6
High - low league position: 3-18
High - low Outlook form figure: 63-46
Final Outlook Index figure: 872

Key Stat: *Redknapp doesn't change but his team does; no club used more players.*

2003/04 Premiership Stats

	Apps	Gls	YC	RC
P Berger	20 (0)	5	3	1
E Berkovic	10 (1)	1	2	0
D Burton	0 (1)	0	0	0
J Curtis	5 (1)	0	0	0
A De Zeeuw	36 (0)	1	7	0
R Duffy	0 (1)	0	0	0
A Faye	27 (0)	0	6	0
H Foxe	8 (2)	1	2	0
K Harper	0 (7)	0	0	0
S Hislop	30 (0)	0	1	0
R Hughes	8 (3)	0	1	0
L LuaLua	10 (5)	4	1	0
I Mornar	3 (5)	1	0	0
G O'Neil	3 (0)	2	0	0
P Pasanen	11 (1)	0	2	0
V Pericard	0 (6)	1	1	0
L Primus	19 (2)	0	0	0
N Quashie	17 (4)	1	5	0
J Roberts	4 (6)	1	0	0
C Robinson	0 (1)	0	0	0
S Schemmel	12 (2)	0	5	0
T Sheringham	25 (7)	9	4	0
T Sherwood	7 (6)	0	6	0
A Smertin	23 (3)	0	2	0
P Srnicek	3 (0)	0	0	0
D Stefanovic	32 (0)	3	4	1
S Stone	29 (3)	2	2	1
M Taylor	18 (12)	0	2	0
S Todorov	1 (0)	0	0	0
H Wapenaar	5 (0)	0	0	0
Yakubu	35 (2)	16	2	0
B Zivkovic	17 (1)	0	3	0

League Stats
Clean sheets 8
Yellow cards 62 Red cards 3
Players used 32
Leading scorer:
Alyegbeni Yakubu 19 (16 league)

Outlook forecast: 16th
Your forecast:

SOUTHAMPTON

Nickname: The Saints
Colours: Red and white
Ground: St Mary's Stadium
Capacity: 32,800
Tel: 0870 2200 000
www.saintsfc.co.uk

ARRIVING at St Mary's late in the season, new boss Paul Sturrock maintained the status quo. Southampton were lying in twelfth place when he arrived in March, and were still there on the last day of the season.

This was thanks to respectable if unspectacular home form coupled with their usual lack of achievement on the road that has seen the Saints fail to win more than five league matches away from home every season since the formation of the Premiership.

As usual, Saints were able to raise their game against some of the bigger sides, beating Man United at St Mary's and completing the double over Liverpool, but inconsistency and some wretched form in their final run-in, from which they took just two points from a possible fifteen, prevented Sturrock's side from replicating the previous season's top ten finish.

James Beattie failed to follow his excellent 2002/03 season which saw him earn a call up to the England squad, but formed an effective partnership with Kevin Phillips. The duo netted 27 times in the league between them.

Marion Pahars spent most of an injury-hit season coming on from the bench but was fit enough to be called up by Latvia for Euro 2004, and may play a greater role over the coming year if Rangers are able to tempt Phillips away from the south coast.

Sturrock is now reunited with Kevin Summerfield, his assistant at Plymouth, and has money available to strengthen the squad.

Longest run without loss: 6
Longest run without win: 5
High - low league position: 4-15
High - low Outlook form figure: 60-35
Final Outlook Index figure: 868
Key Stat: *Firing blanks: Saints failed to score 18 times in 42 games.*

2003/04 Premiership Stats

	Apps	Gls	YC	RC
C Baird	1 (3)	0	1	0
J Beattie	32 (5)	14	3	0
A Blayney	2 (0)	0	0	0
S Crainey	5 (0)	0	0	0
M Cranie	1 (0)	0	0	0
R Delap	26 (1)	1	1	0
A Delgado	0 (4)	0	0	0
J Dodd	27 (1)	0	2	0
F Fernandes	21 (6)	1	2	0
Y Folly	9 (0)	0	1	0
L Griffit	2 (3)	2	0	0
F Hall	7 (4)	0	1	0
D Higginbotham	24 (3)	0	3	0
P Jones	8 (0)	0	0	0
D Kenton	3 (4)	0	0	0
G Le Saux	19 (0)	0	4	0
C Lundekvam	31 (0)	1	2	0
C Marsden	9 (4)	0	4	0
N McCann	9 (9)	0	4	0
A Niemi	28 (0)	0	1	0
M Oakley	7 (0)	0	2	0
B Ormerod	14 (8)	5	1	0
M Pahars	6 (8)	2	0	0
K Phillips	28 (6)	13	2	1
D Prutton	22 (5)	1	4	1
A Svensson	17 (13)	0	6	0
M Svensson	26 (0)	2	6	1
P Telfer	33 (4)	0	3	0
J Tessem	1 (2)	0	0	0

League Stats
Clean sheets 12
Yellow cards 53 Red cards 3
Players used 29
Leading scorer:
James Beattie 17 (14 league)

Outlook forecast: 12th
Your forecast:

TOTTENHAM HOTSPUR

Nickname: Spurs
Colours: White and navy blue
Ground: White Hart Lane
Capacity: 36,236
Tel: 020 8365 5000
www.spurs.co.uk

AFTER a wretched season under caretaker boss David Pleat, and the long and drawn out search for a manager, there has been something of a revolution behind the scenes at Spurs this summer.

If Giovanni Trapattoni and Martin O'Neill both looked like unrealistic targets to replace Glenn Hoddle, France boss Jacques Santini looked an absolutely outlandish candidate. Nonetheless Santini has joined new sporting director Frank Arnesen at White Hart Lane. New assistant coach Martin Jol completes the fashionably European back room line up.

Not surprisingly, a number of French players are now being linked to the club, including Sylvain Wiltord and Bixente Lizarazu.

Whilst a mood of optimism and relief has replaced the uncertainty that cast a shadow over White Hart Lane, it would be unwise to expect a quick fix for Tottenham's problems. An FA Cup in 1991 and a League Cup in 1999 are the only pieces of silverware Spurs have won since the glory days of the early eighties, and for all the expectation and talk of sleeping giants at White Hart Lane, they have been a mid-table club for over a decade.

Santini brought Lyon their first silverware since the seventies, and the first league title in their history in 2002, but in reality the revolution had been started in 1987 when the industrialist Jean-Michel Aulas began to invest in the club, with European football his declared ambition. Lyon-style success will not come overnight to Spurs.

Longest run without loss: 6
Longest run without win: 8
High - low league position: 10-18
High - low Outlook form figure: 66-33
Final Outlook Index figure: 866

Key Stat: *Clean up please. No team in the top-flight committed more fouls (563).*

2003/04 Premiership Stats

	Apps	Gls	YC	RC
D Anderton	16 (4)	1	4	0
J Blondel	0 (1)	0	1	0
M Brown	17 (0)	1	1	0
G Bunjevcevic	3 (4)	0	0	0
S Carr	32 (0)	1	8	1
S Dalmat	12 (10)	3	2	0
S Davies	17 (0)	2	2	0
J Defoe	14 (1)	7	1	0
G Doherty	16 (1)	0	3	0
A Gardner	33 (0)	0	8	0
J Jackson	9 (2)	1	0	0
F Kanoute	19 (8)	7	0	0
R Keane	31 (3)	14	1	0
K Keller	38 (0)	0	0	0
S Kelly	7 (4)	0	0	0
L King	28 (1)	1	1	0
P Konchesky	10 (2)	0	3	0
M Mabizela	0 (6)	1	2	0
D Marney	1 (2)	0	1	0
H Postiga	9 (10)	1	0	0
G Poyet	12 (8)	3	1	0
J Redknapp	14 (3)	1	6	0
D Richards	23 (0)	0	3	0
R Ricketts	12 (12)	1	3	0
M Taricco	31 (1)	1	8	0
M Yeates	1 (0)	0	0	0
B Zamora	6 (10)	0	1	0
C Ziege	7 (1)	0	2	0

League Stats
Clean sheets 8
Yellow cards 61 Red cards 1
Players used 28
Leading scorer:
Robbie Keane 16 (14 league)

Outlook forecast: 9th
Your forecast:

WEST BROM

Nickname: The Baggies
Colours: Navy blue and white
Ground: The Hawthorns
Capacity: 27,877
Tel: 0121 525 8888
www.wba.co.uk

A LACK of firepower was the Baggies' Achilles heel when they were relegated from the top flight in 2003, after just one season with the elite.

They had won promotion by virtue of finishing second behind free-scoring Man City thanks to a string of 1-0 wins, but their attack proved too listless and their defence too porous to cut it at the highest level and relegation followed.

Now West Brom are back having won promotion in second place behind free-scoring Norwich thanks to a string of 1-0 wins. In fact, there were less single-goal victories (eight as opposed to seventeen in all competitions during their 2002 promotion year) but the Baggies were still shot-shy, scoring just three more than in 2001/02.

Manager Gary Megson has learnt from the experience and a new striker tops his summer shopping list. However, attempts to land Paul Dickov, Kanu and Mateja Kezman have already fallen through and the new faces at The Hawthorns include defenders Darren Purse, Martin Albrechtsen and Riccardo Scimeca.

A tighter defence is needed, as they conceded more than twice as many goals as they scored in their relegation season, but since only bottom club Sunderland scored fewer than West Brom's paltry haul of 29, buying defenders is only addressing half the problem.

Unless Megson can find a quality striker, or a less conservative way to play, the Baggies seem doomed to relegation once again.

Longest run without loss: 11
Longest run without win: 6
High - low league position: 1-10
High - low Outlook form figure: 67-42
Final Outlook Index figure: 838

Key Stat: *Unusually for a promoted side, they never won by more than three goals.*

2003/04 Division One Stats

	Apps	Gls	YC	RC
S Berthe	2 (1)	0	0	0
A Chambers	1 (0)	0	0	0
J Chambers	13 (3)	0	1	0
N Clement	25 (10)	2	1	0
D Dichio	5 (6)	0	1	0
S Dobie	14 (17)	5	2	0
L Dyer	2 (15)	2	0	0
D Facey	2 (7)	0	0	0
T Gaardsoe	45 (0)	4	5	1
P Gilchrist	16 (1)	0	1	0
S Gregan	40 (3)	1	7	0
B Haas	36 (0)	1	8	0
G Horsfield	20 (0)	7	2	0
R Hoult	44 (0)	0	0	0
L Hughes	21 (11)	11	4	0
R Hulse	29 (4)	10	3	1
A Johnson	33 (4)	2	2	1
M Kinsella	15 (3)	1	2	0
J Koumas	37 (5)	10	4	2
D Moore	20 (2)	2	1	0
J Murphy	2 (2)	0	0	0
A N'Dour	2 (0)	0	0	0
J O'Connor	27 (3)	0	4	0
P Robinson	30 (1)	0	8	0
A Sakiri	6 (19)	1	0	0
L Sigurdsson	5 (0)	0	2	0
M Skoubo	0 (2)	0	0	0
J Volmer	10 (5)	0	1	0
R Wallwork	4 (1)	0	3	0

League Stats
Clean sheets 19
Yellow cards 57 Red cards 5
Players used 29
Leading scorer:
Rob Hulse 13 (10 league)

Outlook forecast: 20th
Your forecast:

BRIGHTON & HOVE ALBION

Nickname: The Seagulls
Colours: Blue and white

Ground: Withdean Stadium
Capacity: 7,053

Tel: 01273 778 855

www.seagulls.co.uk

MARK MCGHEE and his players fulfilled their part of the bargain in winning May's Division 2 play-off final. Now's the time for Deputy Prime Minister John Prescott to cement that with approval for the move to a purpose-built 23,000-capacity stadium in Falmer.

Otherwise, it could go sour pretty rapidly down on the south coast, with little prospect of any significant loans for on-pitch reinforcements back in the new 'Championship'.

The Seagulls' success last term was based on solid home form - conceding the least in the section and sharing the most wins honours with champions Plymouth - but honest endeavour in front of crowds of just 7,000 at the Withdean will do little more than keep heads above the relegation waterline in what looks an ultra-competitive if hardly top-notch division.

Longest run without loss: 7
Longest run without win: 4
High - low league position: 1-8
High - low Outlook form figure: 65-39
Key Stat: *Seven clean sheets in their last eight games.*

Outlook forecast: 20th

Final Outlook Index figure: 772
Clean sheets 22
Yellow cards 81 Red cards 3
Players used 32
Leading scorer:
Leon Knight 26 (25 league)

Your forecast:

BURNLEY

Nickname: The Clarets
Colours: Claret and blue

Ground: Turf Moor
Capacity: 22,546

Tel: 0870 443 1882

www.burnleyfootballclub.co.uk

RELEGATION, relegation, relegation and, of course, its avoidance - that will be the sole priority in season 2004/05 for new manager Steve Cotterill, and all concerned with the Clarets.

Taking over the Turf Moor reins from Stan Ternent was never going to be an easy task but an opening month fixture list containing clashes with promotion hopefuls Sheffield United, Wolves and West Ham plus fellow survival-seekers Rotherham,

Watford and Gillingham looks a severe start. Especially, for a coach rumoured to have 'lost' the dressing room when assistant to Howard Wilkinson at Sunderland.

Two years ago Burnley let in the most goals on their own patch and finished just two points off the drop last term. The arrival of stalwart stopper John McGreal from Ipswich should help - the continued attacking-player drain from East Lancashire won't.

Longest run without loss: 6
Longest run without win: 8
High - low league position: 8-24
High - low Outlook form figure: 61-38
Key Stat: *Only eight players were under contract when Steve Cotterill took over.*

Outlook forecast: 21st

Final Outlook Index figure: 784
Clean sheets 10
Yellow cards 82 Red cards 3
Players used 28
Leading scorer:
Robert Blake 22 (19 league)

Your forecast:

CARDIFF CITY

Nickname: The Bluebirds
Colours: Blue

Ground: Ninian Park
Capacity: 20,000

Tel: 02920 221001

www.cardiffcityfc.co.uk

EVER-OPTIMISTIC owner Sam Hammam will claim that last season was only a 'sighter' in terms of the Bluebirds making it into the promised land of the Premiership, and that his bid to steer a second club from bottom to top flight football remains on course.

However, it will surely prove to be their sole chance as, contrary to last pre-season's boasts, cash has not proved plentiful for manager Lennie Lawrence - mid-table mediocrity at best beckons.

Hotshot Robert Earnshaw does remain despite much speculation about a move onwards and upwards but it can't help that other decent performers, such as Danny Gabbidon and midfielder Graham Kavanagh, are also linked with transfers.

And it doesn't bode well that relegated Bradford, Walsall and Wimbledon all avoided defeat at Ninian Park despite the intimidating atmosphere.

Longest run without loss: 8
Longest run without win: 6
High - low league position: 6-14
High - low Outlook form figure: 63-32
Key Stat: *Just one defeat in their last six away games.*

Final Outlook Index figure: 798
Clean sheets 14
Yellow cards 65 Red cards 6
Players used 27
Leading scorer:
Robert Earnshaw 26 (21 league)

Outlook forecast: 14th

Your forecast:

COVENTRY CITY

Nickname: The Sky Blues
Colours: Sky blue

Ground: Highfield Road
Capacity: 23,627

Tel: 024 76234000

www.ccfc.co.uk

DESPITE losing two managers in the course of last season, original boss Gary McAllister and then caretaker Eric Black, and the departure since of at least ten players spirits should be high in the Sky Blues camp.

For, while Suffo, Adebola, Barrett, Morrell and McSheffrey remain at Highfield Road, there should be little chance of the dreaded 'r' word rearing its ugly head, even with the uninspiring Peter Reid at the helm.

Rumours persist of a £200m takeover bid and only such an investment will engender a promotion push, as a defence marshalled by veteran Steve Staunton must be a massive negative, whatever the promise of youngsters such as full-back Stuart Giddings.

Reid is said to be trying to bring error-prone, free-agent Phil Babb 'back home' to plug the gaps. Has Reidy learnt owt? Who next Gary Breen?

Longest run without loss: 8
Longest run without win: 8
High - low league position: 10-21
High - low Outlook form figure: 63-43
Key Stat: *They fired in the most shots (671) and most on target (359) in Div One.*

Final Outlook Index figure: 802
Clean sheets 13
Yellow cards 66 Red cards 4
Players used 33
Leading scorer:
Gary McSheffrey 21 (19 league)

Outlook forecast: 11th

Your forecast:

CREWE ALEXANDRA

Nickname: The Railwaymen
Colours: Red and white

Ground: Gresty Road
Capacity: 10,066

Tel: 01270 213014

www.crewealex.net

CONDEMNING a team coached by Dario Gradi is always a view voiced with a heavy heart for, whatever his fiscal restrictions, the remarkable 'Italian' - now 21 years at Gresty Road - has always produced footballing outfits with the accent on youth and intricate passing.

But The Railwaymen can't keep flogging their best assets and look prime candidates for the drop. Alex have already accepted a £500k bid for defend-er David Wright and are set to receive offers for club captain Dave Brammer and front-man Dean Ashton before long.

The latter, still only 20, notched 20 times in all competitions last term.

Seven defeats in their final 12 games suggest a downward spiral that can't be arrested with only fine-tuning and a sprinkling of capable senior pros such as Clayton Ince, Adie Moses, Kenny Lunt and Steve Jones.

Longest run without loss: 5	*Final Outlook Index figure: 777*
Longest run without win: 6	*Clean sheets 11*
High - low league position: 9-18	*Yellow cards 33 Red cards 1*
High - low Outlook form figure: 60-40	*Players used 28*
Key Stat: *Less than two cards every three games and the least fouls too.*	*Leading scorer:* *Dean Ashton 20 (19 league)*
Outlook forecast: 24th	**Your forecast:**

DERBY COUNTY

Nickname: The Rams
Colours: White and black

Ground: Pride Park
Capacity: 33,597

Tel: 0870 444 1884

www.dcfc.co.uk

AFTER two seasons of shelling p's - places, players and points - since falling out of the Premiership, Rams' chairman Lionel Pickering has to give manager George Burley the financial support he deserves.

And about time too, for Pride Park is certainly not a fitting venue for lower league football, while Burley is an astute tactician well up to matching the majority of his current adversaries if given the right resources.

Hitman Tommy Smith is a cracking capture from Sunderland and centre-half Mo Konjic a sneaky steal from Coventry but the best bit of close-season business were the new contracts signed by Ian Taylor, Junior and 17-year-old Lee Holmes.

A measure of the turnaround in Derby's fortunes with the use of such quality young players is that although they beat the drop by only a point, they won eight of their last 11 home games.

Longest run without loss: 5	*Final Outlook Index figure: 782*
Longest run without win: 8	*Clean sheets 10*
High - low league position: 16-24	*Yellow cards 74 Red cards 4*
High - low Outlook form figure: 60-38	*Players used 36*
Key Stat: *An impressive 13,500 season tickets had been sold by June 6.*	*Leading scorer:* *Ian Taylor 12 (11 league)*
Outlook forecast: 13th	**Your forecast:**

GILLINGHAM

Nickname: The Gills
Colours: Blue and black

Ground: Priestfield Stadium
Capacity: 11,582

Tel: 01634 851854/300000

www.gillinghamfootballclub.com

IF it wasn't for the remarkable Mr Dowie and his unstoppable Crystal Palace, everyone would have been going crazy over Andy Hessenthaler keeping the Gills in this new-fangled Championship, despite the mid-season sale of main marksman Marlon King and Paul Shaw.

Unfortunately, the Priestfield fire-sale does not look to have been stopped, with Kevin James following Marlon King to Nottingham Forest and the 'reluctant'

hawking of midfield gem Danny Spiller to the highest bidder.

So for all his hard work and frank-speaking - player-boss Hess begins the new campaign with a three-match touchline ban - survival is unlikely to be achieved with just the arrival of Norwich striker Iwan Roberts as player-coach.

Expect the odd upset, like last term's duffing up of an arrogant West Ham, but ultimately not enough consistent results.

Longest run without loss: 4
Longest run without win: 5
High - low league position: 7-22
High - low Outlook form figure: 56-36
Key Stat: *The Gills conceded more at home than they did away last season.*

Outlook forecast: 22nd

Final Outlook Index figure: 768
Clean sheets 13
Yellow cards 69 Red cards 5
Players used 26
Leading scorer: Agyemang, Sidibe, Shaw and Spiller 6 (all league, Sidibe 5 league)

Your forecast:

IPSWICH TOWN

Nickname: Town or Tractor Boys
Colours: Blue and white

Ground: Portman Road
Capacity: 30,300

Tel: 01473 400500

www.itfc.co.uk

HAVING comprehensively out-fought and out-thought West Ham in their 1-0 Portman Road May play-off semi-final first leg win, Darren Bent fluffed an early opportunity to shatter the Irons and silence the feverish Upton Park crowd in the second leg.

The rest as they say is history and this season's section will be even tougher to escape for a Town outfit that at its most fluent bullied the minnows but was turned over twice by Norwich, West

Brom and Wigan.

Marcus Bent, Jermaine Wright, John McGreal and Martijn Reuser are confirmed departures, while ex-Wigan stopper Jason de Vos is the sole concrete recruit, so the final weeks of pre-season are bound to be busy for manager Joe Royle.

Darren Bent, Kuqi, Counago and Bowditch will score plenty of goals but last season only bottom-placed Wimbledon conceded more times at home.

Longest run without loss: 6
Longest run without win: 5
High - low league position: 4-24
High - low Outlook form figure: 65-40
Key Stat: *3.4 goals per Ipswich game last season - and 3.7 per home game.*

Outlook forecast: 7th

Final Outlook Index figure: 813
Clean sheets 6
Yellow cards 72 Red cards 2
Players used 25
Leading scorer:
Shefki Kuqi 17 (16 league)

Your forecast:

LEEDS UNITED

Nickname: United
Colours: White

Ground: Elland Road
Capacity: 40,204

Tel: 0113 367 6000

www.leedsunited.com

ARE the Leeds creditors the only ones fooled by this name change to the Coca-Cola Championship?

I think we should be told because how else can new Elland Road gaffer Kevin Blackwell justify all his new recruits, even with the departures of Mark Viduka, Dominic Matteo and James Milner.

The Whites were dreadful in the Premiership last season so it is a big ask, with their debts, low morale and personnel changes, to expect them to bounce back automatically.

However, Blackwell - rated extremely highly on the circuit as a coach - has not been slow in addressing the relevant issues for a successful campaign in a section long of brawn and short of artistry.

His aquisitions, which include Brian Deane, Michael Ricketts, and Julian Joachim, can see an unlikely challenge emerge for a return to Premiership football.

Longest run without loss: 5
Longest run without win: 9
High - low league position: 11-20
High - low Outlook form figure: 54-29
Key Stat: *Their debt remains huge at over eight figures.*

Final Outlook Index figure: 846
Clean sheets 3
Yellow cards 71 Red cards 5
Players used 30
Leading scorer:
Mark Viduka 12 (11 league)

Outlook forecast: 3rd

Your forecast:

LEICESTER CITY

Nickname: The Foxes
Colours: Blue and white

Ground: The Walkers Stadium
Capacity: 32,500

Tel: 0870 0406000

www.lcfc.co.uk

MICKY ADAMS led the Foxes back up to the Premiership at the first attempt two seasons ago and should be wholeheartedly backed to do so again.

The current financial circumstances are by no means as dire as those in the immediate weeks and months of that previous relegation and in comparison this is nowhere near as classy a league.

Naturally most of Leicester's most influential playing assets have been stripped during the summer - no Muzzy Izzet, no Paul Dickov, no Riccardo Scimeca to name three - but Adams has already made some astute signings in the shape of young Nottingham Forest midfield schemer Gareth Williams and ex-Manchester City utility man Danny Tiatto.

The fixture-computer appears to have been played its part too, with just three clashes with the other realistic title contenders in their first 13 games.

Longest run without loss: 6
Longest run without win: 15
High - low league position: 11-20
High - low Outlook form figure: 63-39
Key Stat: *Outfoxed - they have not enjoyed successive wins since November.*

Final Outlook Index figure: 852
Clean sheets 9
Yellow cards 57 Red cards 7
Players used 30
Leading scorer: Les Ferdinand and Paul Dickov 14 (12 & 11 league)

Outlook forecast: 1st

Your forecast:

MILLWALL

Nickname: The Lions
Colours: Blue and white

Ground: The New Den
Capacity: 20,146

Tel: 020 7232 1222

www.millwallfc.co.uk

DESPITE the best efforts of manager Dennis Wise and assistant Ray Wilkins there can be little doubt that reaching the FA Cup Final completely distracted the Lions from their main objective, a play-off spot and potential promotion to the Premiership.

But who can begrudge them that May day out in Cardiff against Manchester United and their Uefa Cup jaunt this autumn?

The Lions had lost just once in twelve league games since the turn of the year prior to beating Sunderland in the April semi-final, but they won just one match (the home finale against condemned Bradford) after.

This remains the poser - with little finalised transfer activity down at the New Den - for punters regarding the Lions.

They undoubtedly have the set-up for success in this section but do they have the mental toughness?

Longest run without loss: 10
Longest run without win: 7
High - low league position: 2-12
High - low Outlook form figure: 64-38
Key Stat: *No team committed more fouls (750) in Division One last season.*

Final Outlook Index figure: 810
Clean sheets 16
Yellow cards 94 Red cards 7
Players used 35
Leading scorer:
Tim Cahill 12 (9 league)

Outlook forecast: 10th

Your forecast:

NOTTINGHAM FOREST

Nickname: Forest
Colours: Red and white

Ground: City Ground
Capacity: 30,602

Tel: 0115 9824444

www.nottinghamforest.co.uk

JOE KINNEAR certainly worked the survival oracle at the City Ground. Forest lost just two of their last 17 matches to achieve lower mid-table respectability on 65 points, just eight off Crystal Palace in the final play-off berth.

But money-matters dominate their immediate future, and although sprightly winger Kevin James has arrived from Gillingham, talented midfielder Gareth Williams has moved to Leicester and any substantial offers for centre-half Michael Dawson or Irish international Andy Reid would have to be listened to.

The same applies to striker David Johnson who, having missed much of last year's campaign with a broken leg and taken seven games to notch on his return, blasted five in four at the finish.

Forest beat Sunderland, Norwich and Sheffield United at home before his injury.

Longest run without loss: 8
Longest run without win: 11
High - low league position: 3-22
High - low Outlook form figure: 63-39
Key Stat: *That best unbeaten run came right at the end of the season.*

Final Outlook Index figure: 812
Clean sheets 11
Yellow cards 61 Red cards 5
Players used 31
Leading scorer:
Andy Reid 13 (all league)

Outlook forecast: 9th

Your forecast:

PLYMOUTH ARGYLE

Nickname: The Pilgrims
Colours: Green

Ground: Home Park
Capacity: 20,134

Tel: 01752 562561

www.pafc.co.uk

BOBBY WILLIAMSON has gone back to his roots in his efforts to build on the Pilgrims' fine effort in winning Division Two by seven clear points and guarantee this is no quick fling with Championship football.

Gerry McCabe has arrived from Hibernian to share first-team coaching duties with John Blackley and used his influence to snatch Scotland international striker Stevie Crawford and SPL regulars Keith Lasley, Math-

ias Doumbe, Steven Milne and Lee Makel from under the noses of clubs both north and south of the border.

Plymouth were reported by the layers to have been a virtual skinner at 20-1 ante-post for glory last term, but there will be no excuses for underestimating their chances of survival this. 52 goals in 17 home victories and nine successes and seven clean sheets on the road are stats not to be crabbed.

Longest run without loss: 10
Longest run without win: 4
High - low league position: 1-16
High - low Outlook form figure: 74-39
Key Stat: *Plymouth won all 17 games where they led at half-time.*
Outlook forecast: 16th

Final Outlook Index figure: 784
Clean sheets 21
Yellow cards 60 Red cards 3
Players used 22
Leading scorer:
David Friio 15 (14 league)
Your forecast:

PRESTON NORTH END

Nickname: Lillywhites
Colours: White and navy

Ground: Deepdale
Capacity: 22,225

Tel: 0870 442 1964

www.pnefc.net

THREE years ago the Lillywhites were a victory away from claiming a play-off spot but it's been all downhill at Deepdale since.

Although Craig Brown's side should still have just enough about them to avoid relegation, nothing more than lower mid-table mediocrity can be expected after a dismal finish to last term of one win in 13, while four away victories all season is plain embarrassing.

Jamaican international Ricardo Fuller's transfer request is unlikely to have been wholly unexpected, but it's never a good sign of a club's ambition when a young midfielder like Michael Keane opts to drop down a league - even if it's Hull - rather than sign a new contract.

Andy Smith has joined from Glentoran in a bid to form a club and country strike-partnership with the ever-reliable David Healy.

Longest run without loss: 9
Longest run without win: 6
High - low league position: 5-22
High - low Outlook form figure: 63-39
Key Stat: *North End caught 61 players off-side last season - the least in England.*
Outlook forecast: 19th

Final Outlook Index figure: 785
Clean sheets 11
Yellow cards 74 Red cards 8
Players used 29
Leading scorer:
Ricardo Fuller 19 (17 league)
Your forecast:

QUEENS PARK RANGERS

Nickname: The R's
Colours: Blue and white hoops

Ground: Loftus Road
Capacity: 19,148

Tel: 020 8743 0262

www.qpr.co.uk

THE boys from the Bush return to the Championship after a three-year leave of absence in Division Two, and there can be little doubt that it was their home form that propelled them into second spot.

The R's were undefeated at Loftus Road and conceded only three goals in 12 games on their own patch before Christmas - one of which was a 3-0 trashing of eventual champions Plymouth.

While not even the most ardent fans will expect it to remain an impenetrable fortress, hopes of more enterprising attacking football are not pie-in-the-sky, especially with the capture of exciting winger Lee Cook from Watford.

However, Clarke Carlisle's decision to quit for Leeds does leave a massive hole in the defence and consolidation rather than a play-off push will be Rangers first priority.

Longest run without loss: 13
Longest run without win: 4
High - low league position: 1-7
High - low Outlook form figure: 65-40

Key Stat: *They are currently 26 league games without defeat. It won't last.*

Outlook forecast: 17th

Final Outlook Index figure: 778
Clean sheets 18
Yellow cards 89 Red cards 3
Players used 30

Leading scorer:
Kevin Gallen 17 (all league)

Your forecast:

READING

Nickname: The Royals
Colours: Blue and white

Ground: Madejski Stadium
Capacity: 24,200

Tel: 01189 681100

www.readingfc.co.uk

THERE can be little doubt that the Royals were badly disrupted in 2003/04 by the messy departure of Alan Pardew.

The hangover from that saga lasted longer than the immediate month of September when they lost five of six matches - including a 1-0 defeat to his future West Ham charges at Upton Park.

But Steve Coppell worked wonders to restore the equilibrium at the Madejski and was rewarded with April's cathartic

beating of the Hammers in the televised reverse.

It is only a fear that the eponymous chairman will not be splashing any cash that suggests this worthy but gaffe-prone outfit (note home loss to Wimbledon) will miss out on the play-offs again.

Harper and Sidwell are two of the section's brightest midfielders while the efforts of forwards Forster, Kitson, Owusu and Goater should not be taken lightly.

Longest run without loss: 6
Longest run without win: 7
High - low league position: 2-13
High - low Outlook form figure: 65-36

Key Stat: *They couldn't score more than three goals in the league or Cup.*

Outlook forecast: 12th

Final Outlook Index figure: 814
Clean sheets 13
Yellow cards 47 Red cards 4
Players used 28

Leading scorer:
Shaun Goater 14 (12 league)

Your forecast:

ROTHERHAM UNITED

Nickname: The Millers
Colours: Red and white

Ground: Millmoor
Capacity: 11,514

Tel: 01709 512434

www.themillers.co.uk

THE on-going uncertainty over Ronnie Moore's tenancy at the Millmoor helm, which first went public after a cruel hoax phone-call, and the exact ramifications of a boardroom take-over means that it is worth a gamble on time being called on Rotherham's stay in this section.

While it is never wise to underestimate the Millers - all the leading contenders bar Ipswich dropped points to them last season, including automatic promotion duo Norwich and West Brom - the mood in the infamous cramped dressing room will not have been lifted by the lack of significant summer signings.

Typically honest outputs are expected from stalwart midfielder John Mullin and new boys at the back Phil Gilchrist and Robbie Stockdale, but that might not be enough to guarantee survival in could be a very competitive scrap at the bottom.

Longest run without loss: 8
Longest run without win: 8
High - low league position: 14-23
High - low Outlook form figure: 63-32
Key Stat: *Only Wimbledon had lower Division One crowds last season.*

Outlook forecast: 23rd

Final Outlook Index figure: 787
Clean sheets 15
Yellow cards 75 Red cards 7
Players used 28
Leading scorer:
Martin Butler 15 (all league)

Your forecast:

SHEFFIELD UNITED

Nickname: The Blades
Colours: Red and white

Ground: Bramall Lane
Capacity: 30,936

Tel: 0114 2215757

www.sufc.co.uk

DESPITE two Cup semi-finals and a play-off final berth in 2002/2003, the Blades never convinced as likely candidates for promotion last term.

The Bramall Lane boys went completely off the boil after Boxing Day, winning only seven league games and just one against a major rival - distracted Millwall - with the sale of regular midfield goalscorer Michael Brown to Spurs no doubt effecting them.

Fiery boss Neil Warnock has decided to overhaul his squad for a decent tilt this campaign. In come John Harley, Barry Hayles, Andy Liddell, Phil Barnes, Leigh Bromby and Alan Quinn - out go veterans Robert Page, Peter Ndlovu and Wayne Allison.

September will be their crucial 'moving' month, with home clashes with West Ham, Coventry and Sunderland, and away days at Leicester and Wigan.

Longest run without loss: 8
Longest run without win: 4
High - low league position: 1-10
High - low Outlook form figure: 62-36
Key Stat: *Two wins in nine saw them drop from third to eighth at the death.*

Outlook forecast: 5th

Final Outlook Index figure: 804
Clean sheets 15
Yellow cards 71 Red cards 4
Players used 34
Leading scorer:
Jack Lester 15 (12 league)

Your forecast:

Sponsored by Stan James

STOKE CITY

Nickname: The Potters
Colours: Red and white

Ground: Britannia Stadium
Capacity: 28,384

Tel: 01782 592222

www.stokecityfc.com

THERE is no substitute for experience so the saying goes, but surely 11th place was beyond the wildest dreams of Tony Pulis when he brought the likes of Carl Asaba, Ed de Goey, Gerry Taggart and Ade Akinbiyi to the Britannia Stadium over the course of last season.

The Potters had finished fourth from bottom on their return to what is now the Championship in 2002/03 and weren't expected to do much more than tread water again. But they proved a constant thorn in the side of many a fashionable operation - particularly in the December/January loan period of ex-Northern Ireland international centre-half Taggart when they won seven of eight league games. The loss, though, of wide men Kriss Commons and Peter Hoekstra means that any further progress is unlikely without more investment. And of that there is little evidence.

Longest run without loss: 7
Longest run without win: 5
High - low league position: 4-22
High - low Outlook form figure: 66-39
Key Stat: *In June the squad's average age was just 22.*

Outlook forecast: 17th

Final Outlook Index figure: 809
Clean sheets 14
Yellow cards 71 Red cards 4
Players used 31
Leading scorer: Ade Akinbiyi and Gifton Noel-Williams 10 (all league)

Your forecast:

SUNDERLAND

Nickname: Mackems or Black Cats
Colours: Red and white

Ground: Stadium Of Light
Capacity: 48,300

Tel: 0191 551 5000

www.safc.com

WHEN you consider that the Black Cats had to avoid defeat against Watford in their third game following Premiership relegation to avoid sharing Darwen's 104-year-old record for the most consecutive losses, third place in the league and a Cup semi-final doesn't represent too bad a season.

Unfortunately for Mick McCarthy, Sunderland failed to perform on both the big occasions - the Mackems barely turned up at Old Trafford against Millwall and failed to close out 10-man Palace in the home play-off semi second leg.

Eight home draws and nine away defeats highlight exactly where Sunderland must improve, but that is no gimme given the lack of cash to splash.

Despite Stephen Caldwell making the rare Tyne-Wear switch and John Oster and Julio Arca staying, others could well quicken past them.

Longest run without loss: 9
Longest run without win: 6
High - low league position: 3-17
High - low Outlook form figure: 63-41
Key Stat: *What potential - last season's record crowd (36,278) was against Walsall.*

Outlook forecast: 8th

Final Outlook Index figure: 826
Clean sheets 18
Yellow cards 75 Red cards 9
Players used 32
Leading scorer:
Marcus Stewart 16 (14 league)

Your forecast:

WATFORD

Nickname: The Hornets
Colours: Yellow and black

Ground: Vicarage Road
Capacity: 22,000

Tel: 01923 496000

www.watfordfc.com

FOLLOWING Iain Dowie and Andy Hessenthaler on last year's sectional managerial honours board should be the Hornets' Ray Lewington.

The real importance of football in the scheme of things was brought home by the death of ex-Man United prospect Jimmy Davis in a road accident on the morning of the then postponed first game.

To then steer to safety his Vicarage Road squad, with purse-strings pulled tight, through the ensuing emotions and poor form on the pitch that inevitably followed was no mean feat.

The Hornets won only one of their first 11 games in all competitions, but having rediscovered their poise they played some decent attacking football.

Helguson, Fitzgerald and Webber should score goals but the departure of Lee Cook for QPR undoubtedly takes away some creativity.

Longest run without loss: 6
Longest run without win: 6
High - low league position: 15-24
High - low Outlook form figure: 61-38
Key Stat: *Watford employ not one but two sports psychologists.*

Outlook forecast: 18th

Final Outlook Index figure: 796
Clean sheets 9
Yellow cards 60 Red cards 7
Players used 29
Leading scorer:
Scott Fitzgerald 11 (10 league)

Your forecast:

WEST HAM UNITED

Nickname: Hammers or Irons
Colours: Claret and blue

Ground: Boleyn Ground
Capacity: 35,500

Tel: 020 8548 2748

www.whufc.co.uk

PITHY slogans and fervent support weren't enough to take West Ham back up via the play-offs to the Premiership, and Alan Pardew would be wise to review his own methods, not just the performances of his players, ahead of another hard slog.

The insistence on using 20-goal a season striker Marlon Harewood as a right-sided midfielder away from Upton Park smacked of wilful intransigence and flew in the face of the formbook.

From mid-February, the Irons won just once on the road and were out-fought and out-thought when visiting Sunderland, Millwall, Reading and twice by Crystal Palace, most critically in the Millennium Stadium.

Michael Carrick will undoubtedly be sold to the highest bidder while Harewood and consistent performers Connolly and Etherington have also been touted for transfer. More disappointment could follow next May.

Longest run without loss: 8
Longest run without win: 9
High - low league position: 2-16
High - low Outlook form figure: 67-40
Key Stat: *Last year they hit the woodwork 16 times and missed 3 out of 4 penalties.*

Outlook forecast: 7th

Final Outlook Index figure: 833
Clean sheets 17
Yellow cards 67 Red cards 6
Players used 35
Leading scorer:
Jermaine Defoe 15 (11 league)

Your forecast:

WIGAN ATHLETIC

Nickname: The Latics
Colours: Blue

Ground: JJB Stadium
Capacity: 25,000

Tel: 01942 774000

www.wiganlatics.co.uk

THE Latics will never be the number one attraction at the JJB Stadium - it is also the domain of a certain Warriors Rugby League outfit, but punters must not overlook Paul Jewell's side.

They were denied a play-off berth only by Brian Deane's late equaliser for West Ham on the final day, and can build upon last season's terrific eighth spot.

Indeed, the chequebook of chairman David Whelan has been put to good use with the recruitment of raw Torquay striker David Graham and Crewe defender David Wright. 19-goal Nathan Ellington, Jason Roberts, Neil, Graham and Lee McCulloch looks a nap hand of attacking talent just itching to take advantage of decent service from Jimmy Bullard, Alan Mahon and Gary Teale.

A thin squad cost Wigan dear last term and is the caveat against tipping them to automatically make the Premiership.

Longest run without loss: 16
Longest run without win: 5
High - low league position: 1-15
High - low Outlook form figure: 68-38
Key Stat: *Suspensions cost them dearly; they were the UK's top red carders.*

Outlook forecast: 4th

Final Outlook Index figure: 809
Clean sheets 17
Yellow cards 64 Red cards 11
Players used 26
Leading scorer:
Nathan Ellington 19 (18 league)

Your forecast:

WOLVERHAMPTON W

Nickname: Wolves
Colours: Gold and black

Ground: Molineux
Capacity: 28,525

Tel: 0870 442 0123

www.wolves.co.uk

AS expected Dave Jones' motley gold crew lasted only the one season in the top flight, after an absence of 20 years, but were not a total embarrassment to the Premiership or their supporters.

They delighted the Molineux faithful with the 1-0 triumph over Man United and a 1-1 draw with Liverpool in the space of four crisp January days.

With so many of their rivals yet to emerge intact from relegation-induced ructions, Wolves can bounce back immediately. Jones will have them prepared for the task and loan strikers Ganea and George Ndah should thrive at this level.

Knockers will highlight that they made only the play-offs in May 2003 and that the squad is drifting apart.

Denis Irwin, Alex Rae and Paul Butler have gone, while Paul Ince, Kenny Miller and Henri Camara have yet to commit.

Longest run without loss: 6
Longest run without win: 8
High - low league position: 15-20
High - low Outlook form figure: 68-38
Key Stat: *Only Henry had more shots on target in the Premiership than Camara.*

Outlook forecast: 2nd

Final Outlook Index figure: 844
Clean sheets 7
Yellow cards 66 Red cards 2
Players used 27
Leading scorer:
Henri Camara 7 (all league)

Your forecast:

AFC BOURNEMOUTH

Nickname: The Cherries
Colours: Red and black

Ground: Dean Court
Capacity: 10,770

Tel: 01202 726300

www.afcb.co.uk

THE Cherries got back into the swing of life in League One after bouncing back via the play-offs.

Although Bournemouth finished just three places off the play-off spots, they were a long way behind the likes of Hartlepool and Swindon, and their campaign is perhaps best viewed as one of consolidation in mid-table rather than promotion chasing.

Warren Feeney, who scored twelve times last season, is on the way to Stockport and will be missed but top scorer James Hayter, whose fourteen goals included the fastest league hat-trick in history against Wrexham in February, has signed for another two years. That he has been top scorer for the past two seasons is all the more remarkable when one considers that last term the versatile 25-year-old played in midfield and defence as well as his usual striking role.

Longest run without loss: 6
Longest run without win: 7
High - low league position: 3-21
High - low Outlook form figure: 65-40
Key Stat: *They won none of their last five homes all against non top 10 teams.*

Outlook forecast: 8th

Final Outlook Index figure: 740
Clean sheets 11
Yellow cards 65 Red cards 2
Players used 22
Leading scorer:
James Hayter 14 (all league)

Your forecast:

BARNSLEY

Nickname: Tykes
Colours: Red and white

Ground: Oakwell
Capacity: 23,186

Tel: 01226 211211

www.barnsleyfc.co.uk

FOLLOWING relegation to League One two seasons ago, the Tykes spent last term fighting to avoid a second drop.

Paul Hart was brought in to replace Gudjon Thordarson, who was unable to reproduce the success he had at Stoke before his controversial dismissal. Between them, they contrived to produce a comfortable mid-table finish.

The close season has seen wholesale changes at Oakwell, with Hart releasing a whole battery of players and bringing in plenty of new faces. Those that remain include versatile youngster Antony Kay, voted player of the season last term. The new arrivals include right back Barry Hassell from Mansfield and striker Barry Conlon.

Conlon, who was top scorer during a difficult campaign at Darlington last season, will be a welcome addition to a squad where only Kevin Betsy was able to break into double figures.

Longest run without loss: 6
Longest run without win: 11
High - low league position: 1-13
High - low Outlook form figure: 62-36
Key Stat: *They won and scored more away than at home - where they drew 12.*

Outlook forecast: 14th

Final Outlook Index figure: 736
Clean sheets 13
Yellow cards 67 Red cards 6
Players used 40
Leading scorer:
Kevin Betsy 11 (10 league)

Your forecast:

BLACKPOOL

Nickname: The Seasiders
Colours: Tangerine and white

Ground: Bloomfield Road
Capacity: 11,295

Tel: 0870 443 1953

www.blackpoolfc.co.uk

FORMER Scotland international Colin Hendry returns as manager to the club where he ended his playing career on loan in 2002/03.

Under Steve McMahon, the Seasiders won promotion to League One and managed a comfortable mid-table finish last season, but their league form was plagued by inconsistency and miserable results at home. Only Peterborough and Wycombe lost more home games.

Hendry will have to contend with a threadbare squad made poorer by the loss of keeper Phil Barnes, who has left for Sheffield United.

Among the new arrivals is Keigan Parker who scored eight times in 15 league appearances for St Johnstone attack last season. If he and Scott Taylor - who scored 27 times in all competitions last term - click Blackpool will have a strikeforce to be reckoned with.

Longest run without loss: 5
Longest run without win: 4
High - low league position: 10-18
High - low Outlook form figure: 62-36
Key Stat: *The Seasiders won 11 Cup ties last season.*

Outlook forecast: 15th

Final Outlook Index figure: 727
Clean sheets 12
Yellow cards 71 Red cards 7
Players used 35
Leading scorer:
Scott Taylor 27 (16 league)

Your forecast:

BRADFORD CITY

Nickname: The Bantams
Colours: Claret and amber

Ground: Valley Parade
Capacity: 25,000

Tel: 01274 773355

www.bradfordcityfc.premiumtv.co.uk

AFTER overstretching themselves during their two seasons in the Premiership, life has been very tough for the Bantams.

Last term they succumbed to relegation after being on the brink of extinction and telling the entire playing staff to look for other clubs. Now Bradford must satisfy the Football League that they can make it through the coming season and confirm where they will be playing their home matches before they even kick a ball.

Manager Bryan Robson left frustrated and is succeeded by Colin Todd against this background, he has a mammoth task to halt the club's sad decline.

Not surprisingly, the list of players going out is much longer than those going in, with Danny Cadamateri, Michael Branch, Robert Wolleaston and Mark Paston amongst those who left over the summer. It will be an achievement if the Bantams can avoid a second successive relegation.

Longest run without loss: 3
Longest run without win: 12
High - low league position: 13-23
High - low Outlook form figure: 57-34
Key Stat: *They hit 23rd spot on November 8 - and remained there.*

Outlook forecast: 24th

League Stats
Clean sheets 7
Yellow cards 87 Red cards 5
Players used 32
Leading scorer: Paul Branch, Andy Gray and Dean Windass 6 (all league, 5 Gray)

Your forecast:

BRENTFORD

Nickname: The Bees
Colours: Red, white and black

Ground: Griffin Park
Capacity: 12,763

Tel: 0208 847 2511

www.brentfordfc.co.uk

THERE were only seven minutes of the season left when substitute Alex Rhodes scored the goal against Bournemouth that ensured Brentford's survival in League One.

Under Wally Downes, the Bees endured their worst opening day league defeat for 48 years - a 4-1 drubbing at Tranmere. By the end of August they were out of the League Cup, second from bottom and had just three points from their opening five games.

Relegation seemed certain when Martin Allen replaced Downes in March, but with Allen at the helm the Bees lost just one of their remaining nine matches to beat the drop.

Scott Fitzgerald, who joined the club on loan from Colchester for the final nine games of the season, has signed a one-year contract. He arrival helped stem the torrent of goals and Allen has added more experience with Andy Myers and Chris Hargreaves.

Longest run without loss: 8
Longest run without win: 11
High - low league position: 13-23
High - low Outlook form figure: 61-31
Key Stat: *Bees were 4 points adrift with 9 games left when Martin Allen came in.*

Outlook forecast: 10th

Final Outlook Index figure: 730
Clean sheets 6
Yellow cards 64 Red cards 8
Players used 29
Leading scorer:
Steve Hunt 12 (11 league)

Your forecast:

BRISTOL CITY

Nickname: The Robins
Colours: Red

Ground: Ashton Gate
Capacity: 21,479

Tel: 0117 9630630

www.bcfc.co.uk

THE ROBINS only missed out on automatic promotion by a single point last term but were beaten in the play-offs for a second season running.

It was too much for the Ashton Gate board, who replaced Danny Wilson with Brian Tinnion, who will combine his managerial duties with a midfield role.

City could boast the best defensive record in the division last term but a lack of goals thwarted Wilson's aim of avoiding the play-offs. They scored fewer goals at home than any other top ten side and in the top ten, only Bournemouth scored fewer times in total.

The drawn out contract negotiations with top scorer Lee Peacock have been the story of the summer at Ashton Gate, and Tinnion is keen to line up a strike partner or if necessary, a replacement. Peacock was the only Robin to hit double figures last season.

Longest run without loss: 11
Longest run without win: 7
High - low league position: 1-14
High - low Outlook form figure: 66-37
Key Stat: *Their record run of 11 wins was followed by just two goals in six games.*

Outlook forecast: 1st

Final Outlook Index figure: 774
Clean sheets 17
Yellow cards 63 Red cards 4
Players used 24
Leading scorer:
Lee Peacock 16 (14 league)

Your forecast:

CHESTERFIELD

Nickname: Spireites
Colours: Blue and white

Ground: Recreation Ground
Capacity: 8,960

Tel: 01246 209765

www.chesterfield-fc.co.uk

FOR the second season in succession, the Spireites avoided the drop by the skin of their teeth. This time, it took a final day victory over Luton combined with defeats for both Rushden and Grimsby for Chesterfield to retain their League One status.

Roy McFarland's side were atrocious away from the Recreation Ground, winning just three times on the road all season. Their toothless attack was able to conjure up only 15 away goals, less than any other side in the division. Glynn Hurst was top gun with a respectable 13 strikes but elsewhere the goals were not forthcoming.

McFarland has brought in Wayne Allison, now 35, but the veteran striker will need to improve significantly on last term's solitary goal from fourteen Championship starts for Sheffield Utd if he is to be the answer to McFarland's prayers.

Longest run without loss: 4
Longest run without win: 14
High - low league position: 17-24
High - low Outlook form figure: 57-30
Key Stat: *Great escape - after 13 games they had no wins and just eight goals.*

Outlook forecast: 21st

Final Outlook Index figure: 721
Clean sheets 10
Yellow cards 92 Red cards 5
Players used 29
Leading scorer:
Glynn Hurst 13 (all league)

Your forecast:

COLCHESTER UNITED

Nickname: The U's
Colours: Blue and white

Ground: Layer Road
Capacity: 7,556

Tel: 0845 330 2975

www.cu-fc.com

AFTER taking charge midway through the 2002/03 season and leading the U's to twelfth place, Colchester manager Phil Parkinson guided them to eleventh spot last time.

Parkinson brought in Wayne Andrews from Oldham and was rewarded by a return of 12 goals over the season but strike partner Scott McGleish, who contributed ten goals to the league campaign, has gone to Northampton.

The manager's immediate job has been to bolster his defence after both Andy Myers and Scott Fitzgerald left for Brentford. He has traded experience for youth and Liam Chilvers joins from Arsenal and George Elokobi from Dulwich Hamlet.

Parkinson will hope the new arrivals can replicate the solid defensive displays of last season but, even with McGleish playing, the U's attack lacked bite and this is a cause for concern.

Longest run without loss: 6
Longest run without win: 5
High - low league position: 4-23
High - low Outlook form figure: 62-41
Key Stat: *No UK side played more Cup games than Colchester's 15 last term.*

Outlook forecast: 11th

Final Outlook Index figure: 746
Clean sheets 11
Yellow cards 68 Red cards 8
Players used 27
Leading scorer:
Scott McGleish 17 (10 league)

Your forecast:

DONCASTER ROVERS

Nickname: Rovers
Colours: Red and white

Ground: Belle Vue
Capacity: 9,706

Tel: 01302 539441

www.doncasterroversfc.co.uk

IN the wake of two successive promotions, Rovers are a club with momentum. Inspired by League Two player of the season Michael McIndoe, the Belle Vue club marched to the title scoring freely along the way.

Doncaster chairman John Ryan has made funds available to manager Dave Penney to strengthen the squad and, so far, the summer signings suggest that more attacking football is to come.

Striker Jermaine McSporran and winger Andy Watson are new to the squad and will complement Gregg Blundell who found the net 18 times during the title charge.

Their goal will be to emulate Plymouth rather than Rushden and if Rovers can adapt to League One as quickly as they adapted following their promotion to the League from the Conference, they will stand a good chance of surviving the drop.

Longest run without loss: 14
Longest run without win: 6
High - low league position: 1-18
High - low Outlook form figure: 68-39
Key Stat: *They did not concede more than one in their last 16 games.*

Outlook forecast: 6th

Final Outlook Index figure: 710
Clean sheets 19
Yellow cards 79 Red cards 4
Players used 27
Leading scorer:
Gregg Blundell 20 (18 league)

Your forecast:

HARTLEPOOL UNITED

Nickname: Pool
Colours: White and blue

Ground: Victoria Park
Capacity: 7,629

Tel: 01429 272584

www.hartlepoolunited.co.uk

HARTLEPOOL carried off the transition to life in League One with aplomb last season but, ultimately, the Monkey Hangers finished up as bridesmaids once again.

Twelve months after they were pipped to the League Two championship by Rushden, a pair of last gasp Bristol City goals robbed them of a place in the League One play-off final.

They can take heart that the progress at

Victoria Park under Neale Cooper has continued in the same vein as when Chris Turner and then Mike Newell were in charge.

Cooper is looking to strengthen the squad and is in the market for a striker. Midfielder Jack Ross has already joined from Clyde but defender Chris Westwood - who made 45 appearances for Pool last season - will miss pre-season training with a foot injury.

Longest run without loss: 5
Longest run without win: 4
High - low league position: 3-19
High - low Outlook form figure: 67-41
Key Stat: *Nine fewer cards than any Div Two side and top away goalscorers too.*

Outlook forecast: 4th

Final Outlook Index figure: 754
Clean sheets 14
Yellow cards 54 Red cards 0
Players used 34
Leading scorer:
Adam Boyd 16 (all league)

Your forecast:

HUDDERSFIELD TOWN

Nickname: The Terriers
Colours: Blue and white

Ground: McAlpine Stadium
Capacity: 24,500

Tel: 01484 484100

www. htafc.com.

A LATE Cheltenham equaliser on the final day of the season was the only thing that separated the Terriers from automatic promotion, but thanks to a penalty shootout victory against Mansfield in the play-off final, they line up in League One after just one season down.

Promotion makes a welcome change for Huddersfield whose rapid descent through the divisions has been remarkable - it is not long ago that they were challenging for promotion to the Premiership. More good news is that after being linked with the Leeds job, manager Peter Jackson has signed a new three-year contract.

But it is hard to imagine that Jonathan Stead will not be missed. He has already scored some vital goals for Blackburn in the Premiership and, despite parting company with the Terriers in February, was their top scorer with 16 goals from 26 games.

Longest run without loss: 7
Longest run without win: 4
High - low league position: 3-19
High - low Outlook form figure: 65-40
Key Stat: *Season ticket sales have brought in over £1m.*

Outlook forecast: 17th

Final Outlook Index figure: 714
Clean sheets 17
Yellow cards 84 Red cards 14
Players used 31
Leading scorer:
Jon Stead 18 (16 league)

Your forecast:

HULL CITY

Nickname: The Tigers
Colours: Amber and black

Ground: Kingston Communication Stadium
Capacity: 25,404

Tel: 0870 8370003

www.hullcityafc.net

THERE must be something about Hull. Peter Taylor has been linked with a role at Tottenham as well as the England Under-21 job but is set to remain with the Tigers instead.

There is a wealth of attacking talent at the club. Hull scored more goals than any other team in League Two last season and missed out on the top spot by only four points.

Daniel Allsopp and Ben Burgess proved a formidable strike force at that level, with Stuart Elliott weighing in with 14 goals from midfield. Even so, Taylor has had an offer for Swindon hitman Sam Parkin turned down and has recruited Delroy Facey from West Brom.

At the other end of the pitch, keepers Paul Musselwhite and Alan Fettis are both on the way out of the club. Young Portuguese goalie Sergio Leite is to take over between the sticks.

Longest run without loss: 16
Longest run without win: 6
High - low league position: 1-10
High - low Outlook form figure: 68-37
Key Stat: *They scored the most at home and conceded least away in Div Three.*

Outlook forecast: 2nd

Final Outlook Index figure: 712
Clean sheets 16
Yellow cards 58 Red cards 1
Players used 27
Leading scorer:
Ben Burgess 18 (all league)

Your forecast:

LUTON TOWN

Nickname: The Hatters
Colours: White and black

Ground: Kenilworth Road
Capacity: 9,975

Tel: 01582 411622

www.lutontown.co.uk

AGAINST a background of financial instability, Mike Newell led the Hatters to a top-ten finish in League One last season.

After coming out of administration following a successful take-over bid in the summer, the talk now is of securing Luton's future by relocating to a new stadium within three years.

Aside from that small matter, most of the activity at the club over the summer has been concentrated on keeping their out of contract players rather than bringing in fresh blood.

Striker Adrian Forbes who scored 14 goals last season has gone to Swansea, and player of the year Emmerson Boyce is keeping his options open.

Nevertheless, in his first season in charge, Newell has surpassed expectations after being controversially appointed ahead of Joe Kinnear by a vote.

Longest run without loss: 6
Longest run without win: 7
High - low league position: 6-15
High - low Outlook form figure: 67-41
Key Stat: *Just one clean sheet in their last 17 games.*

Outlook forecast: 9th

Final Outlook Index figure: 739
Clean sheets 9
Yellow cards 86 Red cards 7
Players used 32
Leading scorer:
Steve Howard 16 (15 league)

Your forecast:

MILTON KEYNES DONS

Nickname: The Dons
Colours: White and gold

Ground: National Hockey Stadium
Capacity: 8,900

Tel: 01908 607090

www.mkdons.com

THERE was time when every small club hoped to 'do a Wimbledon' but following the grubby business of the club's relocation and renaming - they are now the Milton Keynes Dons - the expression has become somewhat tarnished.

The Dons were awful last season. Atrocious form in front of tiny crowds at the National Hockey Stadium - just over a thousand turning up for the home defeat to Wigan - resulted in just three 'home' wins. They finished rock bottom and, after the best of the squad had departed for pastures new, were left fielding youngsters and cast-offs.

Off the pitch, the Inland Revenue have opted not to take a case to recover a debt of over £500,000 to the House of Lords, clearing the way for Pete Winkleman's consortium to finally take over the club. But with no funds to strengthen the squad, 1988 seems a long time ago.

Longest run without loss: 3
Longest run without win: 13
High - low league position: 17-24
High - low Outlook form figure: 57-31
Key Stat: *The Dons had the worst defence in England last season.*

Outlook forecast: 22nd

Final Outlook Index figure: 742
Clean sheets 5
Yellow cards 63 Red cards 7
Players used 36
Leading scorer:
Patrick Agyemang 7 (all league)

Your forecast:

OLDHAM ATHLETIC

Nickname: The Latics
Colours: Blue

Ground: Boundary Park
Capacity: 13,659

Tel: 0870 753 2000

www.oldhamathletic.co.uk

A MID-TABLE finish belies the anxiety that overshadowed much of the Latics' campaign. In the end, they won their relegation battle comfortably and with the club coming out of administration following a takeover in February and Brian Talbot taking over managerial duties from John Eyre in March, it turned into a transitional season.

Oldham proved hard to beat last season but also found it hard to win. They drew 21 times (almost half of their games) more than any other side in the league, 13 of those away from Boundary Park. It will be Talbot's challenge to turn some of those draws into wins next season.

At least he will not face the difficulties that Iain Dowie did, when the cream of the squad were sold to ease the club's financial burden. Talbot has been busy making sure his players will be at Boundary Park this season.

Longest run without loss: 9
Longest run without win: 6
High - low league position: 9-22
High - low Outlook form figure: 62-36
Key Stat: *Winger David Eyres was voted Player Of The Year, aged 40!*

Final Outlook Index figure: 750
Clean sheets 9
Yellow cards 91 Red cards 6
Players used 34
Leading scorer:
Scott Vernon 14 (12 league)

Outlook forecast: 13th

Your forecast:

PETERBOROUGH UNITED

Nickname: Posh
Colours: Blue

Ground: London Road
Capacity: 15,314

Tel: 08700 550 442

www.theposh.com

ALWAYS one for doing things his way, Barry Fry became Peterborough's majority shareholder last October after eight years as Posh manager.

The first season under the new regime did not go exactly according to plan, with Fry's side finishing just two points away from the relegation places.

The sale of Leon McKenzie to Norwich undoubtedly helped keep the club afloat financially, but on the pitch he was missed with nobody else able to match his ten league goals.

However, Leon Constantine has joined from Southend, where he bagged 21 goals last season, and both Andy Clarke and Calum Willock are set to stay at London Road.

Head coach Bobby Gould has also pledged his future to the club after agreeing to a two-year deal. As usual, survival will be the goal.

Longest run without loss: 5
Longest run without win: 9
High - low league position: 11-22
High - low Outlook form figure: 62-39
Key Stat: *They stayed up by only losing at two promoted sides in their last 9 aways.*

Final Outlook Index figure: 736
Clean sheets 10
Yellow cards 64 Red cards 5
Players used 30
Leading scorer:
Andy Clarke 12 (9 league)

Outlook forecast: 19th

Your forecast:

PORT VALE

Nickname: The Valiants
Colours: White and black

Ground: Vale Park
Capacity: 23,.000

Tel: 01782 655800

www.port-vale.co.uk

IT was disappointment all round at Nene Park on the final day of last season. Port Vale's 2-0 victory condemned Rushden to the drop but Vale also missed out on the play-offs on goal difference after Swindon's win at Brighton.

But it was much better than the relegation battle that had come before it in a season that was marred by talk of a proposed merger with Potteries rivals Stoke.

Manager Martin Foyle is keen to bring new players to the club, but the Valiants will not be taking financial risks in order to mount a promotion bid this season and he will have to work within a tight budget.

Lee Matthews has joined from Bristol City but 27-goal striker Stephen McPhee has joined Portuguese side Beira Mar. Marc Bridge-Wilkinson and Neil Brisco have also left, but at least Micky Cummins stays.

Longest run without loss: 5
Longest run without win: 4
High - low league position: 1-12
High - low Outlook form figure: 59-41
Key Stat: *They failed to score just once in their final 26 games.*

Outlook forecast: 16th

Final Outlook Index figure: 752
Clean sheets 12
Yellow cards 62 Red cards 2
Players used 30
Leading scorer:
Stephen McPhee 27 (25 league)

Your forecast:

SHEFFIELD WEDNESDAY

Nickname: The Owls
Colours: Blue and white

Ground: Hillsborough
Capacity: 39,814

Tel: 0114 221 2121

www.swfc.co.uk

WEDNESDAY were unable to build on the momentum achieved under Chris Turner during the second half of their 2002/03 campaign and, rather than challenging for promotion, finished the season just three points above the relegation zone.

Although the Owls were below average on the road, it was their performances at home that proved to be their Achilles heel. Despite having the highest average attendance in the division, the cavernous Hillsborough was rarely more than half-full and in front of the empty seats they won just seven times at home.

Wednesday have been busy in the transfer market; new acquisitions include Guy Branston, Paul Heckingbottom, Chris Marsden and Lee Bullen.

Off the pitch, the acrimonious will-he-won't-he Ken Bates takeover saga has kept the Owls in the news.

Longest run without loss: 6
Longest run without win: 7
High - low league position: 2-18
High - low Outlook form figure: 58-40
Key Stat: *The biggest home crowds in the division yet the fewest home goals.*

Outlook forecast: 12th

Final Outlook Index figure: 721
Clean sheets 11
Yellow cards 79 Red cards 7
Players used 35
Leading scorer:
Guylain Ndumbu-Nsungu 10 (9 league)

Your forecast:

STOCKPORT COUNTY

Nickname: County
Colours: Blue

Ground: Edgeley Park
Capacity: 11,540

Tel: 0161 286 8888

www.stockportcounty.com

CARLTON PALMER didn't last long into the season as Stockport boss - just eight league matches.

When Sammy McIlroy took the reins at Edgeley Park, County were fifth from bottom with just 11 points to show from the first 13 games of their campaign.

McIlroy did bring about improvement over the course of the season and at the final reckoning they finished sixth from bottom. Under McIlroy, County were more resilient than they had been previously and until a final-day defeat at home to Barnsley, went 11 games unbeaten. That run gives County reason to be optimistic, but with limited resources it will take another stubborn season to ensure survival in League One.

Stuart Barlow and Mark Robertson have agreed new contracts while Lee Mair joins from Dundee together with Bournemouth striker Warren Feeney.

Longest run without loss: 11
Longest run without win: 9
High - low league position: 17-23
High - low Outlook form figure: 62-37
Key Stat: *Country lost fewer than a third of their aways last season.*

Outlook forecast: 18th

Final Outlook Index figure: 742
Clean sheets 10
Yellow cards 71 Red cards 3
Players used 34
Leading scorer:
Rickie Lambert 13 (12 league)

Your forecast:

SWINDON TOWN

Nickname: The Robins
Colours: Red and white

Ground: County Ground
Capacity: 15,728

Tel: 0870 443 1969

www.swindontownfc.co.uk

A HEART-BREAKING penalty shootout defeat saw the Robins pipped to the play-off final by Brighton and the Swindon faithful will consider a return of play-off football to the County Ground as a minimum requirement for manager Andy King.

The good news is that Sam Parkin - whose 19 league goals were a major factor in a decent campaign - looks likely to stay after interest from Leeds amongst others. The bad news is that

SWINDON TOWN FC

Parkin's strike partner Tommy Mooney is on the way out - Mooney matched Parkin's tally goal for goal.

Midfielders Stefani Miglioranzi and David Duke have both signed new contracts whilst in terms of new acquisitions, King is putting his faith in youth rather than experience. 20-year-old Striker Lloyd Opara has joined on a free transfer from Cambridge, whilst defender Jerel Ifil, 21, is to join the Robins from Watford.

Longest run without loss: 12
Longest run without win: 7
High - low league position: 4-15
High - low Outlook form figure: 64-36
Key Stat: *A yo-yo season: 11th-4th, 15th-9th, 14th-5th in less than five months*

Outlook forecast: 7th

Final Outlook Index figure: 754
Clean sheets 14
Yellow cards 71 Red cards 7
Players used 27
Leading scorer:
Sam Parkin 22 (19 league)

Your forecast:

TORQUAY UNITED

Nickname: The Gulls
Colours: Yellow and blue

Ground: Plainmoor
Capacity: 6,003

Tel: 01803 328666

www.torquayunited.com

TORQUAY managed to sustain their promotion push throughout last season, and a final-day victory against Southend meant that they just beat Huddersfield to the final automatic promotion place.

Defensively the Gulls were very solid, and it was their superior goal difference that ultimately displaced the Terriers.

That goal difference was also aided significantly by the fact that striker David Gra-ham bagged 22 league goals. Sadly for the Plainmoor club, the Scot has left for Wigan after the Latics saw off competition from Leeds.

The move puts a bit of money in the bank, but Graham will be sorely missed. Jo Kuffour, who scored ten alongside Graham, has signed a two-year extension to his current contract. However, without an adequate replacement for Graham, Torquay could struggle.

Longest run without loss: 8
Longest run without win: 5
High - low league position: 3-13
High - low Outlook form figure: 63-42
Key Stat: *Just one week at third in March, before snatching it back on final day.*

Outlook forecast: 20th

Final Outlook Index figure: 710
Clean sheets 14
Yellow cards 77 Red cards 3
Players used 26
Leading scorer:
David Graham 23 (22 league)

Your forecast:

TRANMERE ROVERS

Nickname: Rovers
Colours: White

Ground: Prenton Park
Capacity: 16,789

Tel: 0151 609 3333

www.tranmererovers.co.uk

FOR the second season running, Rovers came close to winning a play-off berth after a storming late run, but that's only part of their story last season.

The campaign will be remembered in Birkenhead for the kind of FA Cup exploits that the Prenton Park side seem to specialise in. They reached the last 16 of the competition, beating Bolton in a replay before losing to eventual finalists Millwall.

Brian Little's side took the momentum from the Cup run into their league form and after the Millwall defeat went on a run that saw them take 26 points out of possible 33, and miss out on the play-offs by two places.

Little has agreed a new three-year contract and has been busy getting out of contract players to re-sign and bringing the likes of centre-back Michael Jackson, midfielders Theodore Whitmore and Mark Rankine and striker Calvin Zola to the club.

Longest run without loss: 12
Longest run without win: 10
High - low league position: 5-21
High - low Outlook form figure: 64-36
Key Stat: *They played eight FA Cup ties; then lost just one of their last 11 games.*

Outlook forecast: 3rd

Final Outlook Index figure: 761
Clean sheets 15
Yellow cards 82 Red cards 5
Players used 27
Leading scorer:
Eugene Dadi 19 (16 league)

Your forecast:

Sponsored by Stan James

WALSALL

Nickname: The Saddlers
Colours: Red, white and black

Ground: Bescot Stadium
Capacity: 9,000

Tel: 01922 622791

www.saddlers.co.uk

FOLLOWING three seasons lurking around the nether regions of the Championship, Walsall were relegated to League One last term, finishing behind Gillingham on goal difference despite victory on the last day of the season.

Player-manager Paul Merson is at the helm, after presiding over the Saddlers death throes in the Championship. Three defeats from his four games in charge did little to help the cause but these were against good sides in Norwich, Crystal Palace and Sheffield United. The damage had already been done before he took over but the jury is still out.

Walsall released nine players including Craig Burley and Jermaine McSporran. Merson has raided cash-strapped Bradford - bringing in Michael Standing and keeper Mark Paston. Neil Emblen and top scorer Jorge Leitao have both re-signed.

Longest run without loss: 4
Longest run without win: 11
High - low league position: 6-22
High - low Outlook form figure: 57-33
Key Stat: *They beat West Brom 4-1 on the opening day. They peaked too early!*

Outlook forecast: 5th

Final Outlook Index figure: 770
Clean sheets 10
Yellow cards 60 Red cards 7
Players used 33
Leading scorer:
Jorge Leitao 9 (7 league)

Your forecast:

WREXHAM

Nickname: Dragons
Colours: Red and white

Ground: Racecourse Ground
Capacity: 15,500

Tel: 01978 262129/290793

www.wrexhamafc.co.uk

WREXHAM'S aim for next season will be simply to survive and a repeat of last term's mid-table finish would be considered a success.

The players and staff had their wages deferred several times over the season, as recently as the end of May, shortly after Mark Guterman resigned as chairman and was replaced by Alex Hamilton. Dragons supporters fear that Hamilton will sell the Racecourse Ground.

To make matters worse, after turning down a £200,000 offer for Carlos Edwards, the winger sustained a knee injury whilst on international duty and will miss most of next season. The club's finances are tied up with keeping their creditors at bay, so there is little money for manager Denis Smith to strengthen the squad. However, Dennis Lawrence, Brian Carey and Shaun Pejic have agreed new deals, as has keeper Andy Dibble.

Longest run without loss: 5
Longest run without win: 6
High - low league position: 2-16
High - low Outlook form figure: 4-39
Key Stat: *Even more erratic than Swindon. 2nd-16th-7th-14th-6th-14th. What a season!*

Outlook forecast: 23rd

Final Outlook Index figure: 722
Clean sheets 14
Yellow cards 62 Red cards 6
Players used 24
Leading scorer:
Hector Sam 12 (10 league)

Your forecast:

BOSTON UNITED

Nickname: The Pilgrims
Colours: Amber and black

Ground: York Street
Capacity: 6,643

Tel: 01205 364406

www.bostonunited.co.uk

BOSTON'S second season in the Nationwide was a tale of two vastly contrasting halves. The Pilgrims started abysmally and for a while it looked like they were on their way back to the Conference.

After 13 games they were just two places off rock bottom, had won only twice, and were averaging less than a goal a game.

The problems were on the road where the Pilgrims took just one point and scored only a single goal in their first six aways.

Incredibly, Steve Evans - back from his ban - managed to steer them to a very respectable 11th. A play-off spot is a realistic aim this year.

There's a Scottish flavour to the Pilgrims close-season signings. Derek Lilley has come in from Livingston, the 30-year-old scored 18 goals last season; Northern Ireland striker Andy Kirk from Hearts; and 24-year-old defender Austin McCann from Clyde.

Longest run without loss: 6	*Final Outlook Index figure: 682*
Longest run without win: 5	*Clean sheets 14*
High - low league position: 10-22	*Yellow cards 110 Red cards 5*
High - low Outlook form figure: 66-38	*Players used 33*
Key Stat: *They have not conceded more than two goals since November.*	*Leading scorer:* *Neil Redfearn 7 (6 league)*
Outlook forecast: 6th	**Your forecast:**

BRISTOL ROVERS

Nickname: The Pirates
Colours: Blue and white

Ground: The Memorial Stadium
Capacity: 11,916

Tel: 0117 909 6648

www.bristolrovers.co.uk

CONSIDERING the acrimonious manner in which Ian Atkins left Oxford, there's reason to think Pirates chairman Geoff Dunford convinced him he was joining a progressive club.

The £17.5m training facilities won't be ready until 2005 but are an indication of their ambition.

There's plenty to improve on though, as the Pirates have been in the bottom half of the table for the last three seasons. Last term they registered back-to-back wins on only two occasions, showing a real lack of consistency.

Atkins has been busy with a host of signings, many tempted by improved terms, showing the money is down.

In come Northampton club captain Paul Trollope, midfielder Craig Disley from Mansfield, Stuart Campbell from Grimsby, striker Jamie Forrester from Hull and Derby County central defender Steve Elliott.

Longest run without loss: 4	*Final Outlook Index figure: 669*
Longest run without win: 10	*Clean sheets 14*
High - low league position: 3-21	*Yellow cards 69 Red cards 9*
High - low Outlook form figure: 56-38	*Players used 33*
Key Stat: *They rose nine places after boss Ray Graydon was sacked.*	*Leading scorer:* *Paul Tait 11 (all league)*
Outlook forecast: 2nd	**Your forecast:**

BURY

Nickname: The Shakers
Colours: White and blue

Ground: Gigg Lane
Capacity: 11,841

Tel: 0161 764 4881

www.buryfc.co.uk

BURY will have to improve on their away record if they are to reverse their slide down the divisions - they were in the old Division One in 1998.

Last term they lost 14 games on the road, only relegated Carlisle lost more. Expectation isn't high as the Shakers don't have the resources, having staved off administration two seasons ago.

They are still paying off creditors and unsurprisingly Graham Barrow has been quiet on the transfer front. He has brought in one-time Ireland under-21 international midfielder Dwayne Mattis from Huddersfield Town on a free.

Defender Lee Connell, midfielder Paul O'Shaughnessy and goalkeeper Lewis Solly have all been released.

Loan players Harpal Singh of Leeds and Preston forward Joe O'Neill have both returned to their clubs after season-long stays at Gigg Lane.

Longest run without loss: 8
Longest run without win: 8
High - low league position: 11-18
High - low Outlook form figure: 56-38
Key Stat: *The Shakers managed to score more than two only three times.*

Outlook forecast: 15th

Final Outlook Index figure: 667
Clean sheets 29
Yellow cards 69 Red cards 9
Players used 29
Leading scorer:
Gareth Seddon 11 (all league)

Your forecast:

CAMBRIDGE UNITED

Nickname: The U's
Colours: Amber and black

Ground: Abbey Stadium
Capacity: 9,617

Tel: 01223 566500

www.cambridge-united.co.uk

CAMBRIDGE are another club for whom 2003 saw financial meltdown narrowly averted. Fans dug deep in December of last year to keep the ground safe for at least a further year, so there hasn't been a big splurge on players.

Striker Jermaine Easter has signed a one-year contract having been released by Hartlepool. Boss Herve Renard has signed unknown French Division Three striker Sully Seychelles, who'll probably need time to adapt. Meanwhile, striker Alex Revell is expected to sign for Southend United.

The U's finished the season well, losing just once in their eight final games, but there was no progress on league position from the previous season (12th). It would have been a different story but for the worst home record in the division, perhaps due to the weight of expectation from those who bailed them out?

Longest run without loss: 4
Longest run without win: 5
High - low league position: 8-22
High - low Outlook form figure: 59-34
Key Stat: *They have not had a win against a top ten side since October 21.*

Outlook forecast: 9th

Final Outlook Index figure: 668
Clean sheets 11
Yellow cards 76 Red cards 3
Players used 36
Leading scorer:
Luke Guttridge 12 (11 league)

Your forecast:

CHELTENHAM TOWN

Nickname: The Robins
Colours: Red and white

Ground: Whaddon Road
Capacity: 7,407

Tel: 01242 573558

www.cheltenhamtownfc.com

JOHN WARD trimmed his squad right down at the end of last season shedding nine players, and will start the new campaign with a thread-bare squad.

He has made some shoe-string replacements; striker Steve Guinan has joined on a free transfer from Conference neighbours Hereford United. Unproven youngster Ashley Vincent has joined from Wolves and 21-year-old Chris Murphy has joined from cash-strapped Telford. Cat

Scott Brown, 19, comes to Whaddon Road after being released by Bristol City. This could be a lean year for the Robins. They won just three on the road and ended the season winning just two of their last twelve games. Having come up from the Conference in 1999, Cheltenham had three successful years, eventually gaining promotion, only to tumble back down in 2002/03. They may go full circle by next season.

Longest run without loss: 7
Longest run without win: 7
High - low league position: 8-22
High - low Outlook form figure: 63-35
Key Stat: *The Robins were England's penalty kings - 11 awarded, all converted.*

Final Outlook Index figure: 676
Clean sheets 10
Yellow cards 61 Red cards 4
Players used 29
Leading scorer:
Grant McCann 12 (8 league)

Outlook forecast: 22nd

Your forecast:

CHESTER CITY

Nickname: City
Colours: Blue and white

Ground: Deva Stadium
Capacity: 6,012

Tel: 01244 371376

www.chester-city.co.uk

EX-ENGLAND defender and Chester boss Mark Wright has worked wonders to get the club back into the Football League after a four year absence.

Having been defeated just four times in the Conference last season, and with a defensive record 10 goals better than the nearest rival, Chester look up to emulating Doncaster Rovers success.

Understandably, expectation is high at the Deva Stadium as Doncaster went on

to win the Division Three title and automatic promotion in their first year back among the big boys.

Wright has landed a real coup in signing ex-Bradford and Everton player Michael Branch on a three-year deal, the same commitment he himself recently made to the club. He has also called on the services of former Macclesfield manager David Moss to serve as his number two, along with eight new players.

Longest run without loss: 13
Longest run without win: 4
High - low league position: 1-10
High - low Outlook form figure: 68-48
Key Stat: *They clinched the Conference title with a 11-2-0 run.*

Final Outlook Index figure: n/a
Clean sheets 20
Yellow cards 67 Red cards 4
Players used 26
Leading scorer:
Daryl Clare 29 (all league)

Outlook forecast: 4th

Your forecast:

DARLINGTON

Nickname: The Quakers
Colours: Black and white

Ground: Feethams
Capacity: 8,500

Tel: 01325 240240

www.darlington-fc.net

THE QUAKERS are another club who last season laboured under a cloud of financial uncertainty.

A saving deal was struck, but the club has few resources for new players. David Hodgson was hoping to bring in Bradford pair Peter Beagrie and Dean Windass, but neither move materialised. Striker Barry Conlon has joined Barnsley.

The Quakers have spent 12 years in this division and in ten of those finished below halfway, including the last four years.

Considering that form and the absence of new players coming in, Darlington are likely to be involved in another scrap at the bottom of the table, the only consolation being that they are used to it.

Mark Proctor, who led Middlesbrough's Youth team to Cup glory, is leaving to work as a coach alongside his ex-Boro team-mate David Hodgson.

Longest run without loss: 4
Longest run without win: 12
High - low league position: 11-24
High - low Outlook form figure: 63-32
Key Stat: *They failed to score only once in their last 19 games.*

Final Outlook Index figure: 673
Clean sheets 12
Yellow cards 86 Red cards 11
Players used 31
Leading scorer:
Barry Conlon 14 (all league)

Outlook forecast: 18th

Your forecast:

GRIMSBY TOWN

Nickname: The Mariners
Colours: Black and white

Ground: Blundell Park
Capacity: 10,003

Tel: 01472 605050

www.gtfc.co.uk

RUSSELL SLADE became Grimsby's third manager of 2004 after his predecessor, Nicky Law, left in March but he failed to save the Mariners from their second successive relegation.

Slade joined from Conference side Scarborough, but has League experience, which he'll need to settle a club in freefall. The Mariners' last away win was in November 2003, one of only three on the road.

Huddersfield have bounced back up, but the Mariners look far more vulnerable and some of the rats are deserting the sinking ship.

Ex-Everton striker Phil Jevons has gone to Yeovil on a free transfer - his 13 goals will be missed - and Stuart Campbell rejected a new deal to join the Pirates.

Slade has made 33-year-old Hull defender Justin Whittle his first signing, but he was unable to get in the Tigers' first team. A hard slog awaits.

Longest run without loss: 4
Longest run without win: 10
High - low league position: 8-22
High - low Outlook form figure: 58-33
Key Stat: *The Mariners conceded more away goals than any team in England.*

Final Outlook Index figure: 717
Clean sheets 12
Yellow cards 59 Red cards 7
Players used 36
Leading scorer: Michael Boulding and Phil Jevons 13 (12 league)

Outlook forecast: 8th

Your forecast:

KIDDERMINSTER

Nickname: The Harriers
Colours: Red and white

Ground: Aggborough
Capacity: 6,293

Tel: 01562 823 931

www.harriers.co.uk

SINCE promotion from the Conference in 2000 the Harriers have enjoyed mid-table mediocrity for four seasons.

After 12 games of last season however, the Harriers had only eight points and were second from bottom. Recovery did follow, but they struggled to score goals all season.

Unsurprisingly, Jan Molby has highlighted the need for a striker and is trying to sign two players who played last sea-son on loan - JJ Melligan (Wolves) who scored 12 goals, and Simon Brown (West Brom).

Molby has been forced into a summer clear-out of players, releasing nine of his squad in May, and after 236 games Craig Hinton is set to leave to join Bristol Rovers. Though financially constrained, Molby has brought in a couple of new faces, but nothing to convince they will be challenging for honours.

Longest run without loss: 4	*Final Outlook Index figure: 678*
Longest run without win: 9	*Clean sheets 11*
High - low league position: 8-23	*Yellow cards 80 Red cards 5*
High - low Outlook form figure: 61-36	*Players used 37*
Key Stat: *Only the bottom side York scored fewer goals than the Harriers.*	*Leading scorer: Dean Bennett 7 (3 league)*
Outlook forecast: 10th	**Your forecast:**

LEYTON ORIENT

Nickname: The O's
Colours: Red and black

Ground: Brisbane Road
Capacity: 13,842

Tel: 020 8926 1111

www.leytonorient.com

THE Orient ensured their league status only in May with a win at York City. That result was their first three points for two months and an amazing 15 games.

Only the two relegated sides had a worse defensive record than the O's, and its no surprise to see Martin Ling sign an experienced defender.

He has landed a coup with Alan White, who was voted player of the year last season at Colchester and was skipper for most of the season. Ling has also captured combative midfielder Michael Simpson (former Wycombe captain) on a two-year deal.

Orient have been stuck in this division for the last nine seasons, and have staved off relegation for the last three.

Despite talk of progress at the club, the disastrous end of season run shows that expectations for next season can be no more than survival.

Longest run without loss: 5	*Final Outlook Index figure: 654*
Longest run without win: 13	*Clean sheets 8*
High - low league position: 10-23	*Yellow cards 100 Red cards 12*
High - low Outlook form figure: 59-40	*Players used 35*
Key Stat: *They scored more than two only twice all season.*	*Leading scorer: Gary Alexander 16 (15 league)*
Outlook forecast: 20th	**Your forecast:**

LINCOLN CITY

Nickname: The Red Imps
Colours: Red, white and black

Ground: Sincil Bank
Capacity: 10,918

Tel: 01522 880011

www.redimps.com

THE Imps lost out narrowly in the play-off semis to eventual winners Huddersfield, but there was no room for sentiment as nine players have subsequently been released by manager Keith Alexander.

The club is still struggling financially after a survival deal just two years ago, so they won't be splashing out. Lincoln are knocking on the door of promotion having made the play-offs in back-to-back seasons. Under Alexander they have become one of the most hard-working clubs in division.

Success has been built on home strength, (just three defeats at Sincil Bank) but they'll be hoping for a better start to the season. Last term they failed to score in six of their opening eight games.

Defender Paul Futcher has left against the club's wishes, along with full back Mark Bailey, leaving the Imps with some defensive headaches.

Longest run without loss: 12
Longest run without win: 5
High - low league position: 4-23
High - low Outlook form figure: 59-40
Key Stat: *Sincil Bank - the Imps won more away than at home last season.*

Outlook forecast: 5th

Final Outlook Index figure: 701
Clean sheets 17
Yellow cards 83 Red cards 4
Players used 28
Leading scorer:
Gary Fletcher 18 (16 league)

Your forecast:

MACCLESFIELD TOWN

Nickname: The Silkmen
Colours: Blue

Ground: Moss Rose
Capacity: 6,335

Tel: 01625 264686

www.mtfc.co.uk

BRIAN HORTON took over in April of this year, when the Silkmen were 23rd in the table with the Conference looming. He staved off relegation with a late season rally, and will clearly hope to maintain that level of performance.

Town have spent the last five seasons in this division, never finishing in the top-half, and that is surely the only realistic goal for Horton.

To tighten up the defence he's brought in Michael Briscoe, a 21-year-old defender who spent a year trying to break into the Coventry first team, and poached Hull keeper Alan Fettis. The cat started last season as the Tigers No.1 before injury and has 25 caps for N Ireland under his belt.

Matthew Tipton has agreed a 12 month extension, which is a real bonus as he's hit 36 goals since joining the club in March 2002, including a club record haul of 19 last season.

Longest run without loss: 5
Longest run without win: 9
High - low league position: 16-23
High - low Outlook form figure: 64-42
Key Stat: *Their crowd average is 600 lower than any other side in the division.*

Outlook forecast: 13th

Final Outlook Index figure: 670
Clean sheets 10
Yellow cards 77 Red cards 11
Players used 32
Leading scorer:
Matthew Tipton 19 (16 league)

Your forecast:

MANSFIELD TOWN

Nickname: The Stags
Colours: Amber and blue

Ground: Field Mill
Capacity: 10,000

Tel: 0870 7563160

www.mansfieldtown.net

THE Stags were promoted to Division One in 2002, but dropped back down the following year.

With the nucleus of the team remaining, they were denied an immediate return on penalties in last season's play-off final.

On the back of that disappointment a mini-exodus has now taken place, with the deserters probably feeling the club has missed the boat.

Keith Curle has yet to fill the vacuum, and will need all of his motivational powers to inspire those players that have stayed on at Field Mill.

He'll be wary of Scunthorpe's demise; having lost in the 2002/03 play-offs, they finished last season one place above relegation.

Craig Disley has moved to Bristol Rovers - sold on their big plans, while 22-goal Liam Lawrence and Bobby Hassell have gone to Sunderland. A long hard season in prospect.

Longest run without loss: 7
Longest run without win: 4
High - low league position: 2-15
High - low Outlook form figure: 68-37
Key Stat: *21 players were out of contract after the play-off final defeat.*

Outlook forecast: 14th

Final Outlook Index figure: 688
Clean sheets 15
Yellow cards 85 Red cards 7
Players used 32
Leading scorer:
Liam Lawrence 22 (19 league)

Your forecast:

NORTHAMPTON TOWN

Nickname: The Cobblers
Colours: Claret and white

Ground: Sixfields Stadium
Capacity: 7,653

Tel: 01604 757773

www.ntfc.co.uk

THE COBBLERS are the bookies' favourites for Coca-Cola Division Two. Colin Calderwood took charge of Northampton in October following a dismal eight game spell with just one win, culminating in a 5-1 humiliation by Hull.

That game was clearly a watershed. Calderwood was brought in with John Deehan as Director of Football (previously working together at Villa). The combination was to work wonders.

They were denied a place in the play-off finals on penalties having won 13 of their final 19 games.

With a new proven management team and recently renovated ground the Cobblers are likely to be thereabouts again.

Calderwood was in Portugal scouting, and has let club captain Paul Trollope go, but has agreed new contracts with Sabin and Asamoah, with further new signings promised.

Longest run without loss: 8
Longest run without win: 9
High - low league position: 5-19
High - low Outlook form figure: 66-39
Key Stat: *They got more points in their last 10 games than the promoted sides.*

Outlook forecast: 1st

Final Outlook Index figure: 713
Clean sheets 15
Yellow cards 77 Red cards 7
Players used 32
Leading scorer:
Martin Smith 15 (11 league)

Your forecast:

NOTTS COUNTY

Nickname: The Magpies
Colours: Black and white

Ground: Meadow Lane
Capacity: 20,300

Tel: 0115 9529000

www.nottscountyfc.co.uk

AFTER gaining promotion in 1998, the Magpies failed to make a real impact in Division Two (as it then was).

Their best placing was eighth which they repeated in 2000 and 2001. They failed to build on those efforts and never managed to finish out of the bottom third thereafter.

This suggests a club in decline. Most clubs find something extra when the threat of relegation materialises, but County managed just one win in their final twelve games; they lost their last five on the road, scoring one and conceding 15.

No surprises then that they had the worse overall defensive record in the league. Inevitably, relegation was followed by a clear out and some defections, and the new faces brought in do not inspire too much confidence. The Magpies will do well to adjust to life in the bottom league and finish above mid-table.

Longest run without loss: 5
Longest run without win: 7
High - low league position: 19-24
High - low Outlook form figure: 60-34
Key Stat: *They conceded four or more seven times last season.*

Outlook forecast: 7th

Final Outlook Index figure: 704
Clean sheets 8
Yellow cards 72 Red cards 3
Players used 35
Leading scorer:
Paul Heffernan 21 (20 league)

Your forecast:

OXFORD UNITED

Nickname: The U's
Colours: Yellow and navy blue

Ground: The Kassam Stadium
Capacity: 12,573

Tel: 01865 337 533

www.oufc.co.uk

OXFORD'S form for the first half of last season was promotion material. From third position in February, however, they went on to record just two wins from the next 16 games, gaining the dubious honour of the longest string of successive away defeats (six) to miss out on the play-offs.

The deterioration in form was linked to back-room rumblings as manager Ian Atkins was suspended before eventually leaving in March.

Graham Rix was brought in for the remaining games but couldn't stop the rot; the last game of the season was the only win of his nine in charge.

Rix has signed defender David Woozley, and striker Lee Bradbury from Walsall. Dean Whitehead - voted player of the year by fans - leaves a hole in midfield, but they've lined up 24-year-old Robert Wolleaston from Bradford (ex Chelsea & Palace). A mid-table finish for United beckons.

Longest run without loss: 9
Longest run without win: 8
High - low league position: 1-9
High - low Outlook form figure: 67-39
Key Stat: *Ambitious? Graham Rix had signed five players by the end of May.*

Outlook forecast: 11th

Final Outlook Index figure: 676
Clean sheets 17
Yellow cards 72 Red cards 3
Players used 28
Leading scorer:
Steve Basham 15 (14 league)

Your forecast:

ROCHDALE

Nickname: The Dale
Colours: Blue

Ground: Spotland Stadium
Capacity: 10,249

Tel: 01706 644648

www.rochdaleafc.co.uk

STEVE PARKIN became Rochdale boss for the second time in January, and helped save the club from the very real threat of relegation.

Following a reasonable start to the season, the Dale lost six straight games from the end of October, failing to score in half those matches, and the writing was on the wall.

Parkin's second era at Spotland was purely about survival and though they spent most of the remainder of the season skirting around the drop zone, he did enough to keep them up.

Home form was a problem throughout the season; Rochdale picked up fewer points in front of their own fans than everyone expect bottom club York.

Parkin has released eight players and although some of the new signings are promising, mid-table mediocrity is probably the best that Dale can hope for.

Longest run without loss: 4
Longest run without win: 6
High - low league position: 5-22
High - low Outlook form figure: 61-38
Key Stat: *The Dale have not lost successive games in 2004.*

Outlook forecast: 17th

Final Outlook Index figure: 661
Clean sheets 12
Yellow cards 94 Red cards 6
Players used 35
Leading scorer:
Kevin Townson 12 (10 league)

Your forecast:

RUSHDEN & DIAMONDS

Nickname: Diamonds
Colours: White and blue

Ground: Nene Park
Capacity: 6,553

Tel: 01933 652000

www.thediamondsfc.com

THE DIAMONDS couldn't handle life in the Division One and have come back down to earth.

Whereas Huddersfield bounced straight back under the same circumstances, Rushden are not in a healthy financial state.

The club have given up hope of finding a new owner and admitted that there are limited resources for new signings.

Their highest profile player Rodney Jack leaves to join Oldham, clearly not enamoured with football in the bottom division. So what now?

Look no further than the words of the man brought in after last season's relegation for an answer. Ernie Tippett has told the fans they cannot expect instant success from his new-look side, as it's virtually a new team. Enough said.

Only Notts County, who last term were also relegated, lost more away games.

Longest run without loss: 4
Longest run without win: 9
High - low league position: 8-22
High - low Outlook form figure: 58-37
Key Stat: *They scored only seven goals in their last 13 games.*

Outlook forecast: 19th

Final Outlook Index figure: 694
Clean sheets 7
Yellow cards 58 Red cards 7
Players used 28
Leading scorer:
Onandi Lowe 15 (all league)

Your forecast:

Sponsored by Stan James

SCUNTHORPE UNITED

Nickname: The Iron
Colours: Claret and white

Ground: Glanford Park
Capacity: 9,183

Tel: 01724 848077

www.scunthorpe-united.co.uk

HAVING gained promotion two seasons ago from this division only to drop straight back down and finish one place above Conference football, all the signs indicate that the Iron Age is over.

To rub salt into the wound Steve Maclean, who scored one third of their goals last season, leaves to one of their Yorkshire rivals Sheffield Wednesday.

This is a real problem as you need to score plenty of goals when you boast last season's worst defensive league record.

Brian Laws has made three signings, goalkeeper Paul Musselwhite from Hull City, Ian Baraclough from Notts County and central defender Andy Crosby from Oxford United - their average age is 33 years and the club have retained the services of Peter Beagrie 38. Experience counts, but that quartet are unlikely to set the section alight.

Longest run without loss: 14
Longest run without win: 9
High - low league position: 8-22
High - low Outlook form figure: 66-34
Key Stat: *They scored and conceded more away goals than any Div Three side.*

Outlook forecast: 21st

Final Outlook Index figure: 648
Clean sheets 8
Yellow cards 117 Red cards 6
Players used 29
Leading scorer:
Steven MacLean 25 (23 league)

Your forecast:

SHREWSBURY TOWN

Nickname: The Shrews
Colours: Blue and amber

Ground: Gay Meadow
Capacity: 8,700

Tel: 01743 360111

www.shrewsburytown.co.uk

THE SHREWS were the surprise package of the play-offs, as everyone expected Hereford to join Chester in climbing out of the Conference.

Jimmy Quinn's side are back in the Football League after just one season and will take heart from Doncaster's meteoric rise, but will perhaps settle for a modest first season avoiding the drop-zone.

Quinn has poached a couple of players from the Conference - including Ben Smith from Hereford - but nothing that really catches the eye. He has managed to hold onto the talismanic forward Luke Rodgers, who along with many of the squad aren't new to League football.

The Shrews maintained the best home defence in the Conference (losing just twice at Gay Meadow). If they can maintain that home strength they should at least live to fight another day in this division.

Longest run without loss: 7
Longest run without win: 3
High - low league position: 3-8
High - low Outlook form figure: 65-46
Key Stat: *They lost successive games only once last season.*

Outlook forecast: 16th

Final Outlook Index figure: n/a
Clean sheets 16
Yellow cards 86 Red cards 5
Players used 24
Leading scorer:
Luke Rodgers 15 (13 league)

Your forecast:

SOUTHEND UNITED

Nickname: The Shrimpers
Colours: Blue

Ground: Roots Hall
Capacity: 12,392

Tel: 01702 304050

www.southendunited.co.uk

THE SHRIMPERS will definitely have to play better at Roots Hall if they are to improve on last season's mid-table finish.

United lost more games at home than any club in the division, finishing the season with a negative home goal difference.

It would also help their cause to be faster out of the blocks as last term they lost seven of their first nine games. They did well not to lose their form later in the season in the wake of their LDV Vans Trophy run which to took them past QPR - now two leagues above them - by a 4-0 margin and all the way to the final in Cardiff.

They ended up losers there but Steve Tilson won the battle for survival and must transfer some of that Cup form into building momentum in the league.

The boss will be pleased to have retained the services of influential club captain Kevin Maher.

Longest run without loss: 6
Longest run without win: 7
High - low league position: 13-23
High - low Outlook form figure: 63-38
Key Stat: *They lost nearly half their home games last season.*

Outlook forecast: 12th

Final Outlook Index figure: 667
Clean sheets 10
Yellow cards 81 Red cards 9
Players used 30
Leading scorer:
Leon Constantine 25 (21 league)

Your forecast:

SWANSEA CITY

Nickname: The Swans
Colours: White

Ground: Vetch Field
Capacity: 11,742

Tel: 01792 633 400

www.swanseacity.net

KENNY JACKETT may have a difficult first full season in charge of Swansea. His predecessor Bryan Flynn saved the Swans from the Conference in 2003, steered them towards the top half of Division Three and a successful FA Cup run last season before leaving the club.

That clearly had an impact on their form, as they ended last term badly. Now Jackett (former assistant manager at QPR and Watford) is struggling to hold on to one of Flynn's most successful signing - top scorer Lee Trundle. If they lose the mercurial striker it could be curtains for the Welsh side.

Another worry for Jackett is their lack of goalkeeping cover as the club currently have only one cat.

The Swans will be moving into a new purpose built stadium - White Rock - in 2005/06 and it will weigh on the new manager's mind that they may be in the Conference by then.

Longest run without loss: 5
Longest run without win: 7
High - low league position: 1-11
High - low Outlook form figure: 60-37
Key Stat: *Just three wins in 2004 - all against bottom-half sides in Div Three.*

Outlook forecast: 23rd

Final Outlook Index figure: 657
Clean sheets 13
Yellow cards 90 Red cards 8
Players used 32
Leading scorer:
Lee Trundle 21 (16 league)

Your forecast:

Sponsored by Stan James

WYCOMBE WANDERERS

Nickname: The Chairboys
Colours: Sky and navy blue

Ground: Adams Park
Capacity: 10,000

Tel: 01494 472100

www.wycombewanderers.co.uk

TONY ADAMS' first season as a league manager was a baptism of fire. The Wanderers won just six of their 46 games, with only a single victory on the road, and were relegated, finishing well adrift from the rest of the pack.

There are no positives to take from that disastrous season and they have now lost their best player Jermaine McSporran, who scored 12 times for them.

The risky appointment of the inexperienced Adams seems to have back-fired and the ex-Arsenal hero will feel the pressure if the Chairboys start badly. It would be no surprise to see him binned before Christmas if they do start poorly.

Having spent a decade in the old Division Two, it's possible that Wycombe could be going full circle back to the Conference from where they emerged in 1993.

Longest run without loss: 5
Longest run without win: 13
High - low league position: 15-24
High - low Outlook form figure: 57-35
Key Stat: *It's 14 games since their last clean sheet.*

Outlook forecast: 24th

Final Outlook Index figure: 708
Clean sheets 8
Yellow cards 67 Red cards 6
Players used 40
Leading scorer:
Jermaine McSporran 12 (7 league)

Your forecast:

YEOVIL TOWN

Nickname: The Glovers
Colours: Green and white

Ground: Huish Park
Capacity: 9,107

Tel: 01935 423662

www.ytfc.net

YEOVIL TOWN's 2003/04 season review DVD best sums up their rookie year in the Football League: 'So Near...'.

The Glovers missed out on a promotion place on goal difference. After a slightly shaky start, when they lost four of the first six games, Town found their feet and rose to third by December, having strung together an impressive 13-game run with just a single defeat.

Cheered on by close to capacity crowds of up to 8,000, their West County stadium was a real fortress. Had they been able to snatch a few more points away from Huish Park they could been facing the likes of Bradford in League One.

The Conference is a breeding ground for progressive clubs; Doncaster have kept on up the league ladder and Yeovil could follow them. Striker Phil Jevons joins from Grimsby, having scored 13 times last season.

Longest run without loss: 8
Longest run without win: 5
High - low league position: 3-18
High - low Outlook form figure: 65-37
Key Stat: *Trouble Chance - no English team drew fewer games last season.*

Outlook forecast: 3rd

Final Outlook Index figure: 701
Clean sheets 16
Yellow cards 73 Red cards 4
Players used 28
Leading scorer:
Kevin Gall 10 (8 league)

Your forecast:

CELTIC

Nickname: The Bhoys
Colours: Green and white
Ground: Celtic Park
Capacity: 60,506
Tel: 0141 556 2611
www.celticfc.co.uk

THE big question surrounding Celtic this season is how much of an impact will the loss of Henrik Larsson have on the team.

The Magnificent Seven scored 242 times in his 315 games for the Bhoys and it is a near impossible task to replace him.

Celtic would almost certainly have won the title last year without Larsson, such was the domination they had over Rangers and the rest.

They won the league with six games to go and were unbeaten at the time, although they did go on to lose twice.

After an opening day draw at Dunfermline they went on to win their next 25 games, setting a new Scottish record.

Martin O'Neill's side completed the League and Cup double when they beat Dunfermline at Hampden, but as the season went on their dominance over the rest appeared to be decreasing.

While this could be put down to them taking their foot of the gas and concentrating on the Uefa Cup, after they'd effectively won the league in January, there were other factors that contributed to this decline.

One of which was the Bhoys' defence. It is by no means watertight and they kept only three clean sheets in their last 18 league games.

With Larsson gone, the goalscoring onus is going to fall on the remainder of the squad. Although O'Neill hasn't brought in anyone to replace him yet, you feel that he must do so as neither Chris Sutton, John Hartson or Shaun Maloney are likely to score 30 goals plus this term.

Longest run without loss: 20
Longest run without win: 3
High - low league position: 1-2
High - low Outlook form figure: 76-46
Final Outlook Index figure: 934

Key Stat: *They beat Rangers five times in a season for the first time ever.*

2003/04 SPL Stats

	Apps	Gls	YC	RC
D Agathe	26 (1)	5	0	1
B Balde	30 (1)	2	2	1
C Beattie	2 (8)	1	1	0
S Crainey	1 (1)	0	0	0
R Douglas	15 (1)	0	0	0
M Gray	2 (5)	0	0	0
J Hartson	14 (1)	8	2	0
M Hedman	12 (0)	0	0	0
J Kennedy	9 (3)	1	1	0
P Lambert	9 (4)	1	0	0
H Larsson	36 (1)	30	2	0
N Lennon	35 (0)	0	4	0
S Maloney	7 (10)	5	1	0
D Marshall	11 (0)	0	0	0
A McGeady	3 (1)	1	0	0
S McManus	5 (0)	0	2	0
J McNamara	26 (1)	1	3	0
L Miller	13 (12)	2	3	0
J Mjallby	10 (3)	0	2	0
S Pearson	16 (1)	3	2	0
S Petrov	33 (2)	6	4	0
J Smith	4 (7)	0	0	0
C Sutton	25 (0)	19	2	0
M Sylla	5 (9)	0	0	0
A Thompson	26 (0)	11	6	0
J Valgaeren	4 (3)	0	0	0
S Varga	35 (0)	6	4	0
R Wallace	4 (4)	1	0	0

League Stats
Clean sheets 17
Yellow cards 42 Red cards 2
Average attendance 57,654
Leading scorer:
Henrik Larsson 50 (30 league)

Outlook forecast: 1st

Your forecast:

RANGERS

Nickname: The Gers
Colours: Blue white and black
Ground: Ibrox Stadium
Capacity: 50,403
Tel: 0870 600 1972
www.rangers.co.uk

ALEX MCLEISH learnt the hard way that you need hard-working determined players to succeed in the SPL.

Big Eck signed players last summer who looked good on the continent but floundered in the Scottish winter and most were gone before the end of the season.

Rangers had started the season strongly but when things started to go wrong they quickly spiralled out of control.

All of a sudden the idea of going to places like Livingston and Motherwell on a cold wet afternoon didn't appeal, and players like Nuno Capucho and Emerson did a disappearing act that David Copperfield would have been proud of.

The title was conceded when they lost at Parkhead on January 3 and their season was over when they lost at the same venue in the Scottish Cup two months later.

McLeish has acknowledged how easily his side were bullied by Celtic last season and has set about trying to stop it happening again. The Bhoys aerial threat was something Rangers just couldn't deal with and in Marvin Andrews and Jean-Alain Boumsong, two big strong centre-backs, they now have players to deal with that danger, while the arrival of Dado Prso gives them a threat of their own.

McLeish has some quality youngsters coming through. Chris Burke left defenders in knots and Alan Hutton and Stephen Hughes also impressed when called upon.

While catching Celtic may be out of the question they are worth a look on the handicap and when playing the Bhoys at Ibrox.

Longest run without loss: 9
Longest run without win: 3
High - low league position: 1-2
High - low Outlook form figure: 71-50
Final Outlook Index figure: 882

Key Stat: *They scored only two in five outings against the Bhoys.*

2003/04 SPL Stats

	Apps	Gls	YC	RC
C Adam	1 (1)	0	0	0
M Arteta	23 (0)	8	2	0
S Arveladze	17 (2)	12	1	0
M Ball	30 (2)	1	7	0
H Berg	20 (0)	0	0	0
C Burke	11 (9)	3	0	0
Capucho	18 (4)	5	2	0
R Davidson	0 (1)	0	0	0
F de Boer	15 (0)	2	2	0
R de Boer	12 (4)	2	1	0
D Duffy	0 (1)	0	0	0
Emerson	13 (1)	0	1	0
B Ferguson	3 (0)	0	1	0
B Fetai	0 (1)	0	0	0
A Hutton	11 (0)	1	3	0
Z Khizanishvili	25 (1)	0	4	0
S Klos	34 (0)	0	1	0
P Lovenkrands	22 (3)	9	3	0
G MacKenzie	0 (2)	0	0	0
R Malcolm	8 (6)	0	1	0
R McCormack	1 (1)	1	0	0
A McGregor	4 (0)	0	0	0
M Mols	29 (6)	9	1	1
C Moore	16 (1)	2	8	0
H Namouchi	4 (3)	3	1	0
C Nerlinger	11 (3)	1	1	0
E Ostenstad	2 (9)	0	0	0
G Rae	9 (1)	2	1	0
F Ricksen	29 (1)	1	6	0
M Ross	10 (10)	1	2	0
S Hughes	17 (5)	3	1	0
S Tompson	9 (7)	8	2	0
P Vanoli	14 (9)	1	1	0
A Walker	0 (2)	0	0	0

League Stats
Clean sheets 16
Yellow cards 54 Red cards 1
Average attendance 48,992
Leading scorer:
Shota Arveladze 15 (12 league)

Outlook forecast: 2nd

Your forecast:

ABERDEEN

Nickname: The Dons
Colours: Red

Ground: Pittodrie
Capacity: 22,199

Tel: 01224 650400

www.afc.co.uk

IT says something that the highlight of the Dons' season was beating an under-strength side after they'd already won the league.

Aberdeen became the first team since May 2001 to win at Parkhead when they stopped Celtic's attempt to go through the season unbeaten.

Aberdeen have come nowhere near the level of success they achieved under Alex Ferguson in the 1980's and, despite being fancied to become the third-force in Scotland, last season they were near-er to relegation than the top six.

Steve Paterson has gone with Jimmy Calderwood moving in from Dunfermline to take the reins.

Many of last season's squad were released or transfer-listed be-fore Paterson left and Calderwood has started to put his own side to-gether, though with all the changes they may need a season to adapt.

Longest run without loss: 6
Longest run without win: 6
High - low league position: 9-11
High - low Outlook form figure: 61-37
Key Stat: *They scored just once in their final five games.*

Outlook forecast: 10th

Final Outlook Index figure: 776
Clean sheets 4
Yellow cards 34 Red cards 3
Average attendance 10,389
Leading scorer:
Scott Booth 10 (8 league)

Your forecast:

DUNDEE

Nickname: The Dark Blues
Colours: Dark blue and white

Ground: Dens Park
Capacity: 12,371

Tel: 01382 889966

www.dundeefc.co.uk

DUNDEE are currently in administration but have avoided a ten-point penalty as they started the process of leaving ad-ministration before the May 31st deadline.

After going into the red last No-vember, the Dees had to let 15 players go, including Fabrizio Ravenelli and Craig Burley. This left them with a thread-bare squad and an injury to Lee Wilkie plus Gavin Rae's sale to Rangers left them really struggling.

They had started the season well and looked set for a top six finish, but in the end only a last-day win over Ab-erdeen secured seventh place.

This season looks like it's go-ing to be even worse. Manager Jim Duffy has agreed to stay but keeper Julian Speroni and star striker Nacho Novo look set to leave. They have brought in central defend-er Bobby Mann from Inverness but they need more then one player to stop the rot.

Longest run without loss: 5
Longest run without win: 6
High - low league position: 4-11
High - low Outlook form figure: 61-37
Key Stat: *The least home goals in the SPL last season.*

Outlook forecast: 11th

Final Outlook Index figure: 810
Clean sheets 7
Yellow cards 64 Red cards 1
Average attendance 7,089
Leading scorer:
Nacho Novo 25 (19 League)

Your forecast:

Sponsored by Stan James

DUNDEE UNITED

Nickname: The Terrors
Colours: Orange and black

Ground: Tannadice Park
Capacity: 14,209

Tel: 01382 833166

www.dundeeunitedfc.co.uk

THE Terrors kept on improving last season, in Ian McCall's first full term in charge. McCall made plenty of changes to the squad last summer, bringing in players from the First Division, where he had plied his trade with Falkirk.

Consequently they made a slow start to the season, winning only two of their first 13 matches, but as the team started to gel their performances improved and they eventually finished fifth.

The club appear to be fighting a losing battle to keep star midfielder Charlie Miller, but players like Mark Kerr and Barry Robson can fill his boots as creative midfielders.

Scotland international goalkeeper Paul Gallacher's move to Norwich is a blow, but James Grady is a good addition to their strikeforce. Continued improvement is on the cards, with the Terrors the most likely challengers to Hearts for third place.

Longest run without loss: 5
Longest run without win: 5
High - low league position: 5-12
High - low Outlook form figure: 64-32
Key Stat: *Last season they took four points off Rangers.*

Final Outlook Index figure: 824
Clean sheets 11
Yellow cards 62 Red cards 2
Average attendance 7,714
Leading scorer:
Jimmy McIntyre 11 (9 league)

Outlook forecast: 4th

Your forecast:

DUNFERMLINE

Nickname: The Pars
Colours: Black and white

Ground: East End Park
Capacity: 12,509

Tel: 01383 724295

www.dafc.co.uk

DUNFERMLINE avoided going into administration last season only when their players agreed to take a 30 per cent pay-cut, but this didn't affect their performance on the field.

The Pars recorded their best ever finish in the SPL, gaining fourth place, and came very close to upsetting Celtic in the Scottish Cup Final.

Their financial problems, however, could catch up with them this term. Manager Jimmy Calderwood has moved to Aberdeen, taking assistant Jimmy Nicholls with him, and star striker Stevie Crawford has been tempted to Plymouth. At least goalkeeper Derek Stillie has re-signed for the club.

The artificial pitch at East End Park means Dunfermline will again be difficult to beat at home, but with Crawford gone and age catching up with Craig Brewster a much more difficult season is in store for the Pars.

Longest run without loss: 6
Longest run without win: 4
High - low league position: 3-8
High - low Outlook form figure: 65-43
Key Stat: *They scored more than two goals in the SPL only once.*

Final Outlook Index figure: 819
Clean sheets 13
Yellow cards 42 Red cards 1
Average attendance 6,230
Leading scorer:
Stevie Crawford 17 (13 league)

Outlook forecast: 8th

Your forecast:

HEARTS

Nickname: Jam Tarts
Colours: Claret and white

Ground: Tynecastle
Capacity: 18,000

Tel: 0131 200 7200

www.heartsfc.co.uk

HEARTS have become the best club outside of the Old Firm, having finished third for the past two seasons, but off-field issues are in danger of affecting their performance on it.

The fans spent much of the second-half of the season protesting over their club's plans to sell Tynecastle rather then supporting the players.

The truth is that in order to compete with the Old Firm they may have to move on from their spiritual home. Like most SPL clubs they are massively in debt and can't afford the best players unless the ground is sold.

The short-term effect, however, will be minimal. They'll still be at Tynecastle this term and only a few players have left.

They have enough quality in the squad to hold onto their third-place spot, but closing the gap on Celtic and Rangers is out of the question.

Longest run without loss: 10
Longest run without win: 5
High - low league position: 3-5
High - low Outlook form figure: 67-42
Key Stat: *They are unbeaten in their last four Old Firm games.*

Final Outlook Index figure: 856
Clean sheets 12
Yellow cards 70 Red cards 1
Average attendance 11,918
Leading scorer:
Mark de Vries 16 (13 league)

Outlook forecast: 3rd

Your forecast:

HIBERNIAN

Nickname: Hibs
Colours: Green and white

Ground: Easter Road
Capacity: 17,500

Tel: 0131 661 2159

www.hibs.co.uk

FORCED to let players go last summer to cut their wage bill and fend off the threat of administration, Hibs have finished just outside the top half for a second season running.

The reduced size of their squad has given youth its chance and Derek Riordan, Garry O'Connor, Stephen Dobbie, Scott Brown and Tam McManus all look to have bright futures.

But the problem with relying on youth is inconsistency and that has stopped the Hibees from becoming a top-six side. They beat both sides of the Old Firm on the way to last season's CIS Cup Final but were just as capable of losing at home to Partick.

Manager Bobby Williamson has gone to Plymouth, with Tony Mowbray taking the reins at Easter Road. If the new manager can get them performing to the same level each week, a top six spot beckons.

Longest run without loss: 6
Longest run without win: 10
High - low league position: 5-10
High - low Outlook form figure: 60-31
Key Stat: *Last season's SPL record against the Old Firm was 0-0-6.*

Final Outlook Index figure: 798
Clean sheets 9
Yellow cards 68 Red cards 3
Average attendance 9,137
Leading scorer:
Derek Riordan 18 (15 league)

Outlook forecast: 6th

Your forecast:

INVERNESS CT

Nickname: Caley
Colours: Blue

Ground: Caledonian Stadium
Capacity: 6,500

Tel: 01463 222880

www.caleythistleonline.com

CALEY THISTLE'S place in the top flight was confirmed only after a second vote by the SPL clubs after a month-long legal battle.

The problems surrounded their ground, Caledonian Stadium, not reaching the SPL's requirement of having a 10,000 capacity. This has been resolved with a ground-share with Aberdeen in place.

Now they have secured their Premiership status, they face a fight to keep it this sea-son. Caley's home record has been out-standing in the past five years. It remains to be seen how they will fare when having to travel 100 miles for each "home" fixture.

Captain Bobby Mann, Steve Hislop and David Bingham have left, and the club were late start-ing to bring in new players due to the uncertainty of which division they would be in. They face a battle with Dundee to avoid relegation.

Longest run without loss: 7
Longest run without win: 2
High - low league position: 1-7
High - low Outlook form figure: 70-45
Key Stat: *They conceded just three in their last eight league games.*

Outlook forecast: 12th

Final Outlook Index figure: 770
Clean sheets 14
Yellow cards 38 Red cards 2
Average attendance 2,378
Leading scorer:
Paul Ritchie 23 (14 league)

Your forecast:

KILMARNOCK

Nickname: Killie
Colours: Blue and white

Ground: Rugby Park
Capacity: 18,128

Tel: 01563 545 300

www.kilmarnockfc.co.uk

KILLIE limped home in tenth place and it could have been even worse had it not been for a reversal in home form to-wards the end of the season.

Their good run coincided with the arrival of Eric Skora on loan from Preston but unfortunately Kil-marnock have not been to get him on a permanent basis for this sea-son.

Manager Jim Jefferies is still looking for a first-choice keeper after Colin Meldrum

and Francois Dubordeau left the club and they also need to find a centre-back to boost their defence. Having kept only three clean sheets, it is easy to spot where they problems lie.

Going forward they are not a bad side and they were the fourth highest scorers in the league last term, while in Kris Boyd they have a young striker with a big future.

If Killie can learn how to defend a top-six finish awaits.

Longest run without loss: 3
Longest run without win: 5
High - low league position: 6-11
High - low Outlook form figure: 57-36
Key Stat: *They had the worst away de-fence in the SPL last season*

Outlook forecast: 9th

Final Outlook Index figure: 796
Clean sheets 3
Yellow cards 56 Red cards 3
Average attendance 6,966
Leading scorer:
Kris Boyd 15 (all league)

Your forecast:

LIVINGSTON

Nickname: Livvy Lions
Colours: White and orange

Ground: Almondvale
Capacity: 10,016

Tel: 01506 417000

www.livingstonfc.co.uk

COACH Allan Preston has already had a tough time at Livvy and the club hasn't even played a game yet!

When he arrived at the start of June, after the Lionheart consortium just beat the deadline to keep the club out of administration, he was left with no players signed on for this season.

Preston is now gradually rebuilding a squad, having re-signed some of the players whose contracts had expired, as well as picking up players released from other clubs.

Livingston picked up their first piece of silverware in their short history when they won the CIS Cup with a 2-0 win over Hibs, but it's difficult to see them having to add an extension to the trophy cabinet this year.

The target for the new owners is to build up a squad that can cement their SPL status and to sort out their finances.

Longest run without loss: 6
Longest run without win: 7
High - low league position: 5-10
High - low Outlook form figure: 63-38
Key Stat: *Dr A W Livingston I presume?*
They drew a third of their SPL games.

Outlook forecast: 7th

Final Outlook Index figure: 792
Clean sheets 11
Yellow cards 70 Red cards 1
Average attendance 5,116
Leading scorer:
Derek Lilley 18 (12 league)

Your forecast:

MOTHERWELL

Nickname: The Well
Colours: Amber and claret

Ground: Fir Park
Capacity: 13,742

Tel: 01698 333333

www.motherwellfc.co.uk

AFTER finishing bottom of the SPL two seasons ago and keeping their top-flight status on a tecnicality (First Division champions Falkirk didn't have a ground that was up to scratch), many expected another tough season for the Well.

However, despite star names James McFadden and Stephen Pearson heading for the door marked exit, they surprised everyone by claiming a top six-spot.

Two years of administration have been tough on the club but, having emerged from that constraint in April, they look a lot stronger. The side has a good blend of youth and experience, and the youngsters who were thrown in at the deep end have coped well with the pressures of the SPL.

Manager Terry Butcher has passed on plenty of his never say die spirit to his squad and, with the team on the up, another good season is expected.

Longest run without loss: 8
Longest run without win: 7
High - low league position: 4-9
High - low Outlook form figure: 63-34
Key Stat: *They fired blanks in half their last 10 league games.*

Outlook forecast: 5th

Final Outlook Index figure: 797
Clean sheets 10
Yellow cards 49 Red cards 1
Average attendance 6,225
Leading scorer:
David Clarkson 14 (12 league)

Your forecast:

SUPER CALY: can the Division One champions bridge the quality gap in the Premiership?

Europe the best forum for Index

ONE of our regular features in the football side of *Racing & Football Outlook* is our exclusive ratings system the *Outlook Index*.

This provides punters with an objective look at the strength of teams across the English and Scottish leagues, as well as the major European leagues and at international level.

One of its greatest strengths is that the *Index* has been designed to allow direct comparison, not just between clubs in the same league as each other, but also between those from different countries.

Within a domestic context, this comparative ability is useful at the start of the season, when it can be used to provide a reasonable estimation (in conjunction with the *Index* Trend values) as to where those clubs who have moved up or down a division fit into their new surroundings.

Similarly, its comparative powers are helpful when looking at Cup matches between sides from different divisions, although in recent seasons one has had to be wary of Cup games in which top-flight sides field second-string line-ups. Even FA Cup matches aren't afforded the same significance as they were less than a decade ago.

In my opinion, however, where the *Index* has been most useful over the years in assessing the relative strengths of teams from different European leagues. In recent seasons, along with

Alex Deacon

a number of other sports-betting writers, I've been making the case for the increasing superiority of Spanish clubs over sides from the other major European leagues.

When one looks to the recent performances of clubs from the Primera Liga, in either of the European competitions, the theory seems to hold true, yet we've been able to get some very fancy prices about the Iberian clubs.

In particular, the value has lain in supporting those Spanish clubs that don't attract the same sort of attention as the likes of Real Madrid, but who are nonetheless of a comparable strength.

While this isn't to say that Spanish league clubs will sweep all before them, it does serve to highlight the fact that

VIVA BARCA! the Catalan giants will be flying the flag for Spain in the Champions League

an objective approach, such as that provided by the *Index*, can give open-minded punters an edge.

For those whose interest in football is concentrated on the English game, such a tool is invaluable, given that most who watch the Premiership tend to rate the quality of the play (as well as the league strength as a whole) at a much higher level within the context of European football than would seem to be justified.

This aspect of the *Index* has, as a consequence, been of particular interest over the past few seasons, with the proliferation of midweek rounds of Champions League football. It becomes even more so this time round, with the expansion of the Uefa Cup, which now features a prolonged group stage.

In a bid to add to the TV lolly generated by the Champions League, the first round of the Uefa Cup now sees 40 teams split into eight groups of five, playing each week between October and December.

After that, the top three from each group move on, along with the eight third-placed Champions League sides, into a knockout stage.

On a footballing front, this has added a lot of broadly unneeded games to an already crowded fixture list, with quantity taking precedence over quality.

It also, however, gives us a lot of interesting betting opportunities.

The Uefa Cup's group stage will feature games that are harder to get an accurate fix on than would be the case with the usual run-of-the-mill domestic games, given that there will be a lot of unfamiliar outfits from the minor European leagues.

It is in the relative obscurity of some of these sides that followers of the *Index* can prosper, as other punters struggle to assess them relative to the bigger names in the competition, who this year include Newcastle, Stuttgart, Parma and Lazio.

While it's unlikely that any of the smaller sides will battle their way to the final in Lisbon, there's plenty of scope for shocks along the way, particularly at the group stage.

Each week in RFO this winter, we'll be using the *Index* to rate the group contestants objectively, and thus identify where the value lies on an outright basis, as well as match by match.

League tables are, quite simply, one of the most deceptive tools a punter can employ in making selections each week, showing as they do the state of a competition at any given point in time.

In their usual format they reveal nothing as to the quality of the opponents each side has met until then. That's where the Outlook Index comes in, showing as it does the relative strength of each side determined by the results of over 38,000 matches and weighted by the strength of the opposition.

Detailed 60-match form is also given for each side so that any trends in a side's playing strength can be readily identified.

Each week of the football season, the Outlook will print updated Index ratings, with the best analysis to help your football betting.

ON THE UP: Pompey finished the season with the most positive Index trend figure

FA Barclaycard Premier League 2003-2004

	Cur	1-6	7-12	13-18	19-24	25-30	31-36	37-42	43-48	49-54	55-60	Home	Away	Trend
		Previous match form												
Arsenal	969	971	976	965	964	966	955	948	954	954	950	970	919	-1
Man United	936	940	948	962	963	963	965	961	948	940	936	942	930	-8
Chelsea	933	935	939	931	938	932	927	914	912	914	920	939	898	-1
Liverpool	909	901	900	908	910	912	920	931	928	928	934	920	882	4
Newcastle	902	904	905	908	910	912	904	919	934	926	917	954	828	-2
Aston Villa	894	893	885	882	871	868	866	873	867	876	870	912	852	6
Bolton	892	888	879	888	882	872	876	874	858	853	854	902	880	5
Fulham	881	876	874	882	890	890	885	874	870	860	859	908	839	2
Blackburn	877	873	872	876	882	879	900	903	894	881	880	876	873	2
Charlton	876	878	883	888	882	886	868	870	889	884	876	872	865	-3
Birmingham	876	877	888	880	877	888	883	870	854	847	853	893	846	-3
Middlesboro	872	880	878	879	877	865	860	875	883	871	882	900	848	-4
Portsmouth	872	866	840	842	846	853	860	847	846	838	834	902	823	14
Southampton	868	874	874	875	878	880	884	875	884	895	892	905	835	-4
Tottenham	866	858	870	866	859	864	862	870	882	888	888	905	838	2
Man City	863	860	864	860	866	880	886	879	876	886	877	888	845	1
Everton	855	870	874	872	872	872	882	889	893	888	889	910	824	-11
Leicester	852	848	856	852	855	846	852	859	859	855	851	897	846	1
Leeds	846	852	846	848	865	865	876	877	873	885	879	887	850	-3
Wolves	844	841	840	841	834	839	830	837	831	822	818	865	820	3

NATIONWIDE DIVISION ONE 2003-2004

Previous match form

	Curr	1-6	7-12	13-18	19-24	25-30	31-36	37-42	43-48	49-54	55-60	Home	Away	Trend
Norwich	854	852	839	837	833	827	821	812	806	805	800	888	812	8
WBA	838	853	843	832	837	838	835	830	821	826	840	850	839	-4
West Ham	833	829	836	839	844	859	876	878	880	870	858	887	808	-1
Crystal P	827	825	809	802	783	781	791	801	797	800	808	845	828	11
Sunderland	826	820	824	813	812	817	816	802	798	815	837	861	815	5
Reading	814	814	812	813	814	823	820	834	826	823	822	833	820	1
Ipswich	813	816	809	818	825	826	824	814	827	834	827	829	822	-1
Nottm F	812	796	785	778	787	802	808	818	814	821	816	864	807	16
Millwall	810	820	833	823	807	811	816	818	821	804	802	858	798	-8
Wigan	809	810	813	822	812	818	822	819	800	801	809	831	805	-3
Stoke	809	803	810	809	791	776	782	788	780	762	748	865	784	3
Sheffield Utd	804	806	819	819	832	828	838	837	828	826	826	844	808	-7
Coventry	802	795	805	794	788	786	782	772	771	781	793	832	822	4
Cardiff	798	798	792	790	793	798	786	780	766	776	779	820	806	3
Watford	796	792	784	785	785	785	778	772	778	780	792	849	800	6
Rotherham	787	785	790	798	801	787	786	789	794	788	794	846	796	-2
Preston	785	788	800	809	811	806	804	794	804	810	805	866	764	-8
Burnley	784	790	790	786	782	782	783	778	777	792	809	834	794	-2
Derby	782	784	782	782	777	772	780	770	776	784	796	850	782	0
Crewe	777	778	781	787	796	789	784	792	786	789	786	809	797	-3
Walsall	770	772	773	780	786	784	777	782	791	785	787	825	777	-3
Gillingham	768	768	778	780	789	787	784	793	795	798	805	808	774	-5
Wimbledon	742	736	734	748	759	770	771	790	809	806	815	782	791	2
Bradford	742	751	756	750	753	759	768	778	780	792	792	792	786	-7

NATIONWIDE DIVISION TWO 2003-2004

Previous match form

	Curr	1-6	7-12	13-18	19-24	25-30	31-36	37-42	43-48	49-54	55-60	Home	Away	Trend
Plymouth	784	777	786	780	780	764	751	747	744	747	746	836	750	3
QPR	778	776	786	784	790	788	784	785	788	772	759	851	751	-2
Bristol City	774	769	779	791	774	764	767	764	771	767	758	838	758	-1
Brighton	772	763	760	756	760	766	784	783	784	781	775	840	734	8
Tranmere	761	754	734	746	748	749	742	756	770	758	752	830	737	11
Swindon	754	758	766	760	742	736	744	745	737	728	739	810	760	-3
Hartlepool	754	754	746	742	734	730	733	728	714	713	730	789	760	5
Port Vale	752	742	739	738	736	732	739	737	728	721	714	823	742	9
Oldham	750	744	736	738	742	747	762	756	769	773	774	778	758	7
Colchester	746	742	732	739	748	754	749	739	736	744	726	795	752	5
Stockport	742	746	726	721	726	726	720	725	731	722	710	768	809	6
Bournem'th	740	742	748	738	724	736	724	710	696	697	700	804	734	0
Luton	739	744	746	758	753	750	748	747	751	751	756	802	746	-8
Peterboro	736	736	724	715	730	731	729	739	740	730	724	773	773	6
Barnsley	736	738	728	742	753	753	745	746	736	738	741	808	762	0
Brentford	730	724	706	718	719	730	726	710	713	718	738	784	758	9
Blackpool	727	734	732	726	728	725	718	718	716	730	752	766	764	-2
Wrexham	722	725	736	740	740	739	741	736	730	710	700	759	755	-7
Chesterfield	721	714	722	717	702	690	690	700	700	700	702	783	721	4
Sheffield W	721	735	750	752	750	760	781	789	789	769	764	760	769	-15
Grimsby	717	718	719	724	734	748	752	754	761	773	766	794	742	-2
Wycombe	708	707	698	698	697	696	698	707	720	726	731	770	744	5
Notts C	704	710	718	711	715	721	717	722	732	740	737	796	732	-6
Rushden	694	704	723	730	734	732	727	734	730	722	715	763	716	-15

NATIONWIDE DIVISION THREE 2003-2004

Previous match form

	Curr	1-6	7-12	13-18	19-24	25-30	31-36	37-42	43-48	49-54	55-60	Home	Away	Trend
Huddersfield	714	722	724	719	708	701	704	701	713	718	730	795	720	-4
Northampton	713	705	692	687	673	672	673	680	683	700	698	762	744	13
Hull	712	705	705	709	698	699	697	682	678	677	670	788	709	5
Doncaster	710	701	-	-	-	-	-	-	-	-	-	752	709	6
Torquay	710	700	703	697	682	689	688	681	684	687	679	788	707	8
Yeovil	701	694	-	-	-	-	-	-	-	-	-	752	735	0
Lincoln	701	711	706	704	703	699	689	680	689	689	690	728	733	-4
Mansfield	688	694	695	702	714	713	709	700	696	701	708	756	714	-6
Boston	682	684	670	668	670	682	676	682	688	681	686	764	702	5
Kidderminstr	678	674	673	663	672	664	661	675	683	685	695	740	719	5
Oxford Utd	676	681	698	711	714	708	700	696	680	680	686	754	693	-12
Cheltenham	676	676	690	689	682	684	695	710	716	719	710	754	712	-4
Darlington	673	670	668	650	643	653	669	665	667	669	672	746	703	7
Macclesfield	670	664	648	661	672	662	672	674	672	662	650	745	720	8
Bristol R	669	663	654	657	666	670	676	682	676	658	652	748	713	7
Cambridge	668	657	648	658	667	670	673	672	676	672	672	728	723	9
Southend	667	674	664	650	644	641	642	652	657	666	731	709	3
Bury	667	668	671	668	668	690	676	688	690	692	695	749	711	-1
Carlisle	664	664	656	641	626	613	629	645	658	657	654	733	702	8
Rochdale	661	660	658	656	656	656	672	673	662	669	678	738	718	2
Swansea	657	660	675	674	682	690	694	686	670	661	652	733	695	-8
L Orient	654	661	675	688	678	672	662	653	657	654	662	754	693	-12
Scunthorpe	648	655	672	675	678	692	692	696	698	692	696	742	682	-12
York	629	635	654	672	688	687	681	687	686	696	686	731	680	-16

BANK OF SCOTLAND SPL 2003-2004

Previous match form

	Curr	1-6	7-12	13-18	19-24	25-30	31-36	37-42	43-48	49-54	55-60	Home	Away	Trend
Celtic	934	949	958	953	945	939	930	929	928	926	932	936	910	-12
Rangers	882	893	900	911	915	919	924	918	923	920	921	916	848	-12
Hearts	856	844	850	847	851	850	850	847	843	830	822	872	798	6
Dundee Utd	824	816	810	803	798	785	780	784	791	789	800	820	808	10
Dunfermline	819	820	820	823	824	815	814	805	811	820	827	860	768	-1
Dundee	810	799	793	800	797	814	811	810	811	802	812	834	800	9
Hibernian	798	804	801	805	803	812	819	816	804	819	820	808	791	-3
Motherwell	797	800	796	785	785	786	766	763	779	782	773	845	774	2
Kilmarnock	796	794	799	799	815	816	825	835	828	822	807	835	772	-1
Livingston	792	792	790	797	793	792	783	794	807	807	805	837	774	0
Aberdeen	776	792	799	800	802	801	813	817	801	801	808	792	790	-13
Partick	764	753	743	746	745	745	762	769	771	775	772	807	740	11

BELL'S SCOTTISH DIVISION ONE 2003-2004

Previous match form

	Curr	1-6	7-12	13-18	19-24	25-30	31-36	37-42	43-48	49-54	55-60	Home	Away	Trend
Clyde	777	785	789	790	776	772	785	778	761	756	754	812	756	-6
Inverness CT	770	758	753	763	754	754	751	752	756	766	769	808	741	9
Queen Sth	745	736	736	744	743	736	724	722	716	714	702	782	739	5
Falkirk	744	745	748	754	769	769	780	775	767	763	752	770	752	-4
St Johnstone	740	755	759	751	760	754	762	772	763	747	744	728	769	-10
Ross County	715	728	726	723	719	719	707	698	711	721	724	757	731	-7
St Mirren	705	694	694	704	704	701	706	716	724	728	734	793	693	6
Ayr	696	690	689	694	704	710	716	726	740	737	739	766	714	3
Raith	675	680	676	672	676	687	675	686	700	705	704	740	679	-1
Brechin	674	669	674	658	655	647	653	664	656	644	654	712	671	5

BELL'S SCOTTISH DIVISION TWO 2003-2004

Previous match form

	Curr	1-6	7-12	13-18	19-24	25-30	31-36	37-42	43-48	49-54	55-60	Home	Away	Trend
Airdrie Utd	682	676	659	658	662	672	454	-	-	-	-	706	681	11
Raith	670	682	701	702	705	703	700	708	710	698	705	745	680	-16
Forfar	662	654	655	660	653	649	659	665	654	661	652	712	686	5
Dumbarton	662	646	641	638	633	633	626	614	611	615	608	710	674	14
Brechin	658	663	660	644	653	642	634	651	653	654	643	706	670	1
Hamilton	657	652	650	648	649	658	666	670	666	671	658	708	680	5
Berwick	653	654	663	676	675	672	676	664	668	665	650	680	698	-6
Stenh'muir	650	657	652	641	630	628	629	637	650	642	650	725	682	1
Stranraer	640	645	651	660	672	662	652	647	657	667	671	707	666	-8
C'denbeath	640	644	644	643	648	668	660	656	651	654	657	702	689	-2

BELL'S SCOTTISH DIVISION THREE 2003-2004

Previous match form

	Curr	1-6	7-12	13-18	19-24	25-30	31-36	37-42	43-48	49-54	55-60	Home	Away	Trend
Stranraer	660	655	652	649	648	645	639	646	652	662	674	715	678	6
Stirling	642	634	636	637	636	633	608	606	600	601	601	689	673	5
Gretna	628	628	620	620	615	600	592	589	600	599	592	642	660	4
Peterhead	622	630	624	629	628	626	638	636	628	615	613	697	639	-3
C'denbeath	617	622	621	626	625	621	632	644	644	643	648	660	680	-3
Montrose	589	581	584	580	570	560	557	566	566	566	583	641	649	6
Albion	579	583	597	594	607	626	644	642	633	630	628	638	658	-8
Queen's P	576	573	573	567	564	569	568	568	574	584	572	645	659	4
Elgin	536	547	537	539	544	558	555	554	566	578	590	651	587	-4
East Stirling	488	483	490	498	507	508	513	523	538	544	550	592	556	-1

CLOSE BUT NO CIGAR: Clyde finished on a high but just missed out on promotion

BUNDESLIGA 2003-2004

Previous match form

	Curr	1-6	7-12	13-18	19-24	25-30	31-36	37-42	43-48	49-54	55-60	Home	Away	Trend
B Munich	955	962	964	962	959	961	966	966	971	967	958	986	914	-4
W Bremen	948	957	956	948	934	923	912	899	906	928	922	938	925	-3
Stuttgart	937	941	932	938	952	939	927	930	932	918	906	939	912	-1
Leverkusen	932	918	901	913	927	916	901	895	900	915	922	928	895	13
Dortmund	919	922	912	914	927	929	928	930	940	946	949	961	866	1
Bochum	915	912	912	905	901	892	880	866	870	870	871	943	873	4
Hamburg	914	908	911	910	902	898	909	909	904	895	885	965	837	4
Schalke	904	913	917	909	898	904	906	920	929	928	932	931	887	-5
Hertha	900	892	888	886	894	906	918	926	920	922	928	936	867	7
H Rostock	888	883	890	880	867	867	874	874	874	876	877	917	853	4
M'gladbach	882	877	870	876	867	873	884	868	861	869	871	942	845	6
K'erslautern	880	880	886	879	891	891	896	898	884	870	876	939	846	-1
Wolfsburg	880	879	884	893	897	906	903	898	890	894	893	926	847	-3
Hannover	877	880	875	889	893	898	896	890	885	883	884	900	894	-3
Freiburg	868	871	878	876	876	876	864	869	892	898	912	924	830	-4
1860 Mun'	861	868	879	883	888	894	894	892	896	902	908	887	876	-10
Frankfurt	859	860	872	861	858	861	865	870	880	884	893	914	838	-3
Cologne	837	837	843	854	848	858	861	855	858	872	877	892	837	-4

LE CHAMPIONNAT 2003-2004

Previous match form

	Curr	1-6	7-12	13-18	19-24	25-30	31-36	37-42	43-48	49-54	55-60	Home	Away	Trend
Lyon	945	944	942	936	938	936	927	934	926	924	933	950	909	3
Paris St-G	939	936	926	918	905	897	886	896	895	900	905	946	894	9
Monaco	922	924	930	938	942	930	922	918	920	912	896	920	897	-5
Auxerre	913	911	916	923	914	908	903	903	895	904	903	930	878	-1
Nantes	912	908	903	897	888	900	902	898	914	903	901	920	883	7
Sochaux	904	914	920	916	920	902	901	898	886	897	898	921	852	-8
Bordeaux	893	900	902	906	901	902	914	918	912	902	892	920	856	-5
Lille	888	889	890	876	873	880	892	877	871	887	900	900	864	2
Lens	883	887	895	890	905	901	905	899	905	906	908	939	857	-5
Rennes	881	872	872	875	869	873	874	870	873	881	873	926	848	6
Marseille	880	885	894	901	907	916	908	904	910	903	899	926	850	-8
Nice	874	873	893	892	893	886	889	886	886	883	887	905	810	-7
Toulouse	872	868	861	850	848	860	865	876	880	882	884	916	853	8
Strasbourg	868	859	858	866	874	879	869	866	866	868	873	900	849	5
Metz	865	861	847	849	846	852	848	849	861	866	865	876	864	9
Ajaccio	863	856	856	858	856	861	864	858	856	856	850	895	817	5
Le Mans	862	851	841	851	849	835	845	851	852	836	834	902	813	10
Guingamp	859	870	870	866	866	872	884	889	864	872	884	892	843	-6
Bastia	854	864	866	862	870	878	870	874	895	895	876	909	816	-7
Montpellier	831	838	834	847	865	867	864	864	858	850	854	870	824	-6

SERIE A 2003-2004

Previous match form

	Curr	1-6	7-12	13-18	19-24	25-30	31-36	37-42	43-48	49-54	55-60	Home	Away	Trend
AC Milan	980	982	981	968	957	946	934	943	949	958	946	997	932	3
Juventus	956	961	975	976	978	984	977	981	982	974	982	986	934	-9
Roma	947	959	961	960	959	945	936	929	924	938	952	977	905	-8
Inter Milan	940	936	924	943	958	945	949	948	958	960	956	935	942	3
Parma	934	933	929	934	936	940	930	929	918	919	920	953	905	2
Lazio	934	934	936	939	946	943	948	940	947	958	954	971	918	-1
Udinese	920	924	923	924	920	917	915	899	900	898	887	942	911	-2
Chievo	912	902	906	910	910	918	919	917	925	928	924	930	909	5
Sampdoria	902	909	912	913	910	900	897	888	887	889	901	943	866	-5
Lecce	899	880	875	856	851	851	860	867	871	877	887	908	901	19
Brescia	897	892	896	898	888	894	900	902	902	892	879	933	880	2
Bologna	893	903	903	905	889	886	893	901	900	914	913	931	852	-6
Perugia	890	875	879	872	880	889	896	903	909	901	898	944	862	10
Reggina	889	884	882	891	891	894	892	888	894	881	877	946	862	3
Siena	881	886	884	893	898	901	-	-	-	-	-	910	880	-4
Empoli	876	882	877	864	857	860	877	877	868	873	873	940	858	2
Modena	872	879	880	882	889	894	885	894	887	889	907	911	876	-5
Ancona	842	842	846	856	873	884	-	-	-	-	-	889	860	-4

PRIMERA LIGA 2003-2004

Previous match form

	Curr	1-6	7-12	13-18	19-24	25-30	31-36	37-42	43-48	49-54	55-60	Home	Away	Trend
Barcelona	966	972	965	940	937	944	947	932	925	927	929	961	940	4
Valencia	961	972	962	962	958	958	949	937	948	968	965	960	944	-3
Deportivo	960	957	955	967	963	976	975	973	980	973	970	996	925	1
R Madrid	948	971	991	992	981	982	981	973	978	969	972	979	930	-22
Sevilla	936	926	926	917	924	931	931	924	927	922	921	949	906	8
R Mallorca	930	912	904	913	925	909	915	922	916	913	929	932	931	13
Ath Bilbao	928	933	931	933	922	926	920	922	909	910	901	946	905	-2
Real Betis	928	922	924	925	914	924	921	910	917	923	930	942	924	4
Albacete	919	911	911	898	896	888	887	901	892	902	898	939	908	9
Villarreal	917	909	900	913	916	906	906	908	906	908	906	962	894	7
R Zaragoza	914	902	904	889	894	891	885	894	899	906	908	963	894	10
R Sociedad	914	910	913	922	925	945	960	964	954	954	962	960	899	0
Ath Madrid	912	911	919	919	922	914	900	906	912	913	908	953	890	-2
Espanyol	910	903	891	877	877	887	901	910	908	899	892	944	877	13
Celta Vigo	910	912	907	917	922	929	939	940	940	933	936	931	921	-1
Malaga	908	916	909	895	908	904	896	912	924	921	923	951	894	0
Osasuna	898	916	922	922	924	924	918	900	894	905	901	903	916	-14
R Santander	894	898	905	909	904	902	896	897	890	883	880	908	912	-5
R Valladolid	894	894	905	915	918	906	906	903	896	898	899	949	872	-6
Real Murcia	882	882	890	903	904	901	914	-	-	-	-	939	880	-5

Man United tick all the right boxes

WAS there ever such universal agreement amongst bookmakers on the fate of those at either end of the Premiership?

The top trio are all between Evens and 3-1 with 14-1 bar, while the three promoted teams are all long odds-on to make an immediate return.

I can't argue with either position, but I would challenge the favourite in each market. Last season I got Arsenal badly wrong here. The development of Cole and Toure made a nonsense of my fears about their defence. They were, however, greatly favoured by fortune when it came to injuries.

Whereas in 2002/03, Ljungberg and Pires suffered, last year it was the turn of Chelsea (Duff) and Man Utd (Solskjaer, Wes Brown and Ferdinand) to lose key players.

Opposing Man Utd here in the past has been a matter of thinking their price is too small. Now, with 3-1 on offer, it seems too big.

Even if Rooney has not been signed, Sir Alex Ferguson now has a batch of strikers at his disposal more varied and skilful than the quartet with which he landed the treble in 1999.

After the Cup Final and Euro 2004, getting Ronaldo for half the Beckham fee is looking a great bit of business. With Pique and Heinz joining the defence, Ferdinand back in early autumn and Keane primed for one last hurrah, United look the value.

Chelsea? At 14-1 or more they gave us a good run for our money in 2003/04. Now they have replaced a man who in many ways never seemed to be quite in control - Ranieri signed 15 midfield players for heaven's sake! - with one used to total control. It will be a culture shock for both parties.

As I write, the Englishmen Kenyon & Co. really want, like Rooney and Gerrard, seem to be eluding them, while

'After the Cup Final and Euro 2004, getting Ronaldo for half the Beckham fee is looking a great bit of business and with Pique and Heinz joining the defence, United look the value'

Kezman, Robben and Ferreira, however stellar, are strangers to the English game like Mourinho himself. I suspect the method and the money will not be blending perfectly until next season.

At the other end, the prices don't reflect the comet-like career of Palace boss Iain Dowie. Blue Square offer the best price against Palace, WBA and

JUMPING FOR JOY: Figaro fancies the Red Devils to snatch the Gunners' Premiership title

Norwich returning whence they came and there will be worse 7-2 shots this season than that. None of that trio seem to be making any significant moves in the market, but presuming Dowie is not poached by a bigger club, Palace look the likeliest to survive.

Everton were dropping like a stone as the season ended and seeing as most of any Rooney money will be clearing debt, they could be the most vulnerable if there's a Palace revelation, and Skybet's 5-1 against them going down could be a useful counterweight to the 7-2.

How ironic that Division One has been re-branded with a name implying greater quality when almost certainly its standard will be the worst for years. Clubs with mon-

ey like Cardiff and Wigan are not splashing the cash. Leeds and Leicester have had to shed their best players just like West Ham did a year ago and Ipswich have this time, while Wolves have been rocked by a transfer request from Kenny Miller.

I'm going with outsiders Nottm Forest and Sheffield Utd more in hope of landing the place money than expectation of winning a pile.

The transformation in Forest after Joe Kinnear's arrival was almost as dramatic as that of Palace under Dowie. Now Kinnear has imposed himself by signing five players and if he has got the blend right, this division is there for the taking.

Neil Warnock has gone one better with

six newcomers at Bramall Lane and, having missed the play-offs by just two points, they look too big at 25-1 with Totesport.

At the other end, take the 2-1 or more available against both Brighton and Burnley dropping down.

In the lower divisions everything could end up ship-shape and Bristol-fashion. City head the Division Two market and they have bought two strikers who scored a bundle for two mediocre teams last year.

What can Miller (pictured right), Heffernan and Maclean do with better supplies? City are blooding a new manager in Brian Tinnion, but the Board must know this City stalwart as well as he himself knows the club, so if they are right 6-1 is a big price.

Tranmere are about right at 8-1 given the impact Brian Little had as manager, while Barnsley and Stockport look the most likely to stir from the depths. Torquay have made the mistake of selling their top scorer. That has ensured an instant return to the basement for others in the past.

Northampton head the Division Three lists on the strength of a final run that made sense of their being last summer's steamer.

As an each-way, I prefer **Oxford**, despite Graham Rix's unimpressive start as a replacement for Ian Atkins who is sure to take **Bristol Rovers** higher. By early July, eleven new players had arrived. They have four good strikers, height, strength and mobility and a strong spine – and a Chairman who is at last talking like a fan.

Keep an eye on improving Boston, whose posse of new Scots includes the SPL striker Derek Lilley from Livingston and two Hearts' reserves. Chester will challenge as well.

The Scottish scene remains confused, confusing and depressing: a further 300 players shown the door, SPL debt projected by PriceWaterhouseCoopers as rising by £55m to £190m by the end of the season, half the SPL top scorers including Larsson on the move, the absurd SPL 'Which Thistle?' promotion saga, born of an obsession with 10,000 plus seater stadia which stay at least half empty 80 per cent of the time, Raith under Claude Anelka's ownership importing at least nine French players, no play-offs = less drama... and to think some Scots tried poking fun at England's Euro 2004 campaign.

Rangers will surely run Celtic closer after a big clear-out, but neither appeal at the odds until we know the identity of any new strikers.

Lower down, Clyde remain full time, but on July 6th, they had only ten players signed up including two keepers and five youngsters. St. Johnstone and Falkirk, playing at their new home, look preferable. Hamilton will be playing on plastic. In the basement, Gretna are full-time and have continued to invest.

And so to the bets. The stated odds were the best available in the first week of July. You should of course go straight to www.racing-post.co.uk and Betfair to get the best current deals.

THE BETS.
3 pts **MAN UTD** (3-1 Skybet)
1 pt e-w both **NOTTM FOR** (16-1 Bet365) and **SHEFF. UTD** (25-1 Totesport)
3 pts **BRISTOL CITY** (6-1 generally)
1 pt **OXFORD** (16-1 Coral).
1 pt e-w **BRISTOL ROVERS** (16-1 available generally)
HANDICAPS: **Middlesbrough, Nottm Forest, Barnsley, Boston**.
ACCA: Any 2 and any 3 of **Man Utd, Bristol City, Oxford, St Johnstone** and **Gretna** = 20 bets.

FA Premier League 2004/05

	BET365	BLUE S	CHANDLR	CORAL	HILLS	LADS	SKYBET	S SOC	S JAMES	STANLEY	TOTE
Arsenal	11-10	6-5	11-8	11-8	6-5	6-5	11-10	5-4	11-8	11-10	Evs
Chelsea	2	15-8	13-8	15-8	2	2	2	15-8	15-8	2	2
Man United	11-4	11-4	11-4	5-2	11-4	5-2	3	11-4	9-4	5-2	11-4
Liverpool	14	12	11	12	12	14	14	14	16	14	14
Newcastle	50	50	66	40	50	50	40	50	66	50	66
Aston Villa	200	200	200	100	200	100	150	250	250	100	150
Tottenham	250	150	250	300	150	250	150	350	400	200	250
Birmingham	200	250	250	200	150	250	150	300	400	200	250
Middlesbrough	125	125	300	300	125	200	500	200	100	250	250
Charlton	750	500	400	500	500	750	750	600	750	500	750
Fulham	750	750	600	500	500	500	750	750	750	500	500
Man City	1000	300	800	750	400	500	1000	750	300	400	750
Bolton	1000	600	800	1000	500	500	1000	1000	500	500	500
Blackburn	1000	500	400	500	500	500	1000	750	500	400	500
Southampton	1000	750	800	1000	750	750	1000	1000	750	500	750
Everton	1000	750	1000	1250	500	750	1000	1000	750	500	1000
Portsmouth	1500	750	1500	1500	1000	750	2000	2000	1000	1000	1000
West Brom	2500	2500	2500	5000	2000	2000	3000	5000	5000	2000	5000
Norwich	5000	5000	2000	5000	2000	2000	2500	6000	3000	2500	5000
Crystal P	5000	5000	2500	5000	2000	2000	4000	7500	3000	3000	5000

Win or each-way (*terms available from individual bookmakers*)

Coca-Cola Championship 2004/05

	BET365	BLUE S	CHANDLR	CORAL	HILLS	LADS	SKYBET	S SOC	S JAMES	STANLEY	TOTE
Wolves	5	6	5	11-2	11-2	9-2	6	9-2	6	5	4
West Ham	6	7	7	7	5	5	6	6	6	11-2	7
Leicester	7	7	8	8	7	7	6	7	7	7	8
Sunderland	9	8	9	8	15-2	8	10	9	9	8	5
Wigan	12	11	8	10	11	12	12	12	12	11	10
Ipswich	12	11	12	8	12	12	10	11	10	12	9
Leeds	12	10	14	12	14	9	10	14	14	12	10
Nottm Forest	16	14	14	16	12	14	12	14	12	14	14
Millwall	20	16	18	16	14	16	16	16	12	16	20
Reading	16	20	20	20	14	16	16	18	18	16	25
Sheffield Utd	20	14	20	20	12	16	14	14	16	16	25
Coventry	25	20	18	16	25	20	25	20	22	20	28
Cardiff	22	20	22	20	25	25	25	22	22	22	28
Plymouth	33	33	33	33	40	33	33	40	40	33	40
Stoke	40	33	33	20	33	25	25	40	25	33	50
QPR	40	33	25	28	28	33	25	33	33	33	66
Preston	40	40	33	33	50	33	33	40	40	33	66
Derby	40	40	28	20	33	50	33	40	33	40	66
Watford	66	66	66	50	50	50	50	66	40	50	100
Brighton	100	100	66	50	80	100	40	80	100	66	200
Rotherham	150	250	150	125	200	200	66	150	100	150	400
Gillingham	150	150	100	200	200	200	66	150	100	150	400
Crewe	150	200	150	200	200	200	66	150	100	125	400
Burnley	100	66	100	66	100	200	50	80	100	80	400

Win or each-way (*terms available from individual bookmakers*)

Coca-Cola Division One 2004/05

	BET365	BLUE S	CHANDLR	CORAL	HILLS	LADS	SKYBET	S SOC	S JAMES	STANLEY	TOTE
Bristol City	5	6	11-2	5	4	5	5	9-2	5	5	4
Tranmere	8	15-2	7	7	7	7	8	8	7	7	13-2
Hull	8	9	10	9	15-2	8	10	9	10	10	8
Swindon	9	11	10	9	10	9	12	10	9	9	8
Sheff Wed	12	11	12	12	7	10	10	9	12	10	10
Wallsall	12	11	10	12	12	9	10	14	12	10	10
Barnsley	12	14	20	16	14	14	16	16	14	16	14
Port Vale	25	18	16	20	22	22	20	18	18	20	25
Hartlepool	25	20	18	20	20	16	16	18	20	18	16
Doncaster	20	16	20	16	20	16	25	22	20	16	14
Luton	20	20	20	16	25	16	16	18	16	18	33
MK Dons	20	20	25	20	25	25	25	25	28	25	33
Bradford	25	18	16	20	33	22	25	25	20	20	33
Huddersfield	25	25	20	20	20	25	33	25	33	25	22
Blackpool	25	28	25	33	28	25	25	25	25	25	33
Stockport	25	20	25	33	20	25	33	33	33	25	28
Bournemouth	25	25	20	20	25	22	25	25	20	20	40
Oldham	33	18	28	33	25	33	33	33	28	33	40
Colchester	33	50	28	33	33	40	33	33	40	33	50
Brentford	40	25	28	40	40	25	25	33	33	40	50
Wrexham	33	40	33	33	33	33	33	40	33	33	66
Torquay	50	50	40	40	50	50	50	50	33	50	66
Peterborough	40	50	33	33	40	40	40	40	40	40	66
Chesterfield	66	66	50	100	80	80	50	80	66	66	200

Win or each-way (*terms available from individual bookmakers*)

Coca-Cola Division Two 2004/05

	BET365	BLUE S	CHANDLR	CORAL	HILLS	LADS	SKYBET	S SOC	S JAMES	STANLEY	TOTE
Northampton	5	9-2	11-2	11-2	5	9-2	5	5	6	5	9-2
Chester	7	8	10	7	8	9	10	9	9	8	6
Yeovil	12	10	11	12	9	10	7	9	11	10	8
Notts County	12	10	12	12	10	10	10	12	8	11	9
Lincoln	14	14	12	14	14	12	14	14	12	14	12
Grimsby	12	12	10	14	11	10	14	12	14	11	14
Oxford	16	14	14	16	14	14	12	16	14	14	16
Wycombe	16	14	11	12	16	12	14	14	16	12	12
Bristol Rovers	12	12	16	14	12	14	16	16	16	16	14
Mansfield	14	16	11	14	12	12	20	14	20	11	14
Boston	16	16	14	20	14	16	20	20	12	16	14
Cambridge	20	25	25	25	20	25	20	25	22	22	20
Cheltenham	25	25	22	25	20	25	33	25	25	25	33
Swansea	25	25	22	20	18	18	20	22	22	18	33
Southend	25	28	28	25	33	16	33	28	28	28	33
Rushden & D	20	16	20	20	33	25	33	22	33	20	33
Shrewsbury	25	25	25	25	25	25	33	33	25	25	33
Scunthorpe	33	33	33	33	33	50	33	33	28	33	50
Macclesfield	40	50	40	33	33	50	40	33	33	40	33
Bury	33	50	28	33	40	33	33	33	33	28	50
Leyton Orient	40	50	25	25	28	33	40	33	33	33	50
Kidderminster	40	40	25	25	50	33	40	33	33	33	50
Rochdale	50	50	50	40	50	66	50	50	33	50	66
Darlington	50	40	33	33	33	40	40	40	40	33	66

Win or each-way (*terms available from individual bookmakers*)

Nationwide Conference 2004/05

	BET365	CHANDLR	CORAL	HILLS	LADS	PREMIER	SKYBET	S SOC	S JAMES	STANLEY	TOTE
Carlisle	7-2	7-2	3	7-2	7-2	7-2	3	3	4	7-2	4
Hereford	4	5	9	5	5	11-2	8	9-2	5	5	9-2
Aldershot	8	9	10	12	10	12	12	11	9	11	8
Exeter	12	10	9	14	12	8	10	11	10	12	14
Stevenage	10	10	10	12	10	11	12	12	12	11	9
Canvey I	12	12	9	10	12	16	14	12	12	10	10
Morecambe	14	14	9	12	10	11	10	12	12	11	10
York	16	16	16	12	12	16	14	14	14	12	16
Barnet	16	16	14	11	12	16	14	14	14	12	16
Dagenham & R	20	20	14	16	25	-	16	20	20	20	25
Accrington	25	20	25	14	16	16	14	20	14	12	12
Woking	33	25	20	16	20	20	25	25	22	20	25
Crawley T	20	25	-	33	25	-	25	25	25	28	-
Halifax	25	33	33	33	33	40	33	28	33	33	33
Scarborough	33	33	40	33	33	25	25	28	28	33	33
Burton	33	25	20	25	40	33	33	33	25	28	33
Gravesend	66	50	25	33	-	33	66	50	40	40	40
Tamworth	66	50	33	25	50	80	66	50	50	50	40
Leigh RMI	66	66	100	66	66	100	66	66	66	66	100
Forest Green	80	66	66	40	50	80	50	66	66	50	100
Farnborough	100	66	50	25	-	125	66	80	66	50	100
Northwich	100	100	80	80	100	150	66	100	100	100	150

Win or each-way (*terms available from individual bookmakers*)

UNITED! Will Hereford be celebrating a promotion to the Football League next May?

FA Cup 2004/05

	BET365	CANBET	CHANDLER	CORAL	HILLS	LADS	SKYBET	S SOCCER	STANLEY	TOTE
Chelsea	5	5	5	5	4	7-2	5	5	9-2	9-2
Arsenal	9-2	6	5	5	6	3	4	5	4	9-2
Man United	11-2	7	6	5	6	9-2	5	5	5	9-2
Liverpool	9	9	7	9	7	7	7	15-2	7	7
Newcastle	11	12	12	10	14	10	11	11	11	12
Tottenham	20	16	14	20	16	25	16	18	20	16
Middlesboro	16	16	20	25	14	25	25	22	25	25
Birmingham	18	25	25	25	33	25	20	22	25	20
Man City	33	20	25	33	25	33	33	33	28	33
Blackburn	33	25	28	33	20	33	33	33	28	33
Fulham	25	25	33	33	20	33	33	33	33	33
Charlton	25	33	33	40	33	40	33	33	33	33
Aston Villa	18	20	18	14	50	14	16	18	16	20
Everton	33	25	28	50	16	40	33	33	33	50
Southampton	33	20	25	50	33	40	33	33	33	33
Bolton	33	33	33	50	33	50	33	33	33	33
Portsmouth	40	40	40	50	20	66	50	50	50	50
West Brom	50	50	50	66	80	80	100	80	80	80
West Ham	66	33	50	66	50	100	100	100	80	100
Sunderland	100	80	80	100	66	100	150	150	100	100
Wolves	66	50	66	66	50	100	150	100	80	100
Leicester	80	66	66	100	50	100	125	100	100	150
Crystal Palace	66	50	66	66	150	100	100	100	100	80
Ipswich	125	100	-	100	66	100	150	150	125	150
Leeds	125	50	66	66	40	100	125	150	100	150
Wigan	125	100	-	-	80	125	200	150	125	200
Nottm Forest	150	100	-	-	100	150	200	150	150	200
QPR	-	-	-	-	125	-	200	200	-	-
Bristol City	-	-	-	-	200	-	-	-	-	-
Tranmere	-	-	-	-	200	-	-	-	-	-
Norwich	66	50	50	66	250	100	66	80	80	80
Millwall	150	80	-	-	100	150	150	150	150	250
Sheff United	150	100	-	-	100	-	200	150	150	250
Reading	150	100	-	-	100	-	200	150	200	250
Coventry	150	100	-	-	80	150	200	200	200	250
Cardiff	150	-	-	-	100	-	250	200	200	250
Sheff Wed	-	-	-	-	250	-	-	-	-	-
Bradford	-	-	-	-	250	-	-	-	-	-
Plymouth	-	-	-	-	-	-	250	250	-	-
Stoke	200	-	-	-	200	-	250	250	-	300
Derby	200	-	-	-	200	-	250	250	-	300
Preston	200	-	-	-	150	-	-	250	-	300
Watford	250	-	-	-	500	-	300	250	-	500
Burnley	250	-	-	-	125	-	250	250	-	500
Rotherham	300	-	-	-	250	-	300	300	-	500
Crewe	300	-	-	-	150	-	300	300	-	500
Gillingham	300	-	-	-	250	-	300	300	-	500

Win or each-way (terms available from individual bookmakers)

ANTE-POST PRICES

Carling Cup 2004/05

ANTE-POST PRICES

	BET365	CANBET	CHANDLER	HILLS	LADS	SKYBET	SP ODDS	STANLEY	S SOCCER	TOTE
Chelsea	7	9	10	8	9-2	10	9	8	10	10
Liverpool	7	9	9	9	6	9	10	8	9	7
Newcastle	8	10	9	10	6	9	11	9	10	10
Man United	12	10	11	12	10	10	9	11	12	10
Aston Villa	14	12	11	12	8	12	12	11	14	12
Arsenal	12	11	11	11	14	10	9	11	12	10
Tottenham	14	14	12	11	16	12	14	14	14	12
Middlesboro	14	12	14	12	14	16	12	14	18	12
Birmingham	14	14	14	14	16	14	16	14	18	14
Southampton	20	22	16	20	20	16	22	20	22	20
Man City	20	18	16	14	18	16	25	16	22	20
Fulham	25	22	25	22	20	20	22	22	22	20
Blackburn	25	20	20	20	20	20	20	20	22	20
Charlton	25	20	20	20	20	20	14	20	22	20
Everton	33	25	20	20	25	25	28	22	22	25
Bolton	25	25	25	20	33	33	22	25	22	20
Portsmouth	33	33	33	33	33	33	40	33	28	33
West Brom	40	50	50	40	50	50	66	50	50	50
Norwich	50	50	40	40	50	50	66	50	50	50
Crystal Palace	66	50	40	40	50	50	66	66	66	50
Leicester	50	66	50	66	66	66	66	66	66	66
West Ham	80	50	50	40	66	66	80	66	66	66
Wolves	50	66	50	40	66	66	80	66	66	66
Sunderland	66	66	66	80	66	66	80	80	80	66
Millwall	100	80	-	80	80	66	80	100	80	100
Ipswich	80	80	-	80	66	66	80	100	80	66
Leeds	100	66	50	66	66	66	80	66	80	66
Wigan	80	-	-	100	80	100	125	100	80	100
Nottm Forest	125	100	-	80	80	100	100	100	80	100
Reading	100	-	-	100	-	100	150	125	80	150
Sheff United	100	100	-	80	-	100	80	100	80	150
Coventry	150	-	-	150	80	100	100	100	100	150
QPR	200	-	-	150	-	100	200	150	100	200
Stoke	150	-	-	150	-	125	200	150	150	200
Preston	150	-	-	200	-	200	200	200	150	200
Plymouth	200	-	-	200	-	125	200	200	150	200
Cardiff	150	-	-	125	-	125	200	125	100	150
Derby	200	-	-	150	-	125	200	150	150	200
Watford	200	-	-	200	-	150	200	200	150	250
Burnley	200	-	-	200	-	125	250	200	150	250
Rotherham	250	-	-	300	-	150	250	300	200	250
Gillingham	250	-	-	300	-	150	250	250	200	250
Bristol City	-	-	-	300	-	250	300	-	-	-
Brighton	250	-	-	300	-	125	250	250	150	250
Crewe	250	-	-	300	-	150	250	250	200	250
Hull	-	-	-	300	-	500	300	-	-	-
Sheff Wed	-	-	-	300	-	500	500	-	-	-

Win or each-way (*terms available from individual bookmakers*)

Scottish Premier League 2004/05

	BET365	CORAL	CHANDLER	HILLS	LADS	PREMIER	SKYBET	SP ODDS	S JAMES	STANLEY	TOTE
Celtic	**4-9**	1-3	1-3	**4-9**	**4-9**	2-5	**4-9**	2-5	2-5	2-5	2-5
Rangers	13-8	**2**	**2**	13-8	13-8	7-4	13-8	7-4	7-4	7-4	7-4
Hearts	250	150	250	200	150	250	150	**300**	250	150	150
Dunfermline	**1000**	300	400	400	350	500	300	750	500	300	500
Dundee Utd	750	500	500	400	500	750	500	**1000**	750	400	750
Hibernian	750	500	750	500	500	**1000**	500	**1000**	500	500	750
Motherwell	1500	1000	1500	1000	750	1500	750	**2000**	1000	750	1000
Aberdeen	1000	1000	500	1000	1000	1500	**2000**	**2000**	1000	1000	1000
Dundee	**2500**	1000	2000	1000	1000	**2500**	1000	**2500**	1500	1000	2000
Kilmarnock	**2500**	2000	1000	1000	1000	**2500**	2000	**2500**	1500	1000	1000
Livingston	2500	2500	**3000**	1500	1500	2500	1000	**3000**	2500	1500	2000
Inverness CT	3000	2500	2500	1500	2000	3000	**5000**	**5000**	2500	1500	2000

Win only

NOT BEFORE TIME: Middlesbrough celebrate winning the club's first major honour

Primera Liga 2004/05

	BET365	BLUE SQ	CORAL	G'BOOKERS	PREMIERBET	STANLEY	TOTE
Real Madrid	11-8	5-4	11-10	5-4	11-10	5-4	5-4
Barcelona	2	2	5-2	7-4	9-4	2	15-8
Valencia	3	3	7-2	4	10-3	13-5	11-4
D La Coruna	13-2	7	13-2	7	8	15-2	8
Ath Madrid	33	50	40	50	50	50	50
Ath Bilbao	66	66	66	40	66	33	40
Seville	100	66	66	80	100	50	66
Real Betis	100	100	66	100	100	66	66
Villarreal	100	80	66	150	150	66	66
R Sociedad	100	150	80	250	200	80	100
R Mallorca	250	200	200	250	200	200	200
Malaga	250	300	400	150	250	150	200
R Zaragoza	350	400	250	500	500	300	350
Espanyol	350	500	500	500	500	300	400
Osasuna	500	500	400	750	500	300	400
Albacete	100	750	500	750	750	500	750
R Santander	500	1000	400	1000	750	500	1000
Numancia	1000	1500	300	1000	1500	100	1500
Levante	1000	2000	750	1500	2000	1000	2500
Letafe	1000	3000	750	2000	2000	2000	2500

Win or each-way (*terms available from individual bookmakers*)

VIVE! Can Lyon make it four in a row?

La Championnat 2004/05

	BET365	BLUE SQ	CORAL	STANLEY	TOTE
Lyon	11-8	7-4	5-4	11-8	5-4
Paris S-G	5-2	5-2	5-2	9-4	12-5
Monaco	10-3	9-2	11-2	11-4	14-5
Marseille	10	6	15-2	10	9
Auxerre	14	16	16	20	20
Bordeaux	25	16	20	33	40
Sochaux	20	28	25	25	33
Nantes	25	33	25	33	33
Lens	33	25	33	80	80
Rennes	50	66	66	100	100
Lille	50	66	80	100	100
Nice	66	100	100	100	100
Metz	150	250	250	200	250
Strasbourg	100	200	150	300	300
St Etienne	500	300	200	150	150
Caen	500	500	300	200	300
Bastia	500	300	150	300	500
Ajaccio	250	500	200	500	750
Toulouse	500	750	250	1000	1500
Istres	750	1000	500	2000	2500

Win or e-w (*individual bookmakers terms apply*)

Sponsored by Stan James

Bundesliga 2004/05

	BET365	CORAL	PREM B	STANLEY	TOTE
B Munich	4-5	8-11	4-6	4-6	8-13
W Bremen	9-2	5	5	4	4
Leverkusen	7	9	7	7	7
B Dortmund	8	8	14	9	9
Stuttgart	9	9	12	8	8
Schalke	12	11	12	12	11
Hamburg	40	50	33	40	50
H Berlin	66	40	40	50	50
Bochum	66	50	80	66	100
Wolfsburg	100	100	100	100	150
K'slautern	150	150	150	150	200
M'gladbach	250	250	200	200	250
H Rostock	150	200	200	300	300
Hannover	350	150	300	300	350
Frieburg	350	200	300	300	500
Nuremberg	500	250	-	-	500
Mainz	750	-	750	500	-
A Bielefeld	500	400	750	-	1000

Win or e-w (*individual bookmakers terms apply*)

KINGPIN: Bayern's Michael Ballack

SHEVCHENKO: Leading the Milan line

Serie A 2004/05

	BET365	CORAL	PREM B	STANLEY	TOTE
AC Milan	6-4	6-4	6-5	5-4	6-5
Juventus	2	2	11-5	2	11-5
Roma	9-2	5	4	3	10-3
Inter Milan	4	9-2	13-2	5	6
Lazio	25	14	20	16	20
Parma	50	50	50	33	33
Udinese	150	150	100	150	200
Sampdoria	150	150	100	200	250
Chievo	250	200	300	300	-
Brescia	350	400	300	500	400
Bologna	350	250	400	250	500
Lecce	350	500	500	500	500
Palermo	1000	150	200	750	750
Fiorentina	500	100	300	500	1000
Cagliari	750	300	400	750	750
Siena	1000	500	1000	1000	2000
Atalanta	750	300	500	1000	2000
Reggina	750	500	1000	1000	2000
Messina	1000	750	500	2000	5000
Livorno	1000	750	1000	2000	3000

Win or e-w (*individual bookmakers terms apply*)

Now's the time for some reputations to be justified

LAST season's Champions League suggested it, and this summer's European Championships has gone a long way to confirming it.

The fact is that those players in the glossy Nike and Adidas adverts (Beckham, Figo, Del Piero, Totti and Raul who are shown performing acts with a football that make a mockery of the life workings of Isaac Newton) are simply no good any more.

It might be going a bit far to suggest that these icons of the modern game are washed up has-beens, but it is worth remembering that none of the aforementioned won a single trophy last term. All have much to do in rebuilding their reputations, and to reverse the recent trend which has seen substance triumph over style.

Last year in Spain, Real Madrid's Galacticos would not have looked out of place on Hackney Marshes, rather than the footballing amphitheatre that is the Bernabeu.

There were no Oscars for the side known as FC Hollywood (Bayern Munich), and in Italy the Old Lady of Juventus looked ready to pick up her free bus pass and pension.

Will the forthcoming season see these fallen giants restore some lost pride? Certainly the close season has seen some drastic changes made at the glamour clubs, in an attempt to wipe out the annus horribilis that was 2004.

At Juve, Marcello Lippi has been replaced by Fabio Capello and it is his task to recover the ground lost to his former clubs Roma and, principally, AC Milan.

There is sure to be a clear out at the Deli Alpi, especially in a defence where Paulo Montero and Ciro Ferrara are too old, and Nicola Legrottaglie simply not good enough.

Parma's unstable financial predicament is likely to mean that talented youngsters Daniel Bonera and Matteo Ferrari, as well as the most exciting attacking talent in Italy, Alberto Gilardino, are likely to be top targets.

Roberto Mancini has become Inter Milan's third manager in a year but he is unlikely to be afforded the same financial clout as his predecessors.

The biggest task facing the former Sampdoria and Lazio legend will be to get the best out of European football's biggest white elephant; the man laughably described as the best midfielder in the world by Claudio Ranieri, Juan Sebastian Veron, who has arrived on a year long loan from Chelsea.

The most pleasing aspect of last season's Spanish campaign was the way in which **Barcelona** awoke from an early season siesta to rival Arsenal as the most watchable side on the continent. Whether the arrival of Ludovic

CHAMPIONS: Pauleta can put his Euro 2004 disappointment by helping PSG lift the title.

Giuly, Deco and Henrik Larsson will disturb the equilibrium of egos, or inspire Barca to bigger and better things remains to be seen.

What is certain though, is that with Valencia still reeling after the resignation of Rafa Benitez and Real Madrid in a similar state of disarray, Barcelona will be the team to beat in Spain this term.

On the subject of Real, it will be interesting to see how Spain's own version of the Spice Boys respond to Jose Camacho's hard nosed style of management.

With Florentino Perez set to dispense with the ludicrous transfer policy of signing one big name per summer, we can expect reinforcements to arrive at the Bernabeu in the coming weeks.

In Germany, the rest better beware of the wounded beast that is **Bayern Munich**. The Bavarian giants have been nursing their pride over the summer, after conceding the Bundesliga title to Werder Bremen and failing to make the quarter finals of the Champions League for the second consecutive year.

The rebuilding process has begun with the appointment of Felix Maggath, the man who worked miracles at Stuttgart, as manager. If he is able to tempt the likes of Phillip Lahm, Andreas Hinkel and Kevin Kuranyi to the Olympic Stadium, and cure Oliver Kahn's sporadic bouts of myopia, it is hard to see anyone stopping Bayern reclaim, their status of top dogs.

The most consistent performers in Europe in recent times have been French side Lyon. They are in the midst of building an Old Trafford like dynasty in France, having secured their third consecutive league title last term, albeit thanks to Monaco stumbling at the final hurdle for the second season running.

With Didier Deschamps' Monaco losing the services of Fernando Morientes, Jerome Rothen and captain Giuly, they will do well to even get into the position of being able to choke for the third year in a row.

If anyone is capable of dislodging Lyon from their lofty perch, **Paris St-Germain** may be the best bet. Most pundits were surprised at their strong showing last season, when they challenged the top two all the way.

In terms of personnel, one South American defender, Gabirel Heinze, has been replaced by another, in Colombian Mario Yepes who arrives from Nantes, but far more significant is the acquisition of Jerome Rothen.

Torturer of Chelsea in the Champions League at Stamford Bridge, the floppy-haired winger was criminally underused by France at Euro 2004.

Supporting him in midfield will be Modest Mbami whose performances at the African Cup of Nations alerted several big name Italian sides and up front they can rely on Pedro Pauletta, whose showing at Euro 2004 should not detract from his fine record at this level.

FA Barclaycard Premiership

Champions:	Arsenal
Runners-up:	Chelsea
Relegated:	Leicester
	Leeds
	Wolves

Nationwide Division One

Champions:	Norwich
Runners-up:	West Brom
Play-off champions:	Crystal Palace
Relegated:	Walsall
	Bradford
	Wimbledon

Nationwide Division Two

Champions:	Plymouth
Runners-up:	QPR
Play-off champions:	Brighton
Relegated:	Grimsby
	Rushden & D
	Notts C
	Wycombe

Nationwide Division Three

Champions:	Doncaster
Runners-up:	Hull
Third:	Torquay
Play-off champions:	Huddersfield
Relegated:	Carlisle
	York

Bank of Scotland Premier League

Champions:	Celtic
Runners-up:	Rangers
Relegated:	Partick

Bell's Scottish Division One

Champions:	Inverness CT
Runners-up:	Clyde
Relegated:	Ayr
	Brechin

Bell's Scottish Division Two

Champions:	Airdrie Utd
Runners-up:	Hamilton
Relegated:	East Fife
	Stenhousemuir

Bell's Scottish Third Division

Champions:	Stranraer
Runners-up:	Stirling
Bottom:	East Stirling

Nationwide Conference

Champions:	Chester City
Play-off champions:	Shrewsbury T
Bottom:	Farnborough
	Leigh RMI
	Northwich

Dr Martens Premier

Champions:	Crawley
Runners-up:	Weymouth
Bottom:	Dover
	Hednesford
	Chippenham
	Grantham

Unibond Premier

Champions:	Hucknell T
Runners-up:	Droylsden
Bottom:	Blyth S
	Frickley
	Wakefield

Ryman Premier

Champions:	Canvey Island
Runners-up:	Sutton Utd
Bottom:	Northwood
	Billericay
	Braintree
	Aylesbury

FA Cup

Winners:	Man United
Runners-up:	Millwall

Carling Cup

Winners:	Middlesbrough
Runners-up:	Bolton

LDV Vans Trophy

Winners:	Blackpool
Runners-up:	Southend

FA Trophy

Winners:	Hednesford T
Runners-up:	Canvey Island

Tennent's Scottish FA Cup

Winners:	Celtic
Runners-up:	Dunfermline

CIS Insurance Cup

Winners:	Livingston
Runners-up:	Hibernian

Bell's Scottish Challenge Cup

Winners:	Inverness CT
Runners-up:	Airdrie Utd

Sponsored by Stan James

Referees can be the bane of players and managers alike but the bookings market is increasingly where spread betting and Fixed Odds punters look to make some profit.

Below are the stats for last sesaon's select group of referees. Their card counts are not exclusive to the Premiership and and that should be borne in mind when weighing up their final scores.

Name	Games	Yellow	Red	Pts	Ave
Styles	34	123	16	1,730	**50.9**
Bennett	30	96	12	1,350	**45**
Dowd	28	104	6	1,220	**43.6**
Knight	30	95	9	1,205	**40.2**
Dunn	29	94	6	1,130	**38.9**
Messias	27	98	2	1,050	**38.9**
D'urso	27	83	6	1,000	**37.0**
Wiley	28	93	3	1,005	**35.9**
Webb	34	92	9	1,155	**33.9**
Rennie	24	79	1	815	**33.9**
Dean	37	98	9	1,255	**33.9**
Foy	23	68	4	775	**33.7**
Barber	28	79	5	935	**33.4**
Barry	35	99	6	1,150	**32.9**
Poll	35	97	3	1,045	**29.9**
Gallagher	34	77	6	940	**27.6**
Durkin	36	87	2	930	**25.8**
Halsey	38	80	5	935	**24.6**
Walton	31	64	4	740	**23.9**
Winter	34	57	3	655	**19.3**
Riley	32	27	5	405	**12.7**

Points are awarded on the basis of ten points for a yellow card and 25 for a red. In the case of a second yellow followed by red the number of points rises to 35, the usual practice in spread betting.

FA BARCLAYCARD PREMIER LEAGUE

	Team	Pld	W	D	L	F	GFA	PGA	Pts
1	Arsenal (1)	38	26	12	0	73	**1.9**	2.37	90
2	Chelsea (2)	38	24	7	7	67	**1.8**	2.08	79
3	Manchester Utd (3)	38	23	6	9	64	**1.7**	1.97	75
4	Liverpool (4)	38	16	12	10	55	**1.4**	1.59	60
5	Manchester C (16)	38	9	14	15	55	**1.4**	1.08	41
6	Newcastle Utd (5)	38	13	17	8	52	**1.4**	1.47	56
7	Fulham (9)	38	14	10	14	52	**1.4**	1.37	52
8	Charlton Ath (7)	38	14	11	13	51	**1.3**	1.39	53
9	Blackburn R (15)	38	12	8	18	51	**1.3**	1.16	44
10	Aston Villa (6)	38	15	11	12	48	**1.3**	1.47	56
11	Bolton W (8)	38	14	11	13	48	**1.3**	1.39	53
12	Leicester (18)	38	6	15	17	48	**1.3**	0.87	33
13	Portsmouth (13)	38	12	9	17	47	**1.2**	1.18	45
14	Tottenham H (14)	38	13	6	19	47	**1.2**	1.18	45
15	Everton (17)	38	9	12	17	45	**1.2**	1.03	39
16	Middlesbrough (11)	38	13	9	16	44	**1.2**	1.26	48
17	Southampton (12)	38	12	11	15	44	**1.2**	1.24	47
18	Birmingham C (10)	38	12	14	12	43	**1.1**	1.31	50
19	Leeds United (19)	38	8	9	21	40	**1.1**	0.87	33
20	Wolves (20)	38	7	12	19	38	**1.0**	0.87	33

- Number in brackets refers to final league finishing position
- GFA: Goals for average per match
- PGA: Average points gained per match

NATIONWIDE LEAGUE DIVISION ONE

	Team	Pld	W	D	L	F	GFA	PGA	Pts
1	Ipswich Town (5)	46	21	10	15	84	**1.8**	1.59	73
2	Norwich City (1)	46	28	10	8	79	**1.7**	2.04	94
3	Crystal Palace (6)	46	21	10	15	72	**1.6**	1.59	73
4	Preston NE (15)	46	15	14	17	69	**1.5**	1.28	59
5	Cardiff City (13)	46	17	14	15	68	**1.5**	1.41	65
6	West Ham (4)	46	19	17	10	67	**1.5**	1.61	74
7	Coventry City (12)	46	17	14	15	67	**1.5**	1.41	65
8	Sheffield Utd (8)	46	20	11	15	65	**1.4**	1.54	71
9	West Brom (2)	46	25	11	10	64	**1.4**	1.87	86
10	Nottm Forest (14)	46	15	15	16	61	**1.4**	1.30	60
11	Sunderland (3)	46	22	13	11	62	**1.3**	1.72	79
12	Wigan (7)	46	18	17	11	60	**1.3**	1.54	71
13	Burnley (19)	46	13	14	19	60	**1.3**	1.15	53
14	Stoke City(11)	46	18	12	16	58	**1.3**	1.43	66
15	Crewe (18)	46	14	11	21	57	**1.2**	1.15	53
16	Reading (9)	46	20	10	16	55	**1.2**	1.52	70
17	Millwall (10)	46	18	15	13	55	**1.2**	1.50	69
18	Watford (16)	46	15	12	19	54	**1.2**	1.24	57
19	Rotherham (17)	46	13	15	18	53	**1.2**	1.17	54
20	Derby County (20)	46	13	13	20	53	**1.2**	1.13	52
21	Gillingham (21)	46	14	9	23	48	**1.0**	1.11	51
22	Walsall (22)	46	13	12	21	45	**1.0**	1.11	51
23	Wimbledon (24)	46	8	5	33	41	**0.9**	0.63	29
24	Bradford City (23)	46	10	6	30	38	**0.8**	0.78	36

Sponsored by Stan James

NATIONWIDE LEAGUE DIVISION TWO

	Team	Pld	W	D	L	F	GFA	PGA	Pts
1	Plymouth A (1)	46	26	12	8	85	**1.8**	1.96	90
2	QPR (2)	46	22	17	7	80	**1.7**	1.80	83
3	Swindon T (5)	46	20	13	13	76	**1.7**	1.59	73
4	Hartlepool (6)	46	20	13	13	76	**1.7**	1.59	73
5	Port Vale (7)	46	21	10	15	73	**1.6**	1.59	73
6	Luton Town (10)	46	17	15	14	69	**1.5**	1.43	66
7	Oldham Ath (15)	46	12	21	13	66	**1.4**	1.24	57
8	Brighton (4)	46	22	11	13	64	**1.4**	1.67	77
9	Stockport C (19)	46	11	19	16	62	**1.3**	1.13	52
10	Rushden & D (22)	46	13	9	24	60	**1.3**	1.04	48
11	Tranmere R (8)	46	17	16	13	59	**1.3**	1.46	67
12	Bristol City (3)	46	23	13	10	58	**1.3**	1.78	82
13	Blackpool (14)	46	16	11	19	58	**1.3**	1.28	59
14	Peterborough (18)	46	12	16	18	58	**1.3**	1.13	52
15	Bournemouth (9)	46	17	15	14	56	**1.2**	1.43	66
16	Grimsby (21)	46	13	11	22	55	**1.2**	1.09	50
17	Barnsley (12)	46	15	17	14	54	**1.2**	1.35	62
18	Colchester Utd (11)	46	17	13	16	52	**1.1**	1.39	64
19	Brentford (17)	46	14	11	21	52	**1.1**	1.15	53
20	Wrexham (13)	46	17	9	20	50	**1.1**	1.30	60
21	Notts C (23)	46	10	12	24	50	**1.1**	0.91	42
22	Wycombe W (24)	46	6	19	21	50	**1.1**	0.80	37
23	Chesterfield (20)	46	12	15	19	49	**1.1**	1.11	51
24	Sheff Wed (16)	46	13	14	19	48	**1.0**	1.15	53

NATIONWIDE LEAGUE DIVISION THREE

	Team	Pld	W	D	L	F	GFA	PGA	Pts
1	Hull City (2)	46	25	13	8	82	**1.8**	1.91	88
2	Doncaster (1)	46	27	11	8	79	**1.7**	2.00	92
3	Mansfield (5)	46	22	9	15	76	**1.7**	1.63	75
4	Yeovil Town (8)	46	23	5	18	70	**1.5**	1.61	74
5	Scunthorpe (22)	46	11	16	19	69	**1.5**	1.10	49
6	Torquay Utd (3)	46	23	12	11	68	**1.5**	1.76	81
7	Huddersfield (4)	46	23	12	11	68	**1.5**	1.76	81
8	Lincoln City (7)	46	19	17	10	68	**1.5**	1.61	74
9	Northampton (6)	46	22	9	15	58	**1.3**	1.63	75
10	Swansea City (10)	46	15	14	17	58	**1.3**	1.28	59
11	Cheltenham (14)	46	14	14	18	57	**1.2**	1.22	56
12	Oxford Utd (9)	46	18	17	11	55	**1.2**	1.54	71
13	Cambridge (13)	46	14	14	18	55	**1.2**	1.22	56
14	Bury (12)	46	15	11	20	54	**1.2**	1.22	56
15	Macclesfield (20)	46	13	13	20	54	**1.2**	1.13	52
16	Darlington (18)	46	14	11	21	53	**1.2**	1.15	53
17	Southend Utd (17)	46	14	12	20	51	**1.1**	1.17	54
18	Boston Utd (11)	46	16	11	19	50	**1.1**	1.28	59
19	Bristol Rovers (15)	46	14	13	19	50	**1.1**	1.20	55
20	Rochdale (21)	46	12	14	20	49	**1.1**	1.10	50
21	Leyton Orient (19)	46	13	14	19	48	**1.0**	1.15	53
22	Carlisle Utd (23)	46	12	9	25	46	**1.0**	1.00	45
23	Kidderminster (16)	46	14	13	19	45	**1.0**	1.20	55
24	York City (24)	46	10	14	22	35	**0.8**	1.00	44

Sponsored by Stan James

TOP SCORERS 2003-2004

NATIONWIDE CONFERENCE

	Team	Pld	W	D	L	F	GFA	PGA	Pts
1	Hereford Utd (2)	42	28	7	7	103	**2.5**	2.17	91
2	Chester City (1)	42	27	11	4	85	**2.0**	2.19	92
3	Aldershot (5)	42	20	10	12	80	**1.9**	1.67	70
4	Exeter City (6)	42	19	12	11	71	**1.7**	1.64	69
5	Gravesend (11)	42	14	15	13	69	**1.6**	1.36	57
6	Acc. Stanley (10)	42	15	13	14	68	**1.6**	1.38	58
7	Shrewsbury (3)	42	20	14	8	67	**1.6**	1.76	74
8	Morecambe (7)	42	20	7	15	66	**1.6**	1.60	67
9	Woking (9)	42	15	16	11	65	**1.5**	1.45	61
10	Barnet (4)	42	19	14	9	60	**1.4**	1.69	71
11	Dag & Red (13)	42	15	9	18	59	**1.4**	1.29	54
12	Stevenage (8)	42	18	9	15	58	**1.4**	1.50	63
13	Forest Green (18)	42	12	12	18	58	**1.4**	1.14	48
14	Burton A (14)	42	15	7	20	57	**1.4**	1.24	52
15	Margate (16)	42	14	9	19	56	**1.3**	1.21	51
16	Farnborough (20)	42	10	9	23	53	**1.3**	0.93	39
17	Scarborough (15)	42	12	15	15	51	**1.2**	1.21	51
18	Telford Utd (12)	42	15	10	17	49	**1.2**	1.31	55
19	Tamworth (17)	42	13	10	19	49	**1.2**	1.17	49
20	Leigh RMI (21)	42	7	8	27	46	**1.1**	0.69	29
21	Halifax Town (19)	42	12	8	22	43	**1.0**	1.05	44
22	Nuneaton B (22)	42	4	11	27	30	**0.7**	0.55	23

BANK OF SCOTLAND SCOTTISH PREMIER LEAGUE

	Team	Pld	W	D	L	F	GFA	PpG	Pts
1	Celtic (1)	38	31	5	2	105	**2.8**	2.58	98
2	Rangers (2)	38	25	6	7	76	**2.0**	2.13	81
3	Hearts (3)	38	19	11	8	56	**1.5**	1.79	68
4	Kilmarnock (10)	38	12	6	20	51	**1.3**	1.11	42
5	Dundee (7)	38	12	10	16	48	**1.3**	1.21	46
6	Livingston (9)	38	10	13	15	48	**1.3**	1.13	43
7	Dundee Utd (5)	38	13	10	15	47	**1.2**	1.29	49
8	Dunfermline (4)	38	14	11	13	45	**1.2**	1.39	53
9	Motherwell (6)	38	12	10	16	42	**1.1**	1.21	46
10	Hibernian (8)	38	11	11	16	41	**1.1**	1.16	44
11	Aberdeen (11)	38	9	7	22	39	**1.0**	0.89	34
12	Partick T (12)	38	6	8	24	39	**1.0**	0.68	26

HAPPY HOME: No side in the Football League scored more goals than Plymouth

FA BARCLAYCARD PREMIER LEAGUE

	Team	Pld	W	D	L	A	GAA	PGA	Pts
1	Arsenal (1)	38	26	12	0	26	0.7	2.37	90
2	Chelsea (2)	38	24	7	7	30	0.8	2.08	79
3	Manchester Utd (3)	38	23	6	9	35	0.9	1.97	75
4	Liverpool (4)	38	16	12	10	37	1.0	1.59	60
5	Newcastle (5)	38	13	17	8	40	1.1	1.47	56
6	Aston Villa (6)	38	15	11	12	44	1.2	1.47	56
7	Southampton (12)	38	12	11	15	45	1.2	1.24	47
8	Fulham (9)	38	14	10	14	46	1.2	1.37	52
9	Birmingham C (10)	38	12	14	12	48	1.3	1.31	50
10	Charlton Ath (7)	38	14	11	13	51	1.3	1.39	53
11	Middlesbrough (11)	38	13	9	16	52	1.4	1.26	48
12	Portsmouth (13)	38	12	9	17	54	1.4	1.18	45
13	Manchester C (16)	38	10	14	14	54	1.4	1.08	41
14	Bolton W (8)	38	14	11	13	56	1.5	1.39	53
15	Tottenham H (14)	38	13	6	19	57	1.5	1.18	45
16	Everton (17)	38	9	12	17	57	1.5	1.03	39
17	Blackburn R (15)	38	12	8	18	59	1.6	1.16	44
18	Leicester C (18)	38	6	15	17	65	1.7	0.87	33
19	Wolverhampton (20)	38	7	12	19	77	2.0	0.87	33
20	Leeds Utd (19)	38	8	9	21	79	2.1	0.87	33

- Number in brackets refers to final league finishing position
- GAA: Goals against average per match
- PGA: Average points gained per match

NATIONWIDE LEAGUE DIVISION ONE

	Team	Pld	W	D	L	A	GAA	PGA	Pts
1	Norwich City (1)	46	28	10	8	39	0.8	2.04	94
2	West Brom (2)	46	25	11	10	42	0.9	1.87	86
3	Sunderland (3)	46	22	13	11	45	1.0	1.72	79
4	West Ham (4)	46	19	17	10	45	1.0	1.61	74
5	Wigan (7)	46	18	17	11	45	1.0	1.54	71
6	Millwall (10)	46	18	15	13	48	1.0	1.50	69
7	Coventry City (12)	46	17	14	15	54	1.2	1.41	65
8	Stoke City (11)	46	18	12	16	55	1.2	1.43	66
9	Sheffield Utd (8)	46	20	11	15	56	1.2	1.54	71
10	Reading (9)	46	20	10	16	57	1.2	1.52	70
11	Cardiff City (13)	46	17	14	15	58	1.3	1.41	65
12	Nottm Forest (13)	46	15	15	16	58	1.3	1.30	60
13	Crystal Palace (6)	46	21	10	15	61	1.3	1.59	73
14	Rotherham (13)	46	13	15	18	61	1.3	1.17	54
15	Walsall (22)	46	13	12	21	65	1.4	1.11	51
16	Crewe (18)	46	14	11	21	66	1.4	1.15	53
17	Derby County (20)	46	13	13	20	67	1.5	1.13	52
18	Gillingham (21)	46	14	9	23	67	1.5	1.11	51
19	Watford (16)	46	15	12	19	68	1.5	1.24	57
20	Bradford (23)	46	10	6	30	69	1.5	0.78	36
21	Preston NE (15)	46	21	10	15	71	1.5	1.59	73
22	Ipswich (5)	46	21	10	15	72	1.6	1.59	73
23	Burnley (19)	46	13	14	19	77	1.7	1.15	53
24	Wimbledon (24)	46	8	5	33	89	1.9	0.63	29

NATIONWIDE LEAGUE DIVISION TWO

	Team	Pld	W	D	L	A	GAA	PGA	Pts
1	Bristol City (3)	46	23	13	10	37	0.8	1.78	82
2	Plymouth A (1)	46	26	12	8	41	0.9	1.96	90
3	Brighton (4)	46	22	11	13	43	0.9	1.67	77
4	QPR (2)	46	22	17	7	45	1.0	1.80	83
5	Bournemouth (9)	46	17	15	14	51	1.1	1.43	66
6	Tranmere R (8)	46	17	16	13	56	1.2	1.46	67
7	Colchester Utd (11)	46	17	13	16	56	1.2	1.39	64
8	Swindon T (5)	46	20	13	13	58	1.3	1.59	73
9	Barnsley (12)	46	15	17	14	58	1.3	1.35	62
10	Peterborough (18)	46	12	16	18	58	1.3	1.13	52
11	Wrexham (13)	46	17	9	20	60	1.3	1.30	60
12	Oldham Ath (15)	46	12	21	13	60	1.3	1.24	57
13	Hartlepool (6)	46	20	13	13	61	1.3	1.59	73
14	Port Vale (7)	46	21	10	15	63	1.4	1.59	73
15	Sheffield Wed (16)	46	13	14	19	64	1.4	1.15	53
16	Blackpool (14)	46	16	11	19	65	1.4	1.28	59
17	Luton Town (10)	46	17	15	14	66	1.4	1.43	66
18	Brentford (17)	46	14	11	21	69	1.5	1.15	53
19	Stockport C (19)	46	11	19	16	70	1.5	1.13	52
20	Chesterfield (20)	46	12	15	19	71	1.5	1.11	51
21	Rushden & D (22)	46	13	9	24	74	1.6	1.04	48
22	Wycombe W (24)	46	6	19	21	75	1.6	0.80	37
23	Notts County (23)	46	10	12	24	78	1.7	0.91	42
24	Grimsby (22)	46	13	11	22	81	1.8	1.09	50

NATIONWIDE LEAGUE DIVISION THREE

	Team	Pld	W	D	L	A	GAA	PGA	Pts
1	Doncaster (1)	46	27	11	8	37	0.8	2.00	92
2	Hull City (2)	46	25	13	8	44	0.9	1.91	88
3	Torquay Utd (3)	46	23	12	11	44	0.9	1.76	81
4	Oxford Utd (9)	46	18	17	11	44	0.9	1.54	71
5	Lincoln City (7)	46	19	17	10	47	1.0	1.61	74
6	Northampton (6)	46	22	9	15	51	1.1	1.63	75
7	Huddersfield (4)	46	23	12	11	52	1.1	1.76	81
8	Boston Utd (11)	46	16	11	19	54	1.2	1.28	59
9	Yeovil Town(8)	46	23	5	18	57	1.2	1.61	74
10	Rochdale (21)	46	12	14	20	58	1.3	1.10	50
11	Kidderminster (16)	46	14	13	19	59	1.3	1.20	55
12	Swansea City (10)	46	15	14	17	61	1.3	1.28	59
13	Bristol Rovers (15)	46	14	13	19	61	1.3	1.20	55
14	Darlington (18)	46	14	11	21	61	1.3	1.15	53
15	Mansfield (5)	46	22	9	15	62	1.3	1.63	75
16	Southend Utd (17)	46	14	12	20	63	1.4	1.17	54
17	Bury (12)	46	15	11	20	64	1.4	1.22	56
18	Leyton Orient (19)	46	13	14	19	65	1.4	1.15	53
19	York City (24)	46	10	14	22	66	1.4	1.00	44
20	Cambridge (13)	46	14	14	18	67	1.5	1.22	56
21	Macclesfield (20)	46	13	13	20	69	1.5	1.13	52
22	Carlisle Utd (23)	46	12	9	25	69	1.5	1.00	45
23	Cheltenham (14)	46	14	14	18	71	1.5	1.22	56
24	Scunthorpe (22)	46	11	16	19	72	1.6	1.10	49

BEST DEFENCE 2003-2004

NATIONWIDE CONFERENCE

	Team	Pld	W	D	L	A	GAA	PGA	Pts
1	Chester City (1)	42	27	11	4	34	0.8	2.19	92
2	Shrewsbury (3)	42	20	14	8	42	1.0	1.76	74
3	Hereford Utd (2)	42	28	7	7	44	1.0	2.17	91
4	Barnet (4)	42	19	14	9	46	1.1	1.69	71
5	Telford Utd (12)	42	15	10	17	51	1.2	1.31	55
6	Stevenage (8)	42	18	9	15	52	1.2	1.50	63
7	Woking (9)	42	15	16	11	52	1.2	1.45	61
8	Scarborough (15)	42	12	15	15	54	1.3	1.21	51
9	Exeter City (6)	42	19	12	11	57	1.4	1.64	69
10	Burton A (14)	42	15	7	20	59	1.4	1.24	52
11	Acc. Stanley (10)	42	15	13	14	61	1.5	1.38	58
12	Dag & Red (13)	42	15	9	18	64	1.5	1.29	54
13	Margate (16)	42	14	9	19	64	1.5	1.21	51
14	Halifax Town (19)	42	12	8	22	65	1.5	1.05	44
15	Morecambe (7)	42	20	7	15	66	1.6	1.60	67
16	Gravesend (11)	42	14	15	13	66	1.6	1.36	57
17	Aldershot (5)	42	20	10	12	67	1.6	1.67	70
18	Tamworth (17)	42	13	10	19	68	1.6	1.17	49
19	Farnborough (20)	42	10	9	23	74	1.8	0.93	39
20	Forest Green (18)	42	12	12	18	80	1.9	1.14	48
21	Nuneaton B (22)	42	4	11	27	80	1.9	0.55	23
22	Leigh RMI (21)	42	7	8	27	97	2.3	0.69	29

BANK OF SCOTLAND SCOTTISH PREMIER LEAGUE

	Team	Pld	W	D	L	A	GAA	PpG	Pts
1	Celtic (1)	38	31	5	2	25	0.7	2.58	98
2	Rangers (2)	38	25	6	7	33	0.9	2.13	81
3	Hearts (3)	38	19	11	8	40	1.1	1.79	68
4	Motherwell (6)	38	12	10	16	49	1.3	1.21	46
5	Dunfermline (4)	38	14	11	13	52	1.4	1.39	53
6	Dundee (7)	38	12	10	16	57	1.5	1.21	46
7	Livingston (9)	38	10	13	15	57	1.5	1.13	43
8	Dundee Utd (5)	38	13	10	15	60	1.6	1.29	49
9	Hibernian (8)	38	11	11	16	60	1.6	1.16	44
10	Aberdeen (11)	38	9	7	22	63	1.7	0.89	34
11	Partick T (12)	38	6	8	24	67	1.8	0.68	26
12	Kilmarnock (10)	38	12	6	20	74	1.9	1.11	42

FIRHILL STADIUM: All the Scottish Premier League sides enjoyed visiting Partick

FA BARCLAYCARD PREMIER LEAGUE

	Team	Pld	CS	CS%
1	Chelsea (2)	38	21	**55.3**
2	Fulham (9)	38	15	**39.5**
3	Arsenal (1)	38	15	**39.5**
4	Liverpool (4)	38	15	**39.5**
5	Birmingham (10)	38	15	**39.5**
6	Man Utd (3)	38	14	**36.8**
7	Middlesbro (11)	38	14	**36.8**
8	Aston Villa (6)	38	12	**31.6**
9	Southampton (12)	38	12	**31.6**
10	Newcastle (6)	38	11	**28.9**
11	Bolton (8)	38	10	**26.3**
12	Charlton (8)	38	10	**26.3**
13	Everton (17)	38	10	**26.3**
14	Leicester (20)	38	9	**23.7**
15	Blackburn (15)	38	8	**21.1**
16	Tottenham (14)	38	8	**21.1**
17	Portsmouth (14)	38	8	**21.1**
18	Wolves (20)	38	7	**18.4**
19	Man City (16)	38	7	**18.4**
20	Leeds (20)	38	3	**7.9**

LEADER:The Blues' John Terry

RECORD WHEN KEEPING A CLEAN SHEET

	Team	Pld	W	D	L	F	GFA	PGA	Pts
1	Blackburn (15)	8	8	0	0	12	1.50	**3.0**	**24**
2	Man Utd (3)	14	12	2	0	27	1.93	**2.7**	**38**
3	Chelsea (2)	21	17	4	0	35	1.67	**2.6**	**55**
4	Arsenal (1)	15	11	4	0	26	1.73	**2.5**	**37**
5	Bolton (8)	10	7	3	0	11	1.10	**2.4**	**24**
6	Charlton (8)	10	7	3	0	11	1.10	**2.4**	**24**
7	Tottenham (14)	8	5	3	0	8	1.00	**2.3**	**18**
8	Portsmouth (14)	8	5	3	0	9	1.13	**2.3**	**18**
9	Fulham (9)	15	9	6	0	19	1.27	**2.2**	**33**
10	Liverpool (4)	15	9	6	0	19	1.27	**2.2**	**33**
11	Aston Villa (6)	12	7	5	0	18	1.50	**2.2**	**26**
12	Birmingham (10)	15	8	7	0	14	0.93	**2.1**	**31**
13	Middlesbro (11)	14	8	6	0	13	0.93	**2.1**	**30**
14	Newcastle (6)	11	6	5	0	13	1.18	**2.1**	**23**
15	Leicester (20)	9	5	4	0	12	1.33	**2.1**	**19**
16	Southampton (12)	12	6	6	0	11	0.92	**2.0**	**24**
17	Everton (17)	10	5	5	0	10	1.00	**2.0**	**20**
18	Wolves (20)	7	3	4	0	4	0.57	**1.9**	**13**
19	Man City (16)	7	3	4	0	6	0.86	**1.9**	**13**
20	Leeds (20)	3	1	2	0	1	0.33	**1.7**	**5**

- Number in brackets refers to final league finishing position
- GFA: Goals against average per match
- PGA: Average points gained per match

Sponsored by Stan James

NATIONWIDE LEAGUE DIVISION ONE

	Team	Pld	CS	CS%
1	West Brom (2)	46	19	**41.3**
2	Norwich (1)	46	18	**39.1**
3	West Ham (4)	46	18	**39.1**
4	Sunderland (3)	46	18	**39.1**
5	Wigan (8)	46	17	**37.0**
6	Millwall (10)	46	16	**34.8**
7	Sheff Utd (8)	46	15	**32.6**
8	Rotherham (17)	46	15	**32.6**
9	Stoke (11)	46	14	**30.4**
10	Cardiff (13)	46	14	**30.4**
11	C Palace (6)	46	14	**30.4**
12	Reading (9)	46	13	**28.3**
13	Coventry (13)	46	13	**28.3**
14	Gillingham (22)	46	13	**28.3**
15	Crewe (19)	46	11	**23.9**
16	Preston (15)	46	11	**23.9**
17	Nottm Forest (14)	46	11	**23.9**
18	Derby (20)	46	10	**21.7**
19	Burnley (19)	46	10	**21.7**
20	Walsall (22)	46	10	**21.7**
21	Watford (16)	46	9	**19.6**
22	Ipswich (6)	46	7	**15.2**
23	Bradford (23)	46	7	**15.2**
24	Wimbledon (24)	46	5	**10.9**

WEST BROM: Tight as a . . .

RECORD WHEN KEEPING A CLEAN SHEET

	Team	Pld	W	D	L	F	GFA	PGA	Pts
1	Norwich (1)	18	15	3	0	29	1.61	**2.7**	**48**
2	Sheff Utd (8)	15	13	2	0	25	1.67	**2.7**	**41**
3	C Palace (6)	14	12	2	0	19	1.36	**2.7**	**38**
4	Ipswich (6)	7	6	1	0	9	1.29	**2.7**	**19**
5	West Brom (2)	19	15	4	0	25	1.32	**2.6**	**49**
6	Burnley (19)	10	8	2	0	16	1.60	**2.6**	**26**
7	Watford (16)	9	7	2	0	11	1.22	**2.6**	**23**
8	Wimbledon (24)	5	4	1	0	6	1.20	**2.6**	**13**
9	Reading (9)	13	10	3	0	16	1.23	**2.5**	**33**
10	Crewe (19)	11	8	3	0	14	1.27	**2.5**	**27**
11	Preston (15)	11	8	3	0	12	1.09	**2.5**	**27**
12	Nottm Forest (14)	11	8	3	0	19	1.73	**2.5**	**27**
13	West Ham (4)	18	13	5	0	31	1.72	**2.4**	**44**
14	Sunderland (3)	18	13	5	0	26	1.44	**2.4**	**44**
15	Wigan (8)	17	12	5	0	24	1.41	**2.4**	**41**
16	Stoke (11)	14	10	4	0	16	1.14	**2.4**	**34**
17	Coventry (13)	13	9	4	0	19	1.46	**2.4**	**31**
18	Walsall (22)	10	7	3	0	8	0.80	**2.4**	**24**
19	Bradford (23)	7	5	2	0	7	1.00	**2.4**	**17**
20	Rotherham (17)	15	9	6	0	17	1.13	**2.2**	**33**
21.	Gillingham (22)	13	8	5	0	13	1.00	**2.2**	**29**
22	Millwall (10)	16	9	7	0	13	0.81	**2.1**	**34**
23	Cardiff (13)	14	8	6	0	20	1.43	**2.1**	**30**
24	Derby (20)	10	5	5	0	8	0.80	**2.0**	**20**

CLEAN SHEETS 2003-2004

NATIONWIDE LEAGUE DIVISION TWO

	Team	Pld	CS	CS%
1	Brighton (4)	46	22	**47.8**
2	Plymouth (1)	46	21	**45.7**
3	QPR (2)	46	18	**39.1**
4	Bristol C (3)	46	17	**37.0**
5	Bournemouth (10)	46	17	**37.0**
6	Tranmere (8)	46	15	**32.6**
7	Swindon (7)	46	14	**30.4**
8	Wrexham (13)	46	14	**30.4**
9	Hartlepool (7)	46	14	**30.4**
10	Barnsley (12)	46	13	**28.3**
11	Grimsby (21)	46	12	**26.1**
12	Port Vale (7)	46	12	**26.1**
13	Sheff Wed (17)	46	11	**23.9**
14	Colchester (11)	46	11	**23.9**
15	Blackpool (14)	46	10	**21.7**
16	Chesterfield (20)	46	10	**21.7**
17	Peterborough (19)	46	10	**21.7**
18	Luton (10)	46	9	**19.6**
19	Oldham (15)	46	9	**19.6**
20	Stockport (19)	46	9	**19.6**
21	Wycombe (24)	46	8	**17.4**
22	Notts Co (23)	46	8	**17.4**
23	Rushden (22)	46	7	**15.2**
24	Brentford (17)	46	6	**13.0**

BRENTFORD: Leaking defence

RECORD WHEN KEEPING A CLEAN SHEET

	Team	Pld	W	D	L	F	GFA	PGA	Pts
1	Swindon (7)	14	13	1	0	27	1.93	**2.9**	**40**
2	QPR (2)	18	15	3	0	33	1.83	**2.7**	**48**
3	Port Vale (7)	12	10	2	0	16	1.33	**2.7**	**32**
4	Brighton (4)	22	18	4	0	35	1.59	**2.6**	**58**
5	Bristol C (3)	17	14	3	0	23	1.35	**2.6**	**45**
6	Plymouth (1)	21	16	5	0	41	1.95	**2.5**	**53**
7	Bournemouth (10)	17	13	4	0	21	1.24	**2.5**	**43**
8	Notts Co (23)	8	6	2	0	9	1.13	**2.5**	**20**
9	Barnsley (12)	13	9	4	0	15	1.15	**2.4**	**31**
10	Blackpool (14)	10	7	3	0	13	1.30	**2.4**	**24**
11	Chesterfield (20)	10	7	3	0	11	1.10	**2.4**	**24**
12	Tranmere (8)	15	10	5	0	16	1.07	**2.3**	**35**
13	Wrexham (13)	14	9	5	0	15	1.07	**2.3**	**32**
14	Hartlepool (7)	14	9	5	0	19	1.36	**2.3**	**32**
15	Colchester (11)	11	7	4	0	9	0.82	**2.3**	**25**
16	Luton (10)	9	6	3	0	9	1.00	**2.3**	**21**
17	Oldham (15)	9	6	3	0	16	1.78	**2.3**	**21**
18	Stockport (19)	9	6	3	0	11	1.22	**2.3**	**21**
19	Brentford (17)	6	4	2	0	8	1.33	**2.3**	**14**
20	Grimsby (21)	12	7	5	0	13	1.08	**2.2**	**26**
21	Sheff Wed (17)	11	6	5	0	10	0.91	**2.1**	**23**
22	Rushden (22)	7	4	3	0	10	1.43	**2.1**	**15**
23	Peterborough (19)	10	4	6	0	6	0.60	**1.8**	**18**
24	Wycombe (24)	8	3	5	0	6	0.75	**1.8**	**14**

NATIONWIDE LEAGUE DIVISION THREE

	Team	Pld	CS	CS%
1	Doncaster (1)	46	19	**41.3**
2	Oxford (9)	46	17	**37.0**
3	Lincoln (8)	46	17	**37.0**
4	Huddersfield (4)	46	17	**37.0**
5	Yeovil (8)	46	16	**34.8**
6	Hull City (2)	46	16	**34.8**
7	Mansfield (6)	46	15	**32.6**
8	Northampton (6)	46	15	**32.6**
9	York (24)	46	14	**30.4**
10	Torquay (4)	46	14	**30.4**
11	Bristol R (16)	46	14	**30.4**
12	Boston Utd (11)	46	14	**30.4**
13	Swansea (11)	46	13	**28.3**
14	Bury (14)	46	12	**26.1**
15	Rochdale (21)	46	12	**26.1**
16	Darlington (19)	46	12	**26.1**
17	Cambridge (14)	46	11	**23.9**
18	Kidderminster (16)	46	11	**23.9**
19	Southend (17)	46	10	**21.7**
20	Cheltenham (14)	46	10	**21.7**
21	Macclesfield (20)	46	10	**21.7**
22	Scunthorpe (22)	46	8	**17.4**
23	Leyton Orient (19)	46	8	**17.4**
24	Carlisle (23)	46	6	**13.0**

CARLISLE: Goals conceded cost them their League status

RECORD WHEN KEEPING A CLEAN SHEET

	Team	Pld	W	D	L	F	GFA	PGA	Pts
1	Yeovil (8)	16	14	2	0	27	1.69	**2.8**	**44**
2	Northampton (6)	15	13	2	0	22	1.47	**2.7**	**41**
3	Darlington (19)	12	10	2	0	19	1.58	**2.7**	**32**
4	Carlisle (23)	6	5	1	0	8	1.33	**2.7**	**16**
5	Doncaster (1)	19	15	4	0	30	1.58	**2.6**	**49**
6	Huddersfield (4)	17	14	3	0	25	1.47	**2.6**	**45**
7	Mansfield (6)	15	12	3	0	26	1.73	**2.6**	**39**
8	Torquay (4)	14	11	3	0	19	1.36	**2.6**	**36**
9	Boston Utd (11)	14	11	3	0	19	1.36	**2.6**	**36**
10	Southend (17)	10	8	2	0	15	1.50	**2.6**	**26**
11	Hull City (2)	16	12	4	0	24	1.50	**2.5**	**40**
12	Leyton Orient (19)	8	6	2	0	9	1.13	**2.5**	**20**
13	Bristol R (16)	14	9	5	0	17	1.21	**2.3**	**32**
14	Rochdale (21)	12	8	4	0	15	1.25	**2.3**	**28**
15	Cambridge (14)	11	7	4	0	12	1.09	**2.3**	**25**
16	Kidderminster (16)	11	7	4	0	11	1.00	**2.3**	**25**
17	Scunthorpe (22)	8	5	3	0	11	1.38	**2.3**	**18**
18	Oxford (9)	17	10	7	0	19	1.12	**2.2**	**37**
19	Bury (14)	12	7	5	0	13	1.08	**2.2**	**26**
20	Macclesfield (20)	10	6	4	0	10	1.00	**2.2**	**22**
21	Lincoln (8)	17	9	8	0	19	1.12	**2.1**	**35**
22	York (24)	14	7	7	0	10	0.71	**2.0**	**28**
23	Swansea (11)	13	6	7	0	11	0.85	**1.9**	**25**
24	Cheltenham (14)	10	3	7	0	4	0.40	**1.6**	**16**

NATIONWIDE CONFERENCE

	Team	Pld	CS	CS%
1	Chester (1)	42	20	**47.6**
2	Shrewsbury (3)	42	16	**38.1**
3	Hereford (2)	42	14	**33.3**
4	Telford (12)	42	13	**31.0**
5	Dag & Red (13)	42	13	**31.0**
6	Barnet (4)	42	12	**28.6**
7	Margate (16)	42	11	**26.2**
8	Woking (9)	42	10	**23.8**
9	Morecambe (7)	42	10	**23.8**
10	Tamworth (17)	42	10	**23.8**
11	Scarborough (16)	42	10	**23.8**
12	Halifax (19)	42	9	**21.4**
13	Accrington (10)	42	9	**21.4**
14	Exeter (6)	42	8	**19.0**
15	Stevenage (8)	42	8	**19.0**
16	Gravesend (11)	42	8	**19.0**
17	Farnborough (20)	42	7	**16.7**
18	Burton (14)	42	6	**14.3**
19	Northwich (22)	42	6	**14.3**
20	Forest Green (18)	42	6	**14.3**
21	Aldershot (5)	42	5	**11.9**
22	Leigh RMI (21)	42	3	**7.1**

AMAZING: Aldershot made the play-offs despite their defence

RECORD WHEN KEEPING A CLEAN SHEET

	Team	Pld	W	D	L	F	GFA	PGA	Pts
1	Morecambe (7)	10	10	0	0	20	2.00	**3.0**	**30**
2	Farnborough (20)	7	7	0	0	14	2.00	**3.0**	**21**
3	Burton (14)	6	6	0	0	11	1.83	**3.0**	**18**
4	Aldershot (5)	5	5	0	0	10	2.00	**3.0**	**15**
5	Leigh RMI (21)	3	3	0	0	3	1.00	**3.0**	**9**
6	Hereford (2)	14	13	1	0	36	2.57	**2.9**	**40**
7	Margate (16)	11	10	1	0	18	1.64	**2.8**	**31**
8	Halifax (19)	9	8	1	0	12	1.33	**2.8**	**25**
9	Exeter (6)	8	7	1	0	15	1.88	**2.8**	**22**
10	Tamworth (17)	10	8	2	0	12	1.20	**2.6**	**26**
11	Shrewsbury (3)	16	12	4	0	21	1.31	**2.5**	**40**
12	Telford (12)	13	10	3	0	18	1.38	**2.5**	**33**
13	Stevenage (8)	8	6	2	0	11	1.38	**2.5**	**20**
14	Gravesend (11)	8	6	2	0	16	2.00	**2.5**	**20**
15	Chester (1)	20	14	6	0	34	1.70	**2.4**	**48**
16	Dag & Red (13)	13	9	4	0	18	1.38	**2.4**	**31**
17	Woking (9)	10	7	3	0	13	1.30	**2.4**	**24**
18	Accrington (10)	9	6	3	0	10	1.11	**2.3**	**21**
19	Northwich (22)	6	4	2	0	4	0.67	**2.3**	**14**
20	Forest Green (18)	6	4	2	0	11	1.83	**2.3**	**14**
21	Barnet (4)	12	7	5	0	12	1.00	**2.2**	**26**
22	Scarborough (16)	10	6	4	0	8	0.80	**2.2**	**22**

CLEAN SHEETS 2003-2004

Sponsored by Stan James

BANK OF SCOTLAND SCOTTISH PREMIER LEAGUE

	Team	Pld	CS	CS%
1	Celtic (1)	38	17	**44.7**
2	Rangers (2)	38	16	**42.1**
3	Dunfermline (4)	38	13	**34.2**
4	Hearts (3)	38	12	**31.6**
5	Dundee Utd (5)	38	11	**28.9**
6	Livingston (9)	38	11	**28.9**
7	Motherwell (7)	38	10	**26.3**
8	Hibernian (8)	38	9	**23.7**
9	Dundee (7)	38	7	**18.4**
10	Partick (12)	38	5	**13.2**
11	Aberdeen (11)	38	5	**13.2**
12	Kilmarnock (10)	38	3	**7.9**

NO 1: Celtic's Rab Douglas

RECORD WHEN KEEPING A CLEAN SHEET

	Team	Pld	W	D	L	F	GFA	PGA	Pts
1	Dundee (7)	7	7	0	0	12	1.71	**3.0**	**21**
2	Kilmarnock (10)	3	3	0	0	8	2.67	**3.0**	**9**
3	Celtic (1)	17	16	1	0	49	2.88	**2.9**	**49**
4	Rangers (2)	16	15	1	0	37	2.31	**2.9**	**46**
5	Motherwell (7)	10	9	1	0	16	1.60	**2.8**	**28**
6	Hearts (3)	12	10	2	0	17	1.42	**2.7**	**32**
7	Hibernian (8)	9	7	2	0	10	1.11	**2.6**	**23**
8	Aberdeen (11)	5	4	1	0	9	1.80	**2.6**	**13**
9	Dundee Utd (5)	11	8	3	0	12	1.09	**2.5**	**27**
10	Livingston (9)	11	7	4	0	14	1.27	**2.3**	**25**
11	Dunfermline (4)	13	8	5	0	14	1.08	**2.2**	**29**
12	Partick (12)	5	3	2	0	4	0.80	**2.2**	**11**

TO THE MAX: Dundee struggled to score but clean sheets always meant three points

FA BARCLAYCARD PREMIER LEAGUE

	Team	Pld	FS	FS%
1	Chelsea (2)	38	25	**65.8**
2	Arsenal (1)	38	24	**63.2**
3	Man Utd (3)	38	22	**57.9**
4	Newcastle (6)	38	20	**52.6**
5	Portsmouth (14)	38	20	**52.6**
6	Liverpool (4)	38	19	**50.0**
7	Bolton (8)	38	18	**47.4**
8	Leicester (20)	38	18	**47.4**
9	Aston Villa (6)	38	18	**47.4**
10	Charlton (8)	38	17	**44.7**
11	Blackburn (15)	38	17	**44.7**
12	Middlesbro (11)	38	16	**42.1**
13	Man City (16)	38	15	**39.5**
14	Southampton (12)	38	15	**39.5**
15	Fulham (9)	38	14	**36.8**
16	Leeds (20)	38	14	**36.8**
17	Tottenham (14)	38	13	**34.2**
18	Birmingham (10)	38	13	**34.2**
19	Everton (17)	38	12	**31.6**
20	Wolves (20)	38	9	**23.7**

ON FIRE: Eidur Gudjohnsen

RECORD WHEN FIRST TO SCORE

	Team	Pld	W	D	L	F	A	PGA	Pts
1	Man Utd (3)	22	20	2	0	53	15	**2.8**	**62**
2	Arsenal (1)	24	19	5	0	53	16	**2.6**	**62**
3	Chelsea (2)	25	20	1	4	48	15	**2.4**	**61**
4	Charlton (8)	17	12	4	1	33	16	**2.4**	**40**
5	Fulham (9)	14	11	1	2	29	9	**2.4**	**34**
6	Southampton (12)	15	11	1	3	28	16	**2.3**	**34**
7	Liverpool (4)	19	13	3	3	39	18	**2.2**	**42**
8	Blackburn (15)	17	11	4	2	34	19	**2.2**	**37**
9	Birmingham (10)	13	9	2	2	21	8	**2.2**	**29**
10	Tottenham (14)	13	9	1	3	34	21	**2.2**	**28**
11	Middlesbro (11)	16	11	1	4	32	19	**2.1**	**34**
12	Everton (17)	12	7	4	1	23	10	**2.1**	**25**
13	Portsmouth (14)	20	12	4	4	40	22	**2.0**	**40**
14	Bolton (8)	18	11	3	4	30	24	**2.0**	**36**
15	Newcastle (6)	20	10	8	2	39	20	**1.9**	**38**
16	Aston Villa (6)	18	10	5	3	34	18	**1.9**	**35**
17	Leeds (20)	14	8	2	4	26	25	**1.9**	**26**
18	Wolves (20)	9	4	4	1	13	11	**1.8**	**16**
19	Man City (16)	15	6	6	3	28	17	**1.6**	**24**
20	Leicester (20)	18	5	6	7	30	26	**1.2**	**21**

- Number in brackets refers to final league finishing position
- PGA: Average points gained per match

Sponsored by Stan James

NATIONWIDE LEAGUE DIVISION ONE

	Team	Pld	FS	FS%
1	West Ham (4)	46	28	**60.9**
2	Sunderland (3)	46	28	**60.9**
3	Wigan (8)	46	27	**58.7**
4	Norwich (1)	46	26	**56.5**
5	C Palace (6)	46	26	**56.5**
6	Sheff Utd (8)	46	25	**54.3**
7	Reading (9)	46	24	**52.2**
8	Burnley (19)	46	24	**52.2**
9	Preston (15)	46	24	**52.2**
10	Stoke (11)	46	23	**50.0**
11	Ipswich (6)	46	22	**47.8**
12	West Brom (2)	46	22	**47.8**
13	Coventry (13)	46	21	**45.7**
14	Millwall (10)	46	21	**45.7**
15	Nottm Forest (14)	46	21	**45.7**
16	Crewe (19)	46	20	**43.5**
17	Walsall (22)	46	20	**43.5**
18	Derby (20)	46	19	**41.3**
19	Watford (16)	46	19	**41.3**
20	Rotherham (17)	46	19	**41.3**
21	Cardiff (13)	46	17	**37.0**
22	Gillingham (22)	46	15	**32.6**
23	Bradford (23)	46	13	**28.3**
24	Wimbledon (24)	46	12	**26.1**

HAMMERS: Quick off the mark

RECORD WHEN FIRST TO SCORE

	Team	Pld	W	D	L	F	A	PGA	Pts
1	Norwich (1)	26	23	3	0	55	15	**2.8**	**72**
2	West Brom (2)	22	19	3	0	40	10	**2.7**	**60**
3	Ipswich (6)	22	17	3	2	52	24	**2.5**	**54**
4	Coventry (13)	21	16	4	1	51	17	**2.5**	**52**
5	Sunderland (3)	28	21	4	3	53	21	**2.4**	**67**
6	C Palace (6)	26	20	3	3	53	23	**2.4**	**63**
7	Cardiff (13)	17	13	1	3	41	17	**2.4**	**40**
8	Stoke (11)	23	16	6	1	41	16	**2.3**	**54**
9	Reading (9)	24	16	6	2	42	24	**2.3**	**54**
10	Millwall (10)	21	15	3	3	37	19	**2.3**	**48**
11	Gillingham (22)	15	11	1	3	25	14	**2.3**	**34**
12	Wigan (8)	27	17	9	1	52	21	**2.2**	**60**
13	Sheff Utd (8)	25	16	7	2	45	19	**2.2**	**55**
14	Nottm Forest (14)	21	14	5	2	45	21	**2.2**	**47**
15	Walsall (22)	20	13	5	2	32	17	**2.2**	**44**
16	West Ham (4)	28	17	7	4	55	25	**2.1**	**58**
17	Crewe (19)	20	13	4	3	35	17	**2.1**	**43**
18	Rotherham (17)	19	12	4	3	34	19	**2.1**	**40**
19	Preston (15)	24	14	7	3	48	27	**2.0**	**49**
20	Derby (20)	19	11	5	3	37	22	**2.0**	**38**
21	Watford (16)	19	11	5	3	31	18	**2.0**	**38**
22	Burnley (19)	24	13	7	4	45	29	**1.9**	**46**
23	Bradford (23)	13	8	1	4	18	12	**1.9**	**25**
24	Wimbledon (24)	12	6	1	5	19	18	**1.6**	**19**

NATIONWIDE LEAGUE DIVISION TWO

	Team	Pld	FS	FS%
1	Swindon (7)	46	30	**65.2**
2	QPR (2)	46	29	**63.0**
3	Bristol C (3)	46	29	**63.0**
4	Port Vale (7)	46	26	**56.5**
5	Oldham (15)	46	24	**52.2**
6	Plymouth (1)	46	24	**52.2**
7	Colchester (11)	46	24	**52.2**
8	Luton (10)	46	23	**50.0**
9	Brighton (4)	46	23	**50.0**
10	Tranmere (8)	46	23	**50.0**
11	Hartlepool (7)	46	22	**47.8**
12	Grimsby (21)	46	20	**43.5**
13	Barnsley (12)	46	20	**43.5**
14	Brentford (17)	46	20	**43.5**
15	Sheff Wed (17)	46	20	**43.5**
16	Wrexham (13)	46	19	**41.3**
17	Blackpool (14)	46	19	**41.3**
18	Stockport (19)	46	19	**41.3**
19	Peterborough (19)	46	19	**41.3**
20	Bournemouth (10)	46	18	**39.1**
21	Chesterfield (20)	46	18	**39.1**
22	Rushden (22)	46	15	**32.6**
23	Wycombe (24)	46	15	**32.6**
24	Notts Co (23)	46	15	**32.6**

HOOPS: R's Kevin Gallen

RECORD WHEN FIRST TO SCORE

	Team	Pld	W	D	L	F	A	PGA	Pts
1	Plymouth (1)	24	22	2	0	65	12	**2.8**	**68**
2	Brighton (4)	23	20	3	0	44	8	**2.7**	**63**
3	Bristol C (3)	29	21	8	0	48	15	**2.4**	**71**
4	Wrexham (13)	19	14	3	2	37	21	**2.4**	**45**
5	Bournemouth (10)	18	14	2	2	32	10	**2.4**	**44**
6	QPR (2)	29	21	5	3	62	22	**2.3**	**68**
7	Colchester (11)	24	16	6	2	43	24	**2.3**	**54**
8	Tranmere (8)	23	15	7	1	42	17	**2.3**	**52**
9	Barnsley (12)	20	13	6	1	36	19	**2.3**	**45**
10	Swindon (7)	30	19	9	2	58	25	**2.2**	**66**
11	Hartlepool (7)	22	15	4	3	46	23	**2.2**	**49**
12	Brentford (17)	20	13	5	2	38	23	**2.2**	**44**
13	Sheff Wed (17)	20	13	4	3	37	23	**2.1**	**43**
14	Blackpool (14)	19	12	4	3	34	18	**2.1**	**40**
15	Chesterfield (20)	18	10	7	1	31	17	**2.1**	**37**
16	Rushden (22)	15	10	2	3	31	18	**2.1**	**32**
17	Notts Co (23)	15	9	4	2	26	13	**2.1**	**31**
18	Port Vale (7)	26	16	4	6	45	26	**2.0**	**52**
19	Luton (10)	23	13	6	4	42	28	**2.0**	**45**
20	Stockport (19)	19	10	7	2	33	21	**1.9**	**37**
21	Peterborough (19)	19	10	6	3	40	25	**1.9**	**36**
22	Oldham (15)	24	11	9	4	50	29	**1.8**	**42**
23	Grimsby (21)	20	11	3	6	38	30	**1.8**	**36**
24	Wycombe (24)	15	4	8	3	26	21	**1.3**	**20**

NATIONWIDE LEAGUE DIVISION THREE

	Team	Pld	FS	FS%
1	Torquay (4)	46	28	**60.9**
2	Hull City (2)	46	28	**60.9**
3	Huddersfield (4)	46	27	**58.7**
4	Doncaster (1)	46	26	**56.5**
5	Mansfield (6)	46	26	**56.5**
6	Northampton (6)	46	25	**54.3**
7	Yeovil (8)	46	23	**50.0**
8	Oxford (9)	46	22	**47.8**
9	Lincoln (8)	46	22	**47.8**
10	Southend (17)	46	22	**47.8**
11	Darlington (19)	46	22	**47.8**
12	Swansea (11)	46	21	**45.7**
13	Rochdale (21)	46	21	**45.7**
14	Boston Utd (11)	46	21	**45.7**
15	Kidderminster (16)	46	20	**43.5**
16	Bury (14)	46	19	**41.3**
17	Cambridge (14)	46	19	**41.3**
18	Scunthorpe (22)	46	19	**41.3**
19	York (24)	46	18	**39.1**
20	Leyton Orient (19)	46	18	**39.1**
21	Bristol R (16)	46	17	**37.0**
22	Macclesfield (20)	46	17	**37.0**
23	Carlisle (23)	46	16	**34.8**
24	Cheltenham (14)	46	12	**26.1**

SHARPEST: Torquay United

RECORD WHEN FIRST TO SCORE

	Team	Pld	W	D	L	F	A	PGA	Pts
1	Doncaster (1)	26	24	0	2	58	13	**2.8**	**72**
2	Hull City (2)	28	24	3	1	67	21	**2.7**	**75**
3	Yeovil (8)	23	19	2	2	49	14	**2.6**	**59**
4	Torquay (4)	28	22	4	2	57	22	**2.5**	**70**
5	Huddersfield (4)	27	21	4	2	52	21	**2.5**	**67**
6	Northampton (6)	25	19	5	1	44	16	**2.5**	**62**
7	Mansfield (6)	26	20	3	3	53	22	**2.4**	**63**
8	Cambridge (14)	19	13	6	0	38	18	**2.4**	**45**
9	Oxford (9)	22	15	4	3	36	17	**2.2**	**49**
10	Boston Utd (11)	21	14	4	3	35	14	**2.2**	**46**
11	Bristol R (16)	17	11	4	2	28	10	**2.2**	**37**
12	Lincoln (8)	22	14	4	4	46	24	**2.1**	**46**
13	Kidderminster (16)	20	12	6	2	33	18	**2.1**	**42**
14	Leyton Orient (19)	18	11	4	3	30	16	**2.1**	**37**
15	Southend (17)	22	12	7	3	40	23	**2.0**	**43**
16	Swansea (11)	21	12	5	4	39	23	**2.0**	**41**
17	Macclesfield (20)	17	10	4	3	32	19	**2.0**	**34**
18	Darlington (19)	22	12	5	5	39	26	**1.9**	**41**
19	Rochdale (21)	21	11	7	3	34	19	**1.9**	**40**
20	Scunthorpe (22)	19	10	6	3	44	24	**1.9**	**36**
21	York (24)	18	10	5	3	24	15	**1.9**	**35**
22	Carlisle (23)	16	8	6	2	26	17	**1.9**	**30**
23	Cheltenham (14)	12	7	1	4	25	19	**1.8**	**22**
24	Bury (14)	19	9	4	6	29	22	**1.6**	**31**

NATIONWIDE CONFERENCE

	Team	Pld	FS	FS%
1	Chester (1)	42	30	**71.4**
2	Hereford (2)	42	30	**71.4**
3	Shrewsbury (3)	42	27	**64.3**
4	Aldershot (5)	42	25	**59.5**
5	Exeter (6)	42	23	**54.8**
6	Gravesend (11)	42	22	**52.4**
7	Telford (12)	42	21	**50.0**
8	Stevenage (8)	42	21	**50.0**
9	Accrington (10)	42	21	**50.0**
10	Halifax (19)	42	20	**47.6**
11	Margate (16)	42	20	**47.6**
12	Morecambe (7)	42	19	**45.2**
13	Tamworth (17)	42	19	**45.2**
14	Woking (9)	42	18	**42.9**
15	Barnet (4)	42	17	**40.5**
16	Burton (14)	42	17	**40.5**
17	Leigh RMI (21)	42	17	**40.5**
18	Scarborough (16)	42	16	**38.1**
19	Forest Green (18)	42	16	**38.1**
20	Dag & Red (13)	42	15	**35.7**
21	Farnborough (20)	42	15	**35.7**
22	Northwich (22)	42	9	**21.4**

DOMINANT: Chester City

RECORD WHEN FIRST TO SCORE

	Team	Pld	W	D	L	F	A	PGA	Pts
1	Dag & Red (13)	15	13	1	1	36	11	**2.7**	**40**
2	Hereford (2)	30	24	5	1	82	23	**2.6**	**77**
3	Barnet (4)	17	14	2	1	37	14	**2.6**	**44**
4	Chester (1)	30	23	5	2	73	25	**2.5**	**74**
5	Morecambe (7)	19	15	3	1	40	14	**2.5**	**48**
6	Shrewsbury (3)	27	19	8	0	56	21	**2.4**	**65**
7	Woking (9)	18	13	4	1	39	16	**2.4**	**43**
8	Aldershot (5)	25	17	6	2	54	30	**2.3**	**57**
9	Exeter (6)	23	15	6	2	50	27	**2.2**	**51**
10	Accrington (10)	21	14	5	2	48	25	**2.2**	**47**
11	Stevenage (8)	21	14	3	4	40	23	**2.1**	**45**
12	Telford (12)	21	14	2	5	37	20	**2.1**	**44**
13	Tamworth (17)	19	12	4	3	31	19	**2.1**	**40**
14	Burton (14)	17	10	4	3	32	18	**2.0**	**34**
15	Scarborough (16)	16	9	5	2	27	18	**2.0**	**32**
16	Farnborough (20)	15	9	3	3	29	16	**2.0**	**30**
17	Gravesend (11)	22	12	6	4	46	28	**1.9**	**42**
18	Halifax (19)	20	11	4	5	30	25	**1.9**	**37**
19	Margate (16)	20	11	4	5	35	21	**1.9**	**37**
20	Northwich (22)	9	4	4	1	11	8	**1.8**	**16**
21	Forest Green (18)	16	7	6	3	30	19	**1.7**	**27**
22	Leigh RMI (21)	17	7	4	6	29	28	**1.5**	**25**

Sponsored by Stan James

BANK OF SCOTLAND SCOTTISH PREMIER LEAGUE

	Team	Pld	FS	FS%
1	Celtic (1)	38	28	**73.7**
2	Rangers (2)	38	25	**65.8**
3	Dundee (7)	38	21	**55.3**
4	Hibernian (8)	38	19	**50.0**
5	Hearts (3)	38	18	**47.4**
6	Dundee Utd (5)	38	18	**47.4**
7	Aberdeen (11)	38	17	**44.7**
8	Livingston (9)	38	16	**42.1**
9	Motherwell (7)	38	15	**39.5**
10	Dunfermline (4)	38	15	**39.5**
11	Partick (12)	38	14	**36.8**
12	Kilmarnock (10)	38	11	**28.9**

RARITY: An early Killie goal

RECORD WHEN FIRST TO SCORE

	Team	Pld	W	D	L	F	A	PGA	Pts
1	Celtic (1)	28	26	1	1	88	15	**2.8**	79
2	Rangers (2)	25	21	3	1	58	11	**2.6**	66
3	Hearts (3)	18	13	4	1	34	13	**2.4**	43
4	Motherwell (7)	15	10	5	0	24	7	**2.3**	35
5	Dundee Utd (5)	18	13	1	4	34	20	**2.2**	40
6	Kilmarnock (10)	11	7	3	1	23	11	**2.2**	24
7	Livingston (9)	16	10	3	3	32	17	**2.1**	33
8	Dunfermline (4)	15	10	2	3	25	15	**2.1**	32
9	Hibernian (8)	19	10	5	4	31	23	**1.8**	35
10	Dundee (7)	21	9	8	4	33	27	**1.7**	35
11	Aberdeen (11)	17	8	5	4	31	19	**1.7**	29
12	Partick (12)	14	5	3	6	24	22	**1.3**	18

HARD TO TAKE: Even when they scored first Rangers were second to Celtic

FINAL
MAN UTD	3-0	MILLWALL

SEMI-FINALS
SUNDERLAND	0-1	MILLWALL
ARSENAL	0-1	MAN UTD

QUARTER-FINAL REPLAY
TRANMERE	1-2	MILLWALL

QUARTER-FINALS
MILLWALL	0-0	TRANMERE
SUNDERLAND	1-0	SHEFF UTD
MAN UTD	2-1	FULHAM
PORTSMOUTH	1-5	ARSENAL

FIFTH ROUND REPLAYS
BIRMINGHAM	0-2	SUNDERLAND
WEST HAM	0-3	FULHAM
PORTSMOUTH	1-0	LIVERPOOL

FIFTH ROUND
ARSENAL	2-1	CHELSEA
LIVERPOOL	1-1	PORTSMOUTH
SHEFF UTD	1-0	COLCHESTER
FULHAM	0-0	WEST HAM
MAN UTD	4-2	MAN CITY
MILLWALL	1-0	BURNLEY
SUNDERLAND	1-1	BIRMINGHAM
TRANMERE	2-1	SWANSEA

FOURTH ROUND REPLAYS
FULHAM	2-1	EVERTON
TOTTENHAM	3-4	MAN CITY
COLCHESTER	3-1	COVENTRY

FOURTH ROUND
EVERTON	1-1	FULHAM
MAN CITY	1-1	TOTTENHAM
NORTHAMPTON	0-3	MAN UTD
NOTTM FOREST	0-3	SHEFF UTD
WOLVES	1-3	WEST HAM
ARSENAL	4-1	MIDDLESBRO
BIRMINGHAM	1-0	WIMBLEDON
BURNLEY	3-1	GILLINGHAM
COVENTRY	1-1	COLCHESTER
IPSWICH	1-2	SUNDERLAND
LIVERPOOL	2-1	NEWCASTLE
LUTON	0-1	TRANMERE
PORTSMOUTH	2-1	SCUNTHORPE
SCARBOROUGH	0-1	CHELSEA
SWANSEA	2-1	PRESTON
TELFORD	0-2	MILLWALL

THIRD ROUND REPLAYS
CHELSEA	4-0	WATFORD
LEICESTER	1-3	MAN CITY
SCARBOROUGH	1-0	SOUTHEND
BOLTON	1-2	TRANMERE
COLCHESTER	2-1	ACCRINGTON
READING	1-2	PRESTON
ROTHERHAM	1-2	NORTHAMPTON
SCUNTHORPE	2-0	BARNSLEY
STOKE	0-1	WIMBLEDON
WOLVES	2-0	KIDDERMINSTER

THIRD ROUND
ASTON VILLA	1-2	MAN UTD
FULHAM	2-1	CHELTENHAM
LEEDS	1-4	ARSENAL

YEOVIL	0-2	LIVERPOOL
ACCRINGTON	0-0	COLCHESTER
BARNSLEY	0-0	SCUNTHORPE
BIRMINGHAM	4-0	BLACKBURN
BRADFORD	1-2	LUTON
CARDIFF	0-1	SHEFF UTD
COVENTRY	2-1	PETERBOROUGH
CREWE	0-1	TELFORD
EVERTON	3-1	NORWICH
GILLINGHAM	3-2	CHARLTON
IPSWICH	3-0	DERBY
KIDDERMINSTER	1-1	WOLVES
MAN CITY	2-2	LEICESTER
MANSFIELD	0-2	BURNLEY
MIDDLESBRO	2-0	NOTTS CO
MILLWALL	2-1	WALSALL
NORTHAMPTON	1-1	ROTHERHAM
NOTTM FOREST	1-0	WEST BROM
PORTSMOUTH	2-1	BLACKPOOL
PRESTON	3-3	READING
SOUTHAMPTON	0-3	NEWCASTLE
SOUTHEND	1-1	SCARBOROUGH
SUNDERLAND	1-0	HARTLEPOOL
SWANSEA	2-1	MACCLESFIELD
TOTTENHAM	3-0	C PALACE
TRANMERE	1-1	BOLTON
WATFORD	2-2	CHELSEA
WIGAN	1-2	WEST HAM
WIMBLEDON	1-1	STOKE

SECOND ROUND REPLAYS
SHEFF WED	0-0	SCUNTHORPE

(0-0 aet Scunthorpe won 3-1 on pens)

BARNSLEY	2-1	BRISTOL C
CAMBRIDGE	2-2	MACCLESFIELD
MANSFIELD	3-2	WYCOMBE
ACCRINGTON	0-0	BOURNEMOUTH

(0-0 aet Accrington won 5-3 on pens)

SECOND ROUND
BURTON	0-1	HARTLEPOOL
PORT VALE	0-1	SCARBOROUGH
BOURNEMOUTH	1-1	ACCRINGTON
BRISTOL C	0-0	BARNSLEY
CHELTENHAM	3-1	LEYTON ORIENT
COLCHESTER	1-0	ALDERSHOT
GRAVESEND	1-2	NOTTS CO
HORNCHURCH	0-1	TRANMERE
MACCLESFIELD	1-1	CAMBRIDGE
NORTHAMPTON	4-1	WESTON S-M
OLDHAM	2-5	BLACKPOOL
PETERBOROUGH	3-2	GRIMSBY
ROCHDALE	0-2	LUTON
SCUNTHORPE	2-2	SHEFF WED
SOUTHEND	3-0	LINCOLN
SWANSEA	2-1	STEVENAGE
TELFORD	3-0	BRENTFORD
WOKING	0-3	KIDDERMINSTER
YEOVIL	5-1	BARNET
WYCOMBE	1-1	MANSFIELD

FIRST ROUND REPLAYS
CANVEY ISL	2-3	SOUTHEND
FORD UTD	1-2	PORT VALE
LUTON	3-1	THURROCK
STALYBRIDGE	0-2	BARNET

FIRST ROUND

ACCRINGTON	1-0	HUDDERSFIELD
BRADFORD PA	2-5	BRISTOL C
HORNCHURCH	2-0	DARLINGTON
NOTTS CO	7-2	SHILDON
SHEFF WED	4-0	SALISBURY
SOUTHEND	1-1	CANVEY ISL
YORK	1-2	BARNSLEY
BARNET	2-2	STALYBRIDGE
BLACKPOOL	4-0	BOREHAM W
BOURNEMOUTH	1-0	BRISTOL R
BRENTFORD	7-1	GAINSBOROUGH
BURY	1-2	ROCHDALE
CHELTENHAM	3-1	HULL CITY
CHESTER	0-1	GRAVESEND
COLCHESTER	1-0	OXFORD
FARNBOROUGH	0-1	WESTON S-M
GRANTHAM	1-2	LEYTON ORIENT
GRAYS	1-2	ALDERSHOT
GRIMSBY	1-0	QPR
HARTLEPOOL	4-0	WHITBY
KIDDERMINSTER	2-1	NORTHWICH
LANCASTER	1-2	CAMBRIDGE
LINCOLN	3-1	BRIGHTON
MACCLESFIELD	3-0	BOSTON UTD
MANSFIELD	6-0	BISHOP'S ST
NORTHAMPTON	3-2	PLYMOUTH
OLDHAM	3-0	CARLISLE
PETERBOROUGH	2-0	HEREFORD
PORT VALE	2-2	FORD UTD
SCARBOROUGH	1-0	DONCASTER
SCUNTHORPE	2-1	SHREWSBURY
STEVENAGE	2-1	STOCKPORT
SWANSEA	3-0	RUSHDEN
TELFORD	3-2	CRAWLEY
TORQUAY	1-2	BURTON
TRANMERE	3-2	CHESTERFIELD
WOKING	3-1	HISTON
WYCOMBE	4-1	SWINDON
YEOVIL	4-1	WREXHAM
THURROCK	1-1	LUTON

BOY WONDER: Cristiano Ronaldo with the Cup his goal helped secure

FOURTH QUALIFYING ROUND REPLAYS

WHITBY	2-1	BROMSGROVE
GRAVESEND	3-3	EXETER
(3-3 aet Gravesend won 6-5 on pens)		
MARGATE	1-1	GRAYS
(1-1 aet Grays won 3-1 on pens)		
STEVENAGE	1-0	EASTBOURNE
TAMWORTH	2-3	TELFORD
WOKING	2-0	EAST THURROCK

FOURTH QUALIFYING ROUND

ACCRINGTON	2-0	LEIGH RMI
ASHTON UTD	1-2	GRANTHAM
BISHOP'S ST	2-0	GLOUCESTER
BLYTH SPTNS	0-1	CHESTER
BOREHAM W	1-0	KETTERING
BRACKNELL T	0-3	BARNET
BROMSGROVE	2-2	WHITBY
BURTON	6-0	BUXTON
CAMBRIDGE C	2-3	FORD UTD
CIRENCESTER	2-4	CRAWLEY
DUNSTON FED	0-1	LANCASTER
EAST THURROCK	1-1	WOKING
EASTBOURNE	2-2	STEVENAGE
EXETER	0-0	GRAVESEND
FARSLEY CELTIC	1-1	GAINSBOROUGH
FOREST GREEN	1-3	ALDERSHOT
GRAYS	3-3	MARGATE
HARROW BOR	1-6	HEREFORD
HORNCHURCH	1-0	PAULTON ROVERS
LEYTON	1-2	HISTON
MANGOTSFIELD	1-2	CANVEY ISL
MORECAMBE	2-4	SHREWSBURY
NORTHWICH	1-0	HALIFAX
OSSETT ALBION	0-1	STALYBRIDGE
RUNCORN	0-1	BRADFORD PA
SALISBURY	5-1	LYMINGTON
SCARBOROUGH	3-1	HINCKLEY UTD
SHILDON	6-0	STOCKSBRIDGE
TELFORD	3-3	TAMWORTH
THAME UTD	1-2	FARNBOROUGH
THURROCK	2-1	DAG & RED
WELLING	2-3	WESTON S-M

FINAL

BOLTON	1-2	MIDDLESBRO

SEMI-FINAL SECOND-LEGS

MIDDLESBRO	2-1	ARSENAL
ASTON VILLA	2-0	BOLTON

SEMI-FINAL FIRST-LEGS

BOLTON	5-2	ASTON VILLA
ARSENAL	0-1	MIDDLESBRO

QUARTER-FINALS

ASTON VILLA	2-1	CHELSEA
TOTTENHAM	1-1	MIDDLESBRO

(1-1 aet Middlesbro won 5-4 on pens)

BOLTON	1-0	SOUTHAMPTON
WEST BROM	0-2	ARSENAL

FOURTH ROUND

ASTON VILLA	3-0	C PALACE
LIVERPOOL	2-3	BOLTON
MIDDLESBRO	0-0	EVERTON

(0-0 aet Middlesbro won 5-4 on pens)

READING	0-1	CHELSEA
TOTTENHAM	3-1	MAN CITY
WEST BROM	2-0	MAN UTD
ARSENAL	5-1	WOLVES
SOUTHAMPTON	2-0	PORTSMOUTH

THIRD ROUND

ASTON VILLA	1-0	LEICESTER
BLACKBURN	3-4	LIVERPOOL
CHELSEA	4-2	NOTTS CO
EVERTON	1-0	CHARLTON
NEWCASTLE	1-2	WEST BROM
NOTTM FOREST	2-4	PORTSMOUTH
TOTTENHAM	1-0	WEST HAM
WIGAN	1-2	MIDDLESBRO
ARSENAL	1-1	ROTHERHAM

(1-1 aet Arsenal win 9-8 on penalties)

BLACKPOOL	1-3	C PALACE
BOLTON	2-0	GILLINGHAM
BRISTOL C	0-3	SOUTHAMPTON
LEEDS	2-3	MAN UTD
QPR	0-3	MAN CITY
READING	1-0	HUDDERSFIELD
WOLVES	2-0	BURNLEY

SECOND ROUND

BOLTON	3-1	WALSALL
COVENTRY	0-3	TOTTENHAM
EVERTON	3-0	STOCKPORT
LEEDS	2-2	SWINDON

(2-2 aet Leeds won 4-3 on pens)

MIDDLESBRO	1-0	BRIGHTON
OXFORD	1-3	READING
BLACKPOOL	1-0	BIRMINGHAM
BRISTOL C	1-0	WATFORD
C PALACE	2-1	DONCASTER
CARDIFF	2-3	WEST HAM
CHARLTON	4-4	LUTON

(4-4 aet Charlton won 8 - 7 on pens)

HARTLEPOOL	1-2	WEST BROM
LEICESTER	1-0	CREWE
NOTTS CO	2-1	IPSWICH
PORTSMOUTH	5-2	NORTHAMPTON
ROTHERHAM	1-0	COLCHESTER
SCUNTHORPE	2-3	BURNLEY
SHEFF UTD	0-2	QPR
STOKE	0-2	GILLINGHAM
SUNDERLAND	2-4	HUDDERSFIELD
TRANMERE	0-0	NOTTM FOREST

(0-0 aet Nottm Forest won 4-1 on pens)

WIGAN	1-0	FULHAM
WOLVES	2-0	DARLINGTON
WYCOMBE	0-5	ASTON VILLA

FIRST ROUND

STOKE	2-1	ROCHDALE
BOSTON UTD	1-3	READING
BRISTOL C	4-1	SWANSEA
COVENTRY	2-0	PETERBOROUGH
IPSWICH	1-0	KIDDERMINSTER
MANSFIELD	1-2	SUNDERLAND
SHEFF WED	2-2	HARTLEPOOL
WEST HAM	3-1	RUSHDEN
BARNSLEY	1-2	BLACKPOOL
BRADFORD	0-0	DARLINGTON

(0-0 aet Darlington won 5-3 on pens)

BRISTOL R	0-1	BRIGHTON
CAMBRIDGE	1-2	GILLINGHAM
CARDIFF	4-1	LEYTON ORIENT
CHELTENHAM	1-2	QPR
CHESTERFIELD	0-0	BURNLEY

(0-0 aet Burnley won 3-2 on pens)

COLCHESTER	2-1	PLYMOUTH
CREWE	2-0	WREXHAM
DONCASTER	3-2	GRIMSBY
HUDDERSFIELD	2-1	DERBY
LINCOLN	0-1	STOCKPORT
LUTON	4-1	YEOVIL
MACCLESFIELD	1-2	SHEFF UTD
MILLWALL	0-1	OXFORD
NORTHAMPTON	1-0	NORWICH
PORT VALE	0-0	NOTTM FOREST

(0-0 aet Nottm Forest won 3-2 on pens)

PRESTON	0-0	NOTTS C

(0-0 aet Notts C won 7-6 on pens)

ROTHERHAM	2-1	YORK
SCUNTHORPE	2-1	OLDHAM
SOUTHEND	2-3	SWINDON
TORQUAY	1-1	C PALACE

(1-1 aet C Palace won 3-1 on pens)

TRANMERE	1-0	BURY
WALSALL	2-1	CARLISLE
WATFORD	1-0	BOURNEMOUTH
WEST BROM	4-0	BRENTFORD
WIGAN	2-0	HULL CITY
WYCOMBE	2-0	WIMBLEDON

FINAL

BLACKPOOL	2-0	SOUTHEND

NORTHERN SECTION FINAL

SHEFF WED	0-2	BLACKPOOL
BLACKPOOL	1-0	SHEFF WED

SOUTHERN SECTION FINAL

SOUTHEND	1-1	COLCHESTER
COLCHESTER	2-3	SOUTHEND

NORTHERN SEMI-FINALS

BLACKPOOL	3-2	HALIFAX
SHEFF WED	4-0	SCUNTHORPE

SOUTHERN SEMI-FINALS

NORTHAMPTON	2-3	COLCHESTER
SOUTHEND	4-0	QPR

NORTHERN QUARTER-FINALS

HALIFAX	1-0	LINCOLN
BURY	0-1	SCUNTHORPE
CARLISLE	0-3	SHEFF WED
STOCKPORT	0-1	BLACKPOOL

SOUTHERN QUARTER-FINALS

NORTHAMPTON	2-1	PETERBOROUGH
SOUTHEND	3-0	LUTON
WYCOMBE	2-3	COLCHESTER
QPR	2-1	BRIGHTON

NORTHERN SECOND ROUND

SHEFF WED	1-0	BARNSLEY
BLACKPOOL	1-0	DONCASTER
CARLISLE	2-0	HUDDERSFIELD
HULL CITY	1-3	SCUNTHORPE
LINCOLN	4-3	CHESTERFIELD
SCARBOROUGH	0-1	HALIFAX
BURY	2-1	OLDHAM

SOUTHERN SECOND ROUND

BRIGHTON	3-1	BOSTON UTD
HEREFORD	1-1	NORTHAMPTON

(1-1 aet Northampton won 4-3 on penalties)

PETERBOROUGH	3-2	BRENTFORD
PLYMOUTH	2-2	WYCOMBE

(2-2 aet Wycombe won 4-2 on pens)

QPR	2-1	DAG & RED
RUSHDEN	1-2	LUTON
SWANSEA	1-2	SOUTHEND
YEOVIL	2-2	COLCHESTER

(2-2 aet Colchester won 4-2 on pens)

NORTHERN FIRST ROUND

NOTTS CO	0-0	BARNSLEY

(0-0 aet Barnsley won 4-2 on pens)

SHEFF WED	1-1	GRIMSBY

(1-1 aet Sheff Wed won 5-4 on pens)

BLACKPOOL	3-2	TRANMERE
CARLISLE	2-0	ROCHDALE
CHESTER	0-1	DONCASTER
CHESTERFIELD	2-1	MACCLESFIELD
DARLINGTON	1-3	HULL CITY
HALIFAX	2-1	YORK
LINCOLN	3-1	TELFORD
MANSFIELD	1-2	STOCKPORT
OLDHAM	3-3	HARTLEPOOL

(3-3 aet Oldham won 5-3 on pens)

SCARBOROUGH	2-1	PORT VALE
SCUNTHORPE	2-1	SHREWSBURY
WREXHAM	4-1	MORECAMBE

SOUTHERN FIRST ROUND

HEREFORD	2-0	EXETER
BOSTON UTD	2-1	SWINDON
DAG & RED	4-1	LEYTON ORIENT
OXFORD	0-1	RUSHDEN
BARNET	3-3	BRENTFORD

(3-3 aet Brentford won 3-1 on pens)

CHELTENHAM	1-3	COLCHESTER
PETERBOROUGH	3-2	TORQUAY
PLYMOUTH	4-0	BRISTOL C
QPR	2-0	KIDDERMINSTER
SOUTHEND	2-1	BRISTOL R
STEVENAGE	0-1	LUTON
WYCOMBE	1-0	CAMBRIDGE
YEOVIL	2-0	BOURNEMOUTH
BRIGHTON	2-0	FOREST GREEN

TANGERINE DREAM: Blackpool enjoy LDV Trophy glory in the Millennium Stadium

FA TROPHY 2003-2004

FINAL
HEDNESFORD	3-2	CANVEY ISL

SEMI-FINAL SECOND-LEGS
CANVEY ISL	2-2	TELFORD

(Aggregate score 2 - 2 Canvey Isl won 4 - 2 on pens)

HEDNESFORD	1-1	ALDERSHOT

SEMI-FINAL FIRST-LEGS
ALDERSHOT	0-2	HEDNESFORD
TELFORD	0-0	CANVEY ISL

QUARTER-FINAL REPLAY
TELFORD	2-1	SHREWSBURY

QUARTER-FINALS
HEDNESFORD	3-1	HORNCHURCH
ALDERSHOT	2-1	EXETER
CANVEY ISL	4-0	MAIDENHEAD
SHREWSBURY	1-1	TELFORD

FIFTH ROUND REPLAYS
CANVEY ISL	4-0	STALYBRIDGE
TAMWORTH	0-2	ALDERSHOT

FIFTH ROUND
ALDERSHOT	1-1	TAMWORTH
ALTRINCHAM	0-1	SHREWSBURY
EXETER	3-0	ARLESEY TOWN
HALIFAX	0-2	MAIDENHEAD
HEDNESFORD	1-0	DOVER
HORNCHURCH	2-1	BURTON
STALYBRIDGE	0-0	CANVEY ISL
TELFORD	3-0	MARGATE

FOURTH ROUND REPLAYS
ARLESEY TOWN	4-2	DAG & RED
DOVER	2-1	FOREST GREEN
KETTERING	1-2	BURTON
MARINE	0-1	STALYBRIDGE
STAINES TOWN	2-3	HALIFAX
WORTHING	1-2	HEDNESFORD

FOURTH ROUND
BLYTH SPTNS	1-3	ALDERSHO
BURTON	1-1	KETTERING
DAG & RED	3-3	ARLESEY TOWN
FOREST GREEN	3-3	DOVER
HALIFAX	1-1	STAINES TOWN
HEDNESFORD	1-1	WORTHING
HORNCHURCH	1-0	STEVENAGE
KING'S LYNN	0-3	EXETER
MAIDENHEAD	5-1	WEALDSTONE
MARGATE	2-0	WORKSOP
MARLOW	0-4	TAMWORTH
SHREWSBURY	2-1	HUCKNALL
STAFFORD RAN	0-2	CANVEY ISL
STALYBRIDGE	1-1	MARINE
TELFORD	4-2	WESTON S-M
WEYMOUTH	0-2	ALTRINCHAM

THIRD ROUND REPLAYS
MARGATE	2-0	DORCHESTER
WESTON S-M	1-0	GRAVESEND
ARLESEY TOWN	1-1	HAYES

(Aggregate score 1 - 1 Arlesley won 4 - 3 on pens)

CRAWLEY	1-2	DAG & RED
WOKING	2-3	KETTERING

GLORY BOYS: Hednesford Town

THIRD ROUND
TELFORD	2-0	ALFRETON
ALTRINCHAM	2-1	RUNCORN
BARNET	3-2	DOVER
BISHOP'S ST	2-4	ALDERSHOT
BLYTH SPTNS	1-0	BARROW
BURSCOUGH	0-1	TAMWORTH
BURTON	4-2	ACCRINGTON
CANVEY ISL	6-0	FARNBOROUGH
CHESTER	1-2	HALIFAX
DAG & RED	0-0	CRAWLEY
DORCHESTER	2-2	MARGATE
EXETER	3-2	HEREFORD
FOLKESTONE INV	1-3	STEVENAGE
FOREST GREEN	4-0	SUTTON UTD
GRAVESEND	2-2	WESTON S-M
GUISELEY	0-2	WORKSOP
HAYES	2-2	ARLESEY TOWN
HEDNESFORD	2-0	GRESLEY R
HISTON	1-3	MAIDENHEAD
HORNCHURCH	2-0	AYLESBURY
HUCKNALL	1-0	BRADFORD PA
KETTERING	0-0	WOKING
KING'S LYNN	3-1	BASINGSTOKE
LEIGH RMI	1-1	STALYBRIDGE
LEWES	5-8	WEYMOUTH
MARINE	1-0	NORTHWICH
MARLOW	3-1	FORD UTD
SCARBOROUGH	1-2	STAFFORD RAN
SHREWSBURY	2-0	MORECAMBE
STAINES TOWN	1-0	BATH CITY
WORTHING	3-0	TAUNTON TOWN
WEALDSTONE	3-2	THURROCK

Sponsored by Stan James

SUPER SOCCER

P.O. BOX 150, 133 SHERLOCK ST., BIRMINGHAM
B5 6LS

FOR ALL YOUR UK & EUROPEAN FOOTBALL BETTING

★ ★ ★ ★ ★

Tel: 0121-666 4511

OR

betsupersoccer.co.uk

★ ★ ★ ★ ★

SWITCH/DELTA/SOLO WELCOME

FINAL
DUNFERMLINE	1-3	CELTIC

SEMI-FINAL REPLAY
DUNFERMLINE	3-2	INVERNESS CT

SEMI-FINALS
LIVINGSTON	1-3	CELTIC
INVERNESS CT	1-1	DUNFERMLINE

QUARTER-FINAL REPLAY
LIVINGSTON	1-0	ABERDEEN

QUARTER-FINALS
CELTIC	1-0	RANGERS
ABERDEEN	1-1	LIVINGSTON
MOTHERWELL	0-1	INVERNESS CT
PARTICK	0-3	DUNFERMLINE

FOURTH ROUND
CLYDE	0-3	DUNFERMLINE
KILMARNOCK	0-2	RANGERS
SPARTANS	0-4	LIVINGSTON
FALKIRK	0-2	ABERDEEN
HEARTS	0-3	CELTIC
MOTHERWELL	3-2	QUEEN OF STH
PARTICK	5-1	HAMILTON
ST MIRREN	0-1	INVERNESS CT

THIRD ROUND REPLAY
DUNDEE	2-3	ABERDEEN

THIRD ROUND
ABERDEEN	0-0	DUNDEE
ARBROATH	1-4	SPARTANS
AYR	1-2	FALKIRK
CELTIC	2-0	ROSS COUNTY
CLYDE	3-0	GRETNA
DUNFERMLINE	3-1	DUNDEE UTD
EAST FIFE	0-1	QUEEN OF STH
HAMILTON	2-0	COWDENBEATH

HEARTS	2-0	BERWICK
HIBERNIAN	0-2	RANGERS
INVERNESS CT	5-1	BRECHIN
LIVINGSTON	1-0	MONTROSE
MORTON	0-3	PARTICK
RAITH	1-3	KILMARNOCK
ST JOHNSTONE	0-3	MOTHERWELL
ST MIRREN	2-0	AIRDRIE UTD

SECOND ROUND REPLAY
SPARTANS	5-3	ALLOA

SECOND ROUND
MONTROSE	1-0	THREAVE R
MORTON	4-0	VALE OF LEITHEN
STRANRAER	0-1	HAMILTON
ALLOA	3-3	SPARTANS
BERWICK	4-2	HUNTLY
EAST STIRLING	0-5	COWDENBEATH
GRETNA	5-1	STENH'SEMUIR
INVERURIE LOC	1-5	AIRDRIE UTD
PETERHEAD	0-2	EAST FIFE
STIRLING	1-2	ARBROATH

FIRST ROUND REPLAYS
ALBION	1-3	MONTROSE
EAST FIFE	3-3	FORFAR

(Aggregate score 3 - 3 East Fife won 4 - 1 on pens)

FIRST ROUND
CLACHNACUDDIN	0-2	STRANRAER
COWDENBEATH	5-2	EDINBURGH C
ELGIN CITY	1-2	PETERHEAD
FORFAR	1-1	EAST FIFE
GRETNA	4-0	DUMBARTON
MONTROSE	1-1	ALBION
SPARTANS	6-1	BUCKIE THISTLE
STIRLING	3-1	QUEEN'S PARK

LAST HURRAH: Henrik Larsson lifts the Scottish Cup in his final game for Celtic

Sponsored by Stan James

CIS CUP FINAL

HIBERNIAN	0-2	LIVINGSTON

SEMI-FINALS

HIBERNIAN	1-1	RANGERS

(1-1 aet Hibernian won 4-3 on pens)

DUNDEE	0-1	LIVINGSTON

QUARTER-FINALS

HIBERNIAN	2-1	CELTIC
DUNDEE	1-0	HEARTS
RANGERS	3-0	ST JOHNSTONE
ABERDEEN	2-3	LIVINGSTON

THIRD ROUND

PARTICK	0-2	CELTIC
CLYDE	2-5	DUNDEE
DUNDEE UTD	0-1	LIVINGSTON
HEARTS	2-1	FALKIRK
ABERDEEN	5-0	BRECHIN
HIBERNIAN	2-1	QUEEN OF STH
RANGERS	6-0	FORFAR
ST JOHNSTONE	3-2	DUNFERMLINE

SECOND ROUND

DUNFERMLINE	2-0	COWDENBEATH
PETERHEAD	2-2	PARTICK

(2-2 aet Partick won 4-3 on pens)

ABERDEEN	3-1	DUMBARTON
ARBROATH	3-4	FALKIRK
BRECHIN	1-0	KILMARNOCK
CLYDE	2-1	AIRDRIE UTD
DUNDEE UTD	3-1	MORTON
FORFAR	3-3	MOTHERWELL

(3-3 aet Forfar win 4 -2 on penalties)

HIBERNIAN	9-0	MONTROSE
QUEEN'S PARK	1-3	LIVINGSTON
ROSS COUNTY	0-3	QUEEN OF STH
ST JOHNSTONE	3-2	HAMILTON

FIRST ROUND

MORTON	2-0	STRANRAER
ARBROATH	1-0	RAITH
AYR	1-2	DUMBARTON
COWDENBEATH	3-0	ALLOA
EAST FIFE	0-2	AIRDRIE UTD
EAST STIRLING	1-2	ROSS COUNTY
ELGIN CITY	0-4	BRECHIN
FORFAR	1-0	BERWICK
GRETNA	1-2	PETERHEAD
HAMILTON	3-2	ALBION
INVERNESS CT	1-2	QUEEN'S PARK
MONTROSE	2-0	STIRLING
ST MIRREN	0-2	ST JOHNSTONE
STENH'SEMUIR	1-2	QUEEN OF STH

LIONS: Livingston's first major trophy

BELL'S CHALLENGE CUP FINAL

INVERNESS CT	2-0	AIRDRIE UTD

SEMI-FINALS

BRECHIN	1-2	AIRDRIE UTD
RAITH	0-4	INVERNESS CT

QUARTER-FINALS

FORFAR	0-2	AIRDRIE UTD
INVERNESS CT	1-0	ROSS COUNTY
RAITH	3-2	ST MIRREN
ST JOHNSTONE	1-2	BRECHIN

SECOND ROUND

BRECHIN	3-1	STIRLING
CLYDE	0-1	ST JOHNSTONE
FORFAR	4-2	ALBION
MORTON	1-2	AIRDRIE UTD
PETERHEAD	1-2	INVERNESS CT
RAITH	2-0	STRANRAER
ROSS COUNTY	5-0	DUMBARTON
ST MIRREN	2-1	BERWICK

FIRST ROUND

AIRDRIE UTD	2-0	MONTROSE
ALBION	1-0	EAST FIFE
ALLOA	1-2	CLYDE
AYR	1-2	STIRLING
BRECHIN	1-0	FALKIRK
COWDENBEATH	1-2	ROSS COUNTY
EAST STIRLING	2-5	RAITH
FORFAR	4-0	ELGIN CITY
GRETNA	0-5	INVERNESS CT
HAMILTON	2-3	ST JOHNSTONE
MORTON	4-3	ARBROATH
ST MIRREN	3-2	QUEEN'S PARK
STENH'SEMUIR	0-3	PETERHEAD
STRANRAER	2-1	QUEEN OF STH

FINAL

PORTO	3-0	MONACO

SEMI-FINAL SECOND-LEGS

CHELSEA	2-2	MONACO
DEPORTIVO	0-1	PORTO

SEMI-FINAL FIRST-LEGS

PORTO	0-0	DEPORTIVO
MONACO	3-1	CHELSEA

QUARTER-FINAL SECOND-LEGS

DEPORTIVO	4-0	AC MILAN
LYON	2-2	PORTO
ARSENAL	1-2	CHELSEA
MONACO	3-1	REAL MADRID

QUARTER-FINAL FIRST-LEGS

CHELSEA	1-1	ARSENAL
REAL MADRID	4-2	MONACO
AC MILAN	4-1	DEPORTIVO
PORTO	2-0	LYON

LAST 16 SECOND-LEGS

ARSENAL	2-0	CELTA VIGO
AC MILAN	4-1	SPARTA PRAGUE
MONACO	1-0	L MOSCOW
REAL MADRID	1-0	B MUNICH
CHELSEA	0-0	STUTTGART
JUVENTUS	0-1	DEPORTIVO
LYON	1-0	R SOCIEDAD
MAN UTD	1-1	PORTO

LAST 16 FIRST-LEGS

DEPORTIVO	1-0	JUVENTUS
PORTO	2-1	MAN UTD
R SOCIEDAD	0-1	LYON
STUTTGART	0-1	CHELSEA
B MUNICH	1-1	REAL MADRID
CELTA VIGO	2-3	ARSENAL
L MOSCOW	2-1	MONACO
SPARTA PRAGUE	0-0	AC MILAN

GROUP A

B MUNICH	1-0	ANDERLECHT
LYON	3-2	CELTIC
ANDERLECHT	1-0	LYON
CELTIC	0-0	B MUNICH
B MUNICH	1-2	LYON
CELTIC	3-1	ANDERLECHT
ANDERLECHT	1-0	CELTIC
LYON	1-1	B MUNICH
ANDERLECHT	1-1	B MUNICH
CELTIC	2-0	LYON
B MUNICH	2-1	CELTIC
LYON	1-0	ANDERLECHT

GROUP B

ARSENAL	2-0	L MOSCOW
DYNAMO KIEV	1-1	INTER MILAN
INTER MILAN	1-5	ARSENAL
L MOSCOW	3-2	DYNAMO KIEV
ARSENAL	1-0	DYNAMO KIEV
INTER MILAN	1-1	L MOSCOW
DYNAMO KIEV	2-1	ARSENAL
L MOSCOW	3-0	INTER MILAN
INTER MILAN	2-1	DYNAMO KIEV
L MOSCOW	0-0	ARSENAL
ARSENAL	0-3	INTER MILAN
DYNAMO KIEV	2-0	L MOSCOW

GROUP C

AEK ATHENS	0-0	MONACO
PSV EINDHOVEN	3-2	DEPORTIVO
DEPORTIVO	3-0	AEK ATHENS
MONACO	1-1	PSV EINDHOVEN
MONACO	8-3	DEPORTIVO
PSV EINDHOVEN	2-0	AEK ATHENS
AEK ATHENS	0-1	PSV EINDHOVEN
DEPORTIVO	1-0	MONACO
DEPORTIVO	2-0	PSV EINDHOVEN
MONACO	4-0	AEK ATHENS
AEK ATHENS	1-1	DEPORTIVO
PSV EINDHOVEN	1-2	MONACO

GROUP D

JUVENTUS	7-0	OLYMPIAKOS
R SOCIEDAD	1-1	GALATASARAY
GALATASARAY	2-0	JUVENTUS
OLYMPIAKOS	2-2	R SOCIEDAD
OLYMPIAKOS	3-0	GALATASARAY
R SOCIEDAD	0-0	JUVENTUS
GALATASARAY	1-0	OLYMPIAKOS
JUVENTUS	4-2	R SOCIEDAD
GALATASARAY	1-2	R SOCIEDAD
OLYMPIAKOS	1-2	JUVENTUS
JUVENTUS	2-1	GALATASARAY
R SOCIEDAD	1-0	OLYMPIAKOS

GROUP E

MAN UTD	2-0	STUTTGART
RANGERS	1-3	PANATHINAIKOS
PANATHINAIKOS	0-1	MAN UTD
STUTTGART	1-0	RANGERS
MAN UTD	3-0	RANGERS
PANATHINAIKOS	1-3	STUTTGART
RANGERS	0-1	MAN UTD
STUTTGART	2-0	PANATHINAIKOS
PANATHINAIKOS	1-1	RANGERS
STUTTGART	2-1	MAN UTD
MAN UTD	5-0	PANATHINAIKOS
RANGERS	2-1	STUTTGART

GROUP F

P BELGRADE	1-1	MARSEILLE
REAL MADRID	1-1	PORTO
MARSEILLE	1-2	REAL MADRID
PORTO	2-1	P BELGRADE
P BELGRADE	0-0	REAL MADRID
PORTO	1-0	MARSEILLE
MARSEILLE	2-3	PORTO
REAL MADRID	1-0	P BELGRADE
MARSEILLE	3-0	P BELGRADE

PORTO	1-3	REAL MADRID
P BELGRADE	1-1	PORTO
REAL MADRID	4-2	MARSEILLE

GROUP G

BESIKTAS	0-2	CHELSEA
S PRAGUE	1-0	LAZIO
CHELSEA	0-0	S PRAGUE
LAZIO	1-1	BESIKTAS
BESIKTAS	1-0	S PRAGUE
LAZIO	0-4	CHELSEA
CHELSEA	2-1	LAZIO
S PRAGUE	2-1	BESIKTAS
CHELSEA	0-2	BESIKTAS
LAZIO	2-2	S PRAGUE
BESIKTAS	0-2	LAZIO
S PRAGUE	0-1	CHELSEA

GROUP H

FC BRUGES	2-1	AJAX
AC MILAN	1-2	CELTA VIGO
AJAX	0-1	AC MILAN
CELTA VIGO	1-1	FC BRUGES
CELTA VIGO	3-2	AJAX
FC BRUGES	0-1	AC MILAN
AJAX	1-0	CELTA VIGO
AC MILAN	0-1	FC BRUGES
AJAX	2-0	FC BRUGES
CELTA VIGO	0-0	AC MILAN
FC BRUGES	1-1	CELTA VIGO
AC MILAN	1-0	AJAX

THIRD ROUND QUALIFYING

AEK ATHENS	3-1	GRASSHOPPERS
AJAX	2-1	GRAZ AK
B DORTMUND	2-1	FC BRUGES
BENFICA	0-1	LAZIO
CSKA SOFIA	0-3	GALATASARAY
CELTIC	1-0	MTK HUNGARIA
DYNAMO ZAGREB	0-2	DYNAMO KIEV
FC COPENHAGEN	1-2	RANGERS
L MOSCOW	3-1	S DONETSK
MARSEILLE	0-0	AUSTRIA VIENNA
NEWCASTLE	0-1	P BELGRADE
SLAVIA PRAGUE	2-0	CELTA VIGO
CHELSEA	3-0	ZILINA
DEPORTIVO	1-0	ROSENBORG
S PRAGUE	2-2	VARDAR SKOPJE
WISLA KRAKOW	0-1	ANDERLECHT
ANDERLECHT	3-1	WISLA KRAKOW
AUSTRIA VIENNA	0-1	MARSEILLE
FC BRUGES	2-1	B DORTMUND
GALATASARAY	3-0	CSKA SOFIA
GRASSHOPPERS	1-0	AEK ATHENS
LAZIO	3-1	BENFICA
MTK HUNGARIA	0-4	CELTIC
P BELGRADE	0-1	NEWCASTLE
RANGERS	1-1	FC COPENHAGEN
ROSENBORG	0-0	DEPORTIVO
S DONETSK	1-0	L MOSCOW
VARDAR SKOPJE	2-3	S PRAGUE
ZILINA	0-2	CHELSEA
CELTA VIGO	3-0	SLAVIA PRAGUE
DYNAMO KIEV	3-1	DYNAMO ZAGREB
GRAZ AK	1-1	AJAX

SECOND ROUND QUALIFYING

ANDERLECHT	3-2	R BUCHAREST
CSKA SOFIA	1-0	PYUNIK YEREVAN
CELTIC	1-0	FBK KAUNAS
DJURGAARDENS	2-2	P BELGRADE
DYNAMO ZAGREB	2-1	NK MARIBOR
GRAZ AK	2-1	SK TIRANA
HJK HELSINKI	1-0	MTK HUNGARIA
MACC TEL AVIV	1-1	ZILINA
OMONIA NICOSIA	2-2	WISLA KRAKOW
ROSENBORG	4-0	B DUBLIN
S DONETSK	2-0	SERIF TIRASPOL
SLAVIA PRAGUE	2-0	LEOTAR
SLIEMA W	0-6	FC COPENHAGEN
VARDAR SKOPJE	1-1	CSKA MOSCOW
B DUBLIN	0-1	ROSENBORG
CSKA MOSCOW	1-2	VARDAR SKOPJE
FBK KAUNAS	0-4	CELTIC
FC COPENHAGEN	4-1	SLIEMA W
LEOTAR	1-2	SLAVIA PRAGUE
MTK HUNGARIA	3-1	HJK HELSINKI
NK MARIBOR	1-1	DYNAMO ZAGREB
P BELGRADE	1-1	DJURGAARDENS
PYUNIK YEREVAN	0-2	CSKA SOFIA
R BUCHAREST	0-0	ANDERLECHT
SK TIRANA	1-5	GRAZ AK
SERIF TIRASPOL	0-0	S DONETSK
WISLA KRAKOW	5-2	OMONIA NICOSIA
ZILINA	1-0	MACC TEL AVIV

FIRST ROUND QUALIFYING

BARRY TOWN	2-1	VARDAR SKOPJE
B DUBLIN	3-0	BATE BORISOV
DINAMO TIRANA	3-0	DYNAMO TBILISI
FBK KAUNAS	4-1	HB TORSHAVN
FLORA TALLINN	1-1	SERIF TIRASPOL
HJK HELSINKI	1-0	GLENTORAN
IRTYSH	1-2	OMONIA NICOSIA
KR REYKJAVIK	1-1	PYUNIK YEREVAN
LEOTAR	2-0	GREVENMACHER
SKONTO RIGA	3-1	SLIEMA W
BATE BORISOV	1-0	B DUBLIN
DYNAMO TBILISI	3-0	DINAMO TIRANA
GLENTORAN	0-0	HJK HELSINKI
GREVENMACHER	0-0	LEOTAR
HB TORSHAVN	0-1	FBK KAUNAS
OMONIA NICOSIA	0-0	IRTYSH
PYUNIK YEREVAN	1-0	KR REYKJAVIK
SERIF TIRASPOL	1-0	FLORA TALLINN
SLIEMA W	2-0	SKONTO RIGA
VARDAR SKOPJE	3-0	BARRY TOWN

FINAL

VALENCIA	2-0	MARSEILLE

SEMI-FINAL SECOND-LEGS

MARSEILLE	2-0	NEWCASTLE
VALENCIA	1-0	VILLARREAL

SEMI-FINAL FIRST-LEGS

NEWCASTLE	0-0	MARSEILLE
VILLARREAL	0-0	VALENCIA

QUARTER-FINAL SECOND-LEGS

INTER MILAN	0-1	MARSEILLE
NEWCASTLE	2-1	PSV EINDHOVEN
VALENCIA	2-1	BORDEAUX
VILLARREAL	2-0	CELTIC

QUARTER-FINAL FIRST-LEGS

BORDEAUX	1-2	VALENCIA
CELTIC	1-1	VILLARREAL
MARSEILLE	1-0	INTER MILAN
PSV EINDHOVEN	1-1	NEWCASTLE

FOURTH ROUND SECOND-LEGS

BARCELONA	0-0	CELTIC
FC BRUGES	0-1	BORDEAUX
INTER MILAN	4-3	BENFICA
MALLORCA	0-3	NEWCASTLE
MARSEILLE	2-1	LIVERPOOL
PSV EINDHOVEN	3-0	AUXERRE
ROMA	2-1	VILLARREAL
VALENCIA	2-0	GENCLERBIRLIGI

FOURTH ROUND FIRST-LEGS

AUXERRE	1-1	PSV EINDHOVEN
BENFICA	0-0	INTER MILAN
BORDEAUX	3-1	FC BRUGES
CELTIC	1-0	BARCELONA
GENCLERBIRLIGI	1-0	VALENCIA
LIVERPOOL	1-1	MARSEILLE
NEWCASTLE	4-1	MALLORCA
VILLARREAL	2-0	ROMA

THIRD ROUND SECOND-LEGS

BARCELONA	2-1	BRONDBY
BESIKTAS	0-2	VALENCIA
BORDEAUX	4-1	G DYSKOBOLIA
DEBRECENI VSC	0-0	FC BRUGES
DNIPRO	0-0	MARSEILLE
GENCLERBIRLIGI	3-0	PARMA
INTER MILAN	0-0	SOCHAUX
LEVSKI SOFIA	2-4	LIVERPOOL
MALLORCA	0-1	SP MOSCOW
NEWCASTLE	3-1	VALERENGA
PSV EINDHOVEN	3-1	PERUGIA
PANATHINAIKOS	0-1	AUXERRE
ROMA	2-0	GAZIANTEPSPOR
ROSENBORG	2-1	BENFICA
TEPLICE	1-0	CELTIC
VILLARREAL	3-0	GALATASARAY

THIRD ROUND FIRST-LEGS

AUXERRE	0-0	PANATHINAIKOS
BENFICA	1-0	ROSENBORG
BRONDBY	0-1	BARCELONA
CELTIC	3-0	TEPLICE
FC BRUGES	1-0	DEBRECENI VSC
GALATASARAY	2-2	VILLARREAL
GAZIANTEPSPOR	1-0	ROMA

G DYSKOBOLIA	0-1	BORDEAUX
LIVERPOOL	2-0	LEVSKI SOFIA
MARSEILLE	1-0	DNIPRO
PARMA	0-1	GENCLERBIRLIGI
PERUGIA	0-0	PSV EINDHOVEN
SOCHAUX	2-2	INTER MILAN
SP MOSCOW	0-3	MALLORCA
VALENCIA	3-2	BESIKTAS
VALERENGA	1-1	NEWCASTLE

SECOND ROUND SECOND-LEGS

MACCABI HAIFA	0-4	VALENCIA
ARIS SALONIKA	1-1	PERUGIA
AUXERRE	4-0	FC UTRECHT
BARCELONA	2-0	PANIONIOS
BRONDBY	2-1	SCHALKE
DEBRECENI VSC	0-0	PAOK SALONIKA
DIN BUCHAREST	3-1	SP MOSCOW
DNIPRO	1-1	DYNAMO ZAGREB
G DYSKOBOLIA	0-0	MAN CITY
HAJDUK SPLIT	1-1	ROMA
HEARTS	0-2	BORDEAUX
LENS	1-3	GAZIANTEPSPOR
LEVSKI SOFIA	0-0	SLAVIA PRAGUE
LIVERPOOL	1-0	S BUCHAREST
MALLORCA	1-1	FC COPENHAGEN
MOLDE	0-2	BENFICA
NEWCASTLE	1-0	FC BASLE
PARMA	5-0	SV SALZBURG
RED STAR BEL	0-1	ROSENBORG
SOCHAUX	4-0	B DORTMUND
SP LISBON	0-3	GENCLERBIRLIGI
TEPLICE	1-1	FEYENOORD
TOR MOSCOW	1-0	VILLARREAL
WISLA KRAKOW	0-0	VALERENGA

SECOND ROUND FIRST-LEGS

B DORTMUND	2-2	SOCHAUX
BENFICA	3-1	MOLDE
BORDEAUX	0-1	HEARTS
DYNAMO ZAGREB	0-2	DNIPRO
FC BASLE	2-3	NEWCASTLE
FC COPENHAGEN	1-2	MALLORCA
FC UTRECHT	0-0	AUXERRE
FEYENOORD	0-2	TEPLICE
GAZIANTEPSPOR	3-0	LENS
GENCLERBIRLIGI	1-1	SP LISBON
MAN CITY	1-1	G DYSKOBOLIA
PAOK SALONIKA	1-1	DEBRECENI VSC
PANIONIOS	0-3	BARCELONA
PERUGIA	2-0	ARIS SALONIKA
ROMA	1-0	HAJDUK SPLIT
SV SALZBURG	0-4	PARMA
SCHALKE	2-1	BRONDBY
SLAVIA PRAGUE	2-2	LEVSKI SOFIA
SP MOSCOW	4-0	DIN BUCHAREST
S BUCHAREST	1-1	LIVERPOOL
VALENCIA	0-0	MACCABI HAIFA
VALERENGA	0-0	WISLA KRAKOW
VILLARREAL	2-0	TOR MOSCOW
ROSENBORG	0-0	RED STAR BE

FIRST ROUND SECOND-LEGS

KARNTEN	0-1	FEYENOORD
SCHALKE	1-0	KAMEN

TEPLICE	1-0	KAISERSLAUTERN
VIKTORIA ZIZKOV	0-1	BRONDBY
ARIS SALONIKA	2-1	FC ZIMBRU
B DORTMUND	1-0	AUSTRIA VIENNA
BARCELONA	8-0	PUCHOV
BENFICA	1-0	LA LOUVIERE
BLACKBURN	1-1	GENCLERBIRLIGI
DEBRECENI VSC	3-2	VARTEKS
DNIPRO	3-0	SV HAMBURG
ESBJERG	1-1	SP MOSCOW
FC BASLE	1-2	MALATYASPOR
FC COPENHAGEN	1-1	FERENCVAROS
GRAZ AK	1-1	VALERENGA
G DYSKOBOLIA	1-0	HERTHA BERLIN
HAJDUK SPLIT	0-0	GRASSHOPPERS
HAPOEL TEL AVIV	0-0	GAZIANTEPSPOR
LENS	5-0	CEMENTARNICA
LEVSKI SOFIA	4-0	H RAMAT-GAN
LIVERPOOL	3-0	O LJUBLJANA
LOKEREN	0-1	MAN CITY
LYN OSLO	0-3	PAOK SALONIKA
MTK HUNGARIA	0-0	DYNAMO ZAGREB
MALLORCA	4-2	APOEL NICOSIA
MALMO	0-1	SP LISBON
MOLDE	3-1	UNIAO LEIRIA
NAC BREDA	0-1	NEWCASTLE
NEC NIJMEGEN	1-2	WISLA KRAKOW
NK PUBLIKUM	2-2	MACCABI HAIFA
N XAMAX	0-1	AUXERRE
NORDSJAELLAND	0-1	PANIONIOS
PARMA	3-0	METALURG D
PERUGIA	1-0	DUNDEE
PETRZALKA	1-1	BORDEAUX
RED STAR BEL	4-3	ODENSE
ROSENBORG	6-0	VENTSPILS
S DONETSK	2-3	DIN BUCHAREST
SLAVIA PRAGUE	2-1	SARTID
SOCHAUX	2-0	MYPA-47
S BUCHAREST	1-0	SOUTHAMPTON
TOR MOSCOW	1-1	CSKA SOFIA
TRABZONSPOR	2-3	VILLARREAL
UDINESE	1-2	SV SALZBURG
VALENCIA	1-0	AIK SOLNA
VARDAR SKOPJE	1-1	ROMA
ZELJEZNICAR	0-0	HEARTS
ZILINA	0-4	FC UTRECHT

FIRST ROUND FIRST-LEGS

BORDEAUX	2-1	PETRZALKA
FEYENOORD	2-1	KARNTEN
KAMEN	0-0	SCHALKE
SV HAMBURG	2-1	DNIPRO
WISLA KRAKOW	2-1	NEC NIJMEGEN
AIK SOLNA	0-1	VALENCIA
APOEL NICOSIA	1-2	MALLORCA
AUSTRIA VIENNA	1-2	B DORTMUND
AUXERRE	1-0	N XAMAX
BRONDBY	1-0	VIKTORIA ZIZKOV
CSKA SOFIA	1-1	TOR MOSCOW
CEMENTARNICA	0-1	LENS
DIN BUCHAREST	2-0	S DONETSK
DUNDEE	1-2	PERUGIA
DYNAMO ZAGREB	3-1	MTK HUNGARIA

FC UTRECHT	2-0	ZILINA
FC ZIMBRU	1-1	ARIS SALONIKA
FERENCVAROS	1-1	FC COPENHAGEN
GAZIANTEPSPOR	1-0	HAPOEL TEL AVIV
GENCLERBIRLIGI	3-1	BLACKBURN
GRASSHOPPERS	1-1	HAJDUK SPLIT
H RAMAT-GAN	0-1	LEVSKI SOFIA
HEARTS	2-0	ZELJEZNICAR
HERTHA BERLIN	0-0	G DYSKOBOLIA
KAISERSLAUTERN	1-2	TEPLICE
LA LOUVIERE	1-1	BENFICA
MACCABI HAIFA	2-1	NK PUBLIKUM
MALATYASPOR	0-2	FC BASLE
MAN CITY	3-2	LOKEREN
METALURG D	1-1	PARMA
MYPA-47	0-1	SOCHAUX
NEWCASTLE	5-0	NAC BREDA
ODENSE	2-2	RED STAR BE
O LJUBLJANA	1-1	LIVERPOO
PAOK SALONIKA	0-1	LYN OSLO
PANIONIOS	2-1	NORDSJAELLAND
PUCHOV	1-1	BARCELONA
ROMA	4-0	VARDAR SKOPJE
SV SALZBURG	0-1	UDINESE
SARTID	1-2	SLAVIA PRAGUE
SOUTHAMPTON	1-1	S BUCHAREST
SP MOSCOW	2-0	ESBJERG
SPORTING LISBON	2-0	MALMO
UNIAO LEIRIA	1-0	MOLDE
VALERENGA	0-0	GRAZ AK
VARTEKS	1-3	DEBRECENI VSC
VENTSPILS	1-4	ROSENBORG
VILLARREAL	0-0	TRABZONSPOR

QUALIFYING SECOND-LEGS

ANORTHOSIS FAM	1-3	ZELJEZNICAR
BANANTS	1-2	HAPOEL TEL AVIV
DEBRECENI VSC	2-1	EKRANAS
DERRY CITY	0-3	APOEL NICOSIA
DINAMO MINSK	0-2	BRONDBY
DNIPRO	1-0	VADUZ
DUNDEE	4-0	V SHKODER
F91 DUDELANGE	0-1	PETRZALKA
FC ZIMBRU	2-0	FC LOVECH
FK BELASICA	0-5	NK PUBLIKUM
FERENCVAROS	1-0	BIRKIRKARA
FYLKIR	0-0	AIK SOLNA
GRINDAVIK	1-1	KARNTEN
HAJDUK SPLIT	1-0	FC HAKA
KI KLAKKSVIK	0-4	MOLDE
KAMEN	7-0	ETZELLA ETTE
KATOWICE	1-1	CEMENTARNICA
LEVSKI SOFIA	2-0	FK ATYRAU
LOKEREN	3-1	DINAMO TIRANA
LYN OSLO	6-0	NSI RUNAVIK
MACCABI HAIFA	3-0	CWMBRAN
M LIEPAJA	1-1	DIN BUCHAREST
N XAMAX	2-0	VALLETTA
NISTRU OTACI	2-3	RED STAR BEL
PORTADOWN	0-2	MALMO
SP DOMAGNANO	0-4	TOR MOSCOW
SANTA COLOMA	1-4	ESBJERG
SARTID	3-0	SARAJEVO

SHELBOURNE	2-3	OLIMPIJA LJUBL
SHIRAK GUMRI	0-2	NORDSJAELLAND
SIONI	0-3	PUCHOV
S BUCHAREST	0-0	NEMAN GRODNO
TNS	0-2	MAN CITY
TVMK TALLINN	0-3	ODENSE
TORPEDO KUTAISI	0-2	LENS
UNIAO LEIRIA	5-0	COLERAINE
VARTEKS	3-2	LEVADIA MAARDU
WISLA PLOCK	2-2	VENTSPILS
YOUNG BOYS	2-2	MYPA-47
ATLANTAS	1-4	G DYSKOBOLIA
ZHENIS ASTANA	1-3	VIKTORIA ZIZKOV

QUALIFYING FIRST- LEGS

AIK SOLNA	1-0	FYLKIR
APOEL NICOSIA	2-1	DERRY CITY
BIRKIRKARA	0-5	FERENCVAROS
BRONDBY	3-0	DINAMO MINSK
CEMENTARNICA	0-0	KATOWICE
COLERAINE	2-1	UNIAO LEIRIA
CWMBRAN	0-3	MACCABI HAIFA
DIN BUCHAREST	5-2	M LIEPAJA
DINAMO TIRANA	0-4	LOKEREN
EKRANAS	1-1	DEBRECENI VSC
ESBJERG	5-0	SANTA COLOMA
E ETTELBRUCK	1-2	KAMEN
FC LOVECH	0-0	FC ZIMBRU
FK ATYRAU	1-4	LEVSKI SOFIA

G DYSKOBOLIA	2-0	ATLANTAS
HAPOEL TEL AVIV	1-1	BANANTS
KARNTEN	2-1	GRINDAVIK
LENS	3-0	TOR KUTAISI
LEVADIA MAARDU	1-3	VARTEKS
MALMO	4-0	PORTADOWN
MAN CITY	5-0	TNS
MOLDE	2-0	KI KLAKKSVIK
MYPA-47	3-2	YOUNG BOYS
NK PUBLIKUM	7-2	FK BELASICA
NSI RUNAVIK	1-3	LYN OSLO
NEMAN GRODNO	1-1	S BUCHAREST
NORDSJAELLAND	4-0	SHIRAK GUMRI
ODENSE	1-1	TVMK TALLINN
O LJUBLJANA	1-0	SHELBOURNE
PETRZALKA	1-0	F91 DUDELANGE
PUCHOV	3-0	SIONI
RED STAR BEL	5-0	NISTRU OTACI
TOR MOSCOW	5-0	SP DOMAGNANO
VADUZ	0-1	DNIPRO
VIKTORIA ZIZKOV	3-0	ZHENIS ASTANA
V SHKODER	0-2	DUNDEE
ZELJEZNICAR	1-0	ANORTHOSIS FAM
VENTSPILS	1-1	WISLA PLOCK
FC HAKA	2-1	HAJDUK SPLIT
SARAJEVO	1-1	SARTID
VALLETTA	0-2	N XAMAX

UEFA Cup Winners
Göteborg 2004

OLE: Valencia dominated the UEFA Cup; this year they're in the Champions League

SPECIAL OFFERS FROM HIGHDOWN

DALGLISH: THE BIOGRAPHY
Stephen Kelly • Paperback
Special price: £7.99
Save £1 off RRP of £8.99
plus FREE post and packing

SUPERMAC: MY AUTOBIOGRAPHY
Malcolm Macdonald • Paperback
Special price: £7.99
Save £1 off RRP of £8.99
plus FREE post and packing

GOAL: THE ART OF SCORING
Jason Thomas • Hardback
Special price: £16.99
Save £2 off RRP of £18.99
plus FREE post and packing
Published in August

JOCK STEIN: THE DEFINITIVE BIOGRAPHY
Archie Macpherson • Hardback
Special price: £16.99
Save £2 off RRP of £18.99
plus FREE post and packing
Published in September

*CLOWN PRINCE OF SOCCER?
THE LEN SHACKLETON STORY*
Colin Malam • Hardback
Special price: £16.99
Save £2 off RRP of £18.99 plus
FREE post and packing
Published in September

FA BARCLAYCARD PREMIER LEAGUE

Pos		P	Home W	D	L	F	A	Away W	D	L	F	A	Pts	Goal Diff
1.	Arsenal	38	15	4	0	40	14	11	8	0	33	12	90	+47
2.	Chelsea	38	12	4	3	34	13	12	3	4	33	17	79	+37
3.	Man. Utd.	38	12	4	3	37	15	11	2	6	27	20	75	+29
4.	Liverpool	38	10	4	5	29	15	6	8	5	26	22	60	+18
5.	Newcastle	38	11	5	3	33	14	2	12	5	19	26	56	+12
6.	Aston Villa	38	9	6	4	24	19	6	5	8	24	25	56	+4
7.	Charlton	38	7	6	6	29	29	7	5	7	22	22	53	0
8.	Bolton	38	6	8	5	24	21	8	3	8	24	35	53	-8
9.	Fulham	38	9	4	6	29	21	5	6	8	23	25	52	+6
10.	Birmingham	38	8	5	6	26	24	4	9	6	17	24	50	-5
11.	Middlesbro	38	8	4	7	25	23	5	5	9	19	29	48	-8
12.	Southampton	38	8	6	5	24	17	4	5	10	20	28	47	-1
13.	Portsmouth	38	10	4	5	35	19	2	5	12	12	35	45	-7
14.	Tottenham	38	9	4	6	33	27	4	2	13	14	30	45	-10
15.	Blackburn	38	5	4	10	25	31	7	4	8	26	28	44	-8
16.	Man. City	38	5	9	5	31	24	4	5	10	24	30	41	+1
17.	Everton	38	8	5	6	27	20	1	7	11	18	37	39	-12
18.	Leicester	38	3	10	6	19	28	3	5	11	29	37	33	-17
19.	Leeds	38	5	7	7	25	31	3	2	14	15	48	33	-39
20.	Wolves	38	7	5	7	23	35	0	7	12	15	42	33	-39

NATIONWIDE LEAGUE DIVISION ONE

Pos		P	Home W	D	L	F	A	Away W	D	L	F	A	Pts	Goal Diff
1	Norwich	46	18	3	2	44	15	10	7	6	35	24	94	+40
2	WBA	46	14	5	4	34	16	11	6	6	30	26	86	+22
3	Sunderland	46	13	8	2	33	15	9	5	9	29	30	79	+17
4	West Ham	46	12	7	4	42	20	7	10	6	25	25	74	+22
5	Ipswich	46	12	3	8	49	36	9	7	7	35	36	73	+12
6	Crystal Pal	46	10	8	5	34	25	11	2	10	38	36	73	+11
7	Wigan	46	11	8	4	29	16	7	9	7	31	29	71	+15
8	Sheff Utd	46	11	6	6	37	25	9	5	9	28	31	71	+9
9	Reading	46	11	6	6	29	25	9	4	10	26	32	70	-2
10	Millwall	46	11	8	4	28	15	7	7	9	27	33	69	+7
11	Stoke	46	11	7	5	35	24	7	5	11	23	31	66	+3
12	Coventry	46	9	9	5	34	22	8	5	10	33	32	65	+13
13	Cardiff	46	10	6	7	40	25	7	8	8	28	33	65	+10
14	Nottm F	46	8	9	6	33	25	7	6	10	28	33	60	+3
15	Preston	46	11	7	5	43	29	4	7	12	26	42	59	-2
16	Watford	46	9	8	6	31	28	6	4	13	23	40	57	-14
17	Rotherham	46	8	8	7	31	27	5	7	11	22	34	54	-8
18	Crewe	46	11	3	9	33	26	3	8	12	24	40	53	-9
19	Burnley	46	9	6	8	37	32	4	8	11	23	45	53	-17
20	Derby	46	11	5	7	39	33	2	8	13	14	34	52	-14
21	Gillingham	46	10	1	12	28	34	4	8	11	20	33	51	-19
22	Walsall	46	8	7	8	29	31	5	5	13	16	34	51	-20
23	Bradford	46	6	3	14	23	35	4	3	16	15	34	36	-31
24	Wimbledon	46	3	4	16	21	40	5	1	17	20	49	29	-48

Sponsored by Stan James

NATIONWIDE LEAGUE DIVISION TWO

Pos		P	Home W	D	L	F	A	Away W	D	L	F	A	Pts	Goal Diff
1	Plymouth	46	17	5	1	52	13	9	7	7	33	28	90	+44
2	QPR	46	16	7	0	47	12	6	10	7	33	33	83	+35
3	Bristol C	46	15	6	2	34	12	8	7	8	24	25	82	+21
4	Brighton	46	17	4	2	39	11	5	7	11	25	32	77	+21
5	Swindon	46	12	7	4	41	23	8	6	9	35	35	73	+18
6	Hartlepool	46	10	8	5	39	24	10	5	8	37	37	73	+15
7	Port Vale	46	15	6	2	45	28	6	4	13	28	35	73	+10
8	Tranmere	46	13	7	3	36	18	4	9	10	23	38	67	+3
9	Bournemouth	46	11	8	4	35	25	6	7	10	21	26	66	+5
10	Luton	46	14	6	3	44	27	3	9	11	25	39	66	+3
11	Colchester	46	11	8	4	33	23	6	5	12	19	33	64	-4
12	Barnsley	46	7	12	4	25	19	8	5	10	29	39	62	-4
13	Wrexham	46	9	6	8	27	21	8	3	12	23	39	60	-10
14	Blackpool	46	9	5	9	31	28	7	6	10	27	37	59	-7
15	Oldham	46	9	8	6	37	25	3	13	7	29	35	57	+6
16	Sheff Weds	46	7	9	7	25	26	6	5	12	23	38	53	-16
17	Brentford	46	9	5	9	34	38	5	6	12	18	31	53	-17
18	Peterboro	46	5	8	10	36	33	7	8	8	22	25	52	0
19	Stockport	46	6	8	9	31	36	5	11	7	31	34	52	-8
20	Chesterfield	46	9	7	7	34	31	3	8	12	15	40	51	-22
21	Grimsby	46	10	5	8	36	26	3	6	14	19	55	50	-26
22	Rushden & D	46	9	5	9	37	34	4	4	15	23	40	48	-14
23	Notts Co	46	6	9	8	32	27	4	3	16	18	51	42	-28
24	Wycombe	46	5	7	11	31	39	1	12	10	19	36	37	-25

NATIONWIDE LEAGUE DIVISION THREE

Pos		P	Home W	D	L	F	A	Away W	D	L	F	A	Pts	Goal Diff
1	Doncaster	46	17	4	2	47	13	10	7	6	32	24	92	+42
2	Hull	46	16	4	3	50	21	9	9	5	32	23	88	+38
3	Torquay	46	15	6	2	44	18	8	6	9	24	26	81	+24
4	Huddersfield	46	16	4	3	42	18	7	8	8	26	34	81	+16
5	Mansfield	46	13	5	5	44	25	9	4	10	32	37	75	+14
6	Northampton	46	13	4	6	30	23	9	5	9	28	28	75	+7
7	Lincoln	46	9	11	3	36	23	10	6	7	32	24	74	+21
8	Yeovil	46	14	3	6	40	19	9	2	12	30	38	74	+13
9	Oxford Utd	46	14	8	1	34	13	4	9	10	21	31	71	+11
10	Swansea	46	9	8	6	36	26	6	6	11	22	35	59	-3
11	Boston	46	11	7	5	35	21	5	4	14	15	33	59	-4
12	Bury	46	10	7	6	29	26	5	4	14	25	38	56	-10
13	Cambridge U	46	6	7	10	26	32	8	7	8	29	35	56	-12
14	Cheltenham	46	11	4	8	37	38	3	10	10	20	33	56	-14
15	Bristol R	46	9	7	7	29	26	5	6	12	21	35	55	-11
16	Kidderminstr	46	9	5	9	28	29	5	8	10	17	30	55	-14
17	Southend	46	8	4	11	27	29	6	8	9	24	34	54	-12
18	Darlington	46	10	4	9	30	28	4	7	12	23	33	53	-8
19	Leyton O	46	8	9	6	28	27	5	5	13	20	38	53	-17
20	Macclesfield	46	8	9	6	28	25	5	4	14	26	44	52	-15
21	Rochdale	46	7	8	8	28	26	5	6	12	21	32	50	-9
22	Scunthorpe	46	7	10	6	36	27	4	6	13	33	45	49	-3
23	Carlisle	46	8	5	10	23	27	4	4	15	23	42	45	-23
24	York	46	7	6	10	22	29	3	8	12	13	37	44	-31

Sponsored by Stan James

Pos		P	Home W	D	L	F	A	Away W	D	L	F	A	Pts	Goal Diff
1.	Chester	42	16	4	1	45	18	11	7	3	40	16	92	+51
2.	Hereford	42	14	3	4	42	20	14	4	3	61	24	91	+59
3.	Shrewsbury	42	13	6	2	38	14	7	8	6	29	28	74	+25
4.	Barnet	42	11	6	4	30	17	8	8	5	30	29	71	+14
5.	Aldershot	42	12	6	3	40	24	8	4	9	40	43	70	+13
6.	Exeter	42	10	7	4	33	24	9	5	7	38	33	69	+14
7.	Morecambe	42	14	4	3	43	25	6	3	12	23	41	67	0
8.	Stevenage	42	10	5	6	29	22	8	4	9	29	30	63	+6
9.	Woking	42	10	9	2	40	23	5	7	9	25	29	61	+13
10.	Accrington	42	13	3	5	46	31	2	10	9	22	30	58	+7
11.	Gravesend	42	7	6	8	34	35	7	9	5	35	31	57	+3
12.	Telford	42	10	3	8	28	28	5	7	9	21	23	55	-2
13.	Burton *	42	7	5	9	30	28	8	3	10	27	30	52	-1
14.	Dagenham & R	42	8	3	10	30	34	6	7	8	28	30	52	-6
15.	Scarborough	42	8	9	4	32	25	4	6	11	19	29	51	-3
16.	Margate	42	8	2	11	30	32	6	7	8	26	32	51	-8
17.	Tamworth	42	9	6	6	32	30	4	4	13	17	38	49	-19
18.	Forest G.	42	6	8	7	32	36	6	4	11	26	44	48	-22
19.	Halifax	42	9	4	8	28	26	3	4	14	15	39	44	-22
20.	Farnborough	42	7	6	8	31	34	3	3	15	22	40	39	-21
21.	Leigh RMI	42	4	6	11	26	44	3	2	16	20	53	29	-51
22.	Northwich	42	2	8	11	15	38	2	3	16	15	42	23	-50

Burton Albion 1 point deducted for fielding an ineligible player

Pos		P	Home W	D	L	F	A	Away W	D	L	F	A	Pts	Goal Diff
1.	Accrington	44	18	4	0	53	20	12	6	4	44	24	100	+53
1.	Hucknall T.	44	15	5	2	38	14	14	3	5	45	24	95	+45
2.	Droylsden	44	15	4	3	51	29	11	4	7	45	35	86	+32
3.	Barrow	44	14	4	4	41	20	8	10	4	41	32	80	+30
4.	Alfreton	44	14	5	3	45	18	9	4	9	28	25	78	+30
5.	Harrogate	44	15	2	5	44	26	9	3	10	34	36	77	+16
6.	Southport	44	10	7	5	36	25	10	3	9	35	27	70	+19
7.	Worksop	44	10	6	6	34	22	9	7	6	35	28	70	+19
8.	Lancaster	44	12	4	6	40	25	8	5	9	22	24	69	+13
9.	Vauxhall M.	44	12	5	5	44	32	7	5	10	35	43	67	+4
10.	Gainsborough	44	12	5	5	46	25	5	8	9	24	27	64	+18
11.	Stalybridge	44	8	6	8	35	33	10	4	8	37	33	64	+6
12.	Altrincham	44	9	8	5	36	24	7	7	8	30	27	63	+15
13.	Runcorn	44	5	9	8	32	32	11	4	7	35	31	61	+4
14.	Ashton Utd.	44	7	5	10	34	44	10	3	9	25	35	59	-20
15.	Whitby	44	9	3	10	24	34	5	8	9	31	36	53	-15
16.	Marine	44	8	5	9	31	30	5	7	10	30	43	51	-12
17.	Bradford Pk.	44	2	9	11	23	32	10	5	7	25	30	50	-14
18.	Spennymoor	44	8	2	12	30	51	6	4	12	25	42	48	-38
19.	Burscough	44	6	8	8	27	30	4	7	11	20	37	45	-20
20.	Radcliffe	44	9	1	12	39	46	3	5	14	35	53	42	-25
21.	Blyth Sp.	44	5	7	10	30	41	5	3	14	24	34	40	-21
22.	Frickley	44	8	4	10	29	32	3	3	16	22	51	40	-32
23.	Wakefield	44	4	2	16	18	45	4	4	14	27	54	30	-54

DR MARTENS PREMIER LEAGUE

Pos		P	Home W	D	L	F	A	Away W	D	L	F	A	Pts	Goal Diff
1.	Crawley	42	13	4	4	45	23	12	5	4	32	20	84	+34
2.	Weymouth	42	10	6	5	37	18	10	6	5	39	29	72	+29
3.	Stafford	42	12	3	6	34	21	7	8	6	21	22	68	+12
4.	Nuneaton	42	11	6	4	34	19	6	9	6	31	30	66	+16
5.	Worcester	42	12	3	6	42	19	6	6	9	29	31	63	+21
6.	Hinckley	42	7	8	6	28	21	8	6	7	27	25	59	+9
7.	Newport AFC	42	6	9	6	23	30	9	5	7	29	19	59	+3
8.	Cambridge C.	42	6	8	7	28	32	8	7	6	26	21	57	+1
9.	Welling	42	10	2	9	32	29	6	6	9	24	29	56	-2
10.	Weston SM	42	10	5	6	31	24	4	8	9	21	28	55	0
11.	Eastbourne	42	7	9	5	25	23	7	4	10	23	33	55	-8
12.	Havant and W	42	8	5	8	35	38	7	5	9	24	32	55	-11
13.	Moor Green	42	7	6	8	21	24	7	6	8	21	30	54	-12
14.	Merthyr	42	7	7	7	28	31	6	7	8	32	35	53	-6
15.	Tiverton	42	7	11	3	35	24	5	4	12	27	40	51	-2
16.	Bath	42	10	4	7	27	20	3	8	10	22	37	51	-8
17.	Dorchester	42	9	5	7	29	23	5	4	12	26	46	51	-14
18.	Chelmsford	42	5	9	7	22	27	6	7	8	24	26	49	-7
19.	Dover	42	9	7	5	33	25	3	6	12	17	33	49	-8
20.	Hednesford	42	7	7	7	35	28	5	5	11	21	41	48	-13
21.	Chippenham	42	4	9	8	23	31	6	8	7	28	32	47	-12
22.	Grantham	42	7	6	8	26	33	3	9	9	19	34	45	-22

RYMAN PREMIER DIVISION

Pos		P	Home W	D	L	F	A	Away W	D	L	F	A	Pts	Goal Diff
1.	Canvey Islnd	46	17	4	2	62	23	15	4	4	44	19	104	+64
2.	Sutton Utd.	46	11	6	6	46	30	14	4	5	48	26	85	+38
3.	Thurrock	46	12	5	6	43	18	12	6	5	44	27	83	+42
4.	Hendon	46	11	6	6	33	24	14	2	7	35	23	83	+21
5.	Hornchurch **	46	16	3	4	34	12	8	8	7	29	23	82	+28
6.	Grays	46	13	10	0	51	16	9	5	9	31	23	81	+43
7.	Carshalton	46	12	5	6	36	31	12	4	7	30	24	81	+11
8.	Hayes	46	11	8	4	29	15	10	3	10	27	31	74	+10
9.	Kettering	46	10	6	7	34	34	10	5	8	29	29	71	0
10.	Bognor	46	13	3	7	45	25	7	7	9	24	42	70	+2
11.	B Stortford	46	11	6	6	45	26	9	3	11	33	35	69	+17
12.	Maidenhead	46	10	4	9	31	36	8	5	10	29	32	63	-8
13.	Ford United	46	11	6	6	42	26	5	8	10	27	37	62	+6
14.	Basingstoke	46	7	3	13	24	37	10	6	7	34	27	60	-6
15.	Bedford	46	11	3	9	41	34	3	10	10	21	29	55	-1
16.	Heybridge	46	7	5	11	31	37	7	6	10	26	41	53	-21
17.	Harrow	46	5	8	10	21	28	7	6	10	26	35	50	-16
18.	Kingstonian	46	5	10	8	21	22	7	3	13	19	34	49	-16
19.	St Albans	46	6	5	12	24	36	6	7	10	31	47	48	-28
20.	Hitchin	46	6	6	11	29	42	7	2	14	26	47	47	-34
21.	Northwood	46	6	4	13	34	45	6	5	12	31	50	45	-30
22.	Billericay	46	5	5	13	20	31	6	6	11	31	35	44	-15
23.	Braintree	46	4	1	18	19	48	7	5	11	22	40	39	-47
24.	Aylesbury	46	3	6	14	17	45	2	8	13	24	56	29	-60

** Hornchurch 1 point deducted for fielding an ineligible player

BANK OF SCOTLAND SCOTTISH PREMIER LEAGUE

Pos		P	Home W	D	L	F	A	Away W	D	L	F	A	Pts	Goal Diff
1.	Celtic	38	15	2	2	62	15	16	3	0	43	10	98	+80
2.	Rangers	38	16	0	3	48	11	9	6	4	28	22	81	+43
3.	Hearts	38	12	5	2	32	17	7	6	6	24	23	68	+16
4.	Dunfermline	38	9	7	3	28	19	5	4	10	17	33	53	-7
5.	Dundee Utd.	38	8	6	5	28	27	5	4	10	19	33	49	-13
6.	Motherwell	38	7	7	5	25	22	5	3	11	17	27	46	-7
7.	Dundee	38	8	3	8	21	20	4	7	8	27	37	46	-9
8.	Hibernian	38	6	5	8	25	28	5	6	8	16	32	44	-19
9.	Livingston	38	6	9	4	24	18	4	4	11	24	39	43	-9
10.	Kilmarnock	38	8	3	8	29	31	4	3	12	22	43	42	-23
11.	Aberdeen	38	5	3	11	22	29	4	4	11	17	34	34	-24
12.	Partick	38	5	4	10	24	32	1	4	14	15	35	26	-28

BELL'S SCOTTISH DIVISION ONE

Pos		P	Home W	D	L	F	A	Away W	D	L	F	A	Pts	Goal Diff
1.	Inv. CT	36	13	4	1	37	12	8	3	7	30	21	70	+34
2.	Clyde	36	11	4	3	34	17	9	5	4	30	23	69	+24
3.	St Johnstone	36	8	5	5	34	27	7	7	4	25	18	57	+14
4.	Falkirk	36	8	4	6	20	16	7	6	5	23	21	55	+6
5.	Queen of Sth	36	9	6	3	24	16	6	3	9	22	32	54	-2
6.	Ross County	36	8	6	4	24	17	4	7	7	25	24	49	+8
7.	St Mirren	36	6	9	3	27	23	3	5	10	12	23	41	-7
8.	Raith	36	5	5	8	18	28	3	5	10	19	29	34	-20
9.	Ayr	36	4	7	7	21	29	2	6	10	16	29	31	-21
10.	Brechin	36	5	3	10	21	33	1	6	11	16	40	27	-36

BELL'S SCOTTISH DIVISION TWO

Pos		P	Home W	D	L	F	A	Away W	D	L	F	A	Pts	Goal Diff
1.	Airdrie Utd.	36	10	6	2	36	19	10	4	4	28	17	70	+28
2.	Hamilton	36	9	3	6	32	21	9	5	4	38	26	62	+23
3.	Dumbarton	36	12	3	3	31	13	6	3	9	25	28	60	+15
4.	Morton	36	8	8	2	37	30	8	3	7	29	28	59	+8
5.	Berwick	36	8	2	8	31	31	6	4	8	30	36	48	-6
6.	Forfar	36	7	4	7	25	30	5	7	6	24	27	47	-8
7.	Alloa	36	6	6	6	33	26	6	2	10	22	29	44	0
8.	Arbroath	36	5	6	7	17	27	6	4	8	24	30	43	-16
9.	East Fife	36	7	2	9	24	24	4	6	8	14	21	41	-7
10.	Stenhsmuir	36	4	1	13	12	29	3	3	12	16	36	25	-37

BELL'S SCOTTISH DIVISION THREE

Pos		P	Home W	D	L	F	A	Away W	D	L	F	A	Pts	Goal Diff
1.	Stranraer	36	13	2	3	51	14	11	5	2	36	16	79	+57
2.	Stirling	36	10	5	3	37	12	13	3	2	41	15	77	+51
3.	Gretna	36	9	5	4	29	18	11	3	4	30	21	68	+20
4.	Peterhead	36	10	5	3	38	13	8	2	8	29	24	61	+30
5.	Cowdenbeath	36	7	3	8	25	27	8	7	3	21	12	55	+7
6.	Montrose	36	7	4	7	31	34	5	8	5	21	29	48	-11
7.	Queen's Park	36	5	5	8	20	24	5	6	7	21	29	41	-12
8.	Albion	36	6	2	10	36	35	6	2	10	30	40	40	-9
9.	Elgin	36	4	5	9	23	34	2	2	14	25	59	25	-45
10.	E. Stirling	36	2	2	14	22	51	0	0	18	8	67	8	-88

Sponsored by Stan James

BUNDESLIGA

Pos		P	Home W	D	L	F	A	Away W	D	L	F	A	Pts	Goal Diff
1	Werder Bremen	34	11	4	2	42	21	11	4	2	37	17	74	+41
2	Bayern Munich	34	13	3	1	43	19	7	5	5	27	20	68	+31
3	Bayer Leverkusen	34	12	1	4	43	18	7	7	3	30	21	65	+34
4	Stuttgart	34	9	7	1	29	13	9	3	5	23	11	64	+28
5	Bochum	34	11	5	1	30	6	4	6	7	27	33	56	+18
6	Borussia Dortmund	34	12	3	2	39	16	4	4	9	20	32	55	+11
7	Schalke	34	7	7	3	28	16	6	4	7	21	26	50	+7
8	Hamburg	34	11	3	3	33	22	3	4	10	14	38	49	-13
9	Hansa Rostock	34	10	1	6	34	18	2	7	8	21	36	44	+1
10	Wolfsburg	34	11	1	5	38	25	2	2	13	17	36	42	-6
11	B. M'gladbach	34	7	6	4	21	16	3	3	11	19	33	39	-9
12	Hertha Berlin	34	6	6	5	26	24	3	6	8	16	35	39	-17
13	Freiburg	34	10	3	4	32	24	0	5	12	10	42	38	-24
14	Hannover	34	5	7	5	27	26	4	3	10	22	37	37	-14
15	Kaiserslautern	34	8	5	4	25	19	3	1	13	14	43	36	-23
16	Eintracht Frankfurt	34	6	4	7	25	24	3	1	13	11	29	32	-17
17	1860 Munich	34	5	4	8	16	25	3	4	10	16	30	32	-23
18	Cologne	34	6	2	9	22	23	0	3	14	10	34	23	-25

PRIMERA LIGA

Pos		P	Home W	D	L	F	A	Away W	D	L	F	A	Pts	Goal Diff
1	Valencia	38	12	3	4	38	16	11	5	3	33	11	77	+44
2	Barcelona	38	10	6	3	33	14	11	3	5	30	25	72	+24
3	Deportivo La Coruna	38	13	3	3	36	15	8	5	6	24	19	71	+26
4	Real Madrid	38	13	2	4	43	26	8	5	6	29	28	70	+18
5	Athletic Bilbao	38	10	5	4	32	20	5	6	8	21	29	56	+4
6	Seville	38	12	2	5	30	15	3	8	8	26	30	55	+11
7	Atletico Madrid	38	11	5	3	30	17	4	5	10	21	36	55	-2
8	Villarreal	38	10	5	4	28	19	5	4	10	19	30	54	-2
9	Real Betis	38	6	9	4	22	20	7	4	8	24	23	52	+3
10	Malaga	38	10	4	5	35	27	5	2	12	15	28	51	-5
11	Mallorca	38	7	5	7	29	32	8	1	10	25	34	51	-12
12	Osasuna	38	6	7	6	24	24	5	8	6	14	13	48	+1
13	Real Zaragoza	38	7	7	5	25	20	6	2	11	21	35	48	-9
14	Albacete	38	9	2	8	25	21	4	6	9	15	27	47	-8
15	Real Sociedad	38	7	7	5	24	22	4	6	9	25	31	46	-4
16	Racing Santander	38	5	4	10	23	32	6	6	7	25	31	43	-15
17	Espanyol	38	8	2	9	24	26	5	2	12	24	38	43	-16
18	Real Valladolid	38	7	6	6	25	23	3	5	11	21	33	41	-10
19	Celta Vigo	38	4	4	11	16	38	5	8	6	32	30	39	-20

Pos		P	Home					Away					Pts	Goal Diff
			W	D	L	F	A	W	D	L	F	A		
1	Lyon	38	13	4	2	39	8	11	3	5	25	18	79	+38
2	Paris St-Germain	38	13	4	2	33	15	9	6	4	17	13	76	+22
3	Monaco	38	11	5	3	35	16	10	7	2	24	14	75	+29
4	Auxerre	38	13	3	3	38	15	6	5	8	22	19	65	+26
5	Sochaux	38	12	4	3	33	17	6	5	8	21	25	63	+12
6	Nantes	38	10	6	4	26	12	7	3	9	21	23	60	+12
7	Marseille	38	12	3	4	34	18	5	3	11	17	27	57	+6
8	Lens	38	10	6	3	21	17	5	2	12	13	31	53	-14
9	Rennes	38	11	6	2	36	15	3	4	12	20	29	52	+12
10	Lille	38	8	6	5	19	15	6	3	10	22	26	51	0
11	Nice	38	8	7	4	24	13	3	10	6	18	26	50	+3
12	Bordeaux	38	10	5	4	26	15	3	6	10	14	28	50	-3
13	Strasbourg	38	7	6	6	26	23	3	7	9	17	27	43	-7
14	Metz	38	6	3	10	18	22	5	6	8	16	20	42	-8
15	Ajaccio	38	8	5	6	18	17	2	5	12	15	38	40	-22
16	Toulouse	38	5	7	7	16	21	4	5	10	15	23	39	-13
17	Bastia	38	8	6	5	22	18	1	6	12	11	31	39	-16
18	Guingamp	38	8	3	8	26	28	2	5	12	10	30	38	-22
19	Le Mans	38	6	7	6	22	18	3	4	12	13	39	38	-22
20	Montpellier	38	6	3	10	22	27	2	4	13	19	47	31	-33

Pos		P	Home					Away					Pts	Goal Diff
			W	D	L	F	A	W	D	L	F	A		
1	AC Milan	34	14	2	1	39	15	11	5	1	26	9	82	+41
2	Roma	34	13	1	3	45	12	8	7	2	23	7	71	+49
3	Juventus	34	13	1	3	40	18	8	5	4	27	24	69	+25
4	Inter Milan	34	9	4	4	31	15	8	4	5	28	22	59	+22
5	Parma	34	9	5	3	32	20	7	5	5	25	26	58	+11
6	Lazio	34	10	4	3	35	19	6	4	7	17	19	56	+14
7	Udinese	34	6	7	4	19	15	7	4	6	25	25	50	+4
8	Sampdoria	34	8	4	5	26	23	3	9	5	14	19	46	-2
9	Chievo	34	5	6	6	17	19	6	5	6	19	18	44	-1
10	Lecce	34	6	4	7	19	23	5	4	8	24	33	41	-13
11	Brescia	34	5	7	5	29	25	4	6	7	23	32	40	-5
12	Bologna	34	7	5	5	26	24	3	4	10	19	29	39	-8
13	Siena	34	7	4	6	23	15	1	6	10	18	39	34	-13
14	Reggina	34	4	8	5	14	17	2	8	7	15	28	34	-16
15	Perugia	34	3	10	4	26	27	3	4	10	18	29	32	-12
16	Modena	34	5	6	6	17	20	1	6	10	10	26	30	-19
17	Empoli	34	6	6	5	19	18	1	3	13	7	36	30	-28
18	Ancona	34	2	6	9	10	24	0	1	16	11	46	13	-49

FA PREMIER LEAGUE 2003-2004 RESULTS

	Arsenal	Aston Villa	Birmingham	Blackburn	Bolton	Charlton	Chelsea	Everton	Fulham	Leeds	Leicester	Liverpool	Man City	Man Utd	Middlesboro	Newcastle	Portsmouth	Southampton	Tottenham	Wolves
Arsenal	*	2-0	0-0	1-0	2-1	2-1	2-1	2-1	0-0	5-0	2-1	4-2	2-1	1-1	4-1	3-2	1-1	2-0	2-1	3-0
Aston Villa	0-2	*	2-2	0-2	1-1	2-1	3-2	0-0	3-0	2-0	3-1	0-0	1-1	0-2	0-2	0-0	2-1	1-0	1-0	3-2
Birmingham	0-3	0-0	*	0-4	2-0	1-2	0-0	3-0	2-2	4-1	0-1	0-3	2-1	1-2	3-1	1-1	2-0	2-1	1-0	2-2
Blackburn	0-2	0-2	1-1	*	3-4	0-1	2-3	2-1	0-2	1-2	1-0	1-3	2-3	1-0	2-2	1-1	1-2	1-1	1-0	5-1
Bolton	1-1	2-2	0-1	2-2	*	0-0	0-2	2-0	0-2	4-1	2-2	2-2	1-3	1-2	2-0	1-0	1-0	0-0	2-0	1-1
Charlton	1-1	1-2	1-1	3-2	1-2	*	4-2	2-2	3-1	0-1	2-2	3-2	0-3	0-2	1-0	0-0	1-1	2-1	2-4	2-0
Chelsea	1-2	1-0	0-0	2-2	1-2	1-0	*	0-0	2-1	1-0	2-1	0-1	1-0	1-0	0-0	5-0	3-0	4-0	4-2	5-2
Everton	1-1	2-0	1-0	0-1	1-2	0-1	0-1	*	3-1	4-0	3-2	0-3	0-0	3-4	1-1	2-2	1-0	0-0	3-1	2-0
Fulham	0-1	1-2	0-0	3-4	2-1	2-0	0-1	2-1	*	2-0	2-0	1-2	2-2	1-1	3-2	2-3	2-0	2-0	2-1	0-0
Leeds	1-4	0-0	0-2	2-1	0-2	3-3	1-1	1-1	3-2	*	3-2	2-2	2-1	0-1	0-3	2-2	1-2	0-0	0-1	4-1
Leicester	1-1	0-5	0-2	2-0	1-1	1-1	0-4	1-1	0-2	4-0	*	0-0	1-1	1-4	0-0	1-1	3-1	2-2	1-2	0-0
Liverpool	1-2	1-0	3-1	4-0	3-1	0-1	1-2	0-0	0-0	3-1	2-1	*	2-1	1-2	2-0	1-1	3-0	1-2	0-0	1-0
Man City	1-2	4-1	0-0	1-1	6-2	1-1	0-1	5-1	0-0	1-1	0-3	2-2	*	4-1	0-1	1-0	1-1	1-3	0-0	3-3
Man Utd	0-0	4-0	3-0	2-1	4-0	2-0	1-1	3-2	1-3	1-1	1-0	0-1	3-1	*	2-3	0-0	3-0	3-2	3-0	1-0
Middlesbro	0-4	1-2	5-3	0-1	2-0	0-0	1-2	1-0	2-1	2-3	3-3	0-0	2-1	0-1	*	0-1	3-1	3-1	3-0	1-0
Newcastle	0-0	1-1	0-1	0-1	0-0	3-1	2-1	4-2	3-1	1-0	3-1	1-1	3-0	1-2	2-1	*	3-0	1-0	4-0	1-1
Portsmouth	1-1	2-1	3-1	1-2	4-0	1-2	0-2	1-2	1-1	6-1	0-2	1-0	4-2	1-0	5-1	1-1	*	1-0	2-0	0-0
Southampton	0-1	1-1	0-0	2-0	1-2	3-2	0-1	3-3	0-0	2-1	0-0	2-0	0-2	1-0	0-1	3-3	3-0	*	1-0	2-0
Tottenham	2-2	2-1	4-1	1-0	0-1	0-1	0-1	3-0	0-3	2-1	4-4	2-1	1-1	1-2	0-0	1-0	4-3	1-3	*	5-2
Wolves	1-3	0-4	1-1	2-2	1-2	0-4	0-5	2-1	2-1	3-1	4-3	1-1	1-0	1-0	2-0	1-1	0-0	1-4	0-2	*

Sponsored by Stan James

NATIONWIDE DIV ONE 2003-2004 RESULTS

Home \ Away	Bradford	Burnley	Cardiff	Coventry	Crewe	Crystal P	Derby	Gillingham	Ipswich	Millwall	Norwich	Nottm F	Preston	Reading	Rotherham	Sheff Utd	Stoke	Sunderland	West Brom	Walsall	Watford	West Ham	Wigan	Wimbledon
Bradford	*	4-0	0-2	0-0	2-2	0-1	3-2	1-0	3-1	1-0	0-1	2-1	1-0	2-2	1-2	2-0	1-0	3-0	2-0	1-0	1-0	1-0	1-0	2-1
Burnley	4-0	*	1-1	1-2	1-0	2-3	2-2	1-0	4-2	1-1	3-5	0-3	1-1	3-0	1-1	3-2	0-1	0-4	1-1	3-1	2-3	1-1	0-2	2-0
Cardiff	0-2	1-3	*	0-1	3-0	0-2	1-0	5-0	2-3	1-3	2-1	0-0	2-2	2-3	3-2	2-1	3-1	4-0	1-0	0-1	3-0	0-0	0-0	1-0
Coventry	0-0	4-0	0-1	*	2-0	2-1	0-0	2-2	1-1	4-0	0-2	1-3	4-1	1-2	1-1	0-1	4-2	1-1	1-1	0-0	0-0	0-0	0-0	1-0
Crewe	2-2	3-1	0-1	3-1	*	2-3	3-0	1-1	1-0	1-2	1-3	3-1	2-1	1-0	0-0	0-1	2-0	1-1	2-2	1-0	0-0	0-3	2-3	1-0
Crystal Pal	0-1	0-0	0-1	3-1	2-3	*	1-1	2-1	3-4	0-1	0-4	3-1	1-1	2-2	1-1	1-2	0-3	3-0	0-1	0-1	0-1	1-0	1-1	3-1
Derby	3-2	1-0	2-2	1-3	0-0	2-1	*	2-1	2-2	2-2	0-4	4-2	5-1	2-3	1-0	2-0	0-3	1-3	0-1	0-1	3-2	0-1	1-1	0-3
Gillingham	1-0	0-3	1-2	2-5	0-0	2-1	2-1	*	2-2	4-3	1-2	2-1	2-0	0-1	2-0	2-0	3-1	1-0	0-1	3-0	1-0	2-0	0-3	1-2
Ipswich	3-1	6-1	1-1	1-3	6-4	1-3	4-3	1-2	*	1-3	1-2	1-2	2-0	0-1	2-1	3-0	3-1	1-0	2-3	2-1	4-1	1-2	1-3	3-1
Millwall	1-0	2-0	0-0	0-0	1-1	1-1	1-2	1-3	0-0	*	0-0	1-2	1-0	0-0	2-1	2-0	1-0	1-0	2-3	2-1	1-2	4-1	1-3	2-0
Norwich	0-1	2-0	4-1	1-1	1-0	2-1	2-1	1-1	3-1	0-0	*	1-0	1-0	2-1	2-0	1-0	1-1	2-1	0-0	5-0	1-1	2-0	1-1	2-0
Nottm F	2-1	1-1	1-2	0-1	2-0	3-2	1-0	1-0	1-1	2-2	1-0	*	3-2	1-1	2-2	3-3	3-1	1-0	0-3	3-3	1-2	1-1	1-0	3-2
Preston	1-0	1-0	2-2	4-2	2-0	4-1	2-0	2-0	1-1	1-2	2-0	0-1	*	2-1	4-1	3-1	1-0	0-2	3-0	0-1	1-1	0-2	1-0	1-0
Reading	2-2	5-3	2-2	4-2	1-0	4-1	3-1	3-0	1-1	1-2	2-1	2-2	0-1	*	4-1	3-3	0-0	0-0	0-0	3-3	2-1	2-0	0-3	6-0
Rotherham	2-2	3-0	2-2	1-2	2-1	0-3	1-0	3-0	1-1	1-2	1-0	2-2	3-1	2-1	*	2-2	0-0	0-2	0-3	1-2	1-1	2-0	1-0	1-0
Sheff Utd.	1-2	2-2	2-1	1-2	2-1	4-1	2-0	3-1	1-1	1-2	0-1	3-0	0-1	5-1	5-0	*	0-1	0-2	0-2	2-0	1-1	2-0	0-0	0-3
Stoke	1-0	2-2	3-1	1-2	2-0	1-1	0-3	3-1	1-1	1-0	1-1	2-2	3-0	1-0	0-2	1-1	*	0-1	0-1	2-0	1-0	2-0	0-3	3-1
Sunderland	3-0	1-0	0-0	0-0	1-1	1-0	3-1	0-0	2-0	3-2	1-0	0-2	1-0	2-0	0-1	0-1	3-1	*	0-1	2-0	1-0	1-1	1-2	0-0
WBA	2-0	1-1	0-0	3-0	1-2	3-1	1-2	0-1	4-1	2-0	2-0	1-2	3-3	0-0	0-1	0-2	1-1	0-0	*	2-0	3-1	2-0	2-1	3-1
Walsall	1-0	0-1	2-1	1-6	0-0	2-1	0-1	1-3	4-1	2-1	2-1	2-1	3-3	5-0	3-2	2-0	1-1	1-3	2-0	*	0-1	1-1	2-0	2-1
Watford	1-0	1-1	1-0	1-1	2-1	1-5	1-0	2-2	1-2	3-1	1-2	1-1	2-0	0-2	1-0	0-0	1-3	2-2	0-1	1-1	*	0-0	2-0	1-0
West Ham	1-0	2-2	1-0	2-0	4-2	3-0	0-0	2-1	1-2	4-2	1-1	1-1	1-2	2-0	2-1	0-0	0-1	3-2	3-4	0-0	4-0	*	4-0	1-1
Wigan	0-1	0-2	0-1	1-1	0-3	0-0	1-1	2-3	1-1	0-3	1-1	0-3	2-4	2-0	1-1	0-3	1-1	1-1	1-1	2-0	0-0	1-1	*	2-0
Wimbledon	2-1	2-2	0-1	0-3	1-3	1-3	1-0	1-2	1-2	0-1	0-1	2-2	3-3	0-3	1-2	1-2	0-1	1-2	0-0	0-1	1-3	1-1	1-1	*

153

NATIONWIDE DIV TWO 2003-2004 RESULTS

	Barnsley	Blackpool	B'mouth	Brentford	Brighton	Bristol C	Chesterfild	Colchester	Grimsby	Hartlepool	Luton	Notts Co	Oldham	Peterboro	Plymouth	Port Vale	QPR	Rushden	Sheff Wed	Stockport	Swindon	Tranmere	Wrexham	Wycombe
Barnsley	*	3-0	1-1	0-2	1-0	0-1	0-1	1-0	0-0	2-2	0-0	1-1	1-1	0-1	1-0	0-0	3-3	2-0	1-1	3-3	1-1	2-0	2-1	0-0
Blackpool	0-2	*	1-2	1-1	3-1	1-0	1-0	0-0	0-1	4-0	0-1	2-1	1-1	0-1	0-1	2-1	0-1	2-3	4-1	1-1	2-2	2-1	0-1	3-2
Bournemouth	2-2	1-2	*	1-0	1-0	0-0	1-0	1-1	0-0	2-2	6-3	1-0	1-0	1-2	0-2	2-1	1-0	2-1	1-0	0-0	0-2	1-5	6-0	1-0
Brentford	2-1	0-0	1-0	*	4-0	1-2	2-2	3-2	1-3	2-1	4-2	2-3	2-1	0-3	1-3	3-2	1-1	0-0	0-3	0-2	2-2	2-2	0-1	1-1
Brighton	1-0	3-0	3-0	1-0	*	1-4	1-1	2-1	3-0	2-0	2-0	1-0	2-1	1-0	2-1	1-1	1-1	2-0	2-0	0-1	2-2	3-0	2-0	4-0
Bristol C	2-1	2-1	2-0	1-4	1-4	*	1-0	1-2	1-3	2-0	1-1	5-0	0-2	2-1	1-0	1-1	2-1	2-0	1-1	0-3	0-3	0-1	1-0	1-1
Chesterfield	0-2	1-0	1-2	1-2	4-0	4-0	*	1-2	4-4	1-1	1-0	4-1	3-3	0-0	1-0	1-0	4-2	2-0	3-1	2-1	3-0	2-2	2-1	1-1
Colchester	1-1	1-1	1-0	1-0	1-2	2-1	1-0	*	2-0	1-2	1-1	2-1	2-1	2-1	1-1	0-2	2-2	2-0	3-1	0-3	3-0	1-1	3-1	2-2
Grimsby	6-1	0-2	1-1	1-0	2-1	1-2	4-0	2-0	*	0-2	3-2	2-0	3-3	0-0	0-2	1-4	1-4	1-0	2-0	2-1	2-1	0-1	1-3	3-1
Hartlepool	1-2	1-1	2-1	1-2	0-0	2-0	2-0	0-0	8-1	*	4-3	4-0	0-0	1-1	1-0	1-2	1-1	2-1	1-1	1-1	3-1	0-0	2-0	3-1
Luton	0-1	3-2	1-1	4-1	2-0	3-2	1-0	1-0	1-2	3-2	*	2-0	1-1	0-1	1-3	2-0	3-3	3-1	3-2	2-2	1-2	2-2	0-1	1-1
Notts Co	1-1	4-1	0-1	2-0	1-2	2-1	1-1	3-0	4-4	1-0	2-0	*	1-1	0-1	1-1	2-0	2-1	1-3	0-0	2-2	4-2	1-1	1-1	1-1
Oldham	1-1	2-3	2-3	1-1	1-3	2-1	2-0	0-0	6-0	0-2	1-1	1-1	*	1-1	0-1	3-1	0-0	3-2	1-0	4-1	0-1	4-2	6-1	1-1
Peterboro	2-3	0-1	0-1	0-0	2-2	0-1	0-2	2-0	0-0	3-4	0-1	2-1	2-2	*	1-1	1-1	1-1	3-1	0-1	2-0	4-2	6-0	0-0	1-1
Plymouth	2-0	1-0	0-0	2-0	3-3	2-2	7-0	2-0	2-0	2-0	0-0	3-0	2-2	1-1	*	0-0	0-1	3-1	3-0	1-2	0-1	2-1	2-1	1-1
Port Vale	3-1	2-1	1-1	1-1	1-1	1-1	1-1	4-3	5-1	2-5	1-2	1-0	3-0	2-0	3-1	*	2-0	3-0	2-2	3-1	1-2	3-3	1-0	1-1
QPR	4-0	5-0	1-0	1-0	2-1	2-1	3-0	1-1	3-0	4-1	1-1	3-2	1-0	1-1	2-1	2-0	*	1-0	3-0	2-2	2-3	2-1	2-0	1-1
Rushden & D	2-3	0-0	0-3	0-1	1-3	1-1	2-1	3-1	3-1	0-2	2-2	2-1	4-1	0-1	2-1	0-2	3-3	*	1-2	2-2	2-0	1-0	2-3	2-0
Sheff Wed	2-1	0-1	0-2	1-1	2-1	1-0	0-0	4-0	0-0	1-0	1-2	2-1	2-2	2-0	2-3	3-1	1-2	1-2	*	1-0	2-3	1-2	2-3	2-0
Stockport	2-3	1-3	3-2	2-0	1-1	0-0	2-0	0-1	2-1	1-2	2-2	2-2	2-1	2-2	2-0	3-1	2-2	2-2	2-2	*	2-4	1-0	0-1	2-0
Swindon	1-1	2-2	2-1	2-2	1-1	0-0	2-0	2-0	2-0	1-1	2-4	4-0	1-2	2-0	2-3	0-0	1-2	2-0	1-0	1-2	*	2-0	1-0	2-1
Tranmere	2-0	1-1	1-1	4-1	1-0	2-1	2-3	2-1	3-0	0-0	1-0	4-0	2-1	2-0	3-0	2-1	3-2	1-2	2-3	3-2	1-0	*	1-2	2-1
Wrexham	1-0	4-2	0-1	1-0	0-2	0-0	0-0	3-0	3-0	1-2	0-1	0-1	4-0	0-0	2-2	2-1	0-2	1-1	2-2	0-0	3-2	0-1	*	0-0
Wycombe	1-2	0-3	2-0	1-2	1-1	3-0	3-3	4-1	4-1	3-4	1-1	1-1	2-5	1-1	0-0	2-1	2-2	0-2	1-2	1-0	0-3	1-2	1-1	*

NATIONWIDE DIV THREE 2003-2004 RESULTS

	Boston	Bristol R	Bury	C'bridge	Carlisle	Cheltenhm	Darlington	Doncaster	Huddersfld	Hull	Kidminstr	Leyton O	Lincoln	Maclesf'ld	Mansfield	North'pton	Oxford Utd	Rochdale	Scunthorpe	Southend	Swansea	Torquay	Yeovil	York
Boston	*	1-0	1-2	1-2	1-0	3-1	0-1	0-0	2-2	1-2	2-2	3-0	0-1	3-1	1-2	1-2	1-1	2-0	1-1	0-2	1-1	4-0	3-2	2-0
Bristol R	2-0	*	1-2	0-2	3-1	1-1	1-1	0-4	5-1	3-0	1-0	1-1	3-1	2-2	1-3	1-2	1-1	0-0	1-2	0-1	2-1	2-2	3-1	3-0
Bury	1-3	0-0	*	1-0	0-0	1-1	1-1	1-3	1-0	0-0	0-0	1-1	2-0	2-0	3-0	1-0	0-4	1-2	2-3	1-1	2-0	2-1	0-1	2-0
Cambridge	0-1	3-1	1-2	*	2-2	2-1	1-1	3-3	1-2	0-2	0-0	1-4	0-0	3-1	1-2	0-1	0-4	0-0	3-2	3-2	0-1	1-1	1-4	2-0
Carlisle	2-1	0-2	2-1	0-0	*	1-1	2-1	0-1	0-2	1-3	2-1	0-1	0-2	2-0	4-2	0-1	2-1	3-1	0-2	0-1	0-1	1-1	3-1	1-2
Cheltenham	1-0	1-2	1-2	0-3	1-1	*	2-1	1-3	2-1	0-2	2-1	1-0	3-2	3-2	4-2	4-3	2-0	3-2	2-1	1-1	3-4	1-3	3-1	1-2
Darlington	3-0	0-4	1-3	3-4	2-1	2-1	*	1-0	0-1	0-0	0-2	1-0	0-0	1-0	1-0	1-2	0-0	1-0	2-1	0-0	1-2	1-1	3-2	3-0
Doncaster	3-0	5-1	3-1	2-0	2-0	2-1	3-1	*	0-1	2-1	5-0	2-1	0-0	1-0	4-2	1-2	2-0	1-0	2-1	0-2	3-1	1-1	1-1	3-1
Huddersfield	2-0	3-0	1-0	2-2	1-0	0-0	0-2	3-1	*	3-1	6-1	3-0	2-1	4-0	1-3	3-0	4-2	1-0	3-2	1-0	3-0	1-0	0-1	3-1
Hull	2-1	3-0	3-0	2-0	2-1	3-3	4-1	0-0	3-1	*	1-1	3-0	1-2	2-2	0-1	2-3	1-1	2-1	2-1	3-2	3-1	1-0	0-0	0-1
Kidderminster	2-0	1-0	0-2	2-2	2-1	0-1	1-0	5-0	6-1	1-1	*	2-1	0-2	1-4	0-1	2-1	0-1	1-0	0-2	1-2	2-0	0-1	0-1	4-1
Leyton O	1-3	1-1	2-0	0-1	1-1	1-4	0-1	2-1	3-0	3-0	2-1	*	0-0	2-0	4-1	2-1	3-1	2-1	1-1	1-1	2-1	0-0	2-3	2-2
Lincoln	1-1	3-1	2-1	2-2	2-0	0-0	1-3	0-0	2-1	3-0	1-1	0-2	*	3-2	4-1	1-1	0-1	3-1	1-1	2-2	2-1	1-3	4-1	3-0
Macclesfield	0-0	2-1	1-0	0-1	1-1	1-2	0-1	3-2	1-0	0-1	1-1	1-0	0-0	*	1-1	0-4	2-1	3-1	2-2	1-0	2-1	1-1	4-1	0-0
Mansfield	2-1	0-0	5-3	1-1	2-3	4-0	3-1	4-2	1-3	1-5	1-0	1-0	1-2	3-2	*	1-2	5-0	1-3	1-0	2-2	1-1	0-1	2-0	2-0
Northampton	2-1	3-2	3-2	1-2	2-0	0-1	3-1	1-2	1-0	0-1	1-0	1-0	1-1	3-2	1-2	*	2-1	3-1	3-2	2-0	1-1	0-1	2-1	2-1
Oxford Utd	0-0	0-0	2-0	2-2	2-1	1-0	2-2	1-0	2-2	1-5	2-1	2-1	0-3	3-1	0-3	1-1	*	2-0	2-0	3-0	3-0	1-0	1-0	0-0
Rochdale	1-0	2-2	0-0	2-2	2-0	1-0	4-2	1-1	1-1	0-2	1-1	3-0	0-3	1-2	3-0	1-1	1-2	*	2-0	1-1	2-2	1-0	1-3	1-2
Scunthorpe	0-1	1-2	0-0	4-0	2-3	5-2	0-1	2-2	1-2	1-1	0-2	1-1	1-3	1-0	0-0	1-0	1-1	2-2	*	1-1	2-2	2-1	3-0	0-0
Southend	0-2	0-1	1-0	1-0	2-2	2-0	3-2	0-2	1-2	2-3	3-0	1-2	0-2	1-0	0-3	0-1	0-1	4-0	4-2	*	1-1	1-2	0-2	0-0
Swansea	3-0	0-0	4-2	0-2	1-2	2-0	2-0	3-0	1-3	1-1	0-0	2-1	2-2	3-0	4-1	0-2	0-0	1-1	4-2	2-3	*	1-2	3-2	3-0
Torquay	2-0	2-1	3-1	4-1	4-1	3-1	1-0	2-1	1-0	1-2	1-1	2-1	3-1	4-1	1-0	3-1	3-0	1-3	1-0	3-0	0-0	*	2-2	1-1
Yeovil	2-0	4-0	2-1	2-0	3-0	0-0	1-0	2-1	0-2	1-0	1-2	1-2	1-4	2-2	2-1	0-2	2-1	1-0	2-1	4-0	2-0	0-2	*	3-0
York	1-1	2-1	1-1	2-0	1-2	0-2	1-1	3-1	1-2	0-1	1-0	1-2	1-4	0-2	1-2	1-0	2-2	1-2	1-3	0-0	0-0	0-0	1-2	*

NATIONWIDE CONFERENCE 2003-2004 RESULTS

	Accrington	Aldershot	Barnet	Burton	Chester	Dagenham	Exeter	Farnboro	Forest G	Gravesend	Halifax	Hereford	Leigh RMI	Margate	Morcambe	Northwich	Scarboro	Sh'wsbury	Stevenage	Tamworth	Telford	Woking
Accrington	*	4-2	2-0	3-1	0-2	2-3	1-2	3-1	4-1	3-3	2-1	2-0	4-1	3-2	1-0	2-2	1-0	0-1	2-1	3-0	1-5	3-3
Aldershot	2-1	*	1-1	3-1	1-1	2-1	2-1	2-0	3-0	2-2	3-1	1-2	2-0	0-2	2-2	4-3	1-2	1-1	2-0	1-1	3-1	2-1
Barnet	0-0	2-1	*	2-1	0-0	2-4	2-3	0-2	5-0	1-0	4-1	1-1	2-1	3-1	2-1	1-0	0-0	0-1	0-0	1-0	2-0	0-0
Burton	1-1	1-4	2-3	*	1-1	0-0	3-4	1-0	2-3	3-0	2-2	4-1	3-2	0-1	0-1	0-1	2-0	0-1	1-1	0-1	2-1	2-0
Chester	3-3	4-2	1-0	3-1	*	2-1	3-2	3-2	1-0	2-2	2-0	0-0	5-0	3-0	2-1	4-0	1-0	2-1	1-2	1-0	0-0	2-0
Dagenham	0-1	2-3	5-2	0-2	0-0	*	0-2	1-0	5-2	2-2	0-1	0-9	1-2	4-0	1-3	2-0	1-0	5-0	1-2	0-0	1-1	2-0
Exeter	3-2	2-1	1-1	2-0	2-1	0-2	*	1-1	2-2	0-1	1-1	0-1	3-2	1-1	4-0	2-0	1-0	3-2	1-0	3-2	1-1	1-0
Farnborough	1-1	4-0	1-1	2-1	1-2	2-2	1-1	*	1-3	1-2	1-0	0-1	1-1	1-1	2-4	2-0	1-2	1-3	2-0	3-2	0-3	1-0
Forest G	2-1	3-1	1-1	1-1	2-1	1-3	2-5	1-3	*	1-2	1-2	0-5	2-2	1-2	1-2	0-0	4-0	1-1	3-1	2-1	0-0	2-2
Gravesend	0-0	1-3	1-1	1-2	0-4	3-0	2-5	1-1	1-1	*	1-0	1-7	3-1	1-2	6-0	2-2	4-0	0-3	2-3	2-0	1-2	2-2
Halifax	1-1	1-2	1-2	1-4	0-3	2-0	1-1	2-0	0-1	1-0	*	1-2	2-1	0-1	1-0	5-3	1-1	0-0	2-1	1-2	1-1	2-2
Hereford	1-0	4-3	2-0	1-2	2-1	1-1	2-0	2-0	5-1	3-3	7-1	*	0-1	2-1	3-0	1-0	2-1	2-1	1-3	1-1	2-1	2-2
Leigh RMI	1-2	2-2	1-4	0-1	2-6	2-1	1-1	0-2	1-2	1-2	1-1	0-5	*	4-2	3-1	1-0	1-4	2-2	1-3	1-1	2-1	0-1
Margate	3-1	1-2	0-1	1-2	1-2	3-3	0-1	3-0	2-0	1-2	2-0	1-3	2-0	*	1-1	3-1	0-2	0-2	1-4	3-2	1-0	1-2
Morecambe	1-0	2-0	1-3	1-2	0-1	3-2	3-2	4-0	2-0	2-2	2-0	2-2	1-0	1-1	*	3-0	2-1	3-3	2-1	4-0	1-0	2-1
Northwich	3-3	1-1	1-1	1-2	0-4	0-1	1-1	1-1	0-4	0-0	0-1	1-5	0-1	0-3	1-1	*	1-1	0-2	1-2	1-0	1-0	1-4
Scarborough	2-1	1-0	2-2	1-2	2-2	2-0	2-3	2-1	2-2	2-0	1-0	3-3	4-1	0-1	1-0	1-0	*	1-1	2-2	0-1	1-1	2-2
Shrewsbury	0-0	1-2	0-1	1-0	0-0	2-1	2-2	3-0	2-0	1-1	2-0	4-1	3-1	1-1	2-0	3-1	4-1	*	3-1	3-1	0-0	1-0
Stevenage	2-1	0-1	1-2	1-0	2-1	0-2	2-1	3-2	2-1	1-0	2-1	4-0	4-3	2-1	2-3	1-0	2-2	2-0	*	3-1	0-1	2-1
Tamworth	1-1	3-3	2-0	1-1	1-5	2-0	2-1	2-1	1-0	1-1	2-1	1-3	2-3	1-1	2-3	2-1	0-0	1-1	3-1	*	2-0	1-0
Telford	1-0	2-5	1-2	2-2	0-2	1-0	2-0	0-2	1-1	3-2	2-2	0-3	5-0	1-1	2-1	0-1	2-1	1-0	1-1	2-0	*	1-0
Woking	2-2	2-2	2-2	1-0	1-2	0-0	1-0	3-2	1-1	3-2	2-2	0-1	2-0	0-0	4-1	3-0	2-1	3-3	1-1	4-0	3-1	*

UNIBOND PREMIER DIV 2003-2004 RESULTS

Home \ Away	Alfreton	Altrincham	Ashton Utd	Barrow	Blyth Sp	Bradford P	Burscough	Droylsden	Frickley	Gainsboro	Harrogate	Hucknall T	Lancaster	Marine	Radcliffe	Runcorn	Southport	Spennymr	Stalybridge	Vauxhall M	Wakefield	Whitby	Worksop
Alfreton	*	0-0	5-0	1-1	2-1	1-1	1-0	4-2	1-2	3-1	2-0	2-1	3-0	4-0	0-0	0-2	0-2	1-1	3-1	5-1	1-2	3-0	2-1
Altrincham	0-1	*	1-2	1-1	1-2	1-0	3-0	1-0	1-1	2-2	0-0	2-3	2-1	3-3	4-1	1-0	1-0	1-1	3-3	3-1	2-3	4-0	2-1
Ashton Utd	1-1	0-2	*	1-2	2-0	0-2	0-0	1-1	3-2	1-1	3-4	1-6	2-1	4-3	3-3	4-2	1-1	1-2	2-1	0-1	3-2	1-3	0-3
Barrow	1-2	2-1	3-0	*	3-0	4-0	3-3	2-1	3-1	3-0	1-2	1-0	4-3	1-1	2-0	1-0	1-1	2-0	0-2	0-1	1-0	0-0	1-0
Blyth Sp	1-0	2-2	2-0	0-2	*	0-0	0-1	1-5	1-3	1-1	3-4	1-2	0-0	5-0	1-0	3-3	1-4	0-2	0-1	3-7	1-0	1-1	3-3
Bradford Pk	0-1	1-1	2-1	2-2	0-0	*	0-2	0-2	0-0	0-0	2-3	1-2	0-2	1-1	1-1	1-1	0-1	0-0	2-3	6-2	1-2	2-3	0-1
Burscough	4-1	3-1	0-0	1-1	0-1	0-2	*	1-3	3-1	2-1	1-0	0-1	0-1	0-0	3-6	1-3	0-3	2-1	0-0	3-1	1-1	1-1	0-0
Droylsden	2-1	1-4	1-1	1-1	1-2	1-1	1-3	*	4-0	0-0	3-1	3-1	0-0	4-2	5-4	1-2	3-2	2-0	2-0	2-1	3-1	2-1	2-2
Frickley	0-3	1-1	1-2	4-2	3-3	3-0	2-0	0-3	*	0-0	0-0	0-1	0-2	4-3	3-0	1-2	1-2	3-2	1-2	0-2	2-1	3-1	1-1
Gainsborough	2-4	2-3	3-0	0-0	2-1	3-3	4-1	1-2	3-0	*	2-0	2-1	3-2	2-0	6-2	0-1	1-2	3-1	0-0	0-0	3-0	2-2	2-1
Harrogate	1-0	1-0	2-1	2-1	2-1	0-0	2-1	4-4	2-1	2-0	*	1-2	2-0	4-1	3-0	1-1	3-1	3-1	4-3	3-2	5-0	1-0	0-2
Hucknall T	3-3	2-1	2-0	3-1	1-0	0-1	2-1	2-1	3-0	2-0	1-0	*	0-1	3-1	1-1	1-0	4-0	2-1	1-3	2-0	0-1	0-1	3-1
Lancaster	0-1	1-1	1-1	0-3	1-1	1-3	4-0	2-1	1-1	0-1	1-4	3-1	*	3-1	4-2	0-1	1-1	6-0	2-1	0-0	3-0	4-3	2-0
Marine	0-1	0-1	0-2	1-2	1-0	2-0	1-2	1-2	2-1	3-1	1-1	1-1	1-1	*	3-2	1-3	1-3	1-3	0-2	3-2	4-1	2-2	2-2
Radcliffe	1-0	1-3	1-2	2-3	2-3	2-0	4-2	4-2	4-2	2-1	3-1	1-6	0-2	3-1	*	1-2	3-2	1-1	3-2	1-2	5-3	0-5	1-2
Runcorn	2-2	0-3	1-2	0-0	1-0	1-2	0-0	2-2	2-0	2-2	4-1	1-2	0-1	0-2	2-2	*	1-1	1-2	3-0	1-1	1-1	1-1	2-3
Southport	1-0	2-2	0-0	1-1	1-0	0-1	2-1	4-1	3-1	2-0	3-2	1-1	3-0	0-0	2-1	0-3	*	2-3	2-3	1-1	1-1	3-0	2-3
Spennymoor	1-0	2-1	3-2	2-4	0-5	2-4	0-2	0-1	3-2	0-6	1-5	1-3	0-1	0-2	3-1	2-1	0-2	*	1-3	2-1	4-4	2-0	1-1
Stalybridge	3-0	1-0	1-1	2-2	2-0	2-0	1-1	2-1	5-0	2-0	1-2	1-2	0-3	1-1	0-2	2-2	2-1	1-3	*	3-4	3-3	1-3	0-3
Vauxhall M	2-0	1-1	1-2	1-1	2-1	6-2	3-2	2-4	2-1	0-2	3-0	1-3	2-1	1-0	0-5	6-0	3-2	0-2	1-1	*	1-0	1-1	4-3
Wakefield	0-3	2-0	1-2	2-5	1-2	0-1	2-2	0-2	0-2	2-1	0-2	0-0	1-0	0-4	2-1	3-5	0-1	2-0	1-3	0-1	*	0-3	1-1
Whitby	0-4	2-3	0-1	3-2	2-1	0-1	1-1	2-1	2-1	0-0	1-0	0-0	2-1	1-2	1-0	1-0	0-5	1-0	0-2	1-1	2-1	*	2-3
Worksop	0-0	0-0	3-0	2-4	1-0	1-2	1-1	1-3	3-0	0-0	1-0	0-3	0-0	1-2	4-1	0-1	1-0	4-0	2-1	4-3	4-0	1-1	*

DR MARTENS PREMIER DIV 2003-2004 RESULTS

	Bath	Cambridge C	Chelmsford	Chippenham	Crawley	Dorchester	Dover	Eastbourne	Grantham	Havant & W	Hednesford	Hinckley	Merthyr	Moor Green	Newport AFC	Nuneaton	Stafford	Tiverton	Welling	Weston SM	Weymouth	Worcester
Bath	*	1-2	0-1	2-2	0-0	0-0	2-1	2-0	5-1	2-0	2-0	0-2	0-2	0-1	1-0	1-3	1-0	2-1	2-0	3-1	0-2	1-1
Cambridge C	0-0	*	2-0	1-1	2-5	4-2	2-1	0-0	1-1	2-3	0-1	1-2	2-2	1-1	0-2	1-3	1-0	6-4	0-3	1-1	0-2	0-0
Chelmsford	0-0	1-1	*	1-3	0-4	2-0	0-0	3-1	0-0	1-1	2-0	0-3	3-1	1-0	0-0	1-2	1-2	3-3	0-1	0-0	1-3	2-2
Chippenham	1-1	0-2	0-0	*	0-1	1-6	0-0	0-1	2-2	3-0	0-0	2-1	3-3	4-0	2-1	1-1	0-3	1-1	0-2	1-1	1-3	1-2
Crawley	2-0	2-0	0-0	3-2	*	2-3	2-0	3-1	4-2	3-1	6-1	0-3	1-2	2-2	1-2	2-2	2-0	2-1	0-0	2-0	2-1	4-0
Dorchester	1-0	0-2	4-1	3-1	2-0	*	0-2	0-1	2-2	1-2	3-4	1-1	1-0	0-1	0-2	0-0	2-0	1-0	3-1	3-2	2-2	3-0
Dover	3-3	0-1	2-2	0-0	2-2	1-2	*	3-1	2-0	0-2	2-1	1-1	2-2	2-0	2-0	3-2	0-0	2-0	1-1	0-2	2-3	2-1
Eastbourne	1-1	1-1	1-1	1-2	1-1	2-1	2-1	*	1-0	0-2	2-1	0-2	1-1	0-1	1-2	0-0	1-1	2-1	3-1	1-0	2-1	1-3
Grantham	1-1	2-1	1-3	0-2	1-1	4-0	3-1	2-2	*	0-2	1-1	0-1	0-1	0-1	2-1	0-5	0-2	1-1	1-1	3-2	1-1	4-3
Havant & W	1-4	2-3	0-2	1-1	1-3	3-2	2-2	0-3	2-1	*	1-2	2-0	4-2	0-0	0-3	5-1	2-2	3-2	2-0	0-1	4-1	0-5
Hednesford	4-0	2-2	2-1	4-1	0-0	2-4	0-1	1-2	2-0	1-0	*	1-1	1-2	4-4	1-4	1-1	1-2	3-1	1-2	2-2	0-0	3-1
Hinckley	1-2	0-0	1-2	0-0	4-0	1-0	3-1	2-2	0-1	2-2	4-0	*	1-2	0-0	1-1	4-3	1-1	2-0	2-0	1-0	1-2	0-0
Merthyr	2-0	1-3	1-0	3-1	2-1	1-0	0-0	2-2	1-0	1-1	2-0	1-1	*	1-2	1-1	2-0	1-2	0-2	2-0	1-2	0-4	0-2
Moor Green	0-3	1-1	1-0	3-2	1-2	1-3	1-0	0-1	0-1	2-1	2-1	0-1	1-1	*	1-1	2-0	3-1	2-0	0-0	0-0	1-2	1-1
Newport AFC	2-1	1-0	1-0	2-2	1-2	0-0	2-1	1-1	2-2	0-2	1-1	0-3	1-1	1-1	*	1-2	0-0	2-1	1-4	2-1	1-1	0-4
Nuneaton	2-1	2-1	1-2	1-1	0-1	2-0	1-1	4-0	1-1	1-2	3-0	2-0	2-1	1-0	2-0	*	0-0	0-1	1-1	1-1	4-3	2-1
Stafford	2-0	2-1	2-0	2-0	0-1	3-0	2-1	4-1	0-1	2-1	1-1	2-0	3-1	1-2	1-0	0-3	*	1-2	2-2	1-1	1-2	2-0
Tiverton	1-1	1-1	3-3	3-1	2-2	1-1	1-0	2-3	1-1	5-1	2-3	3-0	2-1	2-1	0-0	0-0	0-0	*	2-2	2-0	1-2	1-1
Welling	2-1	0-1	1-0	1-3	0-3	6-1	2-1	1-2	0-1	1-1	2-0	2-3	0-3	2-1	0-2	2-1	2-1	4-0	*	2-1	2-2	0-1
Weston SM	1-0	1-0	0-0	1-2	1-2	1-1	3-0	2-1	2-0	2-0	3-2	2-2	3-2	2-3	0-0	1-1	5-1	1-3	2-1	*	0-2	1-0
Weymouth	3-3	2-1	2-2	0-1	0-1	8-0	3-0	2-1	1-0	0-1	3-2	2-2	2-2	3-0	2-1	1-1	0-1	1-1	1-2	0-0	*	3-1
Worcester	7-0	0-2	1-0	0-0	0-1	1-0	5-1	2-1	4-1	1-2	0-1	0-0	2-0	3-0	1-5	4-0	0-1	1-2	3-1	3-0	2-2	*

RYMAN PREMIER DIV 2003-2004 RESULTS

Home \ Away	Aylesbury	B Storford	Basingstke	Bedford	Billericay	Bognor	Braintree	Canvey I	Carshalton	Ford Utd	Grays	Harrow	Hayes	Hendon	Heybridge	Hitchin	H'church	Kettering	Kingstnian	Maidhead	Northwood	St Albans	Sutton Utd	Thurrock
Aylesbury	*	4-4	2-0	4-1	2-2	4-0	2-0	4-0	3-0	4-1	2-1	0-2	3-0	1-1	1-2	2-2	1-0	2-2	0-0	1-3	1-2	0-2	0-6	2-4
B Stortford	0-1	*	1-2	3-1	1-0	0-1	2-0	5-1	1-2	3-0	3-1	1-0	3-0	2-0	0-1	1-0	0-1	3-2	2-1	2-1	6-0	2-2	1-1	1-3
Basingstoke	2-0	1-2	*	3-0	2-1	0-1	2-1	1-2	1-2	1-1	0-2	0-1	0-0	1-4	2-3	2-3	2-1	2-2	0-0	2-1	2-0	1-1	0-5	0-3
Bedford	4-1	0-0	3-1	*	0-0	2-4	4-1	0-0	0-3	1-0	3-2	2-1	4-0	1-2	2-0	2-0	2-1	1-0	1-2	0-1	1-4	1-0	0-1	0-0
Billericay	2-2	2-1	3-1	0-3	*	1-1	4-1	0-3	0-1	1-0	2-1	4-0	0-2	3-1	1-2	2-0	0-2	2-0	2-0	0-1	1-4	2-2	1-1	1-1
Bognor	4-0	2-0	0-1	1-1	1-0	*	4-1	0-0	3-2	2-1	2-1	4-0	0-2	1-2	2-0	2-0	3-0	3-1	0-1	0-3	5-2	2-2	0-2	6-1
Braintree	2-0	2-2	0-1	0-2	4-1	0-3	*	0-3	0-1	3-2	2-1	4-0	1-2	1-3	2-0	3-1	3-0	1-0	6-1	1-2	2-5	2-4	0-3	1-0
Canvey Islnd	4-0	5-1	3-1	4-1	0-3	3-1	4-1	*	3-0	3-1	1-1	2-1	2-0	1-0	4-1	4-0	0-2	1-1	2-1	3-1	1-1	4-0	1-3	4-3
Carshalton	3-0	1-2	0-2	2-1	1-1	1-3	2-1	0-3	*	1-1	0-2	3-2	0-3	1-3	5-3	2-1	3-2	0-0	0-1	3-2	1-0	1-1	2-2	0-3
Ford United	4-1	3-0	1-1	1-0	1-0	1-3	3-2	3-1	1-1	*	3-0	0-1	0-0	0-1	5-3	3-0	0-0	0-2	1-0	1-1	3-0	2-2	2-4	2-3
Grays	2-1	3-1	3-1	1-1	1-1	2-3	1-1	0-0	0-2	2-0	*	2-2	4-0	1-2	4-0	5-1	0-0	1-1	1-0	1-1	2-1	9-1	3-2	1-1
Harrow	0-2	1-0	2-1	1-0	2-1	0-0	1-1	1-1	3-2	1-1	0-0	*	2-0	3-1	2-0	5-1	0-0	0-1	2-0	1-1	2-2	3-1	2-4	1-2
Hayes	3-0	2-1	1-2	0-2	1-2	2-0	4-0	2-0	2-0	3-2	1-2	2-2	*	0-0	3-2	1-2	3-0	0-3	3-1	3-1	1-1	1-0	0-0	0-2
Hendon	1-1	3-1	2-0	1-2	1-3	1-2	1-3	2-0	1-3	1-2	1-3	3-1	0-0	*	4-1	1-1	0-2	4-1	0-2	1-1	1-1	0-2	0-2	1-1
Heybridge	1-2	1-0	0-3	2-0	1-2	2-0	2-0	1-0	5-3	2-2	0-1	2-0	1-2	0-0	*	4-2	0-2	0-0	1-0	0-0	3-2	1-0	2-2	1-2
Hitchin	2-2	1-0	0-3	2-0	1-3	1-0	3-2	0-1	0-1	1-1	2-0	2-3	1-2	1-4	4-2	*	0-2	1-1	1-1	2-0	3-1	0-1	2-4	1-1
Hornchurch	1-0	2-0	2-0	2-1	0-0	3-1	1-4	0-0	0-3	2-0	2-0	1-1	0-3	4-1	4-1	4-0	*	3-2	1-0	1-0	3-1	2-0	3-0	2-0
Kettering	2-2	3-2	0-3	1-0	1-4	1-2	2-2	1-2	0-1	0-2	1-1	1-0	1-0	4-1	1-1	1-0	3-2	*	1-1	3-1	2-1	2-0	0-1	2-1
Kingstonian	0-0	2-0	0-0	2-1	2-0	1-0	2-1	1-2	3-1	1-0	1-0	0-1	1-1	0-1	1-0	1-1	1-1	1-0	*	3-1	0-1	1-2	1-2	1-1
Maidenhead	4-2	0-4	0-2	4-0	1-0	0-2	4-0	1-1	2-4	2-1	1-0	1-2	2-0	2-1	0-4	2-1	1-0	1-2	0-4	*	3-1	4-2	2-0	1-4
Northwood	1-1	2-3	0-2	3-1	4-5	1-2	3-1	1-1	1-2	1-0	2-0	0-4	3-4	2-0	2-1	1-0	1-2	0-1	2-0	3-1	*	3-4	1-2	0-3
St Albans	3-1	3-2	0-3	1-3	0-2	3-0	0-0	4-1	1-3	2-3	1-1	3-1	1-1	1-2	1-1	1-2	1-1	0-1	4-1	1-2	3-0	*	1-0	0-2
Sutton Utd	2-2	2-2	2-2	1-1	1-1	1-1	1-0	3-0	3-1	1-0	3-0	2-0	4-1	2-0	5-1	1-3	1-0	2-1	4-1	0-3	0-0	4-2	*	0-3
Thurrock	5-0	1-1	0-3	1-1	1-0	6-0	3-1	4-3	1-3	3-1	2-0	1-2	2-0	2-0	1-1	2-0	1-3	4-1	4-1	3-1	6-0	2-0	0-1	*

SCOTTISH PREMIER LEAGUE 2003-2004 RESULTS

	Aberdeen	Celtic	Dundee	Dundee U	D'fermline	Hearts	Hibs	K'marnock	Livingston	Motherwell	Partick	Rangers
Aberdeen	*	1-3	2-2 1-2	3-0 0-1	2-0 1-2	0-1	3-1 0-1	3-1	0-3 1-2	0-3 0-2	2-1 0-0	1-1 2-3
Celtic	4-0 1-2	*	3-2	2-1 5-0 2-1	2-1 5-0 1-2	2-2 5-0	6-0	5-1	5-1 5-1	3-0 1-1	3-1	3-0 1-0
Dundee	1-1 2-0	0-1 1-2	*	2-1	2-1	1-2	2-2 1-1	1-2 2-0	1-0 2-1	1-0 0-2	2-1 1-0	0-2
Dundee Utd	3-2	1-5	1-1 2-2	*	1-0 3-2	2-1 0-2	1-2 0-0	4-1 1-1	2-0	1-0 0-2	0-0	1-3 2-0 3-3
Dunfermline	2-2	1-4 0-0	2-0	1-1 2-0	*	2-1 0-0	0-0 1-1	2-1 2-3	2-2	1-0 3-0	1-0 2-1	2-0 2-3
Hearts	1-0 2-0	0-1 1-1	3-1 2-2	3-1 3-0	1-0 2-1	*	2-0	2-1	1-1 3-1	0-0 3-2	2-0	1-1 0-4
Hibernian	0-1 1-1	1-2 0-4	1-1 1-0	2-2	1-2	0-1 0-1	*	3-0 3-1	0-2 2-0	0-2 3-3	3-2 1-2	0-1
Kilmarnock	3-1 1-3 4-0	0-5 0-1	4-2 1-1	0-2	1-1	0-2 1-1	0-2 2-0	*	3-1 0-2	2-0	2-4 2-0	2-3
Livingston	1-1 2-0	0-2	1-1	0-0 2-3	0-0 0-0	2-3	1-0 4-1	1-2 1-1	*	0-3 4-2	2-0 2-2	0-0 1-1
Motherwell	1-0	0-2 1-1	5-3 0-3	3-1 0-1	2-2 1-0	1-1 1-0	0-1	1-0 2-1	0-3 4-2	*	3-0 2-2	1-1 0-1
Partick	0-3 2-0	1-2 1-4	1-2 0-1	1-1 0-2	4-1	1-4 1-0	1-1 0-1	2-4 2-0	1-1 5-2	3-1 1-0	*	0-1
Rangers	3-0	0-1 1-2	4-0 3-1	2-1	4-0 4-1	2-1 0-1	3-0 5-2	2-0 4-0	1-0	1-0 4-0	2-0 3-1	*

SCOTTISH DIVISION ONE 2003-2004 RESULTS

	Ayr	Brechin	Clyde	Falkirk	Inv CT	Queen S	Raith	Ross C	St J'stone	St Mirren
Ayr	*	1-2 3-2	1-1 2-2	1-1 2-3	1-1 0-3	1-1 1-4	1-0 1-0	1-3 1-2	1-1 1-1	0-2 2-0
Brechin	3-1 0-3	*	1-3 2-5	2-2 0-1	2-4 0-2	0-1 2-1	0-3 1-1	1-0 4-2	0-2 0-1	2-0 1-1
Clyde	2-1 3-0	0-0 2-1	*	4-2 1-2	1-2 1-0	3-1 2-0	0-0 4-1	2-2 1-0	2-0 2-3	2-2 2-0
Falkirk	0-1 0-0	3-0 5-0	0-2 1-1	*	2-1 2-1	0-2 0-0	1-0 3-2	2-0 0-2	0-3 0-1	0-0 1-0
Inv CT	2-1 1-0	5-0 1-0	0-0 3-1	2-1 1-2	*	2-1 4-1	2-1 3-0	1-0 3-3	1-0 3-1	1-1 2-0
Queen of Sth	0-0 1-0	1-0 2-2	4-1 1-2	2-0 1-0	3-2 2-1	*	1-1 0-2	1-0 1-1	1-1 1-1	1-0 1-2
Raith	2-1 1-1	2-1 1-1	0-1 0-3	2-0 0-1	1-3 0-1	0-1 3-1	*	1-7 0-0	1-4 1-1	1-0 2-0
Ross County	1-1 2-2	2-1 4-0	0-1 0-0	1-1 1-2	1-0 1-1	1-0 1-2	3-2 1-1	*	0-3 2-0	1-1 2-0
St Johnstone	1-1 3-0	2-2 3-1	1-3 3-0	0-4 2-1	3-2 1-2	2-2 4-1	5-2 0-1	1-1 1-1	*	1-0 2-0
St Mirren	3-2 4-1	3-3 0-0	2-3 2-1	0-0 1-1	0-4 0-0	3-1 1-2	1-1 2-1	1-1 2-0	1-1 1-1	*

SCOTTISH DIVISION TWO 2003-2004 RESULTS

	Airdrie Utd	Alloa	Arbroath	Berwick	Dumbarton	East Fife	Forfar	Hamilton	Morton	Stenhsmuir
Airdrie Utd	*	2-1 1-0	0-1 2-1	1-1 6-0	1-1 2-0	1-1 2-1	3-3 2-2	1-1 3-0	2-0 1-6	4-0 2-0
Alloa	1-4	*	4-0 2-2	4-2 2-3	3-0 1-2	1-1 2-0	4-0 1-1	1-3 1-1	3-3 0-1	1-0 2-2
Arbroath	0-4 1-1	2-1 3-1	*	1-2 1-0	0-3 2-1	0-0 0-1	0-1 0-0	0-2 2-2	2-2 0-4	2-1 1-1
Berwick	0-1 1-1	3-1 3-2	1-3 3-0	*	1-4 1-2	0-2 1-1	3-1 0-4	2-4 3-1	2-3 2-0	3-0 2-1
Dumbarton	1-2 2-0	3-1 1-0	1-0 1-1	4-1 1-1	*	3-1 1-0	1-1 2-1	2-0 0-3	1-0 3-0	0-1 4-0
East Fife	0-1 3-1	0-1 0-1	0-1 1-2	2-2 3-1	1-0 1-3	*	2-0 2-3	2-3 2-3	1-0 0-0	1-0 3-2
Forfar	1-1 1-3	1-1 2-0	1-2 2-2	1-5 0-2	1-0 3-1	1-0 0-1	*	0-4 4-3	2-1 2-3	1-0 2-0
Hamilton	0-1 2-1	3-4 0-1	2-2 2-0	2-0 2-2	2-1 2-0	1-0 2-2	1-2 2-1	*	6-1 1-2	1-1 2-0
Morton	3-1 1-1	2-1 2-2	6-4 1-0	1-3 2-1	3-2 2-2	1-1 2-1	1-1 1-1	2-2 1-1	*	1-4 5-2
Stenhsmuir	0-1 0-3	0-1 1-3	1-0 0-3	3-1 0-3	1-1 1-2	0-1 3-0	0-2 2-0	0-3 0-2	0-1 0-2	*

SCOTTISH DIVISION THREE 2003-2004 RESULTS

	Albion	C'beath	Elgin	E Stirling	Gretna	Montrose	Peterhead	Queens P	Stirling	Stranraer
Albion	*	2-4 1-2	1-2 1-2	5-1 5-1	1-2 1-3	3-0 0-1	2-0 3-3	3-1 3-1	3-5 0-3	1-1 1-4
Cowdenbeath	1-1 1-4	*	3-2 2-0	2-0 2-1	1-2 0-1	3-3 0-0	1-0 0-3	5-1 0-1	0-5 2-0	0-1 1-2
Elgin	1-2 1-5	0-4 0-0	*	3-0 3-1	1-1 3-3	2-1 2-3	1-0 2-3	1-3 2-2	0-2 0-1	0-0 1-3
E Stirling	3-4 1-8	0-1 1-1	2-1 3-1	*	2-4 0-1	1-4 1-1	0-3 1-3	1-2 2-4	0-3 2-4	1-4 1-2
Gretna	3-0 3-1	0-1 1-0	2-1 2-2	2-1 5-1	*	1-2 1-1	3-2 3-2	0-1 1-1	0-1 1-0	0-0 1-1
Montrose	3-1 1-0	1-1 1-3	4-3 3-3	1-0 5-1	2-0 1-4	*	2-1 0-1	1-1 0-0	1-4 2-3	1-4 2-4
Peterhead	2-1 5-0	0-0 0-1	5-1 3-1	6-0 2-0	2-1 2-0	1-2 0-0	*	4-1 1-1	0-0 2-2	2-0 1-2
Queens Park	1-1 0-1	1-2 0-0	4-0 5-2	3-0 1-0	1-1 0-1	1-1 1-1	1-0 0-2	*	1-4 0-2	0-2 0-4
Stirling	3-0 2-1	1-1 0-0	3-0 6-1	6-0 5-1	1-1 3-0	1-1 3-0	0-2 3-1	0-0 1-0	*	2-2 1-0
Stranraer	4-0 5-0	2-0 1-0	6-0 4-3	7-1 4-0	1-2 3-2	2-0 6-0	1-1 0-2	3-1 1-0	1-1 0-1	*

Hereford can reclaim their League status

CHESTER CITY reclaimed their Football League status, after a four season absence status, by just getting the better of luckless Hereford in a thrilling Nationwide League Conference last season.

Hereford, who missed out by a point, and finished 17 points clear of the third-placed team, went out in the play-offs, beaten 4-2 on penalties by Aldershot.

The other team to earn promotion to the Football League was Shrewsbury, who made a quick return following relegation in 2002/2003. Jimmy Quinn's side triumphed over the aforementioned Aldershot, also via penalties, in the play-off final.

Our fancies Telford, who had splashed the cash around pre-season and had been full-time for a couple of years, paid the price. Despite finishing 12th in the Conference, they went into administration and have been demoted to Unibond Division 1.

It was a sad day for Non-League football as a whole, except perhaps if you were a Northwich fan. But for Telford's demise, they would have been relegated to Conference North.

Leigh RMI and Farnborough are other sides who would normally have been relegated from the Conference but Margate have chosen to play in Conference South and Hucknall Town's ground did not pass Conference requirements, so both sides have been reprieved.

The fall from grace of Telford has not stopped other teams going full-time in the Conference, with both Accrington and Aldershot joining the professional ranks in time for the coming season.

The Non-League pyramid has also been altered with two divisions, Conference North and Conference South feeding into the Conference rather than the previous three.

Three teams will be promoted to the National Conference, with the Champions of North and South followed by one team via a series of play-offs, involving the second to fifth plaCed teams in both divisions.

As to who may emerge victorious in the respective divisions, it is hard to make predictions at this stage with so much more transfer activity sure to take place between now and the start of the season.

In the Conference, Carlisle currently head the betting but **Hereford** make more appeal. The gap between the Conference and Football League is narrowing all the time and, although Hereford have lost a few players, they have kept the majority of their squad together and have made a couple of useful signings, most notably Adam Stansfield from Yeovil.

Other sides who should be thereabouts include: Barnet, who finished fourth last year and have made a couple of decent acquisitions, notably Matt Hocking from Boston; Canvey Island, who ran away with the Ryman League in 2003/2004; Stevenage, who won the race to sign the very promising Jon Nurse from Sutton United; and Aldershot who have brought in a

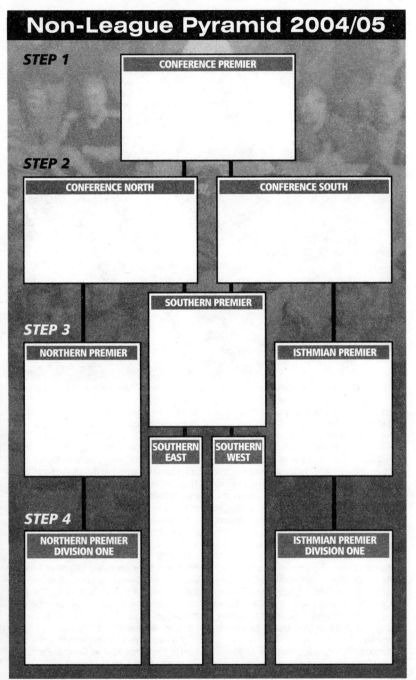

Non-League Pyramid 2004/05

STEP 1

CONFERENCE PREMIER

STEP 2

CONFERENCE NORTH

CONFERENCE SOUTH

SOUTHERN PREMIER

STEP 3

NORTHERN PREMIER

ISTHMIAN PREMIER

SOUTHERN EAST

SOUTHERN WEST

STEP 4

NORTHERN PREMIER DIVISION ONE

ISTHMIAN PREMIER DIVISION ONE

THE REAL DEAL: AFC Wimbledon's players and fans celebrate winning the 2003/04 CCL title

couple of useful players, particularly Nick Crittenden from Yeovil.

Probably the best non-league investment at this stage is **Hornchurch** to win Conference South. Gary Hill's side are a full-time outfit and they have certainly made some telling signings thus far in the close season. Mark Venus, Tarkan Mustafa, Ashley Bayes, Lee Elam and Simon Wormhull, amongst others, have all joined The Urchins in recent weeks, and they should step up considerably on last season's fifth placing, particularly as this league may not be that competitive.

Steve Claridge's Weymouth may prove the biggest dangers but last year's Ryman League runners-up Sutton United could struggle to repeat that performance, having lost three of their better players in the close season.

Hucknall Town, who won the Unibond League last season, have lost their manager and a number of players in the close season, including goalkeeper Paul Pettinger to rivals Harrogate. In the circumstances, **Southport** may prove a better bet.

The Sandgrounders finished sixth in 2003/2004 but they had a lot of new players to integrate at the start of last term. They have managed to keep most of their squad together and they can bear the fruits of that policy this season.

Finally, it is worth keeping an eye on the progress of **AFC Wimbledon** who start this season in Isthmian League Division One.

Having completed a League and Cup double in the Combined Counties League last season, it would be no surprise to see them continue their progress up the football pyramid, especially with experienced manager Dave Anderson, who was at Hendon last season, at the helm.

Their success last year was in direct contrast to the Milton Keynes Dons or Franchise FC or whatever they are called, and I'm sure many football fans hope it remains that way.

Sponsored by Stan James

FINAL BRITISH DRAWS CHART 2003-2004

X = Score draw
O = 0-0 draw
V = Void match
* = Pools panel

Pools No	Aug 9	Aug 16	Aug 23	Aug 30	Sep 6	Sep 13	Sep 20	Sep 27	Oct 4	Oct 11	Oct 18	Oct 25	Nov 1	Nov 8	Nov 15	Nov 22	Nov 29	Dec 6	Dec 13	Dec 20	Dec 27	Jan 3	Jan 10	Jan 17	Jan 24	Jan 31	Feb 7	Feb 14	Feb 21	Feb 28	Mar 6	Mar 13	Mar 20	Mar 27	Apr 3	Apr 10	Apr 17	Apr 24	May 1	May 8	O	X
1	X	X	-	-	-	-	-	-	-	-	-	-	-	-	-	-	-	-	-	-	-	-	-	-*	-	X	-	-	-	X*	-	-	-	-	-	V	-	*	-	X	2	4
2	-	-	X	-	*	-	X	-	-	-	O	-	X	-	O	O	-	X	X	X	X	X	-	-	-	-	X	X	-	X*	-	-	O	X	-	-*	-*	*	-	-	3	4
3	-	-	-	X	-	-	-	-	-	O	-	-	O	-	-	-	-	-	-	O	X	-	-	X	X	-	-	-	X	X	-	-	X	-	-	X	-	X	-	-	1	8
4	X	X	X	-	*	-	-	-	X	X	-	-	-	X	X	X	-	X	-	O	-	-	-	X	X*	-	O	-	X	-	O	-	-	X	O	O	X	-	X	-	4	10
5	-	-*	O	-	-*	-	-*	-	-	-	-	-	-	-	-	X	-	O	-	X	-	-	*	*	-*	O	-	O	X	O	*	-	-	X	-	X*	-	X	-	-	5	6
6	O	X	-	O	-	-	-	X	-	-	-	-	X	X	X	O	-	-	X	-	-	X	-	-	*	O	O	-	-	*	O	-	-	O	-	X*	-	-	-	-	6	4
7	O	-	-	-	-*	-	X*	-	-	-	-	X	X	X	O	X	-	X	-	O	X	O	O	*	*	O	-	X	-	-	-	-	-	X	X*	-	-	-	X	-	5	5
8	-	-	-	O	-	-	-	-	-	-	X	-	X	X	X	X	-	O	-	-	X	-	O	*	*	O	-	-	*,	-	-	-	-	-	-	-	X	-	-	-	2	6
9	-	O	-	-*	-	X*	-	-	-	-	-	-	-	-	O	X	X	O	O	-	-	X	-	-	-	-	-	-	-	*	O	-	X	X	-	X	-	-	X	-	2	9
10	-	-	-	X*	-	-*	X	-	-	-	X	-	X	X	X	X	X	X	O	-	-	-	X	-	-	-	-	X	-	-	-	-	-	-	-	O	-	-	-	X	1	4
11	-	O	X	O	X	O	-	X	-	-	-	X	-	-	-	O	-	O	-	-	X	-	-	X	-	-	X	X	-	-	-	-	X	X	X	-	-	X	X	-	3	8
12	O	-	X	-	-	-	-	-	-	O	-	X	-	-	-	O	-	-	-	-	X	O	O	-	-	-	-	-	X	-	-	O	O	-	-	-	O	-	-	-	4	7
13	-	-	-	-	X	-	X	-	X	-	X	-	X	-	X	-	X	X	-	X	X	-	O	-	-	-	X	-	X	-	O	O	-	-	-	-	X	-	-	-	3	5
14	-	-	-	O	X*	-	X	-	-	O	-	-	-	-	O	O	-	-	-	-	X	X	O	-	X	O	-	-	*,	-	-	-	X	X	X	X	-	X	-	-	1	7
15	X	X	X	-	X*	X	-	X	X	-	X	X	X	X	X	X	X	X	X	-	X	X	X	X	-	O	X	X	X	-	-	-	X	-	-	X	X	-	X	-	4	9
16	X	X	X	X*	X	X	X	-	X	O	O	X	O	O	O	X	X	X	X	-	-	X	-	-	-	-	X	X	-	-	-	-	X	X	-	O	O	X	X	X	3	10
17	-	-	-	X	O	O	-	-	O	X	O	X	-	O	O	O	X	-	O	O	-	X	O	-	X	-	X	X	-	-	-	O	-	-	-	-	X	-	-	-	5	9
18	-	-	X	-	X*	-	X	-	X	O	-	X	-	-	-	O	-	X	X	X	X	X	-	-	-	-	-	X	-	-	X	O	-	-	X	X	X	-	-	X	1	9
19	-	-	-	X	-	O	-	O	-	X	X	X	-	X	-	-	X	X	O	O	-	X	-	-	-	X	X	X	X	-	X	X*	X	X	-	X	X	-	-	X	7	9
20	-	X	X	-	-	-	X	-	X	-	X	X	-	-	-	-	-	X	O	-	X	X	X	-	-	X	-	X	-	-	O	-	-	X	-	-	X	-	X	X	2	8

Sponsored by Stan James

How to read the results

Alongside each fixture are the results for the corresponding league match over the last six seasons. The most recent result (ie 2003/04) is on the right. The final figure on each fixture line is, from left to right the number of home wins draws and away wins between the two sides dating back to 1988/89.

Where Scottish clubs have met more than once in the same season each result is divided by an oblique stroke, the most recent of the matches appearing to the right.

Please note that SKY television coverage and weather conditions will cause alterations to the fixture list.

The Scottish Premier League will also spilt into top and bottom six sections later in the season. These fixtures cover the period until that split.

SATURDAY 7 AUGUST 2004

COCA-COLA CHAMPIONSHIP

Home		Away							Record
Burnley	v	Sheff Utd	-	-	2-0	2-0	0-1	3-2	04-00-01
Coventry	v	Sunderland	-	3-2	1-0	-	-	1-1	02-03-00
Crewe	v	Cardiff	-	-	-	-	1-1	0-1	01-04-01
Ipswich	v	Gillingham	-	-	-	-	0-1	3-4	00-00-02
Leeds	v	Derby	4-1	0-0	0-0	3-0	-	-	04-03-00
Leicester	v	West Ham	0-0	1-3	2-1	1-1	-	-	03-02-05
Plymouth	v	Millwall	-	-	-	-	-	-	03-01-00
Preston	v	Watford	-	-	3-2	1-1	1-1	2-1	03-03-00
QPR	v	Rotherham	-	-	-	-	-	-	00-00-00
Reading	v	Brighton	-	-	-	0-0	1-2	-	02-01-01
Wigan	v	Nottm F	-	-	-	-	-	2-2	00-01-00

COCA-COLA LEAGUE DIVISION ONE

Home		Away							Record
Bristol C	v	Torquay	-	-	-	-	-	-	00-00-00
Chesterfield	v	Brentford	-	1-0	-	0-1	0-2	1-2	01-03-04
Doncaster	v	Blackpool	-	-	-	-	-	-	01-00-01
Hartlepool	v	Bradford	-	-	-	-	-	-	02-00-01
Hull	v	Bournemouth	-	-	-	-	3-1	-	04-02-02
Luton	v	Oldham	2-0	1-1	0-0	-	0-0	1-1	03-06-00
Milton K	v	Barnsley	-	-	1-1	0-1	-	-	01-01-01
Peterboro	v	Tranmere	-	-	-	5-0	0-0	0-0	01-05-00
Sheff Wed	v	Colchester	-	-	-	-	-	0-1	00-00-01
Stockport	v	Huddersfield	1-1	1-1	0-0	-	2-1	-	04-04-01
Walsall	v	Port Vale	-	0-0	2-1	-	-	-	01-01-00
Wrexham	v	Swindon	-	-	1-1	2-2	-	3-2	02-02-00

COCA-COLA LEAGUE DIVISION TWO

Boston	v	Oxford Utd	-	-	-	-	1-3	1-1	00-01-01
Bury	v	Yeovil	-	-	-	-	-	2-1	01-00-00
Darlington	v	Grimsby	-	-	-	-	-	-	00-01-00
Leyton O	v	Macclesfield	-	0-0	2-1	2-0	3-2	2-0	04-02-00
Mansfield	v	Bristol R	-	-	-	2-0	-	0-0	02-01-01
Notts Co	v	Chester	-	-	-	-	-	-	00-02-01
Rushden & D	v	Kidderminstr	1-1	5-3	-	0-2	3-1	-	03-02-01
Scunthorpe	v	Rochdale	0-1	-	0-0	2-1	3-1	2-2	09-03-03
Shrewsbury	v	Lincoln	-	1-2	3-2	1-1	1-2	-	02-01-04
Southend	v	Cheltenham	-	2-1	0-1	0-1	-	2-0	02-00-02
Swansea	v	Northampton	-	4-1	1-1	-	-	0-2	03-02-01
Wycombe	v	Cambridge U	-	1-0	0-2	2-0	-	-	03-00-01

BANK OF SCOTLAND SCOTTISH PREMIER LEAGUE

Aberdeen	v	Rangers	1-1/2-4	1-5/1-1	1-2	0-3/0-1	2-2	2-3/1-1	07-10-14
Celtic	v	Motherwell	2-0/1-0	0-1/4-0	1-0/1-0	2-0	3-1	3-0/1-1	16-08-06
Dundee	v	Hearts	1-0/2-0	1-0/0-0	1-1/0-0	1-1	1-1/1-2	1-2	06-07-05
Dunfermline	v	Dundee Utd	2-1/2-2	-	1-0/3-1	1-1	4-1	2-0/1-1	08-04-04
Hibernian	v	Kilmarnock	-	0-3/2-2	1-1/1-1	2-2/2-2	2-0	3-1/3-0	07-08-04
Livingston	v	Inv CT	2-1/4-3	2-2/1-1	3-1/4-1	-	-	-	04-04-02

BELL'S SCOTTISH FIRST DIVISION

Airdrie Utd	v	St Johnstone	-	-	-	-	-	-	01-05-07
Clyde	v	Partick	1-2/0-1	2-0/1-0	-	3-1/2-1	-	-	06-02-03
Hamilton	v	Raith	3-2/1-2	-	-	-	0-4/0-0	-	05-05-05
Queen Sth	v	Ross C	-	0-2/0-3	-	-	2-0/1-0	1-0/1-1	03-01-02
St Mirren	v	Falkirk	0-2/0-3	2-1/1-0	-	1-5/0-0	4-4/1-2	0-0/1-1	05-05-08

BELL'S SCOTTISH SECOND DIVISION

Berwick	v	Morton	-	-	-	2-0/0-0	-	2-3/2-0	03-01-02
Dumbarton	v	Ayr	-	-	-	-	-	-	01-03-02
Forfar	v	Brechin	-	0-0/2-0	-	-	2-1/1-5	-	04-02-03
Stirling	v	Arbroath	0-1/2-1	3-4/1-1	0-0/1-1	-	-	-	03-04-03
Stranraer	v	Alloa	-	0-0/2-2	-	1-1/0-2	-	-	02-07-03

BELL'S SCOTTISH THIRD DIVISION

East Fife	v	Montrose	-	0-0/2-0	3-1/1-0	1-2/2-0	2-0/2-0	-	10-04-04
Gretna	v	Albion	-	-	-	-	2-0/1-2	3-1/3-0	03-00-01
Peterhead	v	E Stirling	-	-	2-4/1-2	3-2/2-1	5-0/6-0	2-0/6-0	06-00-02
Queens P	v	C'denbeath	2-0/2-1	1-0/3-1	-	-	-	0-0/1-2	11-03-07
Stenhsmuir	v	Elgin	-	-	-	-	-	-	00-00-00

SUNDAY 8 AUGUST 2004
COCA-COLA CHAMPIONSHIP

Stoke	v	Wolves	-	-	-	-	0-2	-	04-02-01

MONDAY 9 AUGUST 2004
COCA-COLA CHAMPIONSHIP

Watford	v	QPR	2-1	-	3-1	-	-	-	02-00-00

TUESDAY 10 AUGUST 2004
COCA-COLA CHAMPIONSHIP

Brighton	v	Plymouth	1-3	1-1	2-0	-	-	2-1	07-03-01
Cardiff	v	Coventry	-	-	-	-	-	0-1	00-00-01
Gillingham	v	Leeds	-	-	-	-	-	-	00-00-00
Millwall	v	Wigan	3-1	3-3	3-1	-	-	2-0	03-02-00
Rotherham	v	Burnley	-	-	-	1-1	0-0	3-0	06-02-01
Sheff Utd	v	Stoke	-	-	-	-	2-1	0-1	04-02-01
Sunderland	v	Crewe	2-0	-	-	-	-	1-1	02-01-00
West Ham	v	Reading	-	-	-	-	-	1-0	01-00-00

COCA-COLA LEAGUE DIVISION ONE

Barnsley	v	Bristol C	2-0	-	-	-	1-4	0-1	04-01-03
Blackpool	v	Sheff Wed	-	-	-	-	-	4-1	01-00-00
Bournemouth	v	Walsall	0-1	-	2-2	-	-	-	02-02-02
Bradford	v	Peterboro	-	-	-	-	-	-	03-00-00
Brentford	v	Doncaster	-	-	-	-	-	-	00-00-00
Colchester	v	Stockport	-	-	-	-	1-0	2-1	02-01-01
Huddersfield	v	Chesterfield	-	-	-	0-0	4-0	-	01-02-00
Oldham	v	Wrexham	3-2	0-0	5-1	3-1	-	1-1	04-02-00
Port Vale	v	Milton K	-	-	-	-	-	-	00-00-00
Torquay	v	Hull	2-0	0-1	1-1	1-1	1-4	1-1	03-04-02
Tranmere	v	Hartlepool	-	-	-	-	-	0-0	01-01-00

COCA-COLA LEAGUE DIVISION TWO

Bristol R	v	Bury	-	0-0	2-0	-	2-1	1-2	04-01-02
Cambridge U	v	Leyton O	1-0	-	-	-	2-1	1-4	07-02-01
Cheltenham	v	Scunthorpe	-	-	1-0	3-3	-	2-1	02-01-00
Chester	v	Wycombe	-	-	-	-	-	-	01-00-01
Grimsby	v	Boston	-	-	-	-	-	-	00-00-00
Kidderminstr	v	Notts Co	-	-	-	-	-	-	00-00-00
Lincoln	v	Southend	-	1-0	3-0	0-1	2-1	2-2	04-01-01
Macclesfield	v	Shrewsbury	-	4-2	2-1	2-1	1-2	-	04-00-01
Northampton	v	Rushden & D	-	-	-	-	-	-	00-00-00
Rochdale	v	Swansea	0-3	0-0	-	2-0	1-2	0-1	02-01-04
Yeovil	v	Darlington	-	-	-	-	-	1-0	01-00-01

WEDNESDAY 11 AUGUST 2004
COCA-COLA CHAMPIONSHIP

Derby	v	Leicester	2-0	3-0	2-0	2-3	1-1	-	06-01-04
Nottm F	v	Ipswich	-	0-1	-	-	2-1	1-1	03-01-02
Wolves	v	Preston	-	-	0-1	2-3	4-0	-	02-00-02

COCA-COLA LEAGUE DIVISION ONE

Swindon	v	Luton	-	-	1-3	-	2-1	2-2	02-01-02

COCA-COLA LEAGUE DIVISION TWO

Oxford Utd	v	Mansfield	-	-	-	3-2	-	1-1	01-01-00

FRIDAY 13 AUGUST 2004
COCA-COLA CHAMPIONSHIP

Cardiff	v	Plymouth	1-0	-	4-1	-	1-1	-	02-01-03

SATURDAY 14 AUGUST 2004
FA BARCLAYCARD PREMIER LEAGUE

Aston Villa	v	Southampton	3-0	0-1	0-0	2-1	0-1	1-0	07-05-04
Blackburn	v	WBA	-	2-1	1-0	-	1-1	-	03-01-02
Bolton	v	Charlton	-	0-2	-	0-0	1-2	0-0	03-02-02
Man City	v	Fulham	3-0	4-0	-	-	4-1	0-0	03-01-00
Middlesbro	v	Newcastle	2-2	2-2	1-3	1-4	1-0	0-1	04-03-05
Norwich	v	Crystal Pal	0-1	0-1	0-0	2-1	2-0	2-1	06-04-03
Portsmouth	v	Birmingham	0-1	2-2	1-1	1-1	-	3-1	03-05-03
Tottenham	v	Liverpool	2-1	1-0	2-1	1-0	2-3	2-1	07-03-06

COCA-COLA CHAMPIONSHIP

Brighton	v	Coventry	-	-	-	-	0-0	-	00-01-00
Derby	v	Ipswich	-	-	1-1	1-3	1-4	2-2	01-03-02
Gillingham	v	Preston	1-1	0-2	4-0	5-0	1-1	0-1	02-06-04
Millwall	v	Leicester	-	-	-	-	2-2	-	03-03-00
Nottm F	v	Crewe	-	1-0	1-0	2-2	-	2-0	04-01-00
Rotherham	v	Stoke	-	-	2-1	-	4-0	3-0	03-01-01

Sponsored by Stan James

Sheff Utd	v	Reading	-	-	-	-	1-3	1-2	03-02-02
Sunderland	v	QPR	1-0	-	-	-	-	-	01-01-01
Watford	v	Burnley	-	-	0-1	1-2	2-1	1-1	03-02-02
West Ham	v	Wigan	-	-	-	-	-	4-0	01-00-00
Wolves	v	Leeds	-	-	-	-	-	3-1	02-00-00

COCA-COLA LEAGUE DIVISION ONE

Barnsley	v	Luton	-	-	-	-	2-3	0-0	04-01-01
Blackpool	v	Stockport	-	-	-	-	1-3	1-1	04-01-03
Bournemouth	v	Bristol C	-	2-3	4-0	1-3	-	0-0	02-02-03
Bradford	v	Doncaster	-	-	-	-	-	-	00-00-00
Brentford	v	Wrexham	-	0-2	1-0	3-0	-	0-1	05-01-03
Colchester	v	Peterboro	-	-	2-2	2-1	1-1	0-0	02-03-02
Oldham	v	Walsall	0-2	-	0-0	-	-	-	01-02-01
Port Vale	v	Hull	-	-	-	-	-	-	01-03-00
Swindon	v	Milton K	-	-	-	-	-	-	00-00-01
Torquay	v	Sheff Wed	-	-	-	-	-	-	00-00-00
Tranmere	v	Chesterfield	-	-	-	0-0	2-1	2-3	01-01-01

COCA-COLA LEAGUE DIVISION TWO

Bristol R	v	Notts Co	1-1	0-1	0-0	-	-	-	03-04-02
Cambridge U	v	Shrewsbury	0-0	-	-	-	5-0	-	04-01-00
Cheltenham	v	Leyton O	-	2-0	1-1	1-1	-	1-0	02-02-00
Chester	v	Mansfield	1-1	5-0	-	-	-	-	04-03-03
Grimsby	v	Bury	0-0	-	-	-	-	-	00-01-01
Kidderminstr	v	Darlington	-	-	0-0	1-0	1-1	1-1	02-03-00
Lincoln	v	Rushden & D	-	-	-	2-4	1-2	-	00-00-02
Macclesfield	v	Swansea	-	1-2	-	1-3	1-3	2-1	02-00-03
Northampton	v	Wycombe	1-1	-	2-2	4-1	0-5	-	02-03-01
Oxford Utd	v	Scunthorpe	-	2-0	-	0-1	0-1	3-2	02-00-02
Rochdale	v	Southend	1-0	2-0	0-1	0-1	1-2	1-1	02-01-04
Yeovil	v	Boston	-	-	2-1	0-1	-	2-0	04-03-01

BANK OF SCOTLAND SCOTTISH PREMIER LEAGUE

Dundee Utd	v	Dundee	0-1/0-2	2-1/1-0	0-2	2-2/1-0	0-0/1-1	1-1/2-2	09-07-06
Hearts	v	Aberdeen	2-0/0-2	3-0/3-0	3-0	1-0/3-1	0-0	2-0/1-0	16-06-08
Kilmarnock	v	Celtic	2-0/0-0	0-1/1-1	0-1/1-0	0-1/0-2	1-1/0-4	0-5/0-1	04-08-10
Motherwell	v	Hibernian	-	2-2/2-0	1-3	1-3/4-0	0-2/2-1	0-1	09-11-08
Rangers	v	Livingston	-	-	-	0-0/3-0	4-3	1-0	03-01-00

BELL'S SCOTTISH FIRST DIVISION

Falkirk	v	Hamilton	2-1/6-1	-	-	-	-	-	05-02-02
Partick	v	Airdrie Utd	-	-	-	1-1/1-1	-	-	04-05-04
Raith	v	Clyde	-	-	1-2/0-1	1-2/0-1	-	0-1/0-3	02-02-07
Ross C	v	St Mirren	-	-	-	0-1/4-1	4-0/2-0	2-0/1-0	05-00-01
St Johnstone	v	Queen Sth	-	-	-	-	2-2/0-1	4-1/2-2	03-02-01

BELL'S SCOTTISH SECOND DIVISION

Alloa	v	Forfar	1-2/3-1	-	-	1-2/2-1	-	1-1/4-0	03-03-08
Arbroath	v	Dumbarton	-	-	-	-	-	2-1/0-3	05-02-03
Ayr	v	Berwick	-	-	-	-	-	-	03-00-01
Brechin	v	Stirling	-	-	-	3-1/2-1	-	-	05-00-04
Morton	v	Stranraer	3-0/1-0	-	-	1-1/2-2	-	-	02-02-00

BELL'S SCOTTISH THIRD DIVISION

Albion	v	East Fife	-	1-3/3-1	0-1/1-2	3-0/2-1	1-5/0-0	-	06-02-08
C'denbeath	v	Stenhsmuir	0-2/0-2	-	-	1-1/2-4	1-0/3-3	-	04-05-05
E Stirling	v	Gretna	-	-	-	-	0-4/1-2	0-1/2-4	00-00-04
Elgin	v	Queens P	-	-	-	2-0/0-1	2-2/0-0	2-2/1-3	01-03-02
Montrose	v	Peterhead	-	-	0-2/2-2	0-3/2-1	0-3/1-2	0-1/2-1	02-01-05

Accrington	v	Burton	-	-	-	3-3	-	3-1	01-01-00
Aldershot	v	York	-	-	-	-	-	-	00-00-00
Barnet	v	Forest G	-	-	-	0-1	2-0	5-0	02-00-01
Carlisle	v	Canvey Islnd	-	-	-	-	-	-	00-00-00
Dagenham	v	Stevenage	-	-	3-0	1-0	3-2	1-2	03-00-03
Exeter	v	Morecambe	-	-	-	-	-	4-0	01-00-00
Gravesend	v	Northwich	-	-	-	-	1-1	2-2	00-02-00
Hereford	v	Farnborough	2-0	-	-	4-2	2-1	2-0	05-00-00
Leigh RMI	v	Crawley	-	-	-	-	-	-	00-00-00
Scarborough	v	Woking	-	3-2	3-2	1-0	1-1	2-2	03-02-00
Tamworth	v	Halifax	-	-	-	-	-	2-0	01-00-00

SUNDAY 15 AUGUST 2004
FA BARCLAYCARD PREMIER LEAGUE

Chelsea	v	Man Utd	0-0	5-0	1-1	0-3	2-2	1-0	05-05-05
Everton	v	Arsenal	0-2	0-1	2-0	0-1	2-1	1-1	04-06-06

BANK OF SCOTLAND SCOTTISH PREMIER LEAGUE

Inv CT	v	Dunfermline	-	1-1/1-2	-	-	-	-	00-01-01

MONDAY 16 AUGUST 2004
COCA-COLA LEAGUE DIVISION ONE

Huddersfield	v	Hartlepool	-	-	-	-	-	-	02-01-00

TUESDAY 17 AUGUST 2004
NATIONWIDE CONFERENCE

Burton	v	Leigh RMI	-	-	-	-	0-1	3-2	01-00-01
Canvey Islnd	v	Gravesend	-	4-1	1-1	0-2	-	-	01-01-01
Crawley	v	Hereford	-	-	-	-	-	-	00-00-00
Farnborough	v	Barnet	-	-	-	2-1	2-2	1-1	01-02-01
Forest G	v	Dagenham	-	-	4-4	2-4	5-2	1-3	01-01-02
Halifax	v	Scarborough	1-2	-	-	-	2-1	1-0	03-00-05
Morecambe	v	Accrington	-	-	-	-	-	1-0	05-00-00
Northwich	v	Carlisle	-	-	-	-	-	-	00-00-00
Stevenage	v	Aldershot	-	-	-	-	-	0-1	00-00-01
Woking	v	Exeter	-	-	-	-	-	1-0	01-00-00
York	v	Tamworth	-	-	-	-	-	-	00-00-00

FRIDAY 20 AUGUST 2004
COCA-COLA CHAMPIONSHIP

Preston	v	Sheff Utd	-	-	3-0	3-0	2-0	3-3	04-01-00

SATURDAY 21 AUGUST 2004
FA BARCLAYCARD PREMIER LEAGUE

Birmingham	v	Chelsea	-	-	-	-	1-3	0-0	00-01-02
Charlton	v	Portsmouth	-	1-1	-	-	-	1-1	07-02-01
Crystal Pal	v	Everton	-	-	-	-	-	-	03-01-02
Fulham	v	Bolton	-	1-1	1-1	3-0	4-1	2-1	03-05-02
Liverpool	v	Man City	-	-	3-2	-	1-2	2-1	06-03-01
Man Utd	v	Norwich	-	-	-	-	-	-	04-01-02
Newcastle	v	Tottenham	1-1	2-1	2-0	0-2	2-1	4-0	06-04-02
Southampton	v	Blackburn	3-3	-	-	1-2	1-1	2-0	05-04-01

COCA-COLA CHAMPIONSHIP

Burnley	v	Wolves	-	-	1-2	2-3	2-1	-	01-00-03
Coventry	v	Millwall	-	-	-	0-1	2-3	4-0	02-01-02
Crewe	v	West Ham	-	-	-	-	-	0-3	00-00-01
Ipswich	v	Cardiff	-	-	-	-	-	1-1	00-01-00

Leeds	v	Nottm F	3-1	-	-	-	-	-	05-00-02
Leicester	v	Watford	-	1-0	-	-	2-0	-	04-04-01
Plymouth	v	Sunderland	-	-	-	-	-	-	02-00-01
Preston	v	Sheff Utd	-	-	3-0	3-0	2-0	3-3	04-01-00
QPR	v	Derby	-	-	-	-	-	-	00-01-02
Reading	v	Rotherham	-	-	2-0	-	3-0	0-0	05-02-00
Stoke	v	Gillingham	0-0	1-1	-	-	0-0	0-0	00-04-00
Wigan	v	Brighton	-	-	-	3-0	-	-	02-00-01

COCA-COLA LEAGUE DIVISION ONE

Bristol C	v	Swindon	3-1	-	0-1	3-1	2-0	2-1	05-03-02
Chesterfield	v	Colchester	3-1	0-1	-	3-6	0-4	1-2	02-03-04
Doncaster	v	Tranmere	-	-	-	-	-	-	00-01-00
Hartlepool	v	Blackpool	-	-	3-1	-	-	1-1	03-01-01
Hull	v	Oldham	-	-	-	-	-	-	00-03-00
Luton	v	Torquay	-	-	-	5-1	-	-	01-00-00
Milton K	v	Bournemouth	-	-	-	-	-	-	00-00-00
Peterboro	v	Brentford	2-4	-	1-1	1-1	5-1	0-0	01-05-04
Sheff Wed	v	Huddersfield	-	-	2-3	-	-	-	00-00-01
Stockport	v	Bradford	1-2	-	-	1-0	-	-	03-01-04
Walsall	v	Barnsley	-	1-4	-	2-1	-	-	01-00-02
Wrexham	v	Port Vale	-	-	1-0	1-3	-	2-1	03-00-01

COCA-COLA LEAGUE DIVISION TWO

Boston	v	Macclesfield	-	-	-	-	2-1	3-1	05-01-01
Bury	v	Chester	-	-	-	-	-	-	03-02-01
Darlington	v	Bristol R	-	-	-	1-0	1-0	0-4	02-00-01
Leyton O	v	Oxford Utd	-	-	-	3-0	1-2	1-0	02-01-01
Mansfield	v	Kidderminstr	-	-	2-1	1-1	-	1-0	02-01-00
Notts Co	v	Yeovil	-	-	-	-	-	-	00-00-00
Rushden & D	v	Grimsby	-	-	-	-	-	3-1	01-00-00
Scunthorpe	v	Lincoln	-	-	2-1	1-1	0-0	1-3	05-05-04
Shrewsbury	v	Northampton	-	1-0	-	-	-	-	03-00-01
Southend	v	Cambridge U	0-1	-	-	-	2-1	1-0	02-04-01
Swansea	v	Cheltenham	-	0-0	-	2-2	-	0-0	00-03-00
Wycombe	v	Rochdale	-	-	-	-	-	-	00-01-00

BANK OF SCOTLAND SCOTTISH PREMIER LEAGUE

Dundee	v	Motherwell	1-0/1-0	0-1/4-1	1-2	3-1/2-0	1-1	0-1	08-03-06
Dunfermline	v	Aberdeen	1-1/1-2	-	0-0/3-2	1-0/0-0	3-0	2-2	04-09-05
Hearts	v	Kilmarnock	2-1/2-2	2-2/0-0	0-2/3-0	2-0	1-1/3-0	2-1	11-07-02
Inv CT	v	Celtic	-	-	-	-	-	-	00-00-00
Livingston	v	Dundee Utd	-	-	-	2-0/1-1	3-0/1-2	0-0/2-3	02-02-02
Rangers	v	Hibernian	-	2-0/5-2	1-0/4-0	2-2/1-1	2-1	5-2/3-0	23-04-02

BELL'S SCOTTISH FIRST DIVISION

Airdrie Utd	v	Raith	0-1/2-2	1-4/0-2	1-1/3-0	2-2/1-1	0-0/1-1	-	05-07-06
Clyde	v	Ross C	-	3-1/0-0	2-2/2-0	3-0/0-0	2-1/1-0	2-2/1-0	06-04-00
Hamilton	v	Partick	-	0-0/0-1	-	-	-	-	00-04-05
Queen Sth	v	Falkirk	-	-	-	-	1-1/2-1	2-0/1-0	03-01-01
St Mirren	v	St Johnstone	-	-	0-1/1-0	-	0-2/1-3	1-1/1-1	02-07-07

BELL'S SCOTTISH SECOND DIVISION

Berwick	v	Brechin	3-0/2-3	2-0/3-1	-	-	0-3/2-0	-	09-04-03
Dumbarton	v	Morton	-	-	-	-	-	1-0/3-0	07-00-03
Forfar	v	Arbroath	1-3/5-2	-	0-1/1-1	-	-	2-2/1-2	04-05-04
Stirling	v	Alloa	4-2/1-1	0-1/1-1	-	-	-	-	03-02-02
Stranraer	v	Ayr	0-1/0-2	-	-	-	-	-	03-01-04

BELL'S SCOTTISH THIRD DIVISION

East Fife	v	C'denbeath	-	2-3/1-1	0-2/1-2	-	-	-	04-03-04
Gretna	v	Montrose	-	-	-	-	4-1/2-2	1-1/1-2	01-02-01

Peterhead	v	Elgin	-	-	1-0/1-1	1-1/1-0	2-2/3-2	5-1/3-1	05-03-00
Queens P	v	Albion	0-0/0-0	2-0/0-1	-	1-2/0-3	2-4/1-1	1-1/0-1	08-12-06
Stenhsmuir	v	E Stirling	1-0/2-2	-	-	-	-	-	07-03-01

NATIONWIDE CONFERENCE

Burton	v	Dagenham	-	-	-	-	0-0	0-0	00-02-00
Canvey Islnd	v	Tamworth	-	-	-	-	-	-	00-00-00
Crawley	v	Aldershot	-	-	-	-	-	-	00-00-00
Farnborough	v	Scarborough	-	-	-	4-2	1-1	1-2	01-01-01
Forest G	v	Carlisle	-	-	-	-	-	-	00-00-00
Halifax	v	Barnet	1-1	1-2	3-0	-	2-4	1-2	02-01-04
Morecambe	v	Gravesend	-	-	-	-	2-0	2-2	01-01-00
Northwich	v	Exeter	-	-	-	-	-	1-1	00-01-00
Stevenage	v	Accrington	-	-	-	-	-	2-1	01-00-00
Woking	v	Leigh RMI	-	-	1-1	1-1	3-0	2-0	02-02-00
York	v	Hereford	-	-	-	-	-	-	04-00-01

SUNDAY 22 AUGUST 2004
FA BARCLAYCARD PREMIER LEAGUE

Arsenal	v	Middlesbro	1-1	5-1	0-3	2-1	2-0	4-1	06-03-01
WBA	v	Aston Villa	-	-	-	-	0-0	-	00-01-00

TUESDAY 24 AUGUST 2004
FA BARCLAYCARD PREMIER LEAGUE

Arsenal	v	Blackburn	1-0	-	-	3-3	1-2	1-0	03-04-03
Birmingham	v	Man City	-	0-1	-	1-2	0-2	2-1	03-00-04
Charlton	v	Aston Villa	0-1	-	3-3	1-2	3-0	1-2	01-02-04
Crystal Pal	v	Chelsea	-	-	-	-	-	-	01-04-02
WBA	v	Tottenham	-	-	-	-	2-3	-	00-00-01

WEDNESDAY 25 AUGUST 2004
FA BARCLAYCARD PREMIER LEAGUE

Fulham	v	Middlesbro	-	-	-	2-1	1-0	3-2	03-00-00
Liverpool	v	Portsmouth	-	-	-	-	-	3-0	01-00-00
Man Utd	v	Everton	3-1	5-1	1-0	4-1	3-0	3-2	11-02-03
Newcastle	v	Norwich	-	-	-	-	-	-	02-00-01
Southampton	v	Bolton	-	-	-	0-0	0-0	1-2	01-02-02

FRIDAY 27 AUGUST 2004
COCA-COLA CHAMPIONSHIP

Gillingham	v	QPR	-	-	0-1	-	-	-	00-00-01

COCA-COLA LEAGUE DIVISION ONE

Tranmere	v	Sheff Wed	-	-	2-0	-	-	2-2	01-01-00

COCA-COLA LEAGUE DIVISION TWO

Bristol R	v	Southend	-	-	-	2-1	0-1	1-1	03-02-02

SATURDAY 28 AUGUST 2004
FA BARCLAYCARD PREMIER LEAGUE

Aston Villa	v	Newcastle	1-0	0-1	1-1	1-1	0-1	0-0	02-05-05
Blackburn	v	Man Utd	0-0	-	-	2-2	1-0	1-0	03-03-04
Chelsea	v	Southampton	1-0	1-1	1-0	2-4	0-0	4-0	07-05-03
Everton	v	WBA	-	-	-	-	1-0	-	01-00-00
Man City	v	Charlton	-	1-1	1-4	-	0-1	1-1	01-03-03
Middlesbro	v	Crystal Pal	-	-	-	-	-	-	00-00-02
Norwich	v	Arsenal	-	-	-	-	-	-	00-06-01
Tottenham	v	Birmingham	-	-	-	-	2-1	4-1	02-00-00

COCA-COLA CHAMPIONSHIP

Home		Away							Record
Brighton	v	Preston	-	-	-	-	0-2	-	01-00-01
Cardiff	v	Stoke	-	1-2	-	2-0	-	3-1	02-00-01
Derby	v	Crewe	-	-	-	-	-	0-0	00-01-00
Millwall	v	Reading	1-1	5-0	2-0	-	0-2	0-1	03-02-02
Nottm F	v	Coventry	1-0	-	-	2-1	1-1	0-1	05-04-03
Rotherham	v	Ipswich	-	-	-	-	2-1	1-3	01-00-01
Sheff Utd	v	Leeds	-	-	-	-	-	-	01-02-02
Sunderland	v	Wigan	-	-	-	-	-	1-1	00-01-00
Watford	v	Plymouth	-	-	-	-	-	-	03-01-02
West Ham	v	Burnley	-	-	-	-	-	2-2	00-01-00
Wolves	v	Leicester	-	-	-	-	1-1	4-3	05-02-01

COCA-COLA LEAGUE DIVISION ONE

Home		Away							Record
Barnsley	v	Hull	-	-	-	-	-	-	01-01-01
Blackpool	v	Luton	1-0	3-3	-	-	5-2	0-1	03-02-01
Bournemouth	v	Wrexham	0-0	1-0	1-2	3-0	2-0	6-0	05-02-04
Bradford	v	Chesterfield	-	-	-	-	-	-	01-00-00
Brentford	v	Stockport	-	-	-	-	1-2	0-2	03-02-02
Colchester	v	Doncaster	-	-	-	-	-	-	05-01-02
Huddersfield	v	Peterboro	-	-	-	3-1	0-1	-	01-01-02
Oldham	v	Milton K	-	-	-	-	-	-	01-01-01
Port Vale	v	Bristol C	3-2	-	1-2	1-0	2-3	2-1	05-01-03
Swindon	v	Hartlepool	-	-	-	-	-	1-1	00-01-00
Torquay	v	Walsall	-	-	-	-	-	-	01-01-02

COCA-COLA LEAGUE DIVISION TWO

Home		Away							Record
Cambridge U	v	Swansea	2-1	-	3-3	-	1-0	0-1	06-01-02
Cheltenham	v	Boston	-	-	-	-	-	1-0	03-02-00
Chester	v	Darlington	1-0	1-2	-	-	-	-	04-01-02
Grimsby	v	Mansfield	-	-	-	-	-	-	01-00-00
Kidderminstr	v	Wycombe	-	-	-	-	-	-	02-00-03
Lincoln	v	Notts Co	0-1	-	-	-	-	-	00-00-02
Macclesfield	v	Scunthorpe	-	-	0-1	4-3	2-3	2-2	02-01-02
Northampton	v	Leyton O	-	2-1	-	-	-	1-0	02-00-03
Oxford Utd	v	Shrewsbury	-	-	-	0-1	2-2	-	02-02-01
Rochdale	v	Bury	-	-	-	-	1-2	0-0	01-02-03
Yeovil	v	Rushden & D	0-1	5-1	0-0	-	-	-	01-01-02

BANK OF SCOTLAND SCOTTISH PREMIER LEAGUE

Home		Away							Record
Aberdeen	v	Livingston	-	-	-	0-3/3-0	0-0/1-0	0-3/1-2	02-01-03
Celtic	v	Rangers	5-1/0-3	1-1/0-1	6-2/1-0	2-1/1-1	3-3/1-0	3-0/1-0	12-07-13
Dundee Utd	v	Inv CT	-	-	-	-	-	-	00-00-00
Hibernian	v	Dundee	-	5-2/1-2	5-1/3-0	1-2/2-2	2-1	1-1/1-0	08-06-03
Motherwell	v	Hearts	3-2/0-4	2-1/0-2	2-0	2-0/1-2	6-1	1-1/1-1	08-08-14

BELL'S SCOTTISH FIRST DIVISION

Home		Away							Record
Falkirk	v	Airdrie Utd	0-1/1-1	2-0/8-0	0-2/1-1	1-2/2-2	-	-	08-07-07
Queen Sth	v	Clyde	2-1/2-1	1-1/3-0	-	-	2-1/1-1	4-1/1-2	09-04-07
Ross C	v	Partick	-	2-1/1-3	-	3-2/0-1	-	-	02-00-02
St Johnstone	v	Raith	-	-	-	-	-	0-1/5-2	04-02-03
St Mirren	v	Hamilton	3-2/1-0	-	-	-	-	-	08-01-05

BELL'S SCOTTISH SECOND DIVISION

Home		Away							Record
Arbroath	v	Stranraer	-	1-2/1-1	1-1/2-1	-	-	-	07-03-03
Ayr	v	Morton	1-0/1-0	3-0/3-2	1-1/3-0	-	-	-	11-04-04
Brechin	v	Alloa	-	-	-	-	-	-	04-00-04
Dumbarton	v	Forfar	-	3-3/0-0	-	-	1-2/1-2	2-1/1-1	01-03-02
Stirling	v	Berwick	-	-	1-1/1-0	-	-	-	08-02-00

Sponsored by Stan James

BELL'S SCOTTISH THIRD DIVISION

Albion	v	Peterhead	-	-	0-0/0-1	1-0/2-1	3-0/0-0	2-0/3-3	04-03-01
C'denbeath	v	E Stirling	2-1/3-2	1-2/0-0	3-0/1-3	-	-	2-1/2-0	14-03-06
East Fife	v	Stenhsmuir	-	-	-	-	-	3-2/1-0	09-03-05
Elgin	v	Montrose	-	-	1-1/0-2	1-2/1-0	0-0/0-2	2-3/2-1	02-02-04
Queens P	v	Gretna	-	-	-	-	1-0/1-2	0-1/1-1	01-01-02

NATIONWIDE CONFERENCE

Accrington	v	Crawley	-	-	-	-	-	-	00-00-00
Aldershot	v	Burton	-	-	-	-	-	3-1	01-00-00
Barnet	v	Northwich	-	-	-	1-0	3-4	1-0	04-01-01
Carlisle	v	Farnborough	-	-	-	-	-	-	00-00-00
Dagenham	v	Woking	-	-	1-2	3-1	1-1	1-0	03-02-03
Exeter	v	Canvey Islnd	-	-	-	-	-	-	00-00-00
Gravesend	v	York	-	-	-	-	-	-	00-00-00
Hereford	v	Stevenage	0-1	1-2	1-1	1-1	2-2	1-0	01-03-03
Leigh RMI	v	Halifax	-	-	-	-	0-2	1-1	00-01-01
Scarborough	v	Morecambe	-	0-2	2-2	0-2	1-0	1-0	02-01-02
Tamworth	v	Forest G	-	-	-	-	-	1-0	01-00-01

SUNDAY 29 AUGUST 2004
FA BARCLAYCARD PREMIER LEAGUE

Bolton	v	Liverpool	-	-	-	2-1	2-3	2-2	01-02-02

BANK OF SCOTLAND SCOTTISH PREMIER LEAGUE

Kilmarnock	v	Dunfermline	0-0/0-0	-	2-1/2-1	0-0	2-2/1-1	1-1	05-08-02

MONDAY 30 AUGUST 2004
FA BARCLAYCARD PREMIER LEAGUE

Portsmouth	v	Fulham	-	0-1	1-1	-	-	1-1	00-02-01

COCA-COLA CHAMPIONSHIP

Burnley	v	Gillingham	0-5	0-3	1-1	2-0	2-0	1-0	05-03-03
Coventry	v	West Ham	0-0	1-0	0-3	-	-	1-1	03-06-02
Ipswich	v	Wolves	2-0	1-0	-	-	2-4	-	04-02-03
Leicester	v	Brighton	-	-	-	-	2-0	-	05-00-00
Plymouth	v	Nottm F	-	-	-	-	-	-	00-00-00
Preston	v	Rotherham	-	-	-	2-1	0-2	4-1	03-01-03
Stoke	v	Derby	-	-	-	-	1-3	2-1	02-02-01
Wigan	v	Cardiff	-	2-0	-	4-0	2-2	3-0	05-02-01

COCA-COLA LEAGUE DIVISION ONE

Bristol C	v	Brentford	-	1-0	1-2	0-2	0-0	3-1	04-03-04
Chesterfield	v	Port Vale	-	-	-	1-1	2-1	1-0	02-01-01
Doncaster	v	Huddersfield	-	-	-	-	-	1-1	00-01-00
Hartlepool	v	Colchester	-	-	-	-	-	0-0	05-01-01
Luton	v	Bournemouth	2-2	1-2	1-0	-	-	1-1	02-02-02
Milton K	v	Torquay	-	-	-	-	-	-	00-00-00
Peterboro	v	Blackpool	-	-	-	3-2	1-0	0-1	04-02-01
Sheff Wed	v	Oldham	-	-	-	-	-	2-2	02-03-00
Stockport	v	Tranmere	0-0	2-1	1-1	-	2-3	1-1	02-04-01
Walsall	v	Swindon	-	0-0	1-0	-	-	-	01-03-00
Wrexham	v	Barnsley	-	-	-	-	-	1-0	01-00-00

COCA-COLA LEAGUE DIVISION TWO

Boston	v	Chester	-	-	0-0	0-1	-	-	00-01-01
Bury	v	Kidderminstr	-	-	-	-	1-1	0-0	00-02-00
Darlington	v	Cambridge U	0-0	-	-	-	1-2	3-4	01-04-02
Leyton O	v	Rochdale	3-0	0-0	1-1	4-2	0-1	2-1	07-02-01
Mansfield	v	Yeovil	-	-	-	-	-	0-1	00-00-01

Sponsored by Stan James

Notts Co	v	Oxford Utd	-	0-1	2-1	-	-	-	03-02-01
Rushden & D	v	Bristol R	-	-	-	3-1	2-1	-	02-00-00
Scunthorpe	v	Northampton	-	-	-	-	-	1-0	06-02-00
Shrewsbury	v	Cheltenham	-	0-2	1-0	2-1	-	-	02-00-01
Southend	v	Macclesfield	-	1-0	3-1	3-0	1-0	1-0	05-00-00
Swansea	v	Lincoln	-	2-1	-	0-0	2-0	2-2	02-03-01
Wycombe	v	Grimsby	-	-	-	-	-	4-1	01-01-00

NATIONWIDE CONFERENCE

Burton	v	Scarborough	-	-	-	-	1-1	2-0	01-01-00
Canvey Islnd	v	Barnet	-	-	-	-	-	-	00-00-00
Crawley	v	Dagenham	-	-	-	-	-	-	00-00-00
Farnborough	v	Exeter	-	-	-	-	-	1-2	00-00-01
Forest G	v	Gravesend	-	-	-	-	2-1	1-2	01-00-01
Halifax	v	Carlisle	1-0	5-2	0-0	2-2	-	-	03-05-01
Morecambe	v	Leigh RMI	-	-	1-2	1-3	2-1	1-0	02-00-02
Northwich	v	Hereford	1-0	0-0	1-0	1-0	2-2	1-5	03-02-02
Stevenage	v	Tamworth	-	-	-	-	-	3-1	01-00-00
Woking	v	Aldershot	-	-	-	-	-	2-2	00-01-00

TUESDAY 31 AUGUST 2004
COCA-COLA CHAMPIONSHIP

Crewe	v	Millwall	-	-	-	1-0	-	1-2	01-01-01
Leeds	v	Watford	-	3-1	-	-	-	-	02-00-01
QPR	v	Sheff Utd	1-2	3-1	1-3	-	-	-	05-01-03
Reading	v	Sunderland	-	-	-	-	-	0-2	01-01-02

COCA-COLA LEAGUE DIVISION TWO

Hull	v	Bradford	-	-	-	-	-	-	03-02-02

NATIONWIDE CONFERENCE

York	v	Accrington	-	-	-	-	-	-	00-00-00

FRIDAY 3 SEPTEMBER 2004
COCA-COLA LEAGUE DIVISION ONE

Tranmere	v	Oldham	-	-	-	2-2	1-2	2-1	03-02-01

COCA-COLA LEAGUE DIVISION TWO

Wycombe	v	Oxford Utd	-	0-1	3-1	-	-	-	02-00-02

SATURDAY 4 SEPTEMBER 2004
COCA-COLA LEAGUE DIVISION ONE

Blackpool	v	Wrexham	1-1	2-1	-	3-0	-	0-1	07-02-02
Bradford	v	Port Vale	4-0	-	-	-	-	-	05-01-00
Brentford	v	Bournemouth	-	0-2	3-2	1-0	-	1-0	06-03-02
Chesterfield	v	Milton K	-	-	-	-	-	-	00-00-00
Colchester	v	Swindon	-	-	0-1	1-3	1-0	0-1	01-00-03
Doncaster	v	Walsall	-	-	-	-	-	-	02-00-03
Hartlepool	v	Barnsley	-	-	-	-	-	1-2	00-00-01
Peterboro	v	Bristol C	-	-	2-1	4-1	1-3	0-1	03-02-03
Sheff Wed	v	Luton	-	-	-	-	-	0-0	02-02-00
Stockport	v	Torquay	-	-	-	-	-	-	02-02-00

COCA-COLA LEAGUE DIVISION TWO

Boston	v	Cambridge U	-	-	-	-	1-3	1-2	00-00-02
Bristol R	v	Shrewsbury	-	-	-	0-0	0-0	-	04-02-00
Bury	v	Lincoln	-	-	-	-	2-0	2-1	05-00-01
Chester	v	Macclesfield	-	1-2	-	-	-	-	00-01-01
Darlington	v	Scunthorpe	3-1	-	2-1	2-1	1-1	2-2	06-06-01

Grimsby	v	Rochdale	-	-	-	-	-	-	00-00-02
Kidderminstr	v	Leyton O	-	-	2-1	0-1	3-2	2-1	03-00-01
Notts Co	v	Cheltenham	-	-	-	-	1-0	-	01-00-00
Rushden & D	v	Southend	-	-	-	0-1	3-0	-	01-00-01
Yeovil	v	Swansea	-	-	-	-	-	2-0	01-00-00

BELL'S SCOTTISH FIRST DIVISION

Airdrie Utd	v	Queen Sth	-	-	-	-	-	-	02-00-00
Clyde	v	St Mirren	-	-	-	1-1/3-1	2-3/3-2	2-0/2-2	04-02-02
Hamilton	v	St Johnstone	-	-	-	-	-	-	03-01-02
Partick	v	Falkirk	-	-	-	5-1/3-0	-	-	07-04-06
Raith	v	Ross C	-	-	4-1/0-4	1-3/0-1	-	1-7/0-0	01-01-04

BELL'S SCOTTISH SECOND DIVISION

Alloa	v	Ayr	-	-	1-1/0-2	-	0-1/2-3	-	00-03-03
Berwick	v	Dumbarton	3-1/0-1	0-1/0-0	-	-	1-2/0-1	1-4/1-2	07-03-10
Forfar	v	Stirling	1-2/3-3	-	1-0/3-1	-	-	-	02-03-03
Morton	v	Arbroath	-	-	-	-	-	6-4/1-0	02-00-00
Stranraer	v	Brechin	-	-	-	-	3-1/2-3	-	03-02-07

BELL'S SCOTTISH THIRD DIVISION

E Stirling	v	Elgin	-	-	0-2/1-0	2-1/0-3	1-2/2-2	3-1/2-1	04-01-03
Gretna	v	C'denbeath	-	-	-	-	1-0/0-1	-	01-00-01
Montrose	v	Albion	1-2/2-3	2-1/1-2	0-2/0-1	1-2/2-0	0-1/1-1	1-0/3-1	12-02-10
Peterhead	v	East Fife	-	-	0-0/2-1	1-3/1-1	0-2/2-2	-	01-03-02
Stenhsmuir	v	Queens P	2-1/4-1	-	1-1/2-0	-	-	-	06-04-03

NATIONWIDE CONFERENCE

Accrington	v	Woking	-	-	-	-	-	3-3	00-01-00
Aldershot	v	Northwich	-	-	-	-	-	4-3	01-00-00
Barnet	v	Morecambe	-	-	-	1-0	1-1	2-1	02-01-00
Carlisle	v	Burton	-	-	-	-	-	-	00-00-00
Dagenham	v	York	-	-	-	-	-	-	00-00-00
Exeter	v	Crawley	-	-	-	-	-	-	00-00-00
Gravesend	v	Stevenage	-	-	-	-	2-1	2-3	01-00-01
Hereford	v	Halifax	-	-	-	-	1-1	7-1	04-02-02
Leigh RMI	v	Forest G	-	-	1-1	1-2	1-0	1-2	01-01-02
Scarborough	v	Canvey Islnd	-	-	-	-	-	-	00-00-00
Tamworth	v	Farnborough	-	-	-	-	-	2-1	01-00-00

SUNDAY 5 SEPTEMBER 2004
COCA-COLA LEAGUE DIVISION ONE

Huddersfield	v	Hull	-	-	-	-	-	3-1	02-02-01

COCA-COLA LEAGUE DIVISION ONE

Mansfield	v	Northampton	-	0-0	-	-	2-1	1-2	04-04-02

SATURDAY 11 SEPTEMBER 2004
FA BARCLAYCARD PREMIER LEAGUE

Aston Villa	v	Chelsea	0-3	0-0	1-1	1-1	2-1	3-2	06-04-05
Bolton	v	Man Utd	-	-	-	0-4	1-1	1-2	00-02-03
Fulham	v	Arsenal	-	-	-	1-3	0-1	0-1	00-00-03
Liverpool	v	WBA	-	-	-	-	2-0	-	01-00-00
Man City	v	Everton	-	-	5-0	-	3-1	5-1	07-00-03
Middlesbro	v	Birmingham	-	-	-	-	1-0	5-3	03-01-00
Newcastle	v	Blackburn	1-1	-	-	2-1	5-1	0-1	06-05-01
Portsmouth	v	Crystal Pal	1-1	3-1	2-4	4-2	1-1	-	02-04-03

COCA-COLA CHAMPIONSHIP

Burnley	v	Crewe	-	-	1-0	3-3	-	1-0	04-02-01

178

Derby	v	Reading	-	-	-	-	3-0	2-3	02-00-02
Gillingham	v	Sunderland	-	-	-	-	-	1-3	00-00-01
Leeds	v	Coventry	2-0	3-0	1-0	-	-	-	08-02-01
Nottm F	v	Cardiff	-	-	-	-	-	1-2	00-00-01
Preston	v	Stoke	3-4	2-1	-	-	4-3	1-0	04-01-02
QPR	v	Plymouth	-	-	-	-	2-2	3-0	01-01-00
Rotherham	v	Leicester	-	-	-	-	1-1	-	00-01-00
Sheff Utd	v	West Ham	-	-	-	-	-	3-3	01-02-01
Watford	v	Brighton	-	-	-	-	1-0	-	02-01-02
Wolves	v	Wigan	-	-	-	-	-	-	01-00-00

COCA-COLA LEAGUE DIVISION ONE

Barnsley	v	Tranmere	1-1	3-0	1-1	-	1-1	2-0	06-05-00
Bournemouth	v	Colchester	2-1	4-0	2-2	0-1	-	1-1	02-02-01
Bristol C	v	Stockport	1-1	-	-	-	1-1	1-0	02-03-00
Hull	v	Blackpool	-	-	0-1	-	-	-	03-01-01
Luton	v	Chesterfield	1-0	1-1	-	-	3-0	1-0	04-01-01
Milton K	v	Doncaster	-	-	-	-	-	-	00-00-00
Oldham	v	Hartlepool	-	-	-	-	-	0-2	00-00-01
Port Vale	v	Huddersfield	2-0	1-2	-	1-1	5-1	-	07-02-01
Swindon	v	Peterboro	-	-	2-1	0-0	1-1	2-0	04-02-00
Torquay	v	Brentford	3-1	-	-	-	-	-	01-01-00
Walsall	v	Sheff Wed	-	-	-	0-3	1-0	-	01-00-01
Wrexham	v	Bradford	-	-	-	-	-	-	00-00-03

COCA-COLA LEAGUE DIVISION TWO

Cambridge U	v	Mansfield	7-2	-	-	-	-	1-2	04-00-02
Cheltenham	v	Yeovil	3-2	-	-	-	-	3-1	05-02-00
Leyton O	v	Bristol R	-	-	-	3-1	1-2	1-1	02-01-03
Lincoln	v	Boston	-	-	-	-	1-1	1-1	00-02-00
Macclesfield	v	Grimsby	-	-	-	-	-	-	00-00-00
Northampton	v	Notts Co	1-1	-	1-0	0-2	2-0	-	02-02-02
Oxford Utd	v	Rushden & D	-	-	-	3-2	3-0	-	02-00-00
Rochdale	v	Darlington	0-0	0-0	1-1	3-1	1-1	4-2	06-07-01
Scunthorpe	v	Chester	2-1	-	-	-	-	-	02-01-02
Shrewsbury	v	Bury	-	-	-	-	4-1	-	04-03-00
Southend	v	Wycombe	-	-	-	-	-	-	00-00-01
Swansea	v	Kidderminstr	-	-	-	2-1	0-4	0-0	01-01-01

BANK OF SCOTLAND SCOTTISH PREMIER LEAGUE

Celtic	v	Dundee	6-1/5-0	6-2/2-2	1-0/2-1/0-2	3-1	2-0/6-2	3-2	14-03-02
Dundee Utd	v	Aberdeen	1-0/3-0	3-1/1-1	3-5/1-1	1-1	1-1/0-2	3-2	10-12-06
Dunfermline	v	Motherwell	1-1/1-2	-	1-2/1-2	5-2/3-1	1-0/3-0	1-0/3-0	09-05-06
Hearts	v	Rangers	2-1/2-3	0-4/1-2	0-1/1-4	2-2/0-2	0-4/0-2	0-4/1-1	06-06-20
Inv CT	v	Hibernian	-	-	-	-	-	-	00-00-00
Livingston	v	Kilmarnock	-	-	-	0-1	0-1/0-4	1-2/1-1	02-03-08

BELL'S SCOTTISH FIRST DIVISION

Clyde	v	Airdrie Utd	-	-	4-1/1-1	0-3/0-1	-	-	02-02-06
Falkirk	v	Raith	1-1/1-0	2-1/1-0	2-1/2-0	1-0/2-1	-	3-2/1-0	13-01-05
Queen Sth	v	Hamilton	-	3-2/1-1	-	0-1/3-1	-	-	03-02-01
Ross C	v	St Johnstone	-	-	-	-	0-0/2-3	0-3/2-0	01-01-02
St Mirren	v	Partick	-	-	-	1-0/0-2	-	-	04-00-02

BELL'S SCOTTISH SECOND DIVISION

Ayr	v	Forfar	-	-	-	-	-	-	03-04-01
Berwick	v	Alloa	-	-	-	0-4/0-1	-	3-2/3-1	04-05-05
Brechin	v	Arbroath	-	-	-	-	-	-	03-03-02
Dumbarton	v	Stranraer	-	-	-	-	3-0/1-1	-	03-05-02
Stirling	v	Morton	-	-	-	-	2-0/0-3	-	05-03-06

BELL'S SCOTTISH THIRD DIVISION

Albion	v	Stenhsmuir	1-3/1-2	-	-	-	-	-	01-03-05

C'denbeath	v	Elgin	-	-	3-1/1-0	-	-	3-2/2-0	04-00-00
East Fife	v	E Stirling	-	1-0/3-1	3-1/4-1	0-4/1-0	4-1/3-0	-	08-07-02
Peterhead	v	Gretna	-	-	-	-	1-1/1-0	2-0/2-1	03-01-00
Queens P	v	Montrose	3-0/1-2	2-1/1-1	-	2-2/0-1	0-1/1-1	1-1/1-1	08-09-07

NATIONWIDE CONFERENCE

Crawley	v	York	-	-	-	-	-	-	00-00-00
Dagenham	v	Accrington	-	-	-	-	-	0-1	00-00-01
Farnborough	v	Canvey Islnd	-	1-2	1-2	-	-	-	00-00-02
Gravesend	v	Hereford	-	-	-	-	3-0	2-5	01-00-01
Halifax	v	Forest G	-	-	-	-	1-1	0-1	00-01-01
Leigh RMI	v	Aldershot	-	-	-	-	-	2-2	00-01-00
Northwich	v	Morecambe	1-1	0-0	1-0	4-3	3-2	1-1	06-03-00
Scarborough	v	Exeter	1-0	-	-	-	-	2-3	03-01-04
Stevenage	v	Burton	-	-	-	-	0-1	1-0	01-00-01
Tamworth	v	Barnet	-	-	-	-	-	2-0	01-00-00
Woking	v	Carlisle	-	-	-	-	-	-	00-00-00

SUNDAY 12 SEPTEMBER 2004
FA BARCLAYCARD PREMIER LEAGUE

| Tottenham | v | Norwich | - | - | - | - | - | - | 06-00-01 |

COCA-COLA CHAMPIONSHIP

| Ipswich | v | Millwall | - | - | - | - | 4-1 | 1-3 | 01-02-02 |

MONDAY 13 SEPTEMBER 2004
FA BARCLAYCARD PREMIER LEAGUE

| Charlton | v | Southampton | 5-0 | - | 1-1 | 1-1 | 2-1 | 2-1 | 03-03-01 |

TUESDAY 14 SEPTEMBER 2004
COCA-COLA CHAMPIONSHIP

Brighton	v	Wolves	-	-	-	-	4-1	-	01-03-00
Cardiff	v	Watford	-	-	-	-	-	3-0	01-00-00
Crewe	v	QPR	0-2	2-1	2-2	-	2-0	-	02-01-02
Leicester	v	Sheff Utd	-	-	-	-	0-0	-	00-01-02
Millwall	v	Derby	-	-	-	-	3-0	0-0	04-03-02
Plymouth	v	Leeds	-	-	-	-	-	-	01-01-00
Reading	v	Preston	2-1	2-2	-	-	5-1	3-2	05-04-00
Stoke	v	Ipswich	-	-	-	-	2-1	2-0	03-03-01
Sunderland	v	Nottm F	-	-	-	-	-	1-0	02-02-01
West Ham	v	Rotherham	-	-	-	-	-	2-1	01-00-00
Wigan	v	Burnley	0-0	1-1	-	-	-	0-0	01-04-00

WEDNESDAY 15 SEPTEMBER 2004
COCA-COLA CHAMPIONSHIP

| Coventry | v | Gillingham | - | - | - | 1-2 | 0-0 | 2-2 | 00-02-01 |

SATURDAY 18 SEPTEMBER 2004
FA BARCLAYCARD PREMIER LEAGUE

Arsenal	v	Bolton	-	-	-	1-1	2-1	2-1	04-01-00
Birmingham	v	Charlton	-	1-0	-	-	1-1	1-2	03-03-02
Blackburn	v	Portsmouth	-	1-1	3-1	-	-	1-2	03-03-01
Crystal Pal	v	Man City	-	1-1	-	2-1	-	-	03-05-01
Everton	v	Middlesbro	5-0	0-2	2-2	2-0	2-1	1-1	05-03-02
Norwich	v	Aston Villa	-	-	-	-	-	-	04-02-01
WBA	v	Fulham	-	0-0	1-3	-	1-0	-	02-01-02

COCA-COLA CHAMPIONSHIP

| Brighton | v | QPR | - | - | - | 2-1 | - | 2-1 | 02-00-00 |

Cardiff	v	Derby	-	-	-	-	-	4-1	01-00-00
Coventry	v	Rotherham	-	-	-	2-0	2-1	1-1	02-01-00
Crewe	v	Leeds	-	-	-	-	-	-	00-00-00
Leicester	v	Burnley	-	-	-	-	0-1	-	00-00-01
Millwall	v	Watford	-	-	-	1-0	4-0	1-2	05-01-05
Plymouth	v	Wolves	-	-	-	-	-	-	02-00-00
Reading	v	Gillingham	0-0	2-2	-	-	2-1	2-1	02-02-01
Stoke	v	Nottm F	-	-	-	-	2-2	2-1	01-02-01
Sunderland	v	Preston	-	-	-	-	-	3-3	00-01-00
West Ham	v	Ipswich	-	-	0-1	3-1	-	1-2	04-01-02
Wigan	v	Sheff Utd	-	-	-	-	-	1-1	00-01-01

COCA-COLA LEAGUE DIVISION ONE

Blackpool	v	Swindon	-	-	-	1-0	0-0	2-2	01-03-00
Bradford	v	Bristol C	5-0	-	-	-	-	-	02-00-00
Brentford	v	Port Vale	-	-	1-1	2-0	1-1	3-2	03-02-01
Chesterfield	v	Walsall	0-1	-	-	-	-	-	03-03-03
Colchester	v	Milton K	-	-	-	-	-	-	00-00-00
Doncaster	v	Oldham	-	-	-	-	-	-	00-00-00
Hartlepool	v	Torquay	4-1	2-0	3-1	4-1	3-2	-	06-06-01
Huddersfield	v	Barnsley	0-1	2-1	1-1	-	1-0	-	03-02-01
Peterboro	v	Hull	1-1	2-1	-	-	-	-	05-01-00
Sheff Wed	v	Bournemouth	-	-	-	-	-	0-2	00-00-01
Stockport	v	Luton	-	-	-	-	2-3	1-2	00-01-02
Tranmere	v	Wrexham	-	-	-	5-0	-	1-2	02-00-01

COCA-COLA LEAGUE DIVISION TWO

Boston	v	Shrewsbury	-	-	-	-	6-0	-	01-00-00
Bristol R	v	Lincoln	3-0	-	-	1-2	2-0	3-1	03-00-01
Bury	v	Scunthorpe	-	3-0	-	-	0-0	2-3	04-02-01
Chester	v	Cambridge U	0-3	-	-	-	-	-	00-03-03
Darlington	v	Northampton	-	0-1	-	-	-	1-2	03-01-04
Grimsby	v	Leyton O	-	-	-	-	-	-	00-02-00
Kidderminstr	v	Macclesfield	-	-	2-1	0-1	0-2	1-4	03-04-06
Mansfield	v	Rochdale	3-1	0-0	1-0	3-1	-	1-0	06-04-01
Notts Co	v	Southend	-	-	-	-	-	-	02-02-00
Rushden & D	v	Cheltenham	1-2	-	-	1-0	-	-	03-00-02
Wycombe	v	Swansea	-	-	2-1	-	-	-	02-00-01
Yeovil	v	Oxford Utd	-	-	-	-	-	1-0	01-00-00

BANK OF SCOTLAND SCOTTISH PREMIER LEAGUE

Dundee	v	Livingston	-	-	-	1-0/2-0	2-1/0-2	2-1/1-0/2-0	09-01-01
Hibernian	v	Celtic	-	0-2/2-1	0-0/2-5	1-4/1-1	0-1	1-2/0-4	05-07-17
Kilmarnock	v	Aberdeen	4-0/4-2	2-0/1-0	1-0/0-0	3-1	2-2/2-0	1-3/3-1/4-0	14-05-03
Motherwell	v	Dundee Utd	1-0/2-0	2-2/1-3	2-1	0-0/2-0	1-2/2-2	3-1/0-1	12-06-11
Rangers	v	Inv CT	-	-	-	-	-	-	00-00-00

BELL'S SCOTTISH FIRST DIVISION

Airdrie Utd	v	Ross C	-	-	5-1/2-2	1-1/0-2	-	-	01-02-01
Hamilton	v	Clyde	-	2-3/1-1	-	-	-	-	06-01-02
Partick	v	Queen Sth	2-2/1-3	2-0/5-4	2-1/0-2	-	-	-	04-01-02
Raith	v	St Mirren	1-0/1-1	0-6/1-2	-	3-0/1-0	-	1-1/2-0	09-03-02
St Johnstone	v	Falkirk	-	-	-	-	0-1/0-1	0-4/2-1	06-02-05

BELL'S SCOTTISH SECOND DIVISION

Alloa	v	Dumbarton	-	-	-	-	-	1-2/3-0	04-00-04
Arbroath	v	Ayr	-	-	-	3-2/0-2	1-1/1-2	-	01-01-02
Forfar	v	Berwick	-	1-1/2-0	3-5/0-1	2-1/0-0	0-2/2-2	1-5/0-2	03-04-08
Morton	v	Brechin	-	-	-	-	-	-	03-02-00
Stranraer	v	Stirling	-	2-1/3-1	1-1/0-3	-	-	0-1/1-1	02-06-05

BELL'S SCOTTISH THIRD DIVISION

E Stirling	v	Queens P	1-1/1-1	1-1/0-1	-	0-1/3-1	0-4/0-2	1-2/2-4	12-06-09
Elgin	v	Albion	-	-	1-2/1-0	2-0/0-0	0-1/1-2	1-5/1-2	02-01-05

Gretna	v	East Fife	-	-	-	-	2-3/3-3	-	00-01-01
Montrose	v	C'denbeath	1-1/1-2	0-1/1-3	1-2/0-1	-	-	1-3/1-1	07-04-10
Stenhsmuir	v	Peterhead	-	-	-	-	-	-	00-00-00

NATIONWIDE CONFERENCE

Accrington	v	Leigh RMI	1-2	-	-	-	-	4-1	01-00-02
Aldershot	v	Dagenham	4-3	1-0	-	-	-	2-1	03-00-00
Barnet	v	Gravesend	-	-	-	-	1-4	1-0	01-00-01
Burton	v	Crawley	1-2	3-0	2-1	-	-	-	09-02-02
Canvey Islnd	v	Halifax	-	-	-	-	-	-	00-00-00
Carlisle	v	Tamworth	-	-	-	-	-	-	00-00-00
Exeter	v	Stevenage	-	-	-	-	-	1-0	01-00-00
Forest G	v	Farnborough	0-0	-	-	1-0	3-1	1-1	02-02-00
Hereford	v	Scarborough	-	4-4	1-1	6-0	0-1	2-1	05-06-03
Morecambe	v	Woking	0-1	1-0	3-0	3-1	5-0	2-1	05-00-04
York	v	Northwich	-	-	-	-	-	-	00-00-00

SUNDAY 19 SEPTEMBER 2004
FA BARCLAYCARD PREMIER LEAGUE

Chelsea	v	Tottenham	2-0	1-0	3-0	4-0	1-1	4-2	10-04-01
Southampton	v	Newcastle	2-1	4-2	2-0	3-1	1-1	3-3	09-03-00

BANK OF SCOTLAND SCOTTISH PREMIER LEAGUE

Dunfermline	v	Hearts	1-1/0-0	-	1-0	0-1/1-1	3-1/0-1	2-1/0-0	07-04-08

MONDAY 20 SEPTEMBER 2004

Man Utd	v	Liverpool	2-0	1-1	0-1	0-1	4-0	0-1	06-06-04

TUESDAY 21 SEPTEMBER 2004
NATIONWIDE CONFERENCE

Barnet	v	Burton	-	-	-	-	2-2	2-1	01-01-00
Canvey Islnd	v	Crawley	-	-	-	-	-	-	00-00-00
Carlisle	v	Scarborough	1-0	-	-	-	-	-	06-02-01
Farnborough	v	Stevenage	1-0	-	-	6-1	0-1	2-0	04-02-02
Forest G	v	Exeter	-	-	-	-	-	2-5	00-00-01
Gravesend	v	Dagenham	2-0	1-2	-	-	1-2	1-2	01-01-03
Halifax	v	Morecambe	-	-	-	-	1-0	1-0	03-02-00
Hereford	v	Aldershot	-	-	-	-	-	4-3	01-00-00
Northwich	v	Accrington	-	-	-	-	-	3-3	00-01-00
Tamworth	v	Woking	-	-	-	-	-	2-0	01-00-00
York	v	Leigh RMI	-	-	-	-	-	-	00-00-00

FRIDAY 24 SEPTEMBER 2004
COCA-COLA CHAMPIONSHIP

Leeds	v	Sunderland	-	2-1	2-0	2-0	0-1	-	07-00-01

SATURDAY 25 SEPTEMBER 2004
FA BARCLAYCARD PREMIER LEAGUE

Aston Villa	v	Crystal Pal	-	-	-	-	-	-	04-01-01
Bolton	v	Birmingham	3-1	3-3	2-2	-	4-2	0-1	05-04-01
Fulham	v	Southampton	-	-	-	2-1	2-2	2-0	02-01-00
Liverpool	v	Norwich	-	-	-	-	-	-	04-01-02
Man City	v	Arsenal	-	-	0-4	-	1-5	1-2	01-02-07
Middlesbro	v	Chelsea	0-0	0-1	1-0	0-2	1-1	1-2	03-03-03
Newcastle	v	WBA	-	-	-	-	2-1	-	02-01-00
Tottenham	v	Man Utd	2-2	3-1	3-1	3-5	0-2	1-2	04-03-09

COCA-COLA CHAMPIONSHIP

Burnley	v	Stoke	0-2	1-0	-	-	2-1	0-1	02-01-03

Sponsored by Stan James

Derby	v	Wigan	-	-	-	-	-	2-2	00-01-00
Gillingham	v	Brighton	-	-	-	-	3-0	-	01-00-00
Ipswich	v	Plymouth	-	-	-	-	-	-	03-01-00
Preston	v	Crewe	-	-	2-1	2-2	-	0-0	03-03-01
QPR	v	Leicester	-	-	-	-	-	-	01-00-00
Rotherham	v	Millwall	-	-	3-2	0-0	1-3	0-0	01-03-01
Sheff Utd	v	Coventry	-	-	-	0-1	0-0	2-1	01-03-03
Watford	v	Reading	-	-	-	-	0-3	1-0	02-01-01
Wolves	v	Cardiff	-	-	-	-	-	-	01-00-00

COCA-COLA LEAGUE DIVISION ONE

Barnsley	v	Chesterfield	-	-	-	-	2-1	0-1	01-00-01
Bournemouth	v	Doncaster	-	-	-	-	-	-	00-00-00
Bristol C	v	Huddersfield	1-2	-	-	1-1	1-0	-	02-02-01
Hull	v	Stockport	-	-	-	-	-	-	00-02-03
Luton	v	Peterboro	-	-	3-2	-	2-3	1-1	03-02-01
Milton K	v	Hartlepool	-	-	-	-	-	-	00-00-00
Oldham	v	Colchester	1-0	1-2	1-1	4-1	2-0	0-0	03-02-01
Port Vale	v	Blackpool	-	-	-	1-1	1-0	2-1	05-01-00
Swindon	v	Bradford	1-4	-	-	-	-	-	04-01-01
Torquay	v	Tranmere	-	-	-	-	-	-	01-00-00
Walsall	v	Brentford	-	-	3-2	-	-	-	03-01-01
Wrexham	v	Sheff Wed	-	-	-	-	-	1-2	00-00-01

COCA-COLA LEAGUE DIVISION TWO

Cambridge U	v	Grimsby	-	-	-	-	-	-	04-00-01
Cheltenham	v	Wycombe	-	-	-	-	0-0	-	02-02-01
Leyton O	v	Boston	-	-	-	-	3-2	1-3	01-00-01
Lincoln	v	Chester	-	4-1	-	-	-	-	01-02-02
Macclesfield	v	Darlington	-	2-1	1-1	1-1	1-0	0-1	03-03-01
Northampton	v	Bristol R	3-1	-	2-1	-	-	2-0	03-01-02
Oxford Utd	v	Bury	0-1	1-1	1-0	-	2-1	1-1	02-03-01
Rochdale	v	Notts Co	-	-	-	-	-	-	00-00-01
Scunthorpe	v	Mansfield	3-2	-	6-0	0-0	-	0-0	03-03-04
Shrewsbury	v	Yeovil	-	-	-	-	-	-	00-00-00
Southend	v	Kidderminstr	-	-	1-1	1-0	0-2	3-0	02-01-01
Swansea	v	Rushden & D	-	-	-	0-0	2-2	-	00-02-00

BANK OF SCOTLAND SCOTTISH PREMIER LEAGUE

Aberdeen	v	Hibernian	-	2-2/4-0	0-2/1-0	2-0	0-1	3-1/0-1	14-06-08
Celtic	v	Dunfermline	5-0/5-0	-	3-1	3-1/5-0/5-0	2-1/1-0	5-0/1-2	17-00-04
Dundee	v	Rangers	0-4/1-1	2-3/1-7	1-1/0-1/0-3	0-0	0-3/2-2	0-2	01-08-10
Hearts	v	Inv CT	-	-	-	-	-	-	00-00-00
Kilmarnock	v	Dundee Utd	2-0/2-0	1-1/1-0	1-0/0-0	2-0/2-2	1-2	0-2	07-05-06
Livingston	v	Motherwell	-	-	-	3-1	3-2/1-0	1-0/3-1	05-00-00

BELL'S SCOTTISH FIRST DIVISION

Falkirk	v	Clyde	-	-	3-2/1-1	1-1/1-6	2-1/3-0	0-2/1-1	08-04-03
Hamilton	v	Ross C	-	1-0/0-3	-	-	-	-	01-00-01
Raith	v	Queen Sth	-	-	-	-	-	0-1/3-1	03-00-01
St Johnstone	v	Partick	-	-	-	-	-	-	04-04-01
St Mirren	v	Airdrie Utd	1-5/3-0	5-0/3-1	-	0-0/2-1	-	-	07-01-10

BELL'S SCOTTISH SECOND DIVISION

Alloa	v	Morton	-	-	2-1/0-3	1-1/4-0	-	0-1/3-3	02-03-02
Ayr	v	Brechin	-	-	-	-	-	3-2/1-2	05-01-01
Berwick	v	Arbroath	-	-	2-1/1-0	-	-	3-0/1-3	09-03-03
Dumbarton	v	Stirling	-	-	-	4-1/2-0	-	-	04-04-04
Forfar	v	Stranraer	-	-	0-0/2-3	1-1/3-2	2-1/4-0	-	06-04-03

BELL'S SCOTTISH THIRD DIVISION

Albion	v	E Stirling	3-1/0-2	1-1/0-1	2-1/2-2	0-4/5-1	6-0/3-1	5-0/5-1	14-06-07

East Fife	v	Queens P	-	0-0/0-0	-	1-4/0-3	1-1/1-0	-	06-07-02
Gretna	v	Elgin	-	-	-	-	0-0/2-1	2-2/2-1	02-02-00
Montrose	v	Stenhsmuir	0-0/1-2	-	-	-	-	-	02-02-07
Peterhead	v	C'denbeath	-	-	3-0/3-0	-	-	0-1/0-0	02-01-01

NATIONWIDE CONFERENCE

Accrington	v	Gravesend	-	-	-	-	-	3-3	00-01-00
Aldershot	v	Carlisle	-	-	-	-	-	-	00-00-00
Burton	v	York	-	-	-	-	-	-	00-00-00
Crawley	v	Forest G	-	-	-	-	-	-	00-01-00
Dagenham	v	Halifax	-	-	-	-	0-0	0-1	01-02-02
Exeter	v	Tamworth	-	-	-	-	-	3-2	01-00-00
Leigh RMI	v	Hereford	-	-	2-1	0-1	0-2	0-5	01-00-03
Morecambe	v	Farnborough	1-0	-	-	1-1	1-1	3-2	02-04-01
Scarborough	v	Barnet	0-0	-	-	3-0	1-1	2-2	02-06-02
Stevenage	v	Northwich	1-3	3-1	3-1	1-0	2-2	1-0	06-02-02
Woking	v	Canvey Islnd	-	-	-	-	-	-	00-00-00

SUNDAY 26 SEPTEMBER 2004
FA BARCLAYCARD PREMIER LEAGUE

Portsmouth	v	Everton	-	-	-	-	-	1-2	00-00-01

COCA-COLA CHAMPIONSHIP

Nottm F	v	West Ham	0-0	-	-	-	-	0-2	00-04-03

MONDAY 27 SEPTEMBER 2004

Charlton	v	Blackburn	0-0	1-2	-	0-2	3-1	3-2	02-02-03

TUESDAY 28 SEPTEMBER 2004
COCA-COLA CHAMPIONSHIP

Burnley	v	Cardiff	-	2-1	-	-	-	1-1	04-01-00
Gillingham	v	Leicester	-	-	-	-	3-2	-	01-00-00
Ipswich	v	Reading	-	-	-	-	3-1	1-1	03-01-01
Leeds	v	Stoke	-	-	-	-	-	-	02-00-00
Preston	v	Plymouth	-	-	-	-	-	-	01-01-02
QPR	v	Coventry	-	-	-	-	-	-	04-04-00
Rotherham	v	Crewe	-	-	-	2-2	-	0-2	00-04-05
Sheff Utd	v	Sunderland	0-4	-	-	-	-	0-1	01-02-04
Watford	v	Wigan	-	-	-	-	-	1-1	01-01-00
Wolves	v	Millwall	-	-	-	1-0	3-0	-	05-03-00

WEDNESDAY 29 SEPTEMBER 2004
COCA-COLA CHAMPIONSHIP

Derby	v	West Ham	0-2	1-2	0-0	0-0	-	0-1	02-02-05
Nottm F	v	Brighton	-	-	-	-	3-2	-	01-00-00

FRIDAY 1 OCTOBER 2004
COCA-COLA LEAGUE DIVISION TWO

Grimsby	v	Cheltenham	-	-	-	-	-	-	00-00-00

SATURDAY 2 OCTOBER 2004
FA BARCLAYCARD PREMIER LEAGUE

Arsenal	v	Charlton	0-0	-	5-3	2-4	2-0	2-1	04-02-01
Birmingham	v	Newcastle	-	-	-	-	0-2	1-1	00-01-02
Blackburn	v	Aston Villa	2-1	-	-	3-0	0-0	0-2	06-02-02
Everton	v	Tottenham	0-1	2-2	0-0	1-1	2-2	3-1	05-07-04
Man Utd	v	Middlesbro	2-3	1-0	2-1	0-1	1-0	2-3	06-01-03
Norwich	v	Portsmouth	0-0	2-1	0-0	0-0	1-0	-	04-04-00

184

| Southampton | v | Man City | - | - | 0-2 | - | 2-0 | 0-2 | 03-02-05 |
| WBA | v | Bolton | 2-3 | 4-4 | 0-2 | - | 1-1 | - | 02-05-02 |

COCA-COLA CHAMPIONSHIP

Brighton	v	Sheff Utd	-	-	-	-	2-4	-	00-01-01
Cardiff	v	Leeds	-	-	-	-	-	-	00-00-00
Coventry	v	Ipswich	-	-	0-1	-	2-4	1-1	02-02-02
Crewe	v	Watford	0-1	-	2-0	1-0	-	0-1	02-00-03
Leicester	v	Preston	-	-	-	-	2-1	-	01-00-00
Millwall	v	Nottm F	-	-	-	3-3	1-2	1-0	02-03-01
Plymouth	v	Gillingham	-	-	-	-	-	-	02-00-01
Reading	v	Burnley	1-1	0-0	-	-	3-0	2-2	03-04-00
Stoke	v	QPR	-	-	-	0-1	-	-	01-01-01
Sunderland	v	Derby	-	1-1	2-1	1-1	-	2-1	06-04-01
West Ham	v	Wolves	-	-	-	-	-	-	02-01-00
Wigan	v	Rotherham	-	-	0-2	-	-	1-2	01-01-03

COCA-COLA LEAGUE DIVISION ONE

Blackpool	v	Bournemouth	0-0	0-0	-	4-3	-	1-2	06-03-01
Bradford	v	Barnsley	2-1	-	-	4-0	-	-	02-02-01
Brentford	v	Oldham	-	2-0	1-1	2-2	0-0	2-1	03-03-00
Chesterfield	v	Bristol C	-	0-2	-	2-1	2-0	1-1	04-03-01
Colchester	v	Port Vale	-	-	0-1	2-0	4-1	1-4	02-00-02
Doncaster	v	Wrexham	-	-	-	-	-	-	02-03-00
Hartlepool	v	Hull	1-0	2-0	0-1	4-0	2-0	-	05-02-03
Huddersfield	v	Walsall	-	1-1	-	-	-	-	01-01-00
Peterboro	v	Torquay	4-0	0-2	-	-	-	-	03-02-02
Sheff Wed	v	Milton K	1-2	5-1	0-5	1-2	4-2	-	05-04-05
Stockport	v	Swindon	2-1	3-0	-	-	2-5	2-4	03-01-02
Tranmere	v	Luton	-	-	-	-	1-3	1-0	04-00-02

COCA-COLA LEAGUE DIVISION TWO

Boston	v	Scunthorpe	-	-	-	-	1-0	1-1	01-01-00
Bristol R	v	Oxford Utd	-	1-0	6-2	1-1	0-2	1-1	06-02-02
Bury	v	Macclesfield	-	-	-	-	2-1	2-0	02-00-00
Chester	v	Swansea	1-1	0-1	-	-	-	-	07-02-01
Darlington	v	Southend	2-1	1-0	1-1	2-2	2-1	0-0	03-03-00
Kidderminstr	v	Cambridge U	-	-	-	-	2-1	2-2	01-01-00
Mansfield	v	Lincoln	-	5-2	2-3	2-1	-	1-2	04-03-03
Notts Co	v	Leyton O	-	-	-	-	-	-	02-00-00
Rushden & D	v	Rochdale	-	-	-	1-1	3-3	-	00-02-00
Wycombe	v	Shrewsbury	-	-	-	-	-	-	03-01-00
Yeovil	v	Northampton	-	-	-	-	-	0-2	00-00-01

BANK OF SCOTLAND SCOTTISH PREMIER LEAGUE

Aberdeen	v	Dundee	2-2/1-2	0-2/0-1	0-2/0-2	0-0	0-0/3-3	2-2/1-2	06-07-06
Dundee Utd	v	Celtic	1-1/1-2	2-1/0-1	1-2/0-4	0-4	0-2	1-5	08-05-14
Dunfermline	v	Hibernian	-	-	1-1/2-1	1-0	1-1	0-0/1-1	04-11-01
Inv CT	v	Motherwell	-	-	-	-	-	-	00-00-00
Rangers	v	Kilmarnock	1-0/1-1	2-1/1-0	0-3/5-1	3-1/5-0	6-1/4-0	4-0/2-0	17-01-04

BELL'S SCOTTISH FIRST DIVISION

Airdrie Utd	v	Hamilton	3-2/1-0	-	-	-	0-0/2-2	3-0/1-1	10-05-02
Clyde	v	St Johnstone	-	-	-	-	1-2/2-1	2-0/2-3	03-00-04
Partick	v	Raith	-	-	-	2-1/1-0	-	-	04-04-06
Queen Sth	v	St Mirren	-	-	-	-	3-0/0-2	1-2/1-0	02-00-02
Ross C	v	Falkirk	-	-	0-2/4-1	1-2/4-2	1-1/0-1	1-2/1-1	02-02-04

BELL'S SCOTTISH SECOND DIVISION

Arbroath	v	Alloa	0-2/1-2	2-2/2-0	-	-	0-1/0-1	3-1/2-1	06-08-09
Brechin	v	Dumbarton	0-0/3-3	0-2/1-2	3-1/1-0	3-2/0-1	1-1/1-1	-	06-07-07
Morton	v	Forfar	-	-	-	1-3/1-4	-	1-1/1-1	01-06-03

Stirling	v	Ayr	-	-	-	-	-	-	03-05-02
Stranraer	v	Berwick	-	-	2-2/1-1	0-2/2-2	1-0/0-0	-	04-09-06

BELL'S SCOTTISH THIRD DIVISION

C'denbeath	v	Albion	2-3/0-2	0-0/5-0	5-0/1-0	-	-	1-4/1-1	08-08-05
E Stirling	v	Montrose	3-1/2-1	2-0/1-0	1-2/0-1	0-1/2-1	1-1/0-3	1-1/1-4	09-04-12
Elgin	v	East Fife	-	-	1-3/1-3	1-1/2-0	1-1/0-1	-	01-02-03
Queens P	v	Peterhead	-	-	-	0-1/2-0	2-0/1-2	0-2/1-0	03-00-03
Stenhsmuir	v	Gretna	-	-	-	-	-	-	00-00-00

NATIONWIDE CONFERENCE

Barnet	v	Woking	-	-	-	3-0	0-0	0-0	01-02-00
Canvey Islnd	v	Morecambe	-	-	-	-	-	-	00-00-00
Carlisle	v	Crawley	-	-	-	-	-	-	00-00-00
Farnborough	v	Accrington	-	-	-	-	-	1-1	00-01-00
Forest G	v	Scarborough	-	0-1	2-3	2-2	0-0	4-0	01-02-02
Gravesend	v	Leigh RMI	-	-	-	-	1-3	3-1	01-00-01
Halifax	v	Exeter	1-1	1-0	3-1	1-1	-	2-0	03-02-02
Hereford	v	Burton	-	-	-	-	4-0	1-2	01-00-01
Northwich	v	Dagenham	-	-	3-0	1-2	0-2	0-1	03-02-03
Tamworth	v	Aldershot	-	-	-	-	-	3-3	00-01-00
York	v	Stevenage	-	-	-	-	-	-	00-00-00

SUNDAY 3 OCTOBER 2004
FA BARCLAYCARD PREMIER LEAGUE

Chelsea	v	Liverpool	2-1	2-0	3-0	4-0	2-1	0-1	09-04-02

BANK OF SCOTLAND SCOTTISH PREMIER LEAGUE

Hearts	v	Livingston	-	-	-	1-3/2-3	2-1	3-1/1-1	02-01-02

MONDAY 4 OCTOBER 2004
FA BARCLAYCARD PREMIER LEAGUE

Crystal Pal	v	Fulham	-	0-0	0-2	-	-	-	00-01-01

TUESDAY 5 OCTOBER 2004
NATIONWIDE CONFERENCE

Accrington	v	Tamworth	-	-	-	-	-	3-0	01-00-00
Aldershot	v	Gravesend	3-0	2-1	1-0	1-2	-	2-2	03-01-01
Burton	v	Halifax	-	-	-	-	2-2	2-2	00-02-00
Crawley	v	Farnborough	-	-	-	-	-	-	01-00-01
Dagenham	v	Hereford	-	-	2-1	1-0	1-0	0-9	03-00-01
Exeter	v	Barnet	1-0	0-0	1-0	-	-	1-1	03-05-01
Leigh RMI	v	Carlisle	-	-	-	-	-	-	00-00-00
Morecambe	v	York	-	-	-	-	-	-	00-00-00
Scarborough	v	Northwich	-	3-0	4-0	1-2	4-1	1-0	04-00-01
Stevenage	v	Canvey Islnd	-	-	-	-	-	-	00-00-00
Woking	v	Forest G	1-1	2-1	2-0	3-4	1-0	1-1	03-02-01

FRIDAY 8 OCTOBER 2004
COCA-COLA LEAGUE DIVISION TWO

Cheltenham	v	Chester	-	1-0	-	-	-	-	01-00-00
Southend	v	Boston	-	-	-	-	4-2	0-2	01-00-01
Swansea	v	Mansfield	1-0	0-1	-	2-0	-	4-1	07-00-03

SATURDAY 9 OCTOBER 2004
COCA-COLA LEAGUE DIVISION ONE

Barnsley	v	Brentford	-	-	-	-	1-0	0-2	02-00-01
Bournemouth	v	Stockport	-	-	-	-	-	0-0	04-03-00
Bristol C	v	Tranmere	1-1	-	-	2-0	2-0	-	04-02-03

Sponsored by Stan James

Luton	v	Hartlepool	-	-	-	2-2	-	3-2	01-01-00
Milton K	v	Bradford	-	3-2	-	1-2	2-2	2-1	02-01-01
Port Vale	v	Doncaster	-	-	-	-	-	-	00-00-00
Swindon	v	Sheff Wed	-	-	-	-	-	2-3	01-00-02
Torquay	v	Huddersfield	-	-	-	-	-	0-1	00-00-02
Walsall	v	Colchester	1-1	-	0-1	-	-	-	01-01-03
Wrexham	v	Peterboro	-	-	2-1	1-2	-	2-0	04-04-01

COCA-COLA LEAGUE DIVISION TWO

Cambridge U	v	Bristol R	-	1-1	0-3	-	3-1	3-1	03-02-03
Leyton O	v	Bury	-	-	-	-	1-2	2-0	03-00-03
Lincoln	v	Kidderminstr	-	-	3-3	0-1	1-0	1-1	01-02-01
Macclesfield	v	Notts Co	0-1	-	-	-	-	-	01-00-01
Northampton	v	Grimsby	-	-	-	-	-	-	01-00-00
Oxford Utd	v	Darlington	-	-	-	1-2	1-1	3-1	01-01-01
Rochdale	v	Yeovil	-	-	-	-	-	1-3	00-00-01
Scunthorpe	v	Wycombe	-	0-1	-	-	-	-	00-01-01
Shrewsbury	v	Rushden & D	-	-	-	0-2	1-1	-	00-01-01

NATIONWIDE CONFERENCE

Accrington	v	Hereford	-	-	-	-	-	2-0	01-00-00
Barnet	v	Dagenham	-	-	-	4-0	2-1	2-4	02-00-01
Burton	v	Gravesend	-	-	-	-	1-1	3-0	04-02-02
Canvey Islnd	v	Forest G	-	-	-	-	-	-	00-00-00
Crawley	v	Northwich	-	-	-	-	-	-	00-00-00
Exeter	v	Carlisle	2-0	1-1	1-0	1-0	1-0	-	06-03-00
Farnborough	v	York	-	-	-	-	-	-	00-00-00
Leigh RMI	v	Stevenage	-	-	1-4	1-2	2-1	1-3	01-00-03
Morecambe	v	Tamworth	-	-	-	-	-	4-0	01-00-00
Scarborough	v	Aldershot	-	-	-	-	-	1-0	01-00-00
Woking	v	Halifax	-	-	-	-	2-1	2-2	02-03-02

SUNDAY 10 OCTOBER 2004
COCA-COLA LEAGUE DIVISION ONE

Oldham	v	Blackpool	3-0	1-1	-	2-1	1-1	2-3	02-02-02
Hull	v	Chesterfield	-	-	3-1	-	-	-	01-01-00

FRIDAY 15 OCTOBER 2004

COCA-COLA CHAMPIONSHIP

Nottm F	v	Wolves	-	1-1	0-0	2-2	2-2	-	01-05-00

COCA-COLA LEAGUE DIVISION TWO

Cambridge U	v	Northampton	-	-	1-2	3-3	-	0-1	00-02-03

SATURDAY 16 OCTOBER 2004
FA BARCLAYCARD PREMIER LEAGUE

Arsenal	v	Aston Villa	1-0	3-1	1-0	3-2	3-1	2-0	08-04-04
Birmingham	v	Man Utd	-	-	-	-	0-1	1-2	00-00-02
Blackburn	v	Middlesbro	0-0	-	-	0-1	1-0	2-2	04-04-02
Bolton	v	Crystal Pal	3-0	2-0	3-3	-	-	-	04-02-00
Everton	v	Southampton	1-0	4-1	1-1	2-0	2-1	0-0	11-03-02
Fulham	v	Liverpool	-	-	-	0-2	3-2	1-2	01-00-02
Man City	v	Chelsea	-	-	1-2	-	0-3	0-1	01-03-07
WBA	v	Norwich	2-0	1-1	2-3	1-0	-	1-0	05-01-02

COCA-COLA CHAMPIONSHIP

Cardiff	v	Rotherham	0-1	-	-	-	-	3-2	04-02-01
Coventry	v	Leicester	1-1	0-1	1-0	-	1-2	-	02-02-03
Crewe	v	Brighton	-	-	-	-	-	-	02-00-00
Derby	v	Watford	-	2-0	-	-	3-0	3-2	04-02-02

Home		Away							Rec
Ipswich	v	Burnley	-	-	-	-	2-2	6-1	01-01-00
Leeds	v	Preston	-	-	-	-	-	-	00-00-00
Plymouth	v	Wigan	-	-	-	-	1-3	-	03-00-01
QPR	v	West Ham	-	-	-	-	-	-	03-02-00
Stoke	v	Reading	0-4	2-1	0-0	2-0	1-0	3-0	06-03-04
Sunderland	v	Millwall	-	-	-	-	-	0-1	04-01-01

COCA-COLA LEAGUE DIVISION ONE

Home		Away							Rec
Blackpool	v	Colchester	2-1	1-1	-	2-1	3-1	0-0	03-02-00
Bournemouth	v	Port Vale	-	-	1-1	0-0	-	2-1	04-02-00
Bristol C	v	Hull	-	-	-	-	-	-	02-00-00
Doncaster	v	Torquay	-	-	-	-	-	1-0	05-01-04
Hartlepool	v	Chesterfield	-	-	1-2	-	-	2-0	03-00-02
Luton	v	Huddersfield	-	-	-	-	3-0	-	01-01-00
Milton K	v	Brentford	-	-	-	-	-	-	00-00-00
Stockport	v	Peterboro	-	-	-	-	2-1	2-2	03-04-02
Swindon	v	Oldham	-	-	3-0	0-2	0-1	1-2	04-02-04
Tranmere	v	Bradford	0-1	-	-	-	-	-	03-00-01
Wrexham	v	Walsall	2-1	-	0-1	-	-	-	05-01-02

COCA-COLA LEAGUE DIVISION TWO

Home		Away							Rec
Boston	v	Wycombe	-	-	-	-	-	-	01-01-03
Darlington	v	Bury	-	-	-	-	3-1	1-3	03-01-03
Grimsby	v	Bristol R	-	-	-	-	-	-	01-00-02
Kidderminstr	v	Scunthorpe	-	-	0-0	1-0	1-3	0-2	01-01-02
Leyton O	v	Shrewsbury	6-1	1-2	2-0	2-4	0-2	-	06-00-04
Mansfield	v	Notts Co	-	-	-	-	3-2	-	01-01-02
Oxford Utd	v	Lincoln	-	-	-	2-1	1-0	0-0	02-01-00
Rochdale	v	Cheltenham	-	0-0	1-1	2-2	-	0-0	00-04-00
Rushden & D	v	Chester	-	-	2-0	-	-	-	01-00-00
Southend	v	Swansea	2-0	2-1	-	4-2	0-2	1-1	04-01-02
Yeovil	v	Macclesfield	-	-	-	-	-	2-2	03-03-02

BANK OF SCOTLAND SCOTTISH PREMIER LEAGUE

Home		Away							Rec
Celtic	v	Hearts	1-1/3-0	4-0/2-3	6-1/1-0	2-0/2-0	4-2/1-0	5-0/2-2	19-10-03
Dundee	v	Kilmarnock	1-1/2-1	0-0/1-2	0-0/2-2/2-1	1-2/2-0	2-1/2-2/0-1	1-2/2-0	08-07-04
Hibernian	v	Dundee Utd	-	3-2/1-0	3-0/1-0	0-1	2-1/1-1	2-2	15-06-05
Inv CT	v	Aberdeen	-	-	-	-	-	-	00-00-00
Livingston	v	Dunfermline	-	0-1/1-0	-	0-0/4-1	1-1	0-0/0-0	03-04-03
Motherwell	v	Rangers	1-0/1-5	1-5/2-0	0-1/1-2	2-2	1-0	1-1/0-1	09-05-16

BELL'S SCOTTISH FIRST DIVISION

Home		Away							Rec
Airdrie Utd	v	Partick	-	-	-	1-0/1-1	-	-	04-08-00
Clyde	v	Raith	-	-	0-0/3-1	3-2/1-2	-	0-0/4-1	04-03-03
Hamilton	v	Falkirk	2-1/0-2	-	-	-	-	-	02-04-03
Queen Sth	v	St Johnstone	-	-	-	-	0-0/1-2	1-1/1-1	00-04-01
St Mirren	v	Ross C	-	-	-	1-0/1-1	1-1/1-0	1-1/2-0	03-03-00

BELL'S SCOTTISH SECOND DIVISION

Home		Away							Rec
Berwick	v	Ayr	-	-	-	-	-	-	01-01-02
Dumbarton	v	Arbroath	-	-	-	-	-	1-1/1-0	03-04-03
Forfar	v	Alloa	1-2/3-1	-	-	0-1/4-1	1-1/2-0	-	07-05-03
Stirling	v	Brechin	-	-	-	1-3/1-3	-	-	04-02-03
Stranraer	v	Morton	2-3/0-1	-	-	1-4/0-0	-	-	00-01-03

BELL'S SCOTTISH THIRD DIVISION

Home		Away							Rec
East Fife	v	Albion	-	1-4/2-1	0-0/2-1	0-0/2-3	0-4/1-1	-	06-05-04
Gretna	v	E Stirling	-	-	-	-	2-2/3-1	2-1/5-1	03-01-00
Peterhead	v	Montrose	-	-	2-0/1-1	4-0/3-1	4-2/3-0	0-0/1-2	05-02-01
Queens P	v	Elgin	-	-	-	0-0/3-0	1-2/3-2	5-2/4-0	04-01-01
Stenhsmuir	v	C'denbeath	1-2/4-1	-	-	0-3/0-1	4-1/1-1	-	04-04-05

NATIONWIDE CONFERENCE

Aldershot	v	Accrington	-	-	-	-	-	2-1	01-00-00
Carlisle	v	Barnet	2-1	3-1	0-2	-	-	-	04-00-03
Dagenham	v	Leigh RMI	-	-	2-1	0-1	3-1	1-2	02-00-02
Forest G	v	Morecambe	2-2	1-2	0-0	3-1	1-0	1-2	02-02-02
Gravesend	v	Exeter	-	-	-	-	-	3-2	01-00-00
Halifax	v	Farnborough	-	-	-	-	1-0	2-0	04-01-01
Hereford	v	Woking	0-1	2-4	0-1	2-2	5-0	0-1	02-01-04
Northwich	v	Burton	-	-	-	-	1-3	1-2	00-00-02
Stevenage	v	Crawley	-	-	-	-	-	-	00-00-00
Tamworth	v	Scarborough	-	-	-	-	-	0-0	00-01-00
York	v	Canvey Islnd	-	-	-	-	-	-	00-00-00

SUNDAY 17 OCTOBER 2004
FA BARCLAYCARD PREMIER LEAGUE

Charlton	v	Newcastle	2-2	-	2-0	1-1	0-2	0-0	03-04-02

COCA-COLA CHAMPIONSHIP

Gillingham	v	Sheff Utd	-	-	4-1	0-1	1-1	0-3	02-01-02

COCA-COLA LEAGUE DIVISION ONE

Sheff Wed	v	Barnsley	-	-	2-1	3-1	-	2-1	05-00-00

MONDAY 18 OCTOBER 2004
FA BARCLAYCARD PREMIER LEAGUE

Portsmouth	v	Tottenham	-	-	-	-	-	2-0	01-00-00

TUESDAY 19 OCTOBER 2004
COCA-COLA CHAMPIONSHIP

Brighton	v	Cardiff	0-2	-	1-0	1-0	-	-	03-01-03
Burnley	v	Coventry	-	-	-	1-0	3-1	1-2	02-00-01
Leicester	v	Ipswich	-	-	2-1	1-1	1-2	-	02-02-05
Millwall	v	Gillingham	3-3	2-2	-	1-2	2-2	1-2	01-03-03
Preston	v	QPR	-	-	5-0	-	-	-	01-00-00
Reading	v	Leeds	-	-	-	-	-	-	00-00-00
Rotherham	v	Plymouth	0-2	1-1	-	-	-	-	01-02-03
Sheff Utd	v	Nottm F	-	2-1	1-3	0-0	1-0	1-2	05-02-02
Watford	v	Sunderland	2-1	2-3	-	-	-	2-2	03-04-03
West Ham	v	Stoke	-	-	-	-	-	0-1	00-01-01
Wigan	v	Crewe	-	-	-	-	2-0	2-3	03-01-01
Wolves	v	Derby	-	-	-	-	1-1	-	01-02-03

COCA-COLA LEAGUE DIVISION ONE

Bradford	v	Blackpool	-	-	-	-	-	-	03-00-01
Brentford	v	Hartlepool	3-1	-	-	-	-	2-1	04-00-00
Colchester	v	Wrexham	1-3	2-2	1-1	2-1	-	3-1	03-02-03
Huddersfield	v	Tranmere	0-0	1-0	3-0	2-1	1-2	-	07-01-02
Oldham	v	Bristol C	-	1-1	0-0	0-1	1-0	1-1	03-03-02
Peterboro	v	Sheff Wed	-	-	-	-	-	0-1	00-00-01
Port Vale	v	Swindon	0-1	2-0	3-0	0-2	1-1	3-3	05-04-03
Torquay	v	Bournemouth	-	-	-	-	4-0	-	02-00-00
Walsall	v	Luton	1-0	-	3-1	-	-	-	03-00-01

COCA-COLA LEAGUE DIVISION TWO

Bristol R	v	Yeovil	-	-	-	-	-	0-1	00-00-01
Bury	v	Boston	-	-	-	-	0-0	1-3	00-01-01
Cheltenham	v	Mansfield	-	1-0	2-2	2-3	3-1	4-2	03-01-01
Chester	v	Kidderminstr	-	-	-	-	-	-	00-00-00
Lincoln	v	Rochdale	-	1-1	1-1	1-1	2-0	1-1	03-06-06
Macclesfield	v	Cambridge U	-	-	-	-	1-1	0-1	01-01-01

Home		Away							Record
Northampton	v	Oxford Utd	-	-	0-1	-	-	2-1	01-00-01
Notts Co	v	Darlington	-	-	-	-	-	-	00-01-00
Scunthorpe	v	Southend	1-1	-	1-1	2-0	4-1	1-1	02-04-00
Shrewsbury	v	Grimsby	-	-	-	-	-	-	00-00-01
Swansea	v	Leyton O	1-1	0-0	-	0-1	0-1	2-1	03-06-04
Wycombe	v	Rushden & D	-	-	-	-	-	0-2	00-00-01

WEDNESDAY 20 OCTOBER 2004
COCA-COLA LEAGUE DIVISION ONE

Home		Away							Record
Barnsley	v	Doncaster	-	-	-	-	-	-	00-00-00
Chesterfield	v	Stockport	-	-	-	-	1-0	0-3	01-02-03
Hull	v	Milton K	-	-	-	-	-	-	00-00-00

FRIDAY 22 OCTOBER 2004
COCA-COLA CHAMPIONSHIP

Home		Away							Record
Burnley	v	Derby	-	-	-	-	2-0	1-0	03-00-00

SATURDAY 23 OCTOBER 2004
FA BARCLAYCARD PREMIER LEAGUE

Home		Away							Record
Aston Villa	v	Fulham	-	-	-	2-0	3-1	3-0	03-00-00
Chelsea	v	Blackburn	1-1	-	-	0-0	1-2	2-2	00-05-06
Crystal Pal	v	WBA	1-1	0-2	2-2	0-1	-	2-2	03-04-02
Liverpool	v	Charlton	3-3	-	3-0	2-0	2-1	0-1	05-01-01
Man Utd	v	Arsenal	1-1	1-1	6-1	0-1	2-0	0-0	07-06-03
Middlesbro	v	Portsmouth	-	-	-	-	-	0-0	03-02-02
Newcastle	v	Man City	-	-	0-1	-	2-0	3-0	04-01-01
Norwich	v	Everton	-	-	-	-	-	-	04-03-00
Southampton	v	Birmingham	-	-	-	-	2-0	0-0	01-01-00
Tottenham	v	Bolton	-	-	-	3-2	3-1	0-1	03-01-01

COCA-COLA CHAMPIONSHIP

Home		Away							Record
Brighton	v	Leeds	-	-	-	-	-	-	01-01-00
Leicester	v	Stoke	-	-	-	-	0-0	-	02-02-01
Millwall	v	Cardiff	-	2-0	-	-	-	0-0	01-01-00
Preston	v	Nottm F	-	-	1-1	2-1	1-1	2-2	01-03-00
Reading	v	Crewe	-	-	-	-	-	1-1	01-03-00
Rotherham	v	Sunderland	-	-	-	-	-	0-2	00-00-01
Sheff Utd	v	Plymouth	-	-	-	-	-	-	01-00-00
Watford	v	Ipswich	1-0	-	-	-	0-2	1-2	02-02-04
West Ham	v	Gillingham	-	-	-	-	-	2-1	01-00-00
Wigan	v	Coventry	-	-	-	-	-	2-1	01-00-00
Wolves	v	QPR	1-2	3-2	1-1	-	-	-	02-02-01

COCA-COLA LEAGUE DIVISION ONE

Home		Away							Record
Barnsley	v	Swindon	1-3	1-0	-	-	1-1	1-1	04-05-02
Bradford	v	Sheff Wed	-	1-1	-	0-2	1-1	-	00-02-01
Brentford	v	Blackpool	-	2-0	-	2-0	5-0	0-0	08-02-01
Chesterfield	v	Doncaster	-	-	-	-	-	-	02-03-01
Colchester	v	Tranmere	-	-	-	2-1	2-2	1-1	01-02-01
Huddersfield	v	Milton K	-	-	0-2	-	-	-	00-00-01
Hull	v	Luton	-	-	-	0-4	-	-	00-00-01
Oldham	v	Bournemouth	2-3	1-0	2-1	3-3	-	1-1	05-02-01
Peterboro	v	Hartlepool	1-1	2-1	-	-	-	3-4	02-03-03
Port Vale	v	Stockport	1-1	1-1	-	-	0-1	2-2	01-05-01
Torquay	v	Wrexham	-	-	-	-	2-1	-	02-02-01
Walsall	v	Bristol C	-	-	0-0	-	-	-	02-02-01

COCA-COLA LEAGUE DIVISION TWO

Home		Away							Record
Bristol R	v	Kidderminstr	-	-	-	2-1	1-2	1-0	02-00-01
Bury	v	Rushden & D	-	-	-	-	0-1	-	00-00-01

190

Cheltenham	v	Cambridge U	-	-	-	-	-	0-3	00-00-01
Chester	v	Grimsby	-	-	-	-	-	-	00-00-01
Lincoln	v	Leyton O	-	0-0	2-3	2-0	1-1	0-0	03-04-02
Macclesfield	v	Oxford Utd	-	-	-	0-1	2-1	2-1	02-00-01
Northampton	v	Rochdale	-	0-1	-	-	-	3-1	04-02-03
Notts Co	v	Boston	-	-	-	-	-	-	00-00-00
Scunthorpe	v	Yeovil	-	-	-	-	-	3-0	01-00-00
Shrewsbury	v	Southend	3-1	2-1	0-1	2-0	0-1	-	03-00-03
Swansea	v	Darlington	2-0	0-0	-	2-0	1-0	1-0	06-02-00
Wycombe	v	Mansfield	-	-	-	-	3-3	-	01-01-00

BANK OF SCOTLAND SCOTTISH PREMIER LEAGUE

Aberdeen	v	Motherwell	1-1/1-1	1-1/2-1	3-3	4-2/1-0	1-1	0-3/0-2	14-11-05
Dundee	v	Dunfermline	1-0/3-1	-	3-0/0-1	2-2	2-3/2-2	0-2/0-1	04-04-07
Hearts	v	Hibernian	-	0-3/2-1	0-0/1-1	1-1	5-1/4-4	2-0	14-11-03
Kilmarnock	v	Inv CT	-	-	-	-	-	-	00-00-00
Livingston	v	Celtic	-	-	-	0-0/1-3	0-2	0-2	00-01-03
Rangers	v	Dundee Utd	2-1/0-1	4-1/3-0	3-0/0-2	3-2	3-0	2-1	19-02-06

BELL'S SCOTTISH FIRST DIVISION

Falkirk	v	St Mirren	1-1/1-0	3-1/2-0	-	3-2/0-0	2-0/3-1	0-0/1-0	12-06-00
Partick	v	Clyde	0-2/0-1	0-0/1-2	-	3-0/2-1	-	-	03-03-04
Raith	v	Hamilton	0-2/1-1	-	-	-	1-1/1-1	-	06-06-03
Ross C	v	Queen Sth	-	1-1/2-0	-	-	2-0/0-3	1-0/1-2	03-01-02
St Johnstone	v	Airdrie Utd	-	-	-	-	-	-	08-04-01

BELL'S SCOTTISH SECOND DIVISION

Alloa	v	Stranraer	-	1-1/4-0	-	2-2/0-0	-	-	03-06-02
Arbroath	v	Stirling	0-3/1-0	2-1/3-2	3-2/1-1	-	-	-	05-01-05
Ayr	v	Dumbarton	-	-	-	-	-	-	01-03-02
Brechin	v	Forfar	-	0-2/1-0	-	-	1-0/3-4	-	04-01-04
Morton	v	Berwick	-	-	-	1-2/3-2	-	1-3/2-1	03-01-02

BELL'S SCOTTISH THIRD DIVISION

Albion	v	Gretna	-	-	-	-	2-1/1-1	1-3/1-2	01-01-02
C'denbeath	v	Queens P	0-3/0-0	0-2/2-3	-	-	-	0-1/5-1	05-06-11
E Stirling	v	Peterhead	-	-	1-3/1-0	2-3/1-0	1-4/1-1	1-3/0-3	02-01-05
Elgin	v	Stenhsmuir	-	-	-	-	-	-	00-00-00
Montrose	v	East Fife	-	1-2/1-1	0-1/1-1	2-1/0-1	0-5/0-2	-	02-04-11

NATIONWIDE CONFERENCE

Barnet	v	York	-	6-3	2-0	-	-	-	03-00-02
Canvey Islnd	v	Leigh RMI	-	-	-	-	-	-	00-00-00
Carlisle	v	Hereford	-	-	-	-	-	-	04-01-03
Exeter	v	Aldershot	-	-	-	-	-	2-1	01-00-00
Farnborough	v	Dagenham	-	2-1	-	1-2	1-0	2-2	03-01-03
Forest G	v	Northwich	3-1	5-1	1-0	2-0	1-0	0-0	05-01-00
Halifax	v	Gravesend	-	-	-	-	2-1	1-0	02-00-00
Morecambe	v	Stevenage	1-1	3-3	1-2	0-3	3-1	2-1	03-02-04
Scarborough	v	Accrington	-	-	-	-	-	2-1	01-00-00
Tamworth	v	Crawley	3-1	3-0	0-2	2-0	1-1	-	04-01-01
Woking	v	Burton	-	-	-	-	2-2	1-0	01-01-00

TUESDAY 26 OCTOBER 2004
BANK OF SCOTLAND SCOTTISH PREMIER LEAGUE

Dundee Utd	v	Hearts	0-0/1-3	0-2/0-1	0-4/1-1	0-2	0-3	2-1/0-2	08-10-10

WEDNESDAY 27 OCTOBER 2004
BANK OF SCOTLAND SCOTTISH PREMIER LEAGUE

Celtic	v	Aberdeen	2-0/3-2	7-0/5-1	6-0	2-0/1-0	7-0	4-0/1-2	21-04-05

Home		Away							Record
Dunfermline	v	Rangers	0-2/0-3	-	0-0	1-4/2-4/1-1	0-6/1-3	2-0/2-3	01-04-15
Hibernian	v	Livingston	-	-	-	0-3	1-0/2-2	0-2/3-1	02-01-02
Inv CT	v	Dundee	-	-	-	-	-	-	00-00-00
Motherwell	v	Kilmarnock	0-0/1-2	0-4/2-0	1-2	2-2/2-0	0-1	2-1/1-0	10-04-06

FRIDAY 29 OCTOBER 2004
COCA-COLA CHAMPIONSHIP

Home		Away							Record
Crewe	v	Sheff Utd	1-2	1-0	1-0	2-2	-	0-1	03-01-02

SATURDAY 30 OCTOBER 2004
FA BARCLAYCARD PREMIER LEAGUE

Home		Away							Record
Arsenal	v	Southampton	1-1	3-1	1-0	1-1	6-1	2-0	12-04-00
Birmingham	v	Crystal Pal	3-1	2-0	2-1	1-0	-	-	05-01-02
Blackburn	v	Liverpool	1-3	-	-	1-1	2-2	1-3	04-03-03
Charlton	v	Middlesbro	1-1	-	1-0	0-0	1-0	1-0	05-03-03
Everton	v	Aston Villa	0-0	0-0	0-1	3-2	2-1	2-0	06-05-05
Fulham	v	Tottenham	-	-	-	0-2	3-2	2-1	02-00-01
Portsmouth	v	Man Utd	-	-	-	-	-	1-0	01-00-00
WBA	v	Chelsea	-	-	-	-	0-2	-	00-00-02

COCA-COLA CHAMPIONSHIP

Home		Away							Record
Cardiff	v	Leicester	-	-	-	-	-	-	00-00-00
Coventry	v	Reading	-	-	-	-	2-0	1-2	01-00-01
Derby	v	Rotherham	-	-	-	-	3-0	1-0	02-00-00
Gillingham	v	Wolves	-	-	1-0	2-3	0-4	-	01-00-03
Ipswich	v	Preston	-	-	-	-	3-0	2-0	02-00-00
Nottm F	v	Watford	-	-	0-2	0-0	0-1	1-1	01-02-02
Plymouth	v	West Ham	-	-	-	-	-	-	00-01-01
QPR	v	Burnley	-	-	0-1	-	-	-	00-00-01
Stoke	v	Millwall	1-0	3-1	3-2	-	0-1	0-0	05-01-02
Sunderland	v	Brighton	-	-	-	-	-	-	03-00-00

COCA-COLA LEAGUE DIVISION ONE

Home		Away							Record
Blackpool	v	Huddersfield	-	-	-	1-2	1-1	-	02-03-02
Bournemouth	v	Barnsley	-	-	-	-	-	2-2	02-01-00
Bristol C	v	Colchester	-	1-1	1-1	3-1	1-2	1-0	02-02-01
Doncaster	v	Peterboro	-	-	-	-	-	-	00-00-04
Hartlepool	v	Port Vale	-	-	-	-	-	2-0	01-01-01
Luton	v	Bradford	-	-	-	-	-	-	00-00-00
Milton K	v	Walsall	-	-	-	2-2	3-2	0-1	01-01-01
Sheff Wed	v	Chesterfield	-	-	-	-	-	0-0	00-01-00
Stockport	v	Oldham	-	-	-	-	1-2	1-1	00-01-01
Swindon	v	Torquay	-	-	-	-	-	-	00-00-00
Tranmere	v	Brentford	-	-	-	1-0	3-1	4-1	05-01-00
Wrexham	v	Hull	-	-	-	-	0-0	-	02-02-00

COCA-COLA LEAGUE DIVISION TWO

Home		Away							Record
Boston	v	Bristol R	-	-	-	-	0-0	1-0	01-01-00
Cambridge U	v	Lincoln	-	-	-	-	0-0	0-0	02-03-02
Darlington	v	Wycombe	-	-	-	-	-	-	00-01-01
Grimsby	v	Swansea	-	-	-	-	-	-	01-00-00
Kidderminstr	v	Shrewsbury	-	-	3-1	1-0	2-2	-	02-01-00
Leyton O	v	Scunthorpe	1-0	-	1-1	0-0	2-0	1-1	04-04-01
Mansfield	v	Bury	-	-	-	-	-	5-3	02-02-03
Oxford Utd	v	Cheltenham	-	-	-	3-0	-	1-0	02-00-00
Rochdale	v	Macclesfield	-	0-1	2-2	1-1	3-1	1-2	02-02-02
Rushden & D	v	Notts Co	-	-	-	-	-	2-1	01-00-00
Southend	v	Northampton	-	2-2	-	-	-	0-1	01-02-01
Yeovil	v	Chester	-	-	2-1	0-1	1-1	-	01-01-01

BANK OF SCOTLAND SCOTTISH PREMIER LEAGUE

Home		Away							Record
Dundee Utd	v	Dunfermline	1-1/1-1	-	3-2/1-0	3-2/0-2	1-2/3-0	1-0/3-2	13-06-03
Hearts	v	Dundee	0-2/1-2	4-0/2-0	3-1/2-0	3-1/2-0	1-2/1-0	2-2/3-1	11-04-05

Sponsored by Stan James

Inv CT	v	Livingston	2-1/3-1	2-0/4-1	2-2/2-3	-	-	-	04-03-03
Kilmarnock	v	Hibernian	-	0-2/1-0	0-1/1-1	0-0/1-0	2-1/6-2	0-2/2-0	08-06-06
Motherwell	v	Celtic	1-2/1-7	3-2/1-1	3-3	1-2/0-4	2-1/0-4	0-2/1-1	07-12-12
Rangers	v	Aberdeen	2-1/3-1	3-0/5-0	3-1/1-0	2-0/2-0	2-0/2-1	3-0	23-06-02

BELL'S SCOTTISH FIRST DIVISION

Airdrie Utd	v	Falkirk	0-3/1-2	0-0/0-2	1-2/1-2	2-1/1-0	-	-	06-07-10
Clyde	v	Queen Sth	2-0/2-1	3-0/3-1	-	-	2-1/2-2	3-1/2-0	14-04-03
Hamilton	v	St Mirren	0-0/0-0	-	-	-	-	-	04-09-01
Partick	v	Ross C	-	0-2/4-2	-	0-0/1-1	-	-	01-02-01
Raith	v	St Johnstone	-	-	-	-	-	1-4/1-1	01-05-03

BELL'S SCOTTISH SECOND DIVISION

Alloa	v	Brechin	-	-	-	-	-	-	04-01-01
Berwick	v	Stirling	-	-	2-2/4-1	-	-	-	03-07-01
Forfar	v	Dumbarton	-	5-0/4-3	-	-	2-0/0-1	3-1/1-0	05-00-01
Morton	v	Ayr	1-2/1-4	0-0/1-2	1-1/0-6	-	-	-	05-04-09
Stranraer	v	Arbroath	-	2-2/0-1	2-1/0-1	-	-	-	08-01-04

BELL'S SCOTTISH THIRD DIVISION

E Stirling	v	C'denbeath	1-1/0-0	0-1/0-4	0-2/0-2	-	-	1-1/0-1	08-07-09
Gretna	v	Queens P	-	-	-	-	2-2/0-1	1-1/0-1	00-02-02
Montrose	v	Elgin	-	-	0-0/2-1	0-2/1-0	1-0/2-0	3-3/4-3	05-02-01
Peterhead	v	Albion	-	-	1-2/1-1	0-0/0-2	2-0/0-0	2-1/5-0	03-03-02
Stenhsmuir	v	East Fife	-	-	-	-	-	3-0/0-1	05-06-06

SUNDAY 31 OCTOBER 2004
FA BARCLAYCARD PREMIER LEAGUE

| Bolton | v | Newcastle | - | - | - | 0-4 | 4-3 | 1-0 | 03-00-02 |

COCA-COLA CHAMPIONSHIP

| Leeds | v | Wigan | - | - | - | - | - | - | 00-00-00 |

MONDAY 1 NOVEMBER 2004
FA BARCLAYCARD PREMIER LEAGUE

| Man City | v | Norwich | - | 3-1 | - | 3-1 | - | - | 08-01-01 |

TUESDAY 2 NOVEMBER 2004
COCA-COLA CHAMPIONSHIP

Cardiff	v	West Ham	-	-	-	-	-	0-0	00-01-00
Crewe	v	Leicester	-	-	-	-	-	-	00-00-00
Gillingham	v	Watford	-	-	0-3	0-0	3-0	1-0	03-02-01
Ipswich	v	Sheff Utd	4-1	1-1	-	-	3-2	3-0	05-05-00
Leeds	v	Burnley	-	-	-	-	-	-	00-00-00
Plymouth	v	Reading	-	-	-	-	-	-	01-01-00
QPR	v	Millwall	-	-	-	-	-	-	00-01-01
Stoke	v	Wigan	2-1	1-1	2-0	2-2	-	1-1	05-03-00
Sunderland	v	Wolves	2-1	-	-	-	-	-	04-03-01

WEDNESDAY 3 NOVEMBER 2004
COCA-COLA CHAMPIONSHIP

Coventry	v	Preston	-	-	-	2-2	1-2	4-1	01-01-01
Derby	v	Brighton	-	-	-	-	1-0	-	02-00-00
Nottm F	v	Rotherham	-	-	-	2-0	3-2	2-2	02-01-00

FRIDAY 5 NOVEMBER 2004
COCA-COLA CHAMPIONSHIP

| Millwall | v | Sunderland | - | - | - | - | - | 2-1 | 04-01-01 |

SATURDAY 6 NOVEMBER 2004

FA BARCLAYCARD PREMIER LEAGUE

Aston Villa	v	Portsmouth	-	-	-	-	2-1	01-00-00
Chelsea	v	Everton	3-1	1-1	2-1	3-0	4-1	0-0	08-05-02
Crystal Pal	v	Arsenal	-	-	-	-	-	00-03-03
Liverpool	v	Birmingham	-	-	-	-	2-2	3-1	01-01-00
Newcastle	v	Fulham	-	-	-	1-1	2-0	3-1	02-01-00
Norwich	v	Blackburn	-	0-2	1-1	-	-	01-03-01
Southampton	v	WBA	-	-	-	-	1-0	-	01-00-00
Tottenham	v	Charlton	2-2	-	0-0	0-1	2-2	0-1	01-04-02

COCA-COLA CHAMPIONSHIP

Brighton	v	Crewe	-	-	-	-	-	00-01-01
Burnley	v	Ipswich	-	-	-	-	1-1	4-2	01-01-00
Leicester	v	Coventry	1-0	1-0	1-3	-	2-1	-	03-02-02
Preston	v	Leeds	-	-	-	-	-	00-00-00
Reading	v	Stoke	2-1	1-0	3-3	1-0	1-1	0-0	07-04-02
Rotherham	v	Cardiff	1-0	-	-	-	-	0-0	04-02-01
Sheff Utd	v	Gillingham	-	-	1-2	0-0	2-2	0-0	01-03-01
Watford	v	Derby	-	0-0	-	-	2-0	2-1	03-03-02
West Ham	v	QPR	-	-	-	-	-	01-03-01
Wigan	v	Plymouth	-	-	-	-	0-1	-	00-01-03
Wolves	v	Nottm F	-	3-0	2-0	1-0	2-1	-	05-01-00

COCA-COLA LEAGUE DIVISION ONE

Barnsley	v	Port Vale	0-2	3-1	-	-	2-1	0-0	04-04-02
Bradford	v	Colchester	-	-	-	-	-	00-00-00
Bristol C	v	Milton K	-	-	-	-	-	00-00-00
Chesterfield	v	Blackpool	1-2	0-0	2-1	2-1	1-0	1-0	05-05-02
Hartlepool	v	Doncaster	-	-	-	-	-	03-01-03
Hull	v	Walsall	-	-	-	-	-	01-01-00
Luton	v	Wrexham	1-2	3-1	3-4	-	-	3-2	02-01-03
Peterboro	v	Bournemouth	-	-	1-2	6-0	-	0-1	03-01-03
Stockport	v	Sheff Wed	-	-	2-1	3-1	-	1-0	03-00-00
Torquay	v	Oldham	-	-	-	-	-	00-00-00
Tranmere	v	Swindon	0-0	3-1	-	0-0	0-1	1-0	06-03-01

COCA-COLA LEAGUE DIVISION TWO

Cheltenham	v	Bury	-	-	-	-	1-2	00-00-01
Chester	v	Leyton O	0-2	1-5	-	-	-	04-02-04
Kidderminstr	v	Boston	-	-	-	-	0-0	2-0	01-02-04
Lincoln	v	Northampton	1-0	2-2	-	-	0-0	05-04-01
Mansfield	v	Macclesfield	-	1-0	4-4	4-0	-	3-2	04-01-00
Notts Co	v	Shrewsbury	-	-	-	-	-	01-02-01
Rochdale	v	Cambridge U	0-2	-	-	-	4-3	2-2	06-01-01
Rushden & D	v	Darlington	-	-	-	2-1	2-0	-	02-00-00
Scunthorpe	v	Grimsby	-	-	-	-	-	00-02-00
Southend	v	Oxford Utd	-	-	-	2-2	2-1	0-1	02-02-03
Swansea	v	Bristol R	-	-	0-0	2-1	0-1	0-0	02-05-02
Wycombe	v	Yeovil	-	-	-	-	-	03-01-01

BANK OF SCOTLAND SCOTTISH PREMIER LEAGUE

Aberdeen	v	Hearts	2-0/2-5	3-1/1-2	1-1/1-0	3-2/2-3	1-1/0-1	0-1	14-07-10
Celtic	v	Kilmarnock	1-1/1-0	5-1/4-2	2-1/6-0	1-0	5-0/2-0	5-1	15-05-00
Dundee	v	Dundee Utd	2-2/1-3	0-2/3-0	3-0/2-3	1-1/0-1	3-2	2-1	05-04-11
Dunfermline	v	Inv CT	-	4-0/1-0	-	-	-	-	02-00-00
Hibernian	v	Motherwell	-	2-2/2-2	2-0/1-1	1-1/4-0	3-1/1-0	0-2/3-3	14-13-03
Livingston	v	Rangers	-	-	-	0-2/2-1	0-2/1-2	0-0/1-1	01-02-03

BELL'S SCOTTISH FIRST DIVISION

Falkirk	v	Partick	-	-	-	1-1/1-4	-	-	05-03-08

Queen Sth	v	Airdrie Utd	-	-	-	-	-	-	00-00-01
Ross C	v	Raith	-	-	0-0/4-0	1-0/4-2	-	3-2/1-1	04-02-00
St Johnstone	v	Hamilton	-	-	-	-	-	-	04-01-00
St Mirren	v	Clyde	-	-	-	4-1/2-2	1-4/1-2	2-1/2-3	03-02-03

BELL'S SCOTTISH SECOND DIVISION

Arbroath	v	Morton	-	-	-	-	-	0-4/2-2	00-01-01
Ayr	v	Alloa	-	-	3-1/4-1	-	3-1/0-1	-	04-00-01
Brechin	v	Stranraer	-	-	-	-	3-1/3-1	-	04-05-03
Dumbarton	v	Berwick	0-0/1-1	2-1/0-2	-	-	1-2/2-2	1-1/4-1	06-08-06
Stirling	v	Forfar	3-1/2-2	-	3-3/1-0	-	-	-	05-02-01

BELL'S SCOTTISH THIRD DIVISION

Albion	v	Montrose	4-1/0-0	1-3/0-2	3-2/2-1	0-0/0-0	1-1/3-0	0-1/3-0	09-06-09
C'denbeath	v	Gretna	-	-	-	-	-	0-1/1-2	00-00-02
East Fife	v	Peterhead	-	-	1-1/2-1	0-1/2-3	3-3/0-2	-	01-02-03
Elgin	v	E Stirling	-	-	1-2/4-2	2-1/2-2	3-1/3-0	3-1/3-0	06-01-01
Queens P	v	Stenhsmuir	0-0/4-1	-	2-0/1-2	-	-	-	05-05-03

NATIONWIDE CONFERENCE

Accrington	v	Exeter	-	-	-	-	-	1-2	00-00-01
Aldershot	v	Morecambe	-	-	-	-	-	2-2	00-01-00
Burton	v	Farnborough	-	-	-	-	2-0	1-0	04-00-00
Crawley	v	Woking	-	-	-	-	-	-	00-00-00
Dagenham	v	Scarborough	-	-	1-0	4-2	1-0	1-0	04-00-00
Gravesend	v	Carlisle	-	-	-	-	-	-	00-00-00
Hereford	v	Barnet	-	-	-	2-1	4-0	2-0	05-03-00
Leigh RMI	v	Tamworth	-	-	-	-	-	1-1	00-01-00
Northwich	v	Canvey Islnd	-	-	-	-	-	-	00-00-00
Stevenage	v	Halifax	-	-	-	-	0-1	1-0	04-00-02
York	v	Forest G	-	-	-	-	-	-	00-00-00

SUNDAY 7 NOVEMBER 2004
FA BARCLAYCARD PREMIER LEAGUE

Man Utd	v	Man City	-	-	1-1	-	1-1	3-1	06-04-00
Middlesbro	v	Bolton	-	-	-	1-1	2-0	2-0	03-01-02

COCA-COLA LEAGUE DIVISION ONE

Huddersfield	v	Brentford	-	-	-	1-1	0-2	-	03-01-04

SATURDAY 13 NOVEMBER 2004
FA BARCLAYCARD PREMIER LEAGUE

Birmingham	v	Everton	-	-	-	-	1-1	3-0	01-01-00
Bolton	v	Aston Villa	-	-	-	3-2	1-0	2-2	02-01-02
Charlton	v	Norwich	-	1-0	-	-	-	-	02-02-02
Fulham	v	Chelsea	-	-	-	1-1	0-0	0-1	00-02-01
Liverpool	v	Crystal Pal	-	-	-	-	-	-	04-01-01
Man City	v	Blackburn	-	2-0	-	-	2-2	1-1	03-03-02
Southampton	v	Portsmouth	-	-	-	-	-	3-0	01-00-00
Tottenham	v	Arsenal	1-3	2-1	1-1	1-1	1-1	2-2	05-08-03

COCA-COLA CHAMPIONSHIP

Burnley	v	Nottm F	-	-	1-0	1-1	1-0	0-3	02-01-01
Coventry	v	Plymouth	-	-	-	-	-	-	00-00-00
Gillingham	v	Derby	-	-	-	-	1-0	0-0	01-01-00
Ipswich	v	Leeds	-	-	1-2	1-2	-	-	02-02-03
Leicester	v	Sunderland	-	5-2	2-0	1-0	-	-	07-02-01
Preston	v	Millwall	0-1	3-2	-	1-0	2-1	1-2	05-00-02
QPR	v	Wigan	-	-	-	1-1	0-1	-	00-01-01
Reading	v	Cardiff	-	0-1	-	1-2	-	2-1	02-01-03

Rotherham	v	Wolves	-	-	-	0-3	0-0	-	00-01-01
Sheff Utd	v	Watford	3-0	-	0-1	0-2	1-2	2-2	03-02-03
Stoke	v	Crewe	-	-	-	-	-	1-1	01-01-01
West Ham	v	Brighton	-	-	-	-	-	-	02-00-00

BANK OF SCOTLAND SCOTTISH PREMIER LEAGUE

Aberdeen	v	Dunfermline	2-1/3-1	-	0-0/1-0	3-2/1-0	3-1/1-0	1-2/2-0	14-03-03
Celtic	v	Inv CT	-	-	-	-	-	-	00-00-00
Dundee Utd	v	Livingston	-	-	-	0-0	2-3/0-1	2-0	01-01-02
Hibernian	v	Rangers	-	0-1/2-2	1-0/0-0	0-3	2-4/0-2	0-1	05-06-17
Kilmarnock	v	Hearts	3-0/1-0	2-2/0-1	0-3/1-1	1-0/3-3	0-1/1-0	0-2/1-1	09-06-07
Motherwell	v	Dundee	2-1/1-2	0-2/0-3	0-2/0-3	4-2/2-1	1-1/1-2	0-3/5-3	09-02-09

BELL'S SCOTTISH FIRST DIVISION

Airdrie Utd	v	Clyde	-	-	1-3/1-0	1-2/2-2	-	-	04-05-02
Hamilton	v	Queen Sth	-	0-3/1-1	-	1-1/3-1	-	-	02-03-01
Partick	v	St Mirren	-	-	-	3-3/1-0	-	-	01-04-01
Raith	v	Falkirk	1-1/2-1	2-1/0-1	0-2/0-0	5-2/5-1	-	0-1/2-0	09-03-06
St Johnstone	v	Ross C	-	-	-	-	1-1/2-0	1-1/1-1	01-03-00

BELL'S SCOTTISH SECOND DIVISION

Alloa	v	Berwick	-	-	-	2-2/1-1	-	2-3/4-2	07-03-03
Arbroath	v	Brechin	-	-	-	-	-	-	02-02-04
Forfar	v	Ayr	-	-	-	-	-	-	04-02-03
Morton	v	Stirling	-	-	-	-	5-1/2-2	-	05-06-03
Stranraer	v	Dumbarton	-	-	-	-	1-0/1-2	-	05-03-02

BELL'S SCOTTISH THIRD DIVISION

E Stirling	v	East Fife	-	0-2/1-0	2-5/1-0	2-1/1-2	1-4/0-4	-	08-01-08
Elgin	v	C'denbeath	-	-	2-3/0-2	-	-	0-4/0-0	00-01-03
Gretna	v	Peterhead	-	-	-	-	1-4/1-1	3-2/3-2	02-01-01
Montrose	v	Queens P	1-0/3-0	2-1/0-2	-	3-1/3-1	1-0/1-1	0-0/1-1	11-07-05
Stenhsmuir	v	Albion	4-1/1-2	-	-	-	-	-	05-02-03

SUNDAY 14 NOVEMBER 2004
FA BARCLAYCARD PREMIER LEAGUE

Newcastle	v	Man Utd	1-2	3-0	1-1	4-3	2-6	1-2	03-04-05
WBA	v	Middlesbro	-	-	-	-	1-0	-	02-02-02

FRIDAY 19 NOVEMBER 2004
COCA-COLA LEAGUE DIVISION TWO

Northampton	v	Chester	-	3-1	-	-	-	-	05-00-01

SATURDAY 20 NOVEMBER 2004
FA BARCLAYCARD PREMIER LEAGUE

Arsenal	v	WBA	-	-	-	-	5-2	-	01-00-00
Chelsea	v	Bolton	-	-	-	5-1	1-0	1-2	04-00-01
Crystal Pal	v	Newcastle	-	-	-	-	-	-	00-00-02
Everton	v	Fulham	-	-	-	2-1	2-0	3-1	03-00-00
Man Utd	v	Charlton	4-1	-	2-1	0-0	4-1	2-0	06-01-00
Middlesbro	v	Liverpool	1-3	1-0	1-0	1-2	1-0	0-0	04-02-04
Norwich	v	Southampton	-	-	-	-	-	-	03-03-01
Portsmouth	v	Man City	-	2-2	-	2-1	-	4-2	03-01-02

COCA-COLA CHAMPIONSHIP

Brighton	v	Burnley	-	-	-	-	2-2	-	02-02-00
Cardiff	v	Preston	-	0-4	-	-	-	2-2	01-02-02
Crewe	v	Gillingham	-	-	2-1	0-0	-	1-1	05-02-00
Derby	v	Sheff Utd	-	-	-	-	2-1	2-0	03-01-01
Leeds	v	QPR	-	-	-	-	-	-	02-02-02

Sponsored by Stan James

Nottm F	v	Reading	-	-	-	-	2-0	0-1	02-00-01
Plymouth	v	Stoke	-	-	-	-	-	-	02-01-00
Watford	v	Rotherham	-	-	-	3-2	1-2	1-0	03-00-01
Wigan	v	Leicester	-	-	-	-	-	-	00-00-00
Wolves	v	Coventry	-	-	-	3-1	0-2	-	01-00-01

COCA-COLA LEAGUE DIVISION ONE

Blackpool	v	Tranmere	-	-	-	1-1	3-0	2-1	02-01-01
Bournemouth	v	Chesterfield	0-0	1-1	-	3-1	-	2-2	04-03-00
Brentford	v	Bradford	-	-	-	-	-	-	04-00-01
Colchester	v	Huddersfield	-	-	-	3-3	2-0	-	01-01-00
Doncaster	v	Stockport	-	-	-	-	-	-	02-01-00
Milton K	v	Luton	-	-	-	-	-	-	03-00-01
Oldham	v	Barnsley	-	-	-	-	2-1	1-1	04-02-02
Port Vale	v	Torquay	-	-	-	-	-	-	00-00-00
Sheff Wed	v	Hartlepool	-	-	-	-	-	1-0	01-00-00
Swindon	v	Hull	-	-	-	-	-	-	03-00-01
Walsall	v	Peterboro	-	-	1-1	-	-	-	01-02-01
Wrexham	v	Bristol C	-	0-1	0-2	0-2	-	0-0	02-02-03

COCA-COLA LEAGUE DIVISION TWO

Boston	v	Mansfield	-	-	-	-	-	1-2	00-00-01
Bristol R	v	Scunthorpe	-	1-1	-	1-1	2-1	1-0	02-02-00
Bury	v	Notts Co	-	1-3	1-1	0-4	-	-	02-02-02
Cambridge U	v	Rushden & D	-	-	-	-	4-1	-	01-00-00
Darlington	v	Lincoln	-	2-0	3-0	2-1	0-0	0-0	07-05-01
Grimsby	v	Kidderminstr	-	-	-	-	-	-	00-00-00
Leyton O	v	Wycombe	-	-	-	-	-	-	00-00-01
Macclesfield	v	Cheltenham	-	1-2	2-1	1-0	-	1-2	04-02-02
Oxford Utd	v	Rochdale	-	-	-	1-2	2-0	2-0	02-00-01
Shrewsbury	v	Swansea	1-0	1-1	-	3-0	0-0	-	02-05-03
Yeovil	v	Southend	-	-	-	-	-	4-0	01-00-00

BANK OF SCOTLAND SCOTTISH PREMIER LEAGUE

Dundee	v	Hibernian	-	3-4/1-0	1-2/0-2	2-1/1-0	2-1/3-0	1-1/2-2	10-04-04
Dunfermline	v	Kilmarnock	0-3/0-6	-	1-0	0-2/2-0	0-2/2-2	2-3/2-1	08-04-05
Hearts	v	Motherwell	3-0/0-2	1-1/0-0	3-0/3-0	3-1	4-2/2-1	0-0/3-2	18-10-03
Inv CT	v	Dundee Utd	-	-	-	-	-	-	00-00-00
Livingston	v	Aberdeen	-	-	-	2-2/0-0	1-2/1-2	1-1/2-0	01-03-02
Rangers	v	Celtic	0-0/2-2	4-2/4-0	5-1/0-3	0-2/1-1	3-2/1-2	0-1/1-2	14-10-08

BELL'S SCOTTISH FIRST DIVISION

Clyde	v	Hamilton	-	2-1/1-0	-	-	-	-	03-02-04
Falkirk	v	St Johnstone	-	-	-	-	1-0/1-1	0-3/0-1	05-04-04
Queen Sth	v	Partick	0-0/2-2	1-2/1-1	1-2/1-3	-	-	-	00-03-05
Ross C	v	Airdrie Utd	-	-	1-1/3-4	0-1/4-1	-	-	01-01-02
St Mirren	v	Raith	2-1/3-1	3-2/3-0	-	1-1/1-0	-	2-1/1-1	06-04-04

NATIONWIDE CONFERENCE

Barnet	v	Accrington	-	-	-	-	-	0-0	00-01-00
Canvey Islnd	v	Hereford	-	-	-	-	-	-	00-00-00
Carlisle	v	Dagenham	-	-	-	-	-	-	00-00-00
Exeter	v	Leigh RMI	-	-	-	-	-	3-2	01-00-00
Farnborough	v	Northwich	1-6	-	-	4-1	3-2	2-0	04-01-06
Forest G	v	Burton	-	-	-	-	2-0	1-1	01-01-01
Halifax	v	Aldershot	-	-	-	-	-	1-2	00-00-01
Morecambe	v	Crawley	-	-	-	-	-	-	00-00-00
Scarborough	v	Stevenage	-	1-3	2-2	1-1	1-2	2-2	00-03-02
Tamworth	v	Gravesend	-	-	-	-	-	1-3	00-00-01
Woking	v	York	-	-	-	-	-	-	00-00-00

SUNDAY 21 NOVEMBER 2004
FA BARCLAYCARD PREMIER LEAGUE

Blackburn	v	Birmingham	-	1-0	2-1	-	1-1	1-1	03-02-00

COCA-COLA CHAMPIONSHIP

Millwall	v	West Ham	-	-	-	-	-	4-1	02-01-01
Sunderland	v	Ipswich	2-1	-	4-1	1-0	-	3-2	07-01-01

MONDAY 22 NOVEMBER 2004
FA BARCLAYCARD PREMIER LEAGUE

Aston Villa	v	Tottenham	3-2	1-1	2-0	1-1	0-1	1-0	10-05-01

FRIDAY 26 NOVEMBER 2004
COCA-COLA LEAGUE DIVISION TWO

Cheltenham	v	Darlington	-	0-0	1-0	0-0	-	2-1	02-02-01
Southend	v	Grimsby	-	-	-	-	-	-	05-01-03

SATURDAY 27 NOVEMBER 2004
FA BARCLAYCARD PREMIER LEAGUE

Birmingham	v	Norwich	0-0	2-0	2-1	4-0	-	-	04-01-02
Bolton	v	Portsmouth	3-1	3-0	2-0	-	-	1-0	05-02-00
Charlton	v	Chelsea	0-1	-	2-0	2-1	2-3	4-2	04-00-02
Fulham	v	Blackburn	-	2-2	2-1	2-0	0-4	3-4	02-01-02
Man City	v	Aston Villa	-	-	1-3	-	3-1	4-1	06-02-02
Southampton	v	Crystal Pal	-	-	-	-	-	-	04-01-01
Tottenham	v	Middlesbro	0-3	2-3	0-0	2-1	0-3	0-0	03-04-03
WBA	v	Man Utd	-	-	-	-	1-3	-	00-00-01

COCA-COLA CHAMPIONSHIP

Burnley	v	Millwall	2-1	4-3	-	0-0	2-2	1-1	03-03-02
Coventry	v	Crewe	-	-	-	1-0	-	2-0	02-00-00
Gillingham	v	Nottm F	-	-	1-3	3-1	1-4	2-1	02-00-02
Ipswich	v	Brighton	-	-	-	-	2-2	-	02-01-02
Leicester	v	Plymouth	-	-	-	-	-	-	03-01-00
Preston	v	Derby	-	-	-	-	4-2	3-0	02-00-00
QPR	v	Cardiff	-	-	-	2-1	0-4	-	01-00-01
Reading	v	Wigan	0-1	0-2	1-0	1-1	-	1-0	06-01-03
Rotherham	v	Leeds	-	-	-	-	-	-	00-00-00
Sheff Utd	v	Wolves	1-1	3-0	1-0	2-2	3-3	-	06-04-01
Stoke	v	Sunderland	-	-	-	-	-	3-1	04-00-03
West Ham	v	Watford	-	1-0	-	-	-	4-0	05-00-00

COCA-COLA LEAGUE DIVISION ONE

Barnsley	v	Blackpool	-	-	-	-	2-1	3-0	02-00-00
Bradford	v	Oldham	-	-	-	-	-	-	01-01-01
Bristol C	v	Sheff Wed	-	-	-	-	-	1-1	00-02-00
Chesterfield	v	Swindon	-	-	-	4-0	2-4	3-0	02-00-02
Hartlepool	v	Bournemouth	-	-	-	-	0-0	2-1	02-02-01
Huddersfield	v	Wrexham	-	-	-	5-1	-	-	03-00-00
Hull	v	Brentford	2-3	-	-	-	-	-	01-00-04
Luton	v	Doncaster	-	-	-	-	-	-	00-00-00
Peterboro	v	Port Vale	-	-	2-0	3-0	1-2	3-1	03-00-01
Stockport	v	Walsall	-	1-1	-	0-2	-	-	02-01-02
Torquay	v	Colchester	-	-	-	-	-	-	01-04-03
Tranmere	v	Milton K	-	-	0-4	-	-	-	00-00-01

COCA-COLA LEAGUE DIVISION TWO

Chester	v	Oxford Utd	-	-	-	-	-	-	01-00-00
Kidderminstr	v	Northampton	-	-	-	-	-	2-1	01-00-00

Lincoln	v	Yeovil	-	-	-	-	-	2-3	00-00-01
Mansfield	v	Leyton O	1-2	1-1	2-0	3-2	-	1-1	04-05-02
Notts Co	v	Cambridge U	-	2-3	0-1	2-1	-	-	03-00-02
Rochdale	v	Boston	-	-	-	-	1-0	1-0	02-00-00
Rushden & D	v	Macclesfield	-	-	-	2-0	3-0	-	02-01-00
Scunthorpe	v	Shrewsbury	3-0	-	2-0	3-1	1-1	-	03-03-01
Swansea	v	Bury	-	-	0-2	-	2-3	4-2	02-01-04
Wycombe	v	Bristol R	1-1	1-1	0-1	-	-	-	02-04-01

BANK OF SCOTLAND SCOTTISH PREMIER LEAGUE

Aberdeen	v	Dundee Utd	0-3/0-4	1-2/3-1	4-1/1-2	2-1/4-0	1-2/3-0	0-1/3-0	14-06-10
Dundee	v	Celtic	1-1/0-3	1-2/0-3	1-2	0-4/0-3	0-1/1-1	0-1/1-2	01-04-14
Hibernian	v	Inv CT	-	-	-	-	-	-	00-00-00
Kilmarnock	v	Livingston	-	-	-	1-5/1-1	2-0	0-3/4-2	07-01-03
Motherwell	v	Dunfermline	0-0/1-1	-	0-1/1-1	1-0	2-1	2-2/1-0	07-06-05
Rangers	v	Hearts	3-0/0-0	1-0/1-0	1-0/2-0	3-1/2-0	2-0/1-0	2-1/0-1	24-06-02

BELL'S SCOTTISH FIRST DIVISION

Falkirk	v	Ross C	-	-	2-3/1-1	4-2/1-4	2-0/3-0	0-2/2-0	04-01-03
Hamilton	v	Airdrie Utd	1-1/0-2	-	-	-	1-0/2-1	2-1/0-1	08-03-06
Raith	v	Partick	-	-	-	1-2/2-0	-	-	06-05-04
St Johnstone	v	Clyde	-	-	-	-	0-1/1-2	3-0/1-3	02-02-03
St Mirren	v	Queen Sth	-	-	-	-	2-1/2-2	1-2/3-1	02-01-01

BELL'S SCOTTISH SECOND DIVISION

Ayr	v	Arbroath	-	-	-	0-1/0-0	1-0/4-0	-	02-01-01
Berwick	v	Forfar	-	2-2/2-0	1-1/1-0	1-1/0-2	2-1/0-0	0-4/3-1	07-05-03
Brechin	v	Morton	-	-	-	-	-	-	00-01-05
Dumbarton	v	Alloa	-	-	-	-	-	1-0/3-1	02-04-03
Stirling	v	Stranraer	-	1-1/2-5	2-0/0-1	-	-	1-0/2-2	06-03-03

BELL'S SCOTTISH THIRD DIVISION

Albion	v	Elgin	-	-	1-1/0-1	4-4/2-2	1-1/1-1	1-2/1-2	00-05-03
C'denbeath	v	Montrose	4-1/1-0	1-1/2-1	2-0/2-1	-	-	3-3/0-0	07-05-07
East Fife	v	Gretna	-	-	-	-	3-2/2-1	-	02-00-00
Peterhead	v	Stenhsmuir	-	-	-	-	-	-	00-00-00
Queens P	v	E Stirling	0-4/2-1	2-1/0-1	-	2-3/1-0	0-2/3-4	3-0/1-0	14-05-08

NATIONWIDE CONFERENCE

Accrington	v	Canvey Islnd	-	-	-	-	-	-	00-00-00
Aldershot	v	Barnet	-	-	-	-	-	1-1	00-01-00
Burton	v	Exeter	-	-	-	-	-	3-4	00-00-01
Crawley	v	Scarborough	-	-	-	-	-	-	00-00-00
Dagenham	v	Morecambe	-	-	3-2	3-2	1-1	1-3	02-02-01
Gravesend	v	Woking	-	-	-	-	4-2	2-2	01-01-00
Hereford	v	Tamworth	-	-	-	-	-	0-1	00-00-00
Leigh RMI	v	Farnborough	-	-	-	3-0	3-2	0-2	02-00-01
Northwich	v	Halifax	-	-	-	-	0-2	0-1	02-02-03
Stevenage	v	Forest G	1-1	1-1	3-1	4-1	0-0	2-1	03-03-00
York	v	Carlisle	-	1-1	0-0	0-0	2-1	2-0	05-06-01

SUNDAY 28 NOVEMBER 2004
FA BARCLAYCARD PREMIER LEAGUE

Liverpool	v	Arsenal	0-0	2-0	4-0	1-2	2-2	1-2	08-03-05
Newcastle	v	Everton	1-3	1-1	0-1	6-2	2-1	4-2	09-01-02

SATURDAY 4 DECEMBER 2004
FA BARCLAYCARD PREMIER LEAGUE

Arsenal	v	Birmingham	-	-	-	-	2-0	0-0	01-01-00
Aston Villa	v	Liverpool	2-4	0-0	0-3	1-2	0-1	0-0	06-05-05

Blackburn	v	Tottenham	1-1	-	-	2-1	1-2	1-0	05-01-04
Chelsea	v	Newcastle	1-1	1-0	3-1	1-1	3-0	5-0	07-04-00
Everton	v	Bolton	-	-	-	3-1	0-0	1-2	03-01-01
Man Utd	v	Southampton	2-1	3-3	5-0	6-1	2-1	3-2	14-02-00
Norwich	v	Fulham	-	1-2	0-1	-	-	-	00-00-02
Portsmouth	v	WBA	2-1	2-0	0-1	1-2	-	-	03-03-06

COCA-COLA CHAMPIONSHIP

Brighton	v	Rotherham	4-1	1-1	-	-	2-0	-	02-03-03
Cardiff	v	Gillingham	-	1-2	-	-	-	5-0	05-00-02
Crewe	v	Ipswich	0-3	1-2	-	-	-	1-0	01-01-02
Derby	v	Coventry	0-0	0-0	1-0	-	1-0	1-3	06-03-01
Leeds	v	Leicester	0-1	2-1	3-1	2-2	-	3-2	06-02-02
Millwall	v	Sheff Utd	-	-	-	2-0	1-0	2-0	05-00-00
Nottm F	v	QPR	-	1-1	1-1	-	-	-	04-06-00
Plymouth	v	Burnley	-	-	-	-	-	-	01-02-01
Sunderland	v	West Ham	-	1-0	1-1	1-0	0-1	2-0	04-03-01
Watford	v	Stoke	-	-	-	-	1-2	1-3	02-02-03
Wigan	v	Preston	2-2	0-1	-	-	-	1-1	02-05-05
Wolves	v	Reading	-	-	-	-	0-1	-	03-01-02

BANK OF SCOTLAND SCOTTISH PREMIER LEAGUE

Aberdeen	v	Kilmarnock	0-1/2-1	2-2/5-1	1-2	2-0/1-1	0-1	3-1	10-05-05
Celtic	v	Hibernian	-	4-0/1-1	3-0/1-1	3-0	1-0/3-2	6-0	17-09-02
Dundee Utd	v	Motherwell	2-2/0-3	0-2/1-2	1-1/2-0/1-0	1-1/1-0	1-1/2-1	0-2/1-0	11-15-05
Hearts	v	Dunfermline	2-1/2-0	-	2-0/7-1	1-1/2-0	2-0/3-0	1-0/2-1	15-03-02
Inv CT	v	Rangers	-	-	-	-	-	-	00-00-00
Livingston	v	Dundee	-	-	-	1-0	1-1	1-1	01-03-02

BELL'S SCOTTISH FIRST DIVISION

Airdrie Utd	v	St Mirren	1-0/0-3	0-2/0-1	-	0-0/2-3	-	-	05-05-08
Clyde	v	Falkirk	-	-	3-1/0-3	1-1/2-3	2-0/0-0	1-2/4-2	04-04-06
Partick	v	St Johnstone	-	-	-	-	-	-	03-02-04
Queen Sth	v	Raith	-	-	-	-	-	0-2/1-1	00-01-02
Ross C	v	Hamilton	-	2-1/0-1	-	-	-	-	01-00-01

BELL'S SCOTTISH SECOND DIVISION

Arbroath	v	Berwick	-	-	0-2/2-0	-	-	1-0/1-2	07-01-07
Brechin	v	Ayr	-	-	-	-	-	3-1/0-3	01-03-04
Morton	v	Alloa	-	-	2-0/1-1	1-1/0-0	-	2-2/2-1	04-04-00
Stirling	v	Dumbarton	-	-	-	4-5/2-1	-	-	06-03-04
Stranraer	v	Forfar	-	-	2-0/3-1	2-0/0-3	2-0/3-2	-	10-02-01

BELL'S SCOTTISH THIRD DIVISION

C'denbeath	v	Peterhead	-	-	2-0/4-0	-	-	2-0/0-3	03-00-01
E Stirling	v	Albion	0-1/4-1	4-3/3-1	1-1/1-0	1-2/1-2	0-3/0-4	3-4/1-8	10-04-14
Elgin	v	Gretna	-	-	-	-	0-2/2-2	3-3/1-1	00-03-01
Queens P	v	East Fife	-	0-1/1-0	-	1-2/2-0	0-0/1-2	-	07-02-06
Stenhsmuir	v	Montrose	4-0/3-1	-	-	-	-	-	07-00-05

NATIONWIDE CONFERENCE

Barnet	v	Leigh RMI	-	-	-	1-1	4-0	2-1	02-01-00
Canvey Islnd	v	Burton	-	-	-	-	-	-	00-00-00
Carlisle	v	Stevenage	-	-	-	-	-	-	00-00-00
Exeter	v	York	-	2-1	3-1	2-1	0-1	-	05-00-02
Farnborough	v	Aldershot	-	0-0	1-0	-	-	4-0	02-01-00
Forest G	v	Accrington	-	-	-	-	-	2-1	01-00-00
Halifax	v	Crawley	-	-	-	-	-	-	00-00-00
Morecambe	v	Hereford	1-0	3-2	1-1	2-2	3-1	2-2	03-03-01
Scarborough	v	Gravesend	-	-	-	-	3-2	2-0	02-00-00
Tamworth	v	Dagenham	-	-	-	-	-	2-0	01-00-00
Woking	v	Northwich	2-1	1-1	1-1	3-1	2-3	3-0	07-04-01

Sponsored by Stan James

SUNDAY 5 DECEMBER 2004
FA BARCLAYCARD PREMIER LEAGUE

Crystal Pal	v	Charlton	-	0-1	-	-	-	-	03-01-01

MONDAY 6 DECEMBER 2004
FA BARCLAYCARD PREMIER LEAGUE

Middlesbro	v	Man City	-	-	1-1	-	3-1	2-1	05-01-00

TUESDAY 7 DECEMBER 2004
COCA-COLA LEAGUE DIVISION ONE

Blackpool	v	Torquay	-	-	5-0	-	-	-	02-00-00
Bournemouth	v	Bradford	-	-	-	-	-	-	04-02-02
Brentford	v	Luton	-	2-0	2-2	-	0-0	4-2	03-03-01
Colchester	v	Barnsley	-	-	-	-	1-1	1-1	00-02-00
Doncaster	v	Bristol C	-	-	-	-	-	-	00-00-00
Milton K	v	Peterboro	-	-	-	-	-	-	00-00-00
Oldham	v	Chesterfield	2-0	1-2	-	1-1	4-0	2-0	04-01-01
Port Vale	v	Tranmere	2-2	1-0	-	1-1	1-4	2-1	04-04-02
Walsall	v	Hartlepool	-	-	-	-	-	-	01-00-01
Wrexham	v	Stockport	-	-	-	-	-	0-0	02-01-05

COCA-COLA LEAGUE DIVISION TWO

Bristol R	v	Chester	-	-	-	-	-	-	03-00-00
Bury	v	Wycombe	-	2-0	1-1	1-1	-	-	02-02-01
Cambridge U	v	Scunthorpe	0-0	1-3	-	-	1-1	3-2	02-03-04
Darlington	v	Mansfield	5-1	0-0	2-1	0-1	-	1-0	04-04-02
Grimsby	v	Notts Co	-	-	-	-	-	2-0	02-02-00
Leyton O	v	Southend	0-3	2-1	0-2	2-1	2-1	2-1	04-00-03
Macclesfield	v	Lincoln	0-0	1-1	2-0	0-1	0-1	0-0	02-03-02
Northampton	v	Cheltenham	-	3-2	-	-	1-2	1-0	02-00-01
Shrewsbury	v	Rochdale	3-2	2-4	0-4	1-0	3-1	-	04-01-03
Yeovil	v	Kidderminstr	3-1	1-0	-	-	-	1-2	05-03-03

NATIONWIDE CONFERENCE

Accrington	v	Carlisle	-	-	-	-	-	-	00-00-00
Aldershot	v	Canvey Islnd	-	3-1	1-0	1-3	1-0	-	03-00-01
Burton	v	Morecambe	-	-	-	-	1-4	0-1	00-00-02
Crawley	v	Barnet	-	-	-	-	-	-	00-00-00
Dagenham	v	Exeter	-	-	-	-	-	0-2	00-00-01
Gravesend	v	Farnborough	-	5-1	2-1	-	0-0	2-0	03-01-01
Hereford	v	Forest G	4-0	1-0	3-1	0-0	1-1	5-1	04-02-00
Leigh RMI	v	Scarborough	-	-	2-0	1-1	0-2	1-4	01-01-02
Northwich	v	Tamworth	-	-	-	-	-	1-0	01-00-00
Stevenage	v	Woking	5-0	0-1	0-3	1-4	1-1	1-1	02-03-05
York	v	Halifax	-	2-0	2-1	1-0	-	-	04-03-01

WEDNESDAY 8 DECEMBER 2004
COCA-COLA LEAGUE DIVISION ONE

Sheff Wed	v	Hull	-	-	-	-	-	-	01-00-00
Swindon	v	Huddersfield	3-0	2-0	-	0-1	0-1	-	03-01-02

COCA-COLA LEAGUE DIVISION TWO

Boston	v	Rushden & D	-	-	1-1	-	1-1	-	00-02-00
Oxford Utd	v	Swansea	-	-	3-1	2-1	1-0	3-0	05-00-01

FRIDAY 10 DECEMBER 2004
COCA-COLA LEAGUE DIVISION ONE

Tranmere	v	Bournemouth	-	-	-	0-0	-	1-1	01-02-00

SATURDAY 11 DECEMBER 2004

FA BARCLAYCARD PREMIER LEAGUE

Crystal Pal	v	Blackburn	-	2-1	2-3	-	-	-	01-02-03
Everton	v	Liverpool	0-0	0-0	2-3	1-3	1-2	0-3	04-06-06
Man City	v	Tottenham	-	-	0-1	-	2-3	0-0	03-03-04
Newcastle	v	Portsmouth	-	-	-	-	-	3-0	05-00-00
Norwich	v	Bolton	2-2	2-1	0-2	-	-	-	01-01-02
Southampton	v	Middlesbro	3-3	1-1	1-3	1-1	0-0	0-1	03-04-03
WBA	v	Charlton	-	2-0	-	-	0-1	-	05-00-03

COCA-COLA CHAMPIONSHIP

Burnley	v	Preston	0-1	0-3	3-0	2-1	2-0	1-1	04-02-03
Cardiff	v	Sunderland	-	-	-	-	-	4-0	01-00-00
Crewe	v	Plymouth	-	-	-	-	0-1	-	01-01-01
Derby	v	Nottm F	1-0	-	-	-	0-0	4-2	03-02-03
Leicester	v	Reading	-	-	-	-	2-1	-	01-01-00
Millwall	v	Brighton	-	-	-	-	1-0	-	02-00-01
QPR	v	Ipswich	1-1	3-1	-	-	-	-	02-03-02
Rotherham	v	Sheff Utd	-	-	-	1-1	1-2	1-1	00-02-01
Stoke	v	Coventry	-	-	-	-	1-2	1-0	01-00-01
Watford	v	Wolves	0-2	-	3-2	1-1	1-1	-	06-03-02
West Ham	v	Leeds	1-5	0-0	0-2	0-0	3-4	-	01-03-08
Wigan	v	Gillingham	4-1	2-0	-	-	-	1-0	06-00-02

COCA-COLA LEAGUE DIVISION ONE

Blackpool	v	Bristol C	-	1-2	-	5-1	0-0	1-0	04-03-02
Bradford	v	Walsall	-	-	-	2-0	1-2	1-1	03-01-01
Colchester	v	Hull	-	-	-	-	-	-	01-01-00
Hartlepool	v	Stockport	-	-	-	-	-	2-2	04-02-01
Luton	v	Port Vale	-	-	1-1	-	0-0	2-0	03-02-00
Milton K	v	Wrexham	-	-	-	-	-	-	00-00-00
Oldham	v	Huddersfield	-	-	-	1-1	4-0	-	02-01-01
Peterboro	v	Chesterfield	-	-	-	1-1	1-0	0-2	02-03-02
Sheff Wed	v	Brentford	-	-	-	-	-	1-1	00-01-00
Swindon	v	Doncaster	-	-	-	-	-	-	00-00-00
Torquay	v	Barnsley	-	-	-	-	-	-	00-00-00

COCA-COLA LEAGUE DIVISION TWO

Bristol R	v	Macclesfield	0-0	-	-	0-2	1-1	2-2	00-03-01
Bury	v	Southend	-	-	-	-	1-3	1-1	01-01-02
Chester	v	Shrewsbury	1-1	0-0	-	-	-	2-1	05-02-02
Darlington	v	Leyton O	1-1	3-1	1-1	3-0	2-2	2-1	05-04-02
Kidderminstr	v	Rochdale	-	-	0-0	4-1	0-0	0-1	01-02-01
Lincoln	v	Cheltenham	-	1-2	1-0	0-1	-	0-0	01-01-02
Mansfield	v	Rushden & D	-	-	-	1-4	-	-	00-00-01
Northampton	v	Boston	-	-	-	-	-	2-0	01-00-00
Notts Co	v	Wycombe	1-0	2-1	0-2	0-1	1-1	1-1	03-02-03
Oxford Utd	v	Cambridge U	-	1-0	1-1	-	1-1	2-2	04-03-00
Scunthorpe	v	Swansea	1-2	-	-	2-2	2-0	2-2	03-02-01
Yeovil	v	Grimsby	-	-	-	-	-	-	00-00-00

BANK OF SCOTLAND SCOTTISH PREMIER LEAGUE

Dundee Utd	v	Kilmarnock	0-2/0-0	0-0/2-2	0-1	0-2/0-2	1-2/2-2	1-1/4-1	02-09-08
Dunfermline	v	Celtic	2-2/1-2	-	1-2/0-3	0-4	1-4/1-4	0-0/1-4	01-06-12
Hibernian	v	Aberdeen	-	2-0/1-0	0-2	2-0/3-4	1-2/2-0/3-1	1-1/0-1	11-07-12
Inv CT	v	Hearts	-	-	-	-	-	-	00-00-00
Motherwell	v	Livingston	-	-	-	0-0/1-2	1-5/6-2	1-1	01-02-02
Rangers	v	Dundee	1-0/6-1	1-2/3-0	0-2	2-0/2-1	3-0/3-1	3-1/4-0	15-02-02

BELL'S SCOTTISH FIRST DIVISION

Airdrie Utd	v	St Johnstone	-	-	-	-	-	-	01-05-07

Sponsored by Stan James

Clyde	v	Partick	1-2/0-1	2-0/1-0	-	3-1/2-1	-	-	06-02-03
Hamilton	v	Raith	3-2/1-2	-	-	-	0-4/0-0	-	05-05-05
Queen Sth	v	Ross C	-	0-2/0-3	-	-	2-0/1-0	1-0/1-1	03-01-02
St Mirren	v	Falkirk	0-2/0-3	2-1/1-0	-	1-5/0-0	4-4/1-2	0-0/1-1	05-05-08

NATIONWIDE CONFERENCE

Crawley	v	Burton	1-1	1-4	2-2	-	-	-	00-08-05
Dagenham	v	Aldershot	0-1	3-1	-	-	-	2-3	01-00-02
Farnborough	v	Forest G	2-2	-	-	3-0	0-3	1-3	01-01-02
Gravesend	v	Barnet	-	-	-	-	2-2	1-1	00-02-00
Halifax	v	Canvey Islnd	-	-	-	-	-	-	00-00-00
Leigh RMI	v	Accrington	1-2	-	-	-	-	1-2	01-00-02
Northwich	v	York	-	-	-	-	-	-	00-00-00
Scarborough	v	Hereford	-	3-0	2-4	3-2	2-1	3-3	06-04-04
Stevenage	v	Exeter	-	-	-	-	-	2-2	00-01-00
Tamworth	v	Carlisle	-	-	-	-	-	-	00-00-00
Woking	v	Morecambe	0-3	0-0	3-1	1-3	0-6	4-1	03-01-05

FRIDAY 17 DECEMBER 2004
COCA-COLA CHAMPIONSHIP

| Brighton | v | Stoke | - | - | - | 1-0 | 1-2 | - | 01-02-02 |
| Nottm F | v | Leicester | 1-0 | - | - | - | 2-2 | - | 03-02-00 |

SUNDAY 12 DECEMBER 2004
FA BARCLAYCARD PREMIER LEAGUE

| Arsenal | v | Chelsea | 1-0 | 2-1 | 1-1 | 2-1 | 3-2 | 2-1 | 11-03-01 |
| Aston Villa | v | Birmingham | - | - | - | - | 0-2 | 2-2 | 00-01-01 |

MONDAY 13 DECEMBER 2004
FA BARCLAYCARD PREMIER LEAGUE

| Fulham | v | Man Utd | - | - | - | 2-3 | 1-1 | 1-1 | 00-02-01 |

SATURDAY 18 DECEMBER 2004
FA BARCLAYCARD PREMIER LEAGUE

Birmingham	v	WBA	4-0	1-1	2-1	0-1	1-0	-	05-02-04
Blackburn	v	Everton	1-2	-	-	1-0	0-1	2-1	05-01-04
Bolton	v	Man City	-	0-1	-	-	2-0	1-3	02-01-02
Chelsea	v	Norwich	-	-	-	-	-	-	01-02-03
Liverpool	v	Newcastle	4-2	2-1	3-0	3-0	2-2	1-1	08-02-02
Man Utd	v	Crystal Pal	-	-	-	-	-	-	05-00-01
Middlesbro	v	Aston Villa	0-0	0-4	1-1	2-1	2-5	1-2	02-03-05
Tottenham	v	Southampton	3-0	7-2	0-0	2-0	2-1	1-3	10-02-04

COCA-COLA CHAMPIONSHIP

Coventry	v	Watford	-	4-0	-	0-2	0-1	0-0	01-01-02
Gillingham	v	Rotherham	-	-	-	2-1	1-1	2-0	04-01-00
Ipswich	v	Wigan	-	-	-	-	-	1-3	00-00-01
Plymouth	v	Derby	-	-	-	-	-	-	00-01-00
Preston	v	West Ham	-	-	-	-	-	1-2	00-00-01
Sheff Utd	v	Cardiff	-	-	-	-	-	5-3	01-00-01
Sunderland	v	Burnley	-	-	-	-	-	1-1	00-02-00
Wolves	v	Crewe	3-0	2-0	0-0	0-1	-	-	03-01-01

COCA-COLA LEAGUE DIVISION ONE

Barnsley	v	Peterboro	-	-	-	-	1-2	0-1	01-00-03
Bournemouth	v	Swindon	-	-	3-0	0-0	-	2-2	01-03-02
Brentford	v	Colchester	-	0-0	1-0	4-1	1-1	3-2	03-02-00
Bristol C	v	Luton	-	0-0	3-1	-	1-1	1-1	04-05-00
Chesterfield	v	Torquay	-	-	3-0	-	-	-	05-01-00

Doncaster	v	Sheff Wed	-	-	-	-	-	-	00-00-00
Huddersfield	v	Bradford	2-1	-	-	-	-	-	02-03-03
Hull	v	Tranmere	-	-	-	-	-	-	00-00-00
Port Vale	v	Oldham	-	-	0-0	3-2	1-1	1-0	06-02-01
Stockport	v	Milton K	-	-	2-2	1-2	-	-	00-01-01
Walsall	v	Blackpool	1-0	-	-	-	-	-	04-03-00
Wrexham	v	Hartlepool	-	-	-	-	2-0	1-2	03-01-02

COCA-COLA LEAGUE DIVISION TWO

Boston	v	Darlington	-	-	-	-	1-0	1-0	02-00-01
Cambridge U	v	Bury	-	3-0	0-1	3-1	1-2	1-2	02-01-04
Cheltenham	v	Kidderminstr	1-0	-	1-3	2-1	-	2-1	05-01-03
Grimsby	v	Oxford Utd	1-0	-	-	-	-	-	03-01-01
Leyton O	v	Yeovil	-	-	-	-	-	2-0	01-00-00
Macclesfield	v	Northampton	0-1	1-0	-	-	-	0-4	01-00-02
Rochdale	v	Bristol R	-	-	-	2-1	1-1	2-2	01-02-00
Rushden & D	v	Scunthorpe	-	-	-	0-0	2-0	-	01-01-00
Shrewsbury	v	Mansfield	1-0	1-2	2-1	3-0	-	-	04-01-03
Southend	v	Chester	0-1	3-1	-	-	-	-	02-01-01
Swansea	v	Notts Co	-	-	0-1	-	-	-	01-02-02
Wycombe	v	Lincoln	4-1	-	-	-	-	-	01-00-01

BANK OF SCOTLAND SCOTTISH PREMIER LEAGUE

Celtic	v	Dundee Utd	2-1/2-1	4-1/2-0	2-1	5-1/1-0	5-0/2-0	5-0/2-1/2-1	23-05-02
Dundee	v	Aberdeen	0-2/1-2	1-3/0-2	2-2	1-4/2-3	1-2	2-0/1-1	02-06-10
Hibernian	v	Dunfermline	-	-	3-0	5-1/1-1	1-4/1-3	1-2	09-04-03
Kilmarnock	v	Rangers	1-3/0-5	1-1/0-2	2-4/1-2	2-2	1-1/0-1	2-3	01-05-14
Livingston	v	Hearts	-	-	-	2-1/2-0	1-1/1-1	2-3	02-02-01
Motherwell	v	Inv CT	-	-	-	-	-	-	00-00-00

BELL'S SCOTTISH FIRST DIVISION

Falkirk	v	Queen Sth	-	-	-	-	3-0/5-0	0-0/0-2	04-01-01
Partick	v	Hamilton	-	0-1/2-2	-	-	-	-	02-05-02
Raith	v	Airdrie Utd	1-3/0-1	1-1/2-0	1-1/5-0	2-2/2-1	0-0/1-0	-	05-08-06
Ross C	v	Clyde	-	2-0/2-2	0-2/2-0	4-0/2-1	1-1/1-1	0-1/0-0	04-04-02
St Johnstone	v	St Mirren	-	-	2-0/2-2	-	2-0/1-1	1-0/1-3	09-04-03

BELL'S SCOTTISH SECOND DIVISION

Alloa	v	Arbroath	1-1/1-2	0-0/2-1	-	-	0-3/3-2	2-2/4-0	09-07-08
Ayr	v	Stirling	-	-	-	-	-	-	05-02-03
Berwick	v	Stranraer	-	-	1-1/0-2	2-2/4-1	3-4/1-0	-	10-03-06
Dumbarton	v	Brechin	1-2/2-0	1-3/2-1	0-2/1-0	1-2/2-1	1-0/1-3	-	11-02-08
Forfar	v	Morton	-	-	-	2-1/2-1	-	2-3/2-1	04-02-05

BELL'S SCOTTISH THIRD DIVISION

Albion	v	C'denbeath	0-1/1-1	1-4/0-3	1-0/0-0	-	-	1-2/2-4	09-02-12
East Fife	v	Elgin	-	-	1-1/1-1	3-0/0-1	4-0/5-0	-	03-02-01
Gretna	v	Stenhsmuir	-	-	-	-	-	-	00-00-00
Montrose	v	E Stirling	2-0/1-0	1-2/0-0	0-1/1-1	2-0/2-0	2-2/5-4	5-1/1-0	14-07-05
Peterhead	v	Queens P	-	-	-	2-1/1-2	3-0/3-1	4-1/1-1	04-01-01

NATIONWIDE CONFERENCE

Accrington	v	Dagenham	-	-	-	-	-	2-3	00-00-01
Aldershot	v	Leigh RMI	-	-	-	-	-	2-0	01-00-00
Barnet	v	Tamworth	-	-	-	-	-	1-0	01-00-00
Burton	v	Stevenage	-	-	-	-	1-2	1-1	00-01-01
Canvey Islnd	v	Farnborough	-	2-0	0-1	-	-	-	01-00-01
Carlisle	v	Woking	-	-	-	-	-	-	00-00-00
Exeter	v	Scarborough	1-0	-	-	-	-	0-0	05-03-00
Forest G	v	Halifax	-	-	-	-	0-2	1-2	00-00-02
Hereford	v	Gravesend	-	-	-	-	3-0	3-3	01-01-00
Morecambe	v	Northwich	3-1	5-0	4-0	2-1	3-1	3-0	08-01-00
York	v	Crawley	-	-	-	-	-	-	00-00-00

SUNDAY 19 DECEMBER 2004
FA BARCLAYCARD PREMIER LEAGUE

Portsmouth	v	Arsenal	-	-	-	-	-	1-1	00-01-00

COCA-COLA CHAMPIONSHIP

Leeds	v	Millwall	-	-	-	-	-	-	00-00-00
Reading	v	QPR	-	-	-	1-0	-	-	02-00-01

MONDAY 20 DECEMBER 2004
FA BARCLAYCARD PREMIER LEAGUE

Charlton	v	Fulham	-	1-0	-	1-1	0-1	3-1	02-01-01

SUNDAY 26 DECEMBER 2004
FA BARCLAYCARD PREMIER LEAGUE

Arsenal	v	Fulham	-	-	-	4-1	2-1	0-0	02-01-00
Birmingham	v	Middlesbro	-	-	-	-	3-0	3-1	03-01-00
Blackburn	v	Newcastle	0-0	-	-	2-2	5-2	1-1	08-03-01
Chelsea	v	Aston Villa	2-1	1-0	1-0	1-3	2-0	1-0	08-02-05
Crystal Pal	v	Portsmouth	4-1	4-0	2-3	0-0	2-3	-	04-02-03
Everton	v	Man City	-	-	3-1	-	2-2	0-0	04-04-02
Man Utd	v	Bolton	-	-	-	1-2	0-1	4-0	02-01-02
Norwich	v	Tottenham	-	-	-	-	-	-	02-02-03
Southampton	v	Charlton	3-1	-	0-0	1-0	0-0	3-2	05-02-00
WBA	v	Liverpool	-	-	-	-	0-6	-	00-00-01

COCA-COLA CHAMPIONSHIP

Brighton	v	Gillingham	-	-	-	-	2-4	-	00-00-01
Cardiff	v	Wolves	-	-	-	-	-	-	00-01-00
Coventry	v	Sheff Utd	-	-	-	1-0	2-1	0-1	03-02-02
Crewe	v	Burnley	-	-	4-2	1-2	-	3-1	05-01-01
Leicester	v	Rotherham	-	-	-	-	2-1	-	01-00-00
Millwall	v	Ipswich	-	-	-	-	1-1	0-0	01-03-01
Plymouth	v	QPR	-	-	-	-	0-1	2-0	01-00-01
Reading	v	Watford	-	-	-	-	1-0	2-1	03-01-00
Stoke	v	Preston	0-1	2-1	-	-	2-1	1-1	04-01-02
Sunderland	v	Leeds	-	1-2	0-2	2-0	1-2	-	02-00-06
West Ham	v	Nottm F	2-1	-	-	-	-	1-1	04-02-01
Wigan	v	Derby	-	-	-	-	-	2-0	01-00-00

COCA-COLA LEAGUE DIVISION ONE

Blackpool	v	Hull	-	-	3-1	-	-	-	03-01-01
Bradford	v	Wrexham	-	-	-	-	-	-	02-01-00
Brentford	v	Torquay	3-2	-	-	-	-	-	02-00-00
Chesterfield	v	Luton	3-1	1-3	-	-	2-1	1-0	03-02-01
Colchester	v	Bournemouth	2-1	3-1	3-1	1-2	-	1-0	04-00-01
Doncaster	v	Milton K	-	-	-	-	-	-	00-00-00
Hartlepool	v	Oldham	-	-	-	-	-	0-0	00-01-00
Huddersfield	v	Port Vale	2-1	2-2	-	2-1	2-2	-	02-04-04
Peterboro	v	Swindon	-	-	4-0	1-1	1-1	4-2	02-03-01
Sheff Wed	v	Walsall	-	-	-	2-1	2-1	-	02-00-00
Stockport	v	Bristol C	2-2	-	-	-	1-4	2-0	01-03-01
Tranmere	v	Barnsley	3-0	2-2	2-3	-	1-0	2-0	06-02-03

COCA-COLA LEAGUE DIVISION TWO

Boston	v	Lincoln	-	-	-	-	2-0	0-1	01-00-01
Bristol R	v	Leyton O	-	-	-	5-3	1-2	1-1	02-03-01
Bury	v	Shrewsbury	-	-	-	-	4-3	-	03-03-01
Chester	v	Scunthorpe	0-2	-	-	-	-	-	03-00-02
Darlington	v	Rochdale	3-0	4-1	1-2	1-0	0-1	1-0	07-02-05

Grimsby	v	Macclesfield	-			-	-	-	00-00-00
Kidderminstr	v	Swansea	-	-	-	0-2	2-2	2-0	01-01-01
Mansfield	v	Cambridge U	1-3	-	-	-	-	1-1	03-02-01
Notts Co	v	Northampton	3-1	-	2-0	0-3	2-1	-	04-00-02
Rushden & D	v	Oxford Utd	-	-	-	2-1	0-2	-	01-00-01
Wycombe	v	Southend	-	-	-	-	-	-	01-00-00
Yeovil	v	Cheltenham	2-2	-	-	-	-	0-0	02-04-01

BELL'S SCOTTISH FIRST DIVISION

Falkirk	v	Airdrie Utd	0-1/1-1	2-0/8-0	0-2/1-1	1-2/2-2	-	-	08-07-07
Queen Sth	v	Clyde	2-1/2-1	1-1/3-0	-	-	2-1/1-1	4-1/1-2	09-04-07
Ross C	v	Partick	-	2-1/1-3	-	3-2/0-1	-	-	02-00-02
St Johnstone	v	Raith	-	-	-	-	-	0-1/5-2	04-02-03
St Mirren	v	Hamilton	3-2/1-0	-	-	-	-	-	08-01-05

NATIONWIDE CONFERENCE

Accrington	v	Halifax	-	-	-	-	-	2-1	01-00-00
Aldershot	v	Forest G	-	-	-	-	-	3-0	01-00-00
Burton	v	Tamworth	2-1	1-1	3-1	-	-	0-1	02-02-01
Crawley	v	Gravesend	-	-	-	-	-	-	02-01-03
Dagenham	v	Canvey Islnd	-	2-0	-	-	-	-	01-00-00
Exeter	v	Hereford	-	-	-	-	-	0-1	02-02-02
Leigh RMI	v	Northwich	-	-	3-0	1-2	1-1	1-0	02-01-01
Morecambe	v	Carlisle	-	-	-	-	-	-	00-00-00
Scarborough	v	York	-	-	-	-	-	-	02-02-01
Stevenage	v	Barnet	-	-	-	3-2	1-2	1-2	01-00-02
Woking	v	Farnborough	4-0	-	-	3-2	1-1	3-2	07-01-01

MONDAY 27 DECEMBER 2004
BANK OF SCOTLAND SCOTTISH PREMIER LEAGUE

Aberdeen	v	Inv CT	-	-	-	-	-	-	00-00-00
Dundee Utd	v	Hibernian	-	3-1/0-0	0-1	3-1/1-2/2-1	1-1/1-2	1-2/0-0	10-11-07
Dunfermline	v	Livingston	-	3-0/4-1	-	1-2/1-0	2-1/2-0	2-2	07-02-02
Hearts	v	Celtic	2-1/2-4	1-2/1-0	2-4/0-3	0-1/1-4	1-4/2-1	0-1/1-1	08-05-20
Kilmarnock	v	Dundee	2-1/0-0	0-2/2-2	2-3	0-1/3-2	2-0	1-1/4-2	08-04-04
Rangers	v	Motherwell	2-1/2-1	4-1/6-2	2-0	3-0/3-0	3-0/2-0	1-0/4-0	27-01-03

BELL'S SCOTTISH SECOND DIVISION

Berwick	v	Morton	-	-	-	2-0/0-0	-	2-3/2-0	03-01-02
Dumbarton	v	Ayr	-	-	-	-	-	-	01-03-02
Forfar	v	Brechin	-	0-0/2-0	-	-	2-1/1-5	-	04-02-03
Stirling	v	Arbroath	0-1/2-1	3-4/1-1	0-0/1-1	-	-	-	03-04-03
Stranraer	v	Alloa	-	0-0/2-2	-	1-1/0-2	-	-	02-07-03

BELL'S SCOTTISH THIRD DIVISION

East Fife	v	Montrose	-	0-0/2-0	3-1/1-0	1-2/2-0	2-0/2-0	-	10-04-04
Gretna	v	Albion	-	-	-	-	2-0/1-2	3-1/3-0	03-00-01
Peterhead	v	E Stirling	-	-	2-4/1-2	3-2/2-1	5-0/6-0	2-0/6-0	06-00-02
Queens P	v	C'denbeath	2-0/2-1	1-0/3-1	-	-	-	0-0/1-2	11-03-07
Stenhsmuir	v	Elgin	-	-	-	-	-	-	00-00-00

TUESDAY 28 DECEMBER 2004
FA BARCLAYCARD PREMIER LEAGUE

Aston Villa	v	Man Utd	1-1	0-1	0-1	1-1	0-1	0-2	03-05-08
Bolton	v	Blackburn	-	3-1	1-4	1-1	1-1	2-2	03-03-01
Charlton	v	Everton	1-2	-	1-0	1-2	2-1	2-2	02-01-04
Fulham	v	Birmingham	-	0-0	0-1	-	0-1	0-0	00-03-04
Liverpool	v	Southampton	7-1	0-0	2-1	1-1	3-0	1-2	09-05-02
Man City	v	WBA	-	2-1	-	0-0	1-2	-	03-02-01
Middlesbro	v	Norwich	-	-	-	-	-	-	01-01-01
Portsmouth	v	Chelsea	-	-	-	-	-	0-2	00-00-02
Tottenham	v	Crystal Pal	-	-	-	-	-	-	00-03-03

COCA-COLA CHAMPIONSHIP

Burnley	v	Wigan	1-1	0-0	-	-	-	0-2	00-02-03
Derby	v	Millwall	-	-	-	-	1-2	2-0	03-02-04
Gillingham	v	Coventry	-	-	-	1-2	0-2	2-5	00-00-03
Ipswich	v	Stoke	-	-	-	-	0-0	1-0	03-03-01
Leeds	v	Plymouth	-	-	-	-	-	-	02-00-00
Nottm F	v	Sunderland	-	-	-	-	-	2-0	02-01-02
Preston	v	Reading	4-0	2-2	-	-	1-0	2-1	06-02-01
QPR	v	Crewe	0-1	1-0	1-0	-	0-0	-	03-01-01
Rotherham	v	West Ham	-	-	-	-	-	1-0	01-00-00
Sheff Utd	v	Leicester	-	-	-	-	2-1	-	01-01-01
Watford	v	Cardiff	-	-	-	-	-	2-1	01-00-00
Wolves	v	Brighton	-	-	-	-	1-1	-	01-01-02

COCA-COLA LEAGUE DIVISION ONE

Barnsley	v	Stockport	1-1	2-1	0-2	2-2	1-0	3-3	02-03-01
Bournemouth	v	Huddersfield	-	-	-	2-3	-	-	01-02-03
Bristol C	v	Hartlepool	-	-	-	-	-	1-1	00-01-00
Luton	v	Colchester	2-0	3-2	0-3	-	1-2	1-0	03-00-02
Milton K	v	Blackpool	-	-	-	-	-	-	00-00-00
Oldham	v	Peterboro	-	-	1-4	2-0	0-0	1-1	01-02-01
Port Vale	v	Sheff Wed	-	-	-	-	-	3-0	01-01-00
Swindon	v	Brentford	-	-	2-3	2-0	2-1	2-1	03-01-02
Torquay	v	Bradford	-	-	-	-	-	-	00-01-00
Walsall	v	Tranmere	-	1-2	-	-	-	-	01-00-01
Wrexham	v	Chesterfield	0-0	1-1	-	0-1	-	0-0	03-05-03

COCA-COLA LEAGUE DIVISION TWO

Cambridge U	v	Yeovil	-	-	-	-	-	1-4	00-00-01
Cheltenham	v	Bristol R	-	-	-	0-0	-	1-2	00-01-01
Leyton O	v	Rushden & D	-	-	-	2-1	0-0	-	01-01-00
Lincoln	v	Grimsby	-	-	-	-	-	-	00-02-00
Macclesfield	v	Wycombe	1-3	-	-	-	-	-	02-02-02
Northampton	v	Bury	-	-	2-1	1-0	-	3-2	06-00-03
Oxford Utd	v	Kidderminstr	-	-	-	1-1	2-1	2-1	02-01-00
Rochdale	v	Chester	3-1	2-1	-	-	-	-	03-01-02
Scunthorpe	v	Notts Co	-	1-0	-	-	-	-	01-00-01
Shrewsbury	v	Darlington	3-0	0-1	1-0	3-0	2-2	-	04-02-03
Southend	v	Mansfield	1-2	1-0	3-1	1-0	-	0-3	04-01-02
Swansea	v	Boston	-	-	-	-	0-0	3-0	01-01-00

NATIONWIDE CONFERENCE

Barnet	v	Scarborough	1-0	-	-	1-1	3-0	0-0	06-03-01
Canvey Islnd	v	Woking	-	-	-	-	-	-	00-00-00
Carlisle	v	Aldershot	-	-	-	-	-	-	00-00-00
Farnborough	v	Morecambe	1-6	-	-	2-1	2-3	2-4	02-01-04
Forest G	v	Crawley	-	-	-	-	-	-	01-00-00
Gravesend	v	Accrington	-	-	-	-	-	0-0	00-01-00
Halifax	v	Dagenham	-	-	-	-	3-3	3-0	02-02-01
Hereford	v	Leigh RMI	-	-	1-1	0-1	0-1	0-1	00-01-03
Northwich	v	Stevenage	0-1	3-3	3-2	2-1	1-1	1-2	02-03-05
Tamworth	v	Exeter	-	-	-	-	-	2-1	01-00-00
York	v	Burton	-	-	-	-	-	-	00-00-00

WEDNESDAY 29 DECEMBER 2004
FA BARCLAYCARD PREMIER LEAGUE

Newcastle	v	Arsenal	1-1	4-2	0-0	0-2	1-1	0-0	04-04-04

COCA-COLA LEAGUE DIVISION ONE

Hull	v	Doncaster	-	-	-	-	-	3-1	03-00-00

BELL'S SCOTTISH FIRST DIVISION

Home		Away							Record
Airdrie Utd	v	Queen Sth	-	-	-	-	-	-	02-00-00
Clyde	v	St Mirren	-	-	-	1-1/3-1	2-3/3-2	2-0/2-2	04-02-02
Hamilton	v	St Johnstone	-	-	-	-	-	-	03-01-02
Partick	v	Falkirk	-	-	-	5-1/3-0	-	-	07-04-06
Raith	v	Ross C	-	-	4-1/0-4	1-3/0-1	-	1-7/0-0	01-01-04

SATURDAY 1 JANUARY 2005
FA BARCLAYCARD PREMIER LEAGUE

Home		Away							Record
Aston Villa	v	Blackburn	1-3	-	-	2-0	3-0	0-2	04-01-05
Bolton	v	WBA	2-1	1-1	0-1	-	1-1	-	04-03-02
Charlton	v	Arsenal	0-1	-	1-0	0-3	0-3	1-1	01-02-04
Fulham	v	Crystal Pal	-	1-0	3-1	-	-	-	02-00-00
Liverpool	v	Chelsea	1-1	1-0	2-2	1-0	1-0	1-2	11-02-02
Man City	v	Southampton	-	-	0-1	-	0-1	1-3	02-03-05
Middlesbro	v	Man Utd	0-1	3-4	0-2	0-1	3-1	0-1	02-02-06
Newcastle	v	Birmingham	-	-	-	-	1-0	0-1	01-01-01
Portsmouth	v	Norwich	1-2	2-1	2-0	1-2	3-2	-	04-01-03
Tottenham	v	Everton	4-1	3-2	3-2	1-1	4-3	3-0	10-06-00

COCA-COLA CHAMPIONSHIP

Home		Away							Record
Burnley	v	Leicester	-	-	-	-	1-2	-	00-00-01
Derby	v	Cardiff	-	-	-	-	-	2-2	00-01-00
Gillingham	v	Reading	2-1	2-2	-	-	0-1	0-1	01-01-03
Ipswich	v	West Ham	-	-	1-1	2-3	-	1-2	01-03-03
Leeds	v	Crewe	-	-	-	-	-	-	00-00-00
Nottm F	v	Stoke	-	-	-	-	6-0	0-0	02-01-01
Preston	v	Sunderland	-	-	-	-	-	0-2	00-00-01
QPR	v	Brighton	-	-	-	0-0	-	2-1	01-01-00
Rotherham	v	Coventry	-	-	-	0-0	1-0	2-0	02-01-00
Sheff Utd	v	Wigan	-	-	-	-	-	1-1	01-01-00
Watford	v	Millwall	-	-	-	1-4	0-0	3-1	04-01-06
Wolves	v	Plymouth	-	-	-	-	-	-	03-00-00

COCA-COLA LEAGUE DIVISION ONE

Home		Away							Record
Barnsley	v	Hartlepool	-	-	-	-	-	2-2	00-01-00
Bournemouth	v	Brentford	-	4-1	2-0	0-2	-	1-0	06-02-03
Bristol C	v	Peterboro	-	-	2-1	1-0	1-0	1-1	05-01-02
Hull	v	Huddersfield	-	-	-	-	-	0-0	03-01-01
Luton	v	Sheff Wed	-	-	-	-	-	3-2	02-01-01
Milton K	v	Chesterfield	-	-	-	-	-	-	00-00-00
Oldham	v	Tranmere	-	-	-	1-1	2-0	1-1	01-03-02
Port Vale	v	Bradford	1-1	-	-	-	-	-	01-04-01
Swindon	v	Colchester	-	-	0-0	1-0	2-2	2-0	02-02-00
Torquay	v	Stockport	-	-	-	-	-	-	03-01-00
Walsall	v	Doncaster	-	-	-	-	-	-	03-00-02
Wrexham	v	Blackpool	1-1	1-1	-	1-1	-	4-2	02-05-04

COCA-COLA LEAGUE DIVISION TWO

Home		Away							Record
Cambridge U	v	Boston	-	-	-	-	1-2	0-1	00-00-02
Cheltenham	v	Notts Co	-	-	-	-	1-4	-	00-00-01
Leyton O	v	Kidderminstr	-	-	0-0	1-3	0-0	1-1	00-03-01
Lincoln	v	Bury	-	-	-	-	1-1	2-1	01-03-02
Macclesfield	v	Chester	-	1-1	-	-	-	-	01-01-00
Northampton	v	Mansfield	-	1-0	-	-	2-0	0-3	05-01-04
Oxford Utd	v	Wycombe	-	0-0	1-2	-	-	-	00-01-03
Rochdale	v	Grimsby	-	-	-	-	-	-	00-00-02
Scunthorpe	v	Darlington	0-1	-	1-1	7-1	0-1	0-1	07-02-04
Shrewsbury	v	Bristol R	-	-	-	0-1	2-5	-	02-01-03
Southend	v	Rushden & D	-	-	-	4-2	2-1	-	02-00-00
Swansea	v	Yeovil	-	-	-	-	-	3-2	01-00-00

BANK OF SCOTLAND SCOTTISH PREMIER LEAGUE

Celtic	v	Livingston	-	-	-	3-2/5-1	2-0/2-1	5-1/5-1	06-00-00
Dundee Utd	v	Rangers	0-0/1-2	0-4/0-2	1-1	1-6/0-1	0-3/1-4	1-3/2-0/3-3	05-07-18
Dunfermline	v	Dundee	2-0/2-0	-	1-0	1-0/2-0	4-2/0-1	2-0	09-02-03
Hibernian	v	Hearts	-	1-1/3-1	6-2/0-0	2-1/1-2	1-2	1-0/1-1	09-10-10
Inv CT	v	Kilmarnock	-	-	-	-	-	-	00-00-00
Motherwell	v	Aberdeen	2-2/1-1	5-6/1-0	1-1/0-1/0-2	3-2	1-2/0-1/2-3	1-0	07-12-13

BELL'S SCOTTISH FIRST DIVISION

Clyde	v	Airdrie Utd	-	-	4-1/1-1	0-3/0-1	-	-	02-02-06
Falkirk	v	Raith	1-1/1-0	2-1/1-0	2-1/2-0	1-0/2-1	-	3-2/1-0	13-01-05
Queen Sth	v	Hamilton	-	3-2/1-1	-	0-1/3-1	-	-	03-02-01
Ross C	v	St Johnstone	-	-	-	-	0-0/2-3	0-3/2-0	01-01-02
St Mirren	v	Partick	-	-	-	1-0/0-2	-	-	04-00-02

BELL'S SCOTTISH SECOND DIVISION

Alloa	v	Stirling	7-0/2-2	4-4/1-0	-	-	-	-	04-02-01
Arbroath	v	Forfar	2-1/2-2	-	3-4/1-1	-	-	0-0/0-1	01-08-04
Ayr	v	Stranraer	7-1/4-0	-	-	-	-	-	06-02-00
Brechin	v	Berwick	1-1/0-3	0-3/1-2	-	-	2-4/2-2	-	06-04-06
Morton	v	Dumbarton	-	-	-	-	-	2-2/3-2	06-02-02

BELL'S SCOTTISH THIRD DIVISION

Albion	v	Queens P	2-1/1-0	2-4/0-3	-	2-1/2-0	0-2/2-1	3-1/3-1	13-05-07
C'denbeath	v	East Fife	-	4-0/1-0	1-0/3-2	-	-	-	06-03-03
E Stirling	v	Stenhsmuir	1-1/1-1	-	-	-	-	-	02-04-05
Elgin	v	Peterhead	-	-	1-3/0-1	4-1/0-3	3-0/0-4	2-3/1-0	03-00-05
Montrose	v	Gretna	-	-	-	-	0-2/0-1	2-0/1-4	01-00-03

NATIONWIDE CONFERENCE

Barnet	v	Stevenage	-	-	-	0-3	0-2	0-0	00-01-02
Canvey Islnd	v	Dagenham	-	3-1	-	-	-	-	01-00-00
Carlisle	v	Morecambe	-	-	-	-	-	-	00-00-00
Farnborough	v	Woking	2-1	-	-	0-1	5-0	1-0	04-00-05
Forest G	v	Aldershot	-	-	-	-	-	3-1	01-00-00
Gravesend	v	Crawley	-	-	-	-	-	-	02-01-03
Halifax	v	Accrington	-	-	-	-	-	1-1	00-01-00
Hereford	v	Exeter	-	-	-	-	-	1-1	03-02-01
Northwich	v	Leigh RMI	-	-	1-1	0-3	0-1	0-1	00-01-03
Tamworth	v	Burton	0-1	1-1	2-3	-	-	1-1	00-03-02
York	v	Scarborough	-	-	-	-	-	-	03-01-01

MONDAY 3 JANUARY 2005
FA BARCLAYCARD PREMIER LEAGUE

Arsenal	v	Man City	-	-	5-0	-	2-1	2-1	08-02-00
Birmingham	v	Bolton	0-0	2-1	1-1	-	3-1	2-0	07-02-01
Blackburn	v	Charlton	1-0	1-1	-	4-1	1-0	0-1	03-02-02
Chelsea	v	Middlesbro	2-0	1-1	2-1	2-2	1-0	0-0	06-03-00
Crystal Pal	v	Aston Villa	-	-	-	-	-	-	02-04-00
Everton	v	Portsmouth	-	-	-	-	-	1-0	01-00-00
Man Utd	v	Tottenham	2-1	3-1	2-0	4-0	1-0	3-0	13-02-01
Norwich	v	Liverpool	-	-	-	-	-	-	02-03-02
Southampton	v	Fulham	-	-	-	1-1	4-2	0-0	01-02-00
WBA	v	Newcastle	-	-	-	-	2-2	-	00-02-01

COCA-COLA CHAMPIONSHIP

Brighton	v	Watford	-	-	-	-	4-0	-	04-00-01
Cardiff	v	Nottm F	-	-	-	-	-	0-0	00-01-00
Coventry	v	Leeds	2-2	3-4	0-0	-	-	-	02-07-02
Crewe	v	Preston	-	-	1-3	2-1	-	2-1	05-01-01
Leicester	v	QPR	-	-	-	-	-	-	00-01-00

Millwall	v	Rotherham	-	-	4-0	1-0	0-6	2-1	04-00-01
Plymouth	v	Ipswich	-	-	-	-	-	-	02-01-01
Reading	v	Derby	-	-	-	-	2-1	3-1	04-00-00
Stoke	v	Burnley	1-4	2-2	-	-	0-1	1-2	01-02-03
Sunderland	v	Gillingham	-	-	-	-	-	2-1	01-00-00
West Ham	v	Sheff Utd	-	-	-	-	-	0-0	01-03-00

COCA-COLA LEAGUE DIVISION ONE

Blackpool	v	Port Vale	-	-	-	4-0	3-2	2-1	04-00-02
Bradford	v	Swindon	3-0	-	-	-	-	-	02-04-00
Brentford	v	Walsall	-	-	2-1	-	-	-	04-01-00
Chesterfield	v	Barnsley	-	-	-	-	1-0	0-2	01-00-01
Colchester	v	Oldham	2-2	0-1	1-1	2-1	0-1	2-1	02-02-02
Doncaster	v	Bournemouth	-	-	-	-	-	-	00-00-00
Hartlepool	v	Milton K	-	-	-	-	-	-	00-00-00
Huddersfield	v	Bristol C	2-2	-	-	1-0	1-2	-	02-01-02
Peterboro	v	Luton	-	-	1-1	-	1-1	1-2	00-03-03
Sheff Wed	v	Wrexham	-	-	-	-	-	2-3	00-00-01
Stockport	v	Hull	-	-	-	-	-	-	02-03-00
Tranmere	v	Torquay	-	-	-	-	-	-	01-00-00

COCA-COLA LEAGUE DIVISION TWO

Boston	v	Leyton O	-	-	-	-	0-1	3-0	01-00-01
Bristol R	v	Northampton	1-1	-	0-1	-	-	1-2	01-02-03
Bury	v	Oxford Utd	1-0	1-2	3-1	-	1-1	0-4	03-01-02
Chester	v	Lincoln	-	1-3	-	-	-	-	03-01-01
Darlington	v	Macclesfield	-	3-0	1-1	0-1	0-0	0-1	02-03-02
Grimsby	v	Cambridge U	-	-	-	-	-	-	02-02-01
Kidderminstr	v	Southend	-	-	2-1	2-0	1-0	1-2	03-00-01
Mansfield	v	Scunthorpe	2-1	-	1-0	2-1	-	5-0	07-01-02
Notts Co	v	Rochdale	-	-	-	-	-	-	01-00-00
Rushden & D	v	Swansea	-	-	-	4-0	1-1	-	01-01-00
Wycombe	v	Cheltenham	-	-	-	-	1-1	-	01-02-02
Yeovil	v	Shrewsbury	-	-	-	-	-	-	00-00-00

BELL'S SCOTTISH SECOND DIVISION

Arbroath	v	Stranraer	-	1-2/1-1	1-1/2-1	-	-	-	07-03-03
Ayr	v	Morton	1-0/1-0	3-0/3-2	1-1/3-0	-	-	-	11-04-04
Brechin	v	Alloa	-	-	-	-	-	-	04-00-04
Dumbarton	v	Forfar	-	3-3/0-0	-	-	1-2/1-2	2-1/1-1	01-03-02
Stirling	v	Berwick	-	-	1-1/1-0	-	-	-	08-02-00

BELL'S SCOTTISH THIRD DIVISION

Albion	v	Peterhead	-	-	0-0/0-1	1-0/2-1	3-0/0-0	2-0/3-3	04-03-01
C'denbeath	v	E Stirling	2-1/3-2	1-2/0-0	3-0/1-3	-	-	2-1/2-0	14-03-06
East Fife	v	Stenhsmuir	-	-	-	-	-	3-2/1-0	09-03-05
Elgin	v	Montrose	-	-	1-1/0-2	1-2/1-0	0-0/0-2	2-3/2-1	02-02-04
Queens P	v	Gretna	-	-	-	-	1-0/1-2	0-1/1-1	01-01-02

TUESDAY 4 JANUARY 2005
COCA-COLA CHAMPIONSHIP

Wigan	v	Wolves	-	-	-	-	-	-	00-01-00

SATURDAY 8 JANUARY 2005
COCA-COLA LEAGUE DIVISION ONE

Blackpool	v	Oldham	3-0	1-2	-	0-2	0-0	1-1	01-03-02
Bradford	v	Milton K	-	3-0	-	3-3	3-5	2-3	01-01-02
Brentford	v	Barnsley	-	-	-	-	1-2	2-1	02-00-01
Chesterfield	v	Hull	-	-	1-0	-	-	-	01-01-00
Colchester	v	Walsall	1-0	-	0-2	-	-	-	03-00-02
Doncaster	v	Port Vale	-	-	-	-	-	-	00-00-00

Home		Away							Record
Hartlepool	v	Luton	-	-	-	1-2	-	4-3	01-00-01
Huddersfield	v	Torquay	-	-	-	-	-	1-0	02-00-00
Peterboro	v	Wrexham	-	-	1-0	2-3	-	6-1	06-01-02
Sheff Wed	v	Swindon	-	-	-	-	-	1-1	01-02-00
Stockport	v	Bournemouth	-	-	-	-	-	3-2	04-01-02
Tranmere	v	Bristol C	1-1	-	-	1-0	1-1	1-0	05-04-00

COCA-COLA LEAGUE DIVISION TWO

Home		Away							Record
Boston	v	Southend	-	-	-	-	1-0	0-2	01-00-01
Bristol R	v	Cambridge U	-	1-0	2-1	-	3-1	0-2	05-02-01
Bury	v	Leyton O	-	-	-	-	0-1	1-1	04-01-01
Chester	v	Cheltenham	-	2-1	-	-	-	-	01-00-00
Darlington	v	Oxford Utd	-	-	-	1-0	0-1	2-0	02-00-01
Grimsby	v	Northampton	-	-	-	-	-	-	01-00-00
Kidderminstr	v	Lincoln	-	-	1-3	1-1	1-1	1-2	00-02-02
Mansfield	v	Swansea	1-0	0-1	-	3-0	-	1-1	05-04-01
Notts Co	v	Macclesfield	1-1	-	-	-	-	-	00-02-00
Rushden & D	v	Shrewsbury	-	-	-	3-0	5-1	-	02-00-00
Wycombe	v	Scunthorpe	-	2-1	-	-	-	-	01-01-00
Yeovil	v	Rochdale	-	-	-	-	-	1-0	01-00-00

NATIONWIDE CONFERENCE

Home		Away							Record
Accrington	v	Farnborough	-	-	-	-	-	3-1	01-00-00
Aldershot	v	Tamworth	-	-	-	-	-	1-1	00-01-00
Burton	v	Hereford	-	-	-	-	2-0	4-1	02-00-00
Crawley	v	Carlisle	-	-	-	-	-	-	00-00-00
Dagenham	v	Northwich	-	-	1-0	1-1	2-0	2-0	04-02-02
Exeter	v	Halifax	2-1	1-0	0-0	0-0	-	1-1	04-03-00
Leigh RMI	v	Gravesend	-	-	-	-	0-0	1-2	00-01-01
Morecambe	v	Canvey Islnd	-	-	-	-	-	-	00-00-00
Scarborough	v	Forest G	-	5-0	1-0	1-1	3-0	2-2	03-02-00
Stevenage	v	York	-	-	-	-	-	-	00-00-00
Woking	v	Barnet	-	-	-	1-3	0-0	2-2	00-02-01

SATURDAY 15 JANUARY 2005
FA BARCLAYCARD PREMIER LEAGUE

Home		Away							Record
Aston Villa	v	Norwich	-	-	-	-	-	-	03-03-01
Bolton	v	Arsenal	-	-	-	0-2	2-2	1-1	01-02-02
Charlton	v	Birmingham	-	1-0	-	-	0-2	1-1	04-03-01
Fulham	v	WBA	-	1-0	0-0	-	3-0	-	02-03-00
Liverpool	v	Man Utd	2-2	2-3	2-0	3-1	1-2	1-2	07-03-06
Man City	v	Crystal Pal	-	2-1	-	1-0	-	-	04-04-01
Middlesbro	v	Everton	2-2	2-1	1-2	1-0	1-1	1-0	04-03-03
Newcastle	v	Southampton	4-0	5-0	1-1	3-1	2-1	1-0	08-02-02
Portsmouth	v	Blackburn	-	1-2	2-2	-	-	1-2	01-03-03
Tottenham	v	Chelsea	2-2	0-1	0-3	2-3	0-0	0-1	00-06-09

COCA-COLA CHAMPIONSHIP

Home		Away							Record
Burnley	v	Reading	1-1	3-0	-	-	2-5	3-0	02-02-03
Derby	v	Sunderland	-	0-5	1-0	0-1	-	1-1	04-02-05
Gillingham	v	Plymouth	-	-	-	-	-	-	03-00-00
Ipswich	v	Coventry	-	-	2-0	-	2-1	1-1	03-02-01
Leeds	v	Cardiff	-	-	-	-	-	-	00-00-00
Nottm F	v	Millwall	-	-	-	1-2	3-3	2-2	02-02-02
Preston	v	Leicester	-	-	-	-	2-0	-	01-00-00
QPR	v	Stoke	-	-	-	1-0	-	-	01-02-00
Rotherham	v	Wigan	-	-	1-1	-	-	0-3	01-01-03
Sheff Utd	v	Brighton	-	-	-	-	2-1	-	02-00-00
Watford	v	Crewe	4-2	-	3-0	0-1	-	2-1	03-00-02
Wolves	v	West Ham	-	-	-	-	-	-	02-01-00

COCA-COLA LEAGUE DIVISION ONE

Home	v	Away							Rec
Barnsley	v	Huddersfield	7-1	4-2	3-1	-	0-1	-	05-00-01
Bournemouth	v	Sheff Wed	-	-	-	-	-	1-0	01-00-00
Bristol C	v	Bradford	2-3	-	-	-	-	-	01-00-01
Hull	v	Peterboro	1-0	2-3	-	-	-	-	02-01-03
Luton	v	Stockport	-	-	-	-	1-1	2-2	00-03-00
Milton K	v	Colchester	-	-	-	-	-	-	00-00-00
Oldham	v	Doncaster	-	-	-	-	-	-	00-00-00
Port Vale	v	Brentford	-	-	1-1	2-1	1-0	1-0	05-01-00
Swindon	v	Blackpool	-	-	-	1-0	1-1	2-2	01-03-00
Torquay	v	Hartlepool	3-0	0-0	1-0	1-0	1-1	-	07-04-02
Walsall	v	Chesterfield	1-1	-	-	-	-	-	04-03-02
Wrexham	v	Tranmere	-	-	-	1-1	-	0-1	00-02-01

COCA-COLA LEAGUE DIVISION TWO

Home	v	Away							Rec
Cambridge U	v	Chester	2-1	-	-	-	-	-	02-03-01
Cheltenham	v	Rushden & D	1-0	-	-	1-1	-	-	03-01-01
Leyton O	v	Grimsby	-	-	-	-	-	-	01-00-01
Lincoln	v	Bristol R	1-0	-	-	0-1	2-1	3-1	03-00-01
Macclesfield	v	Kidderminstr	-	-	1-0	0-1	2-0	1-1	02-06-05
Northampton	v	Darlington	-	0-3	-	-	-	1-0	04-01-03
Oxford Utd	v	Yeovil	-	-	-	-	-	1-0	01-00-00
Rochdale	v	Mansfield	1-0	2-1	1-0	3-1	-	3-0	06-03-02
Scunthorpe	v	Bury	-	0-2	-	-	0-1	0-0	02-02-03
Shrewsbury	v	Boston	-	-	-	-	1-2	-	00-00-01
Southend	v	Notts Co	-	-	-	-	-	-	03-01-00
Swansea	v	Wycombe	-	-	3-1	-	-	-	01-01-01

BANK OF SCOTLAND SCOTTISH PREMIER LEAGUE

Home	v	Away							Rec
Aberdeen	v	Celtic	3-2/1-5	0-5/0-6	1-1/0-1	2-0/0-1	0-4/1-1	1-3	06-13-12
Dundee	v	Inv CT	-	-	-	-	-	-	00-00-00
Hearts	v	Dundee Utd	0-1/4-1	3-0/1-2	3-1	1-2/1-2	2-0/2-1	3-0/3-1	19-05-05
Kilmarnock	v	Motherwell	0-0/0-1	0-1/0-2	3-2/1-2	2-0/1-4	0-3/1-0	2-0	08-03-10
Livingston	v	Hibernian	-	-	-	1-0/0-3	1-2/1-2	1-0/4-1	03-00-03
Rangers	v	Dunfermline	1-1/1-0	-	4-1/2-0	4-0	3-0/6-1	4-0/4-1	17-02-00

BELL'S SCOTTISH FIRST DIVISIONß

Home	v	Away							Rec
Airdrie Utd	v	Ross C	-	-	5-1/2-2	1-1/0-2	-	-	01-02-01
Hamilton	v	Clyde	-	2-3/1-1	-	-	-	-	06-01-02
Partick	v	Queen Sth	2-2/1-3	2-0/5-4	2-1/0-2	-	-	-	04-01-02
Raith	v	St Mirren	1-0/1-1	0-6/1-2	-	3-0/1-0	-	1-1/2-0	09-03-02
St Johnstone	v	Falkirk	-	-	-	-	0-1/0-1	0-4/2-1	06-02-05

BELL'S SCOTTISH SECOND DIVISION

Home	v	Away							Rec
Alloa	v	Ayr	-	-	1-1/0-2	-	0-1/2-3	-	00-03-03
Berwick	v	Dumbarton	3-1/0-1	0-1/0-0	-	-	1-2/0-1	1-4/1-2	07-03-10
Forfar	v	Stirling	1-2/3-3	-	1-0/3-1	-	-	-	02-03-03
Morton	v	Arbroath	-	-	-	-	-	6-4/1-0	02-00-00
Stranraer	v	Brechin	-	-	-	-	3-1/2-3	-	03-02-07

BELL'S SCOTTISH THIRD DIVISION

Home	v	Away							Rec
E Stirling	v	Elgin	-	-	0-2/1-0	2-1/0-3	1-2/2-2	3-1/2-1	04-01-03
Gretna	v	C'denbeath	-	-	-	-	-	1-0/0-1	01-00-01
Montrose	v	Albion	1-2/2-3	2-1/1-2	0-2/0-1	1-2/2-0	0-1/1-1	1-0/3-1	12-02-10
Peterhead	v	East Fife	-	-	0-0/2-1	1-3/1-1	0-2/2-2	-	01-03-02
Stenhsmuir	v	Queens P	2-1/4-1	-	1-1/2-0	-	-	-	06-04-03

SATURDAY 22 JANUARY 2005
FA BARCLAYCARD PREMIER LEAGUE

Home	v	Away							Rec
Arsenal	v	Newcastle	3-0	0-0	5-0	1-3	1-0	3-2	08-01-03
Birmingham	v	Fulham	-	2-2	1-3	-	0-0	2-2	02-04-01

Sponsored by Stan James

Blackburn	v	Bolton	-	3-1	1-1	1-1	0-0	3-4	03-03-01
Chelsea	v	Portsmouth	-	-	-	-	-	3-0	01-01-00
Crystal Pal	v	Tottenham	-	-	-	-	-	-	01-01-04
Everton	v	Charlton	4-1	-	3-0	0-3	1-0	0-1	05-00-02
Man Utd	v	Aston Villa	2-1	3-0	2-0	1-0	1-1	4-0	10-06-00
Norwich	v	Middlesbro	-	-	-	-	-	-	00-02-01
Southampton	v	Liverpool	1-2	1-1	3-3	2-0	0-1	2-0	06-04-06
WBA	v	Man City	-	0-2	-	4-0	1-2	-	02-00-04

COCA-COLA CHAMPIONSHIP

Brighton	v	Nottm F	-	-	-	-	1-0	-	01-00-00
Cardiff	v	Burnley	-	1-2	-	-	-	2-0	03-00-02
Coventry	v	QPR	-	-	-	-	-	-	02-02-04
Crewe	v	Rotherham	-	-	-	2-0	-	0-0	04-02-03
Leicester	v	Gillingham	-	-	-	-	2-0	-	01-00-00
Millwall	v	Wolves	-	-	-	1-0	1-1	-	06-01-01
Plymouth	v	Preston	-	-	-	-	-	-	03-00-01
Reading	v	Ipswich	-	-	-	-	3-1	1-1	02-01-02
Stoke	v	Leeds	-	-	-	-	-	-	00-01-01
Sunderland	v	Sheff Utd	0-0	-	-	-	-	3-0	04-02-01
West Ham	v	Derby	5-1	1-1	3-1	4-0	-	0-0	03-06-00
Wigan	v	Watford	-	-	-	-	-	1-0	02-00-00

COCA-COLA LEAGUE DIVISION ONE

Blackpool	v	Milton K	-	-	-	-	-	-	00-00-00
Bradford	v	Torquay	-	-	-	-	-	-	01-00-00
Brentford	v	Swindon	-	-	0-1	2-0	3-1	0-2	02-01-03
Chesterfield	v	Wrexham	2-1	0-3	-	3-2	-	2-1	06-03-02
Colchester	v	Luton	2-2	3-0	3-1	-	0-5	1-1	02-02-01
Doncaster	v	Hull	-	-	-	-	-	0-0	01-02-00
Hartlepool	v	Bristol C	-	-	-	-	-	1-2	00-00-01
Huddersfield	v	Bournemouth	-	-	-	1-0	-	-	02-02-02
Peterboro	v	Oldham	-	-	0-0	2-2	0-1	2-2	00-03-01
Sheff Wed	v	Port Vale	-	-	-	-	-	2-3	00-01-01
Stockport	v	Barnsley	0-1	1-3	2-0	1-3	4-1	2-3	02-00-04
Tranmere	v	Walsall	-	1-1	-	-	-	-	01-01-00

COCA-COLA LEAGUE DIVISION TWO

Boston	v	Swansea	-	-	-	-	1-0	1-1	01-01-00
Bristol R	v	Cheltenham	-	-	-	1-2	-	2-0	01-00-01
Bury	v	Northampton	-	-	1-0	2-1	-	1-0	05-02-02
Chester	v	Rochdale	1-1	0-2	-	-	-	-	02-02-02
Darlington	v	Shrewsbury	1-0	2-2	3-0	3-3	5-1	-	04-03-02
Grimsby	v	Lincoln	-	-	-	-	-	-	02-00-00
Kidderminstr	v	Oxford Utd	-	-	-	0-0	1-3	1-1	00-02-01
Mansfield	v	Southend	0-0	3-1	1-1	0-0	-	1-0	03-03-01
Notts Co	v	Scunthorpe	-	3-0	-	-	-	-	02-00-00
Rushden & D	v	Leyton O	-	-	-	1-0	2-0	-	02-00-00
Wycombe	v	Macclesfield	3-0	-	-	-	-	-	01-03-02
Yeovil	v	Cambridge U	-	-	-	-	-	4-1	01-00-00

BANK OF SCOTLAND SCOTTISH PREMIER LEAGUE

Aberdeen	v	Rangers	1-1/2-4	1-5/1-1	1-2	0-3/0-1	2-2	2-3/1-1	07-10-14
Celtic	v	Motherwell	2-0/1-0	0-1/4-0	1-0/1-0	2-0	3-1	3-0/1-1	16-08-06
Dundee	v	Hearts	1-0/2-0	1-0/0-0	1-1/0-0	1-1	1-1/1-2	1-2	06-07-05
Dunfermline	v	Dundee Utd	2-1/2-2	-	1-0/3-1	1-1	4-1	2-0/1-1	08-08-04
Hibernian	v	Kilmarnock	-	0-3/2-2	1-1/1-1	2-2/2-2	2-0	3-1/3-0	07-08-04
Livingston	v	Inv CT	2-1/4-3	2-2/1-1	3-1/4-1	-	-	-	04-04-02

BELL'S SCOTTISH FIRST DIVISION

Falkirk	v	Clyde	-	-	3-2/1-1	1-1/1-6	2-1/3-0	0-2/1-1	08-04-03
Hamilton	v	Ross C	-	1-0/0-3	-	-	-	-	01-00-01

Raith	v	Queen Sth	-	-	-	-	-	0-1/3-1	03-00-01
St Johnstone	v	Partick	-	-	-	-	-	-	04-04-01
St Mirren	v	Airdrie Utd	1-5/3-0	5-0/3-1	-	0-0/2-1	-	-	07-01-10

BELL'S SCOTTISH SECOND DIVISION

Ayr	v	Forfar	-	-	-	-	-	-	03-04-01
Berwick	v	Alloa	-	-	-	0-4/0-1	-	3-2/3-1	04-05-05
Brechin	v	Arbroath	-	-	-	-	-	-	03-03-02
Dumbarton	v	Stranraer	-	-	-	-	3-0/1-1	-	03-05-02
Stirling	v	Morton	-	-	-	-	2-0/0-3	-	05-03-06

BELL'S SCOTTISH THIRD DIVISION

Albion	v	Stenhsmuir	1-3/1-2	-	-	-	-	-	01-03-05
C'denbeath	v	Elgin	-	-	3-1/1-0	-	-	3-2/2-0	04-00-00
East Fife	v	E Stirling	-	1-0/3-1	3-1/4-1	0-4/1-0	4-1/3-0	-	08-07-02
Peterhead	v	Gretna	-	-	-	-	1-1/1-0	2-0/2-1	03-01-00
Queens P	v	Montrose	3-0/1-2	2-1/1-1	-	2-2/0-1	0-1/1-1	1-1/1-1	08-09-07

NATIONWIDE CONFERENCE

Barnet	v	Exeter	0-1	2-2	1-1	-	-	2-3	03-03-03
Canvey Islnd	v	Stevenage	-	-	-	-	-	-	00-00-00
Carlisle	v	Leigh RMI	-	-	-	-	-	-	00-00-00
Farnborough	v	Crawley	-	-	-	-	-	-	01-00-01
Forest G	v	Woking	0-2	0-0	0-0	2-1	3-2	2-2	02-03-01
Gravesend	v	Aldershot	2-1	1-1	2-0	-	-	1-3	02-01-01
Halifax	v	Burton	-	-	-	-	0-1	1-4	00-00-02
Hereford	v	Dagenham	-	-	0-1	1-0	2-1	1-1	02-01-01
Northwich	v	Scarborough	-	2-0	3-0	1-1	0-2	1-1	02-02-01
Tamworth	v	Accrington	-	-	-	-	-	1-1	00-01-00
York	v	Morecambe	-	-	-	-	-	-	00-00-00

FRIDAY 28 JANUARY 2005
COCA-COLA LEAGUE DIVISION TWO

Cheltenham	v	Grimsby	-	-	-	-	-	-	00-00-00

SATURDAY 29 JANUARY 2005
COCA-COLA LEAGUE DIVISION ONE

Barnsley	v	Bradford	0-1	-	-	3-3	-	-	02-02-01
Bournemouth	v	Blackpool	1-1	2-0	-	0-1	-	1-2	05-02-03
Bristol C	v	Chesterfield	-	3-0	-	3-0	4-0	4-0	08-00-00
Hull	v	Hartlepool	4-0	0-3	0-0	1-1	2-0	-	06-02-02
Luton	v	Tranmere	-	-	-	-	0-0	3-1	03-02-01
Milton K	v	Sheff Wed	2-1	0-2	4-1	1-1	3-0	-	07-05-02
Oldham	v	Brentford	-	3-0	3-0	3-2	2-1	1-1	04-02-00
Port Vale	v	Colchester	-	-	3-1	3-1	1-0	4-3	04-00-00
Swindon	v	Stockport	2-3	1-1	-	-	0-1	1-2	00-03-03
Torquay	v	Peterboro	0-1	2-1	-	-	-	-	04-02-01
Walsall	v	Huddersfield	-	2-0	-	-	-	-	01-00-01
Wrexham	v	Doncaster	-	-	-	-	-	-	01-03-01

COCA-COLA LEAGUE DIVISION TWO

Cambridge U	v	Kidderminstr	-	-	-	-	0-2	0-0	00-01-01
Leyton O	v	Notts Co	-	-	-	-	-	-	00-01-01
Lincoln	v	Mansfield	-	3-0	0-2	1-4	-	4-1	05-01-04
Macclesfield	v	Bury	-	-	-	-	0-0	1-0	01-01-00
Northampton	v	Yeovil	-	-	-	-	-	2-0	01-00-00
Oxford Utd	v	Bristol R	-	0-5	0-1	0-0	0-1	0-0	02-04-04
Rochdale	v	Rushden & D	-	-	-	0-0	0-1	-	00-01-01
Scunthorpe	v	Boston	-	-	-	-	2-0	0-1	01-00-01
Shrewsbury	v	Wycombe	-	-	-	-	-	-	01-03-00
Southend	v	Darlington	2-1	1-2	0-2	1-0	2-0	3-2	04-00-02

Sponsored by Stan James

Swansea	v	Chester	1-1	2-1	-	-	-	-	07-02-01

BANK OF SCOTLAND SCOTTISH PREMIER LEAGUE

Dundee Utd	v	Dundee	0-1/0-2	2-1/1-0	0-2	2-2/1-0	0-0/1-1	1-1/2-2	09-07-06
Hearts	v	Aberdeen	2-0/0-2	3-0/3-0	3-0	1-0/3-1	0-0	2-0/1-0	16-06-08
Inv CT	v	Dunfermline	-	1-1/1-2	-	-	-	-	00-01-01
Kilmarnock	v	Celtic	2-0/0-0	0-1/1-1	0-1/1-0	0-1/0-2	1-1/0-4	0-5/0-1	04-08-10
Motherwell	v	Hibernian	-	2-2/2-0	1-3	1-3/4-0	0-2/2-1	0-1	09-11-08
Rangers	v	Livingston	-	-	-	0-0/3-0	4-3	1-0	03-01-00

BELL'S SCOTTISH FIRST DIVISION

Airdrie Utd	v	Hamilton	3-2/1-0	-	-	-	0-0/2-2	3-0/1-1	10-05-02
Clyde	v	St Johnstone	-	-	-	-	1-2/2-1	2-0/2-3	03-00-04
Partick	v	Raith	-	-	-	2-1/1-0	-	-	04-04-06
Queen Sth	v	St Mirren	-	-	-	-	3-0/0-2	1-2/1-0	02-00-02
Ross C	v	Falkirk	-	-	0-2/4-1	1-2/4-2	1-1/0-1	1-2/1-1	02-02-04

BELL'S SCOTTISH SECOND DIVISION

Alloa	v	Dumbarton	-	-	-	-	-	1-2/3-0	04-00-04
Arbroath	v	Ayr	-	-	-	3-2/0-2	1-1/1-2	-	01-01-02
Forfar	v	Berwick	-	1-1/2-0	3-5/0-1	2-1/0-0	0-2/2-2	1-5/0-2	03-04-08
Morton	v	Brechin	-	-	-	-	-	-	03-02-00
Stranraer	v	Stirling	-	2-1/3-1	1-1/0-3	-	-	0-1/1-1	02-06-05

BELL'S SCOTTISH THIRD DIVISION

E Stirling	v	Queens P	1-1/1-1	1-1/0-1	-	0-1/3-1	0-4/0-2	1-2/2-4	12-06-09
Elgin	v	Albion	-	-	1-2/1-0	2-0/0-0	0-1/1-2	1-5/1-2	02-01-05
Gretna	v	East Fife	-	-	-	-	2-3/3-3	-	00-01-01
Montrose	v	C'denbeath	1-1/1-2	0-1/1-3	1-2/0-1	-	-	1-3/1-1	07-04-10
Stenhsmuir	v	Peterhead	-	-	-	-	-	-	00-00-00

NATIONWIDE CONFERENCE

Accrington	v	Northwich	-	-	-	-	-	2-2	00-01-00
Aldershot	v	Hereford	-	-	-	-	-	1-2	00-00-01
Burton	v	Barnet	-	-	-	-	0-3	2-3	00-00-02
Crawley	v	Canvey Islnd	-	-	-	-	-	-	00-00-00
Dagenham	v	Gravesend	0-0	2-1	-	-	4-0	0-4	03-01-01
Exeter	v	Forest G	-	-	-	-	-	2-2	00-01-00
Leigh RMI	v	York	-	-	-	-	-	-	00-00-00
Morecambe	v	Halifax	-	-	-	-	2-0	2-0	03-01-01
Scarborough	v	Carlisle	3-0	-	-	-	-	-	02-04-03
Stevenage	v	Farnborough	3-1	-	-	1-2	5-0	3-2	06-01-01
Woking	v	Tamworth	-	-	-	-	-	4-0	01-00-00

TUESDAY 1 FEBRUARY 2005
FA BARCLAYCARD PREMIER LEAGUE

Arsenal	v	Man Utd	3-0	1-2	1-0	3-1	2-2	1-1	08-05-03
Birmingham	v	Southampton	-	-	-	-	3-2	2-1	02-00-00
Bolton	v	Tottenham	-	-	-	1-1	1-0	2-0	02-02-01
Charlton	v	Liverpool	1-0	-	0-4	0-2	2-0	3-2	03-00-04
Portsmouth	v	Middlesbro	-	-	-	-	-	5-1	04-02-01
WBA	v	Crystal Pal	3-2	0-0	1-0	2-0	-	2-0	06-01-02

WEDNESDAY 2 FEBRUARY 2005
FA BARCLAYCARD PREMIER LEAGUE

Blackburn	v	Chelsea	3-4	-	-	0-0	2-3	2-3	05-03-03
Everton	v	Norwich	-	-	-	-	-	-	03-02-02
Fulham	v	Aston Villa	-	-	-	0-0	2-1	1-2	01-01-01
Man City	v	Newcastle	-	-	0-1	-	1-0	1-0	03-02-01

FRIDAY 4 FEBRUARY 2005
COCA-COLA LEAGUE DIVISION TWO

Northampton	v	Cambridge U	-	-	0-2	2-2	-	1-2	01-01-03
Swansea	v	Southend	3-1	3-1	-	3-2	1-0	2-3	05-00-02

SATURDAY 5 FEBRUARY 2005
FA BARCLAYCARD PREMIER LEAGUE

Aston Villa	v	Arsenal	3-2	1-1	0-0	1-2	1-1	0-2	05-06-05
Chelsea	v	Man City	-	-	2-1	-	5-0	1-0	04-05-02
Crystal Pal	v	Bolton	2-2	0-0	0-2	-	-	-	00-05-01
Liverpool	v	Fulham	-	-	-	0-0	2-0	0-0	01-02-00
Man Utd	v	Birmingham	-	-	-	-	2-0	3-0	02-00-00
Middlesbro	v	Blackburn	2-1	-	-	1-3	1-0	0-1	05-01-04
Newcastle	v	Charlton	0-0	-	0-1	3-0	2-1	3-1	03-02-04
Norwich	v	WBA	1-1	2-1	0-1	2-0	-	0-0	02-04-02
Southampton	v	Everton	2-0	2-0	1-0	0-1	1-0	3-3	06-06-04
Tottenham	v	Portsmouth	-	-	-	-	-	4-3	01-00-00

COCA-COLA CHAMPIONSHIP

Brighton	v	Derby	-	-	-	-	1-0	-	01-00-01
Burnley	v	Leeds	-	-	-	-	-	-	00-00-00
Leicester	v	Crewe	-	-	-	-	-	-	00-00-00
Millwall	v	QPR	-	-	-	-	-	-	01-00-01
Preston	v	Coventry	-	-	-	4-0	2-2	4-2	02-01-00
Reading	v	Plymouth	-	-	-	-	-	-	02-00-00
Rotherham	v	Nottm F	-	-	-	1-2	2-2	1-1	00-02-01
Sheff Utd	v	Ipswich	1-2	2-2	-	-	0-0	1-1	02-05-03
Watford	v	Gillingham	-	-	0-0	2-3	0-1	2-2	00-03-03
West Ham	v	Cardiff	-	-	-	-	-	1-0	01-00-00
Wigan	v	Stoke	2-3	1-2	1-1	6-1	-	2-1	04-02-02
Wolves	v	Sunderland	1-1	-	-	-	-	-	04-02-02

COCA-COLA LEAGUE DIVISION ONE

Barnsley	v	Sheff Wed	-	-	1-0	3-0	-	1-1	03-02-00
Bradford	v	Tranmere	2-0	-	-	-	-	-	02-00-02
Brentford	v	Milton K	-	-	-	-	-	-	00-00-00
Chesterfield	v	Hartlepool	-	-	0-0	-	-	1-2	02-01-02
Colchester	v	Blackpool	2-2	1-1	-	1-1	0-2	1-1	00-04-01
Huddersfield	v	Luton	-	-	-	-	0-1	-	01-00-01
Hull	v	Bristol C	-	-	-	-	-	-	00-00-02
Oldham	v	Swindon	-	-	1-0	2-0	4-0	0-1	06-03-01
Peterboro	v	Stockport	-	-	-	-	2-0	1-2	04-01-04
Port Vale	v	Bournemouth	-	-	2-1	0-0	-	2-1	04-02-00
Torquay	v	Doncaster	-	-	-	-	-	1-0	07-00-03
Walsall	v	Wrexham	1-0	-	2-3	-	-	-	03-02-03

COCA-COLA LEAGUE DIVISION TWO

Bristol R	v	Grimsby	-	-	-	-	-	-	00-00-03
Bury	v	Darlington	-	-	-	-	2-2	1-1	03-04-00
Cheltenham	v	Rochdale	-	0-2	0-2	1-1	-	0-2	00-01-03
Chester	v	Rushden & D	-	-	1-2	-	-	-	00-00-01
Lincoln	v	Oxford Utd	-	-	-	1-0	0-1	0-1	01-00-02
Macclesfield	v	Yeovil	-	-	-	-	-	4-1	03-01-04
Notts Co	v	Mansfield	-	-	-	-	2-2	-	03-01-00
Scunthorpe	v	Kidderminstr	-	-	2-0	1-0	1-1	0-2	02-01-01
Shrewsbury	v	Leyton O	1-1	1-0	1-1	1-0	2-1	-	06-02-02
Wycombe	v	Boston	-	-	-	-	-	-	04-01-00

BELL'S SCOTTISH SECOND DIVISION

Alloa	v	Morton	-	-	2-1/0-3	1-1/4-0	-	0-1/3-3	02-03-02
Ayr	v	Brechin	-	-	-	-	-	3-2/1-2	05-01-01

Sponsored by Stan James

Berwick	v	Arbroath	-	-	2-1/1-0	-	-	3-0/1-3	09-03-03
Dumbarton	v	Stirling	-	-	-	4-1/2-0	-	-	04-04-04
Forfar	v	Stranraer	-	-	0-0/2-3	1-1/3-2	2-1/4-0	-	06-04-03

BELL'S SCOTTISH THIRD DIVISION

Albion	v	E Stirling	3-1/0-2	1-1/0-1	2-1/2-2	0-4/5-1	6-0/3-1	5-0/5-1	14-06-07
East Fife	v	Queens P	-	0-0/0-0	-	1-4/0-3	1-1/1-0	-	06-07-02
Gretna	v	Elgin	-	-	-	-	0-0/2-1	2-2/2-1	02-02-00
Montrose	v	Stenhsmuir	0-0/1-2	-	-	-	-	-	02-02-07
Peterhead	v	C'denbeath	-	-	3-0/3-0	-	-	0-1/0-0	02-01-01

NATIONWIDE CONFERENCE

Accrington	v	Scarborough	-	-	-	-	-	1-0	01-00-00
Aldershot	v	Exeter	-	-	-	-	-	2-1	01-00-00
Burton	v	Woking	-	-	-	-	0-2	2-0	01-00-01
Crawley	v	Tamworth	1-0	3-0	0-2	1-2	1-0	-	04-00-02
Dagenham	v	Farnborough	-	3-2	-	2-1	1-0	1-0	05-01-01
Gravesend	v	Halifax	-	-	-	-	1-0	1-0	02-00-00
Hereford	v	Carlisle	-	-	-	-	-	-	04-02-02
Leigh RMI	v	Canvey Islnd	-	-	-	-	-	-	00-00-00
Northwich	v	Forest G	1-0	0-0	0-0	2-2	2-1	0-4	02-03-01
Stevenage	v	Morecambe	2-0	1-2	1-1	3-1	1-1	0-1	03-03-03
York	v	Barnet	-	1-0	1-0	-	-	-	03-01-01

FRIDAY 11 FEBRUARY 2005
COCA-COLA LEAGUE DIVISION ONE

Hartlepool	v	Peterboro	1-2	1-0	-	-	-	1-0	05-01-02

COCA-COLA LEAGUE DIVISION TWO

Southend	v	Scunthorpe	0-1	-	1-0	2-0	1-2	4-2	03-01-02

SATURDAY 12 FEBRUARY 2005
FA BARCLAYCARD PREMIER LEAGUE

Arsenal	v	Crystal Pal	-	-	-	-	-	-	05-00-01
Birmingham	v	Liverpool	-	-	-	-	2-1	0-3	01-00-01
Blackburn	v	Norwich	-	1-1	3-2	-	-	-	02-02-01
Bolton	v	Middlesbro	-	-	-	1-0	2-1	2-0	05-01-00
Charlton	v	Tottenham	1-4	-	1-0	3-1	0-1	2-4	02-01-04
Everton	v	Chelsea	0-0	1-1	2-1	0-0	1-3	0-1	04-06-05
Fulham	v	Newcastle	-	-	-	3-1	2-1	2-3	02-00-01
Man City	v	Man Utd	-	-	0-1	-	3-1	4-1	03-03-04
Portsmouth	v	Aston Villa	-	-	-	-	-	2-1	01-00-00
WBA	v	Southampton	-	-	-	-	1-0	-	01-00-00

COCA-COLA CHAMPIONSHIP

Cardiff	v	Brighton	2-0	-	1-1	1-1	-	-	03-04-00
Coventry	v	Burnley	-	-	-	0-2	0-1	4-0	01-00-02
Crewe	v	Wigan	-	-	-	-	0-1	2-3	03-00-02
Derby	v	Wolves	-	-	-	-	1-4	-	01-02-03
Gillingham	v	Millwall	1-1	2-0	-	1-0	1-0	4-3	04-01-02
Ipswich	v	Leicester	-	-	2-0	2-0	6-1	-	07-02-00
Leeds	v	Reading	-	-	-	-	-	-	00-00-00
Nottm F	v	Sheff Utd	-	0-0	2-0	1-1	3-0	3-1	05-02-02
Plymouth	v	Rotherham	1-0	1-1	-	-	-	-	04-02-00
QPR	v	Preston	-	-	0-0	-	-	-	00-01-00
Stoke	v	West Ham	-	-	-	-	-	0-2	00-01-01
Sunderland	v	Watford	4-1	2-0	-	-	-	2-0	06-02-02

COCA-COLA LEAGUE DIVISION ONE

Blackpool	v	Brentford	-	0-1	-	1-3	1-0	1-1	04-02-05

Bournemouth	v	Oldham	2-0	3-0	1-1	3-2	-	1-0	05-03-00
Bristol C	v	Walsall	-	-	1-3	-	-	-	03-00-02
Doncaster	v	Chesterfield	-	-	-	-	-	-	02-01-03
Luton	v	Hull	-	-	-	0-1	-	-	00-00-01
Milton K	v	Huddersfield	-	-	1-1	-	-	-	00-01-00
Sheff Wed	v	Bradford	-	2-0	-	1-1	2-1	-	02-01-00
Stockport	v	Port Vale	4-2	1-0	-	-	1-1	2-2	05-02-00
Swindon	v	Barnsley	1-3	1-2	-	-	3-1	1-1	04-04-03
Tranmere	v	Colchester	-	-	-	0-0	1-1	1-1	00-04-00
Wrexham	v	Torquay	-	-	-	-	2-1	-	04-01-00

COCA-COLA LEAGUE DIVISION TWO

Boston	v	Bury	-	-	-	-	1-1	1-0	01-01-00
Cambridge U	v	Macclesfield	-	-	-	-	3-1	3-1	02-01-00
Darlington	v	Notts Co	-	-	-	-	-	-	00-00-01
Grimsby	v	Shrewsbury	-	-	-	-	-	-	01-00-00
Kidderminstr	v	Chester	-	-	-	-	-	-	00-00-00
Leyton O	v	Swansea	1-1	0-1	-	2-2	3-1	1-2	05-03-05
Mansfield	v	Cheltenham	-	0-1	2-1	2-1	0-2	4-0	03-00-02
Oxford Utd	v	Northampton	-	-	3-1	-	-	3-0	02-00-00
Rochdale	v	Lincoln	-	1-1	3-1	2-2	0-1	0-3	06-06-03
Rushden & D	v	Wycombe	-	-	-	-	-	2-0	01-00-00
Yeovil	v	Bristol R	-	-	-	-	-	4-0	01-00-00

BANK OF SCOTLAND SCOTTISH PREMIER LEAGUE

Dundee	v	Motherwell	1-0/1-0	0-1/4-1	1-2	3-1/2-0	1-1	0-1	08-03-06
Dunfermline	v	Aberdeen	1-1/1-2	-	0-0/3-2	1-0/0-0	3-0	2-2	04-09-05
Hearts	v	Kilmarnock	2-1/2-2	2-2/0-0	0-2/3-0	2-0	1-1/3-0	2-1	11-07-02
Inv CT	v	Celtic	-	-	-	-	-	-	00-00-00
Livingston	v	Dundee Utd	-	-	-	2-0/1-1	3-0/1-2	0-0/2-3	02-02-02
Rangers	v	Hibernian	-	2-0/5-2	1-0/4-0	2-2/1-1	2-1	5-2/3-0	23-04-02

BELL'S SCOTTISH FIRST DIVISION

Falkirk	v	Hamilton	2-1/6-1	-	-	-	-	-	05-02-02
Partick	v	Airdrie Utd	-	-	-	1-1/1-1	-	-	04-05-04
Raith	v	Clyde	-	-	1-2/0-1	1-2/0-1	-	0-1/0-3	02-02-07
Ross C	v	St Mirren	-	-	-	0-1/4-1	4-0/2-0	2-0/1-0	05-00-01
St Johnstone	v	Queen Sth	-	-	-	-	2-2/0-1	4-1/2-2	03-02-01

BELL'S SCOTTISH SECOND DIVISION

Arbroath	v	Alloa	0-2/1-2	2-2/2-0	-	-	0-1/0-1	3-1/2-1	06-08-09
Brechin	v	Dumbarton	0-0/3-3	0-2/1-2	3-1/1-0	3-2/0-1	1-1/1-1	-	06-07-07
Morton	v	Forfar	-	-	-	1-3/1-4	-	1-1/1-1	01-06-03
Stirling	v	Ayr	-	-	-	-	-	-	03-05-02
Stranraer	v	Berwick	-	-	2-2/1-1	0-2/2-2	1-0/0-0	-	04-09-06

BELL'S SCOTTISH THIRD DIVISION

C'denbeath	v	Albion	2-3/0-2	0-0/5-0	5-0/1-0	-	-	1-4/1-1	08-08-05
E Stirling	v	Montrose	3-1/2-1	2-0/1-0	7-0/1-0	0-1/2-1	1-1/0-3	1-1/1-4	09-04-12
Elgin	v	East Fife	-	-	1-3/1-3	1-1/2-0	1-1/0-1	-	01-02-03
Queens P	v	Peterhead	-	-	-	0-1/2-0	2-0/1-2	0-2/1-0	03-00-03
Stenhsmuir	v	Gretna	-	-	-	-	-	-	00-00-00

NATIONWIDE CONFERENCE

Barnet	v	Hereford	-	-	-	2-0	2-1	1-1	04-02-02
Canvey Islnd	v	Northwich	-	-	-	-	-	-	00-00-00
Carlisle	v	Gravesend	-	-	-	-	-	-	00-00-00
Exeter	v	Accrington	-	-	-	-	-	3-2	01-00-00
Farnborough	v	Burton	-	-	-	-	5-1	2-1	04-00-00
Forest G	v	York	-	-	-	-	-	-	00-00-00
Halifax	v	Stevenage	-	-	-	-	1-0	2-1	04-00-02
Morecambe	v	Aldershot	-	-	-	-	-	2-0	01-00-00

Scarborough	v	Dagenham	-	-	0-1	0-0	0-1	0-0	00-02-02
Tamworth	v	Leigh RMI	-	-	-	-	-	4-3	01-00-00
Woking	v	Crawley	-	-	-	-	-	-	00-00-00

SATURDAY 19 FEBRUARY 2005
COCA-COLA CHAMPIONSHIP

Brighton	v	Sunderland	-	-	-	-	-	-	01-01-01
Burnley	v	QPR	-	-	2-1	-	-	-	01-00-00
Leicester	v	Cardiff	-	-	-	-	-	-	00-00-00
Millwall	v	Stoke	2-0	1-0	2-0	-	3-1	1-1	05-02-01
Preston	v	Ipswich	-	-	-	-	0-0	1-1	00-02-00
Reading	v	Coventry	-	-	-	-	1-2	1-2	00-00-02
Rotherham	v	Derby	-	-	-	-	2-1	0-0	01-01-00
Sheff Utd	v	Crewe	3-1	1-1	1-0	1-0	-	2-0	05-01-00
Watford	v	Nottm F	-	-	3-0	1-2	1-1	1-1	01-02-02
West Ham	v	Plymouth	-	-	-	-	-	-	01-01-00
Wigan	v	Leeds	-	-	-	-	-	-	00-00-00
Wolves	v	Gillingham	-	-	1-1	2-0	6-0	-	03-01-00

COCA-COLA LEAGUE DIVISION ONE

Barnsley	v	Bournemouth	-	-	-	-	-	1-1	01-01-01
Bradford	v	Luton	-	-	-	-	-	-	00-00-00
Brentford	v	Tranmere	-	-	-	4-0	1-2	2-2	01-01-04
Chesterfield	v	Sheff Wed	-	-	-	-	-	3-1	01-00-00
Colchester	v	Bristol C	-	3-4	4-0	0-0	2-2	2-1	02-02-01
Huddersfield	v	Blackpool	-	-	-	2-4	0-0	-	02-04-01
Hull	v	Wrexham	-	-	-	-	1-2	-	01-02-01
Oldham	v	Stockport	-	-	-	-	2-0	2-0	02-00-00
Peterboro	v	Doncaster	-	-	-	-	-	-	02-01-01
Port Vale	v	Hartlepool	-	-	-	-	-	2-5	02-00-01
Torquay	v	Swindon	-	-	-	-	-	-	00-00-00
Walsall	v	Milton K	-	-	-	2-1	2-0	1-0	03-00-00

COCA-COLA LEAGUE DIVISION TWO

Bristol R	v	Boston	-	-	-	-	1-1	2-0	01-01-00
Bury	v	Mansfield	-	-	-	-	-	3-0	03-02-02
Cheltenham	v	Oxford Utd	-	-	-	2-0	-	0-0	01-01-00
Chester	v	Yeovil	-	-	2-1	1-1	2-2	-	01-02-00
Lincoln	v	Cambridge U	-	-	-	-	2-2	2-2	02-04-01
Macclesfield	v	Rochdale	-	1-2	0-0	0-1	3-2	2-1	03-01-02
Northampton	v	Southend	-	2-0	-	-	-	2-2	02-02-00
Notts Co	v	Rushden & D	-	-	-	-	-	1-3	00-00-01
Scunthorpe	v	Leyton O	2-0	-	1-1	4-1	2-1	1-1	05-03-01
Shrewsbury	v	Kidderminstr	-	-	1-0	4-0	2-3	-	02-00-01
Swansea	v	Grimsby	-	-	-	-	-	-	00-01-00
Wycombe	v	Darlington	-	-	-	-	-	-	01-00-01

BANK OF SCOTLAND SCOTTISH PREMIER LEAGUE

Aberdeen	v	Livingston	-	-	-	0-3/3-0	0-0/1-0	0-3/1-2	02-01-03
Celtic	v	Rangers	5-1/0-3	1-1/0-1	6-2/1-0	2-1/1-1	3-3/1-0	3-0/1-0	12-07-13
Dundee Utd	v	Inv CT	-	-	-	-	-	-	00-00-00
Hibernian	v	Dundee	-	5-2/1-2	5-1/3-0	1-2/2-2	2-1	1-1/1-0	08-06-03
Kilmarnock	v	Dunfermline	0-0/0-0	-	2-1/2-1	0-0	2-2/1-1	1-1	05-08-02
Motherwell	v	Hearts	3-2/0-4	2-1/0-2	2-0	2-0/1-2	6-1	1-1/1-1	08-08-14

BELL'S SCOTTISH FIRST DIVISION

Airdrie Utd	v	Raith	0-1/2-2	1-4/0-2	1-1/3-0	2-2/1-1	0-0/1-1	-	05-07-06
Clyde	v	Ross C	-	3-1/0-0	2-2/2-0	3-0/0-0	2-1/1-0	2-2/1-0	06-04-00
Hamilton	v	Partick	-	0-0/0-1	-	-	-	-	00-04-05
Queen Sth	v	Falkirk	-	-	-	-	1-1/2-1	2-0/1-0	03-01-01
St Mirren	v	St Johnstone	-	-	0-1/1-0	-	0-2/1-3	1-1/1-1	02-07-07

Berwick	v	Brechin	3-0/2-3	2-0/3-1	-	-	0-3/2-0	-	09-04-03
Dumbarton	v	Morton	-					1-0/3-0	07-00-03
Forfar	v	Arbroath	1-3/5-2	-	0-1/1-1	-	-	2-2/1-2	04-05-04
Stirling	v	Alloa	4-2/1-1	0-1/1-1	-	-	-	-	03-02-02
Stranraer	v	Ayr	0-1/0-2	-	-	-	-	-	03-01-04

BELL'S SCOTTISH THIRD DIVISION

East Fife	v	C'denbeath	-	2-3/1-1	0-2/1-2	-			04-03-04
Gretna	v	Montrose	-	-	-	-	4-1/2-2	1-1/1-2	01-02-01
Peterhead	v	Elgin	-	-	1-0/1-1	1-1/1-0	2-2/3-2	5-1/3-1	05-03-00
Queens P	v	Albion	0-0/0-0	2-0/0-1	-	1-2/0-3	2-4/1-1	1-1/0-1	08-12-06
Stenhsmuir	v	E Stirling	1-0/2-2	-	-	-			07-03-01

NATIONWIDE CONFERENCE

Accrington	v	Barnet	-	-	-	-	-	2-0	01-00-00
Aldershot	v	Halifax	-	-	-	-	-	3-1	01-00-00
Burton	v	Forest G	-	-	-	-	2-3	2-3	01-00-02
Crawley	v	Morecambe	-	-	-	-	-	-	00-00-00
Dagenham	v	Carlisle	-	-	-	-	-	-	00-00-00
Gravesend	v	Tamworth	-	-	-	-	-	2-0	01-00-00
Hereford	v	Canvey Islnd	-	-	-	-	-	-	00-00-00
Leigh RMI	v	Exeter	-	-	-	-	-	1-1	00-01-00
Northwich	v	Farnborough	3-0	-	-	1-2	2-2	1-1	02-05-04
Stevenage	v	Scarborough	-	0-1	1-1	2-0	1-1	2-2	01-03-01
York	v	Woking	-	-	-	-	-	-	00-00-00

TUESDAY 22 FEBRUARY 2005
COCA-COLA CHAMPIONSHIP

Cardiff	v	Millwall	-	1-1	-	-	-	1-3	00-01-01
Crewe	v	Reading	-	-	-	-	-	1-0	03-01-00
Gillingham	v	West Ham	-	-	-	-	-	2-0	01-00-00
Ipswich	v	Watford	3-2	-	-	-	4-2	4-1	06-01-01
Leeds	v	Brighton	-	-	-	-	-	-	02-00-00
Plymouth	v	Sheff Utd	-	-	-	-	-	-	00-00-00
QPR	v	Wolves	0-1	1-1	2-2	-	-	-	00-04-01
Stoke	v	Leicester	-	-	-	-	0-1	-	02-01-02
Sunderland	v	Rotherham	-	-	-	-	-	0-0	00-01-00

COCA-COLA LEAGUE DIVISION ONE

Blackpool	v	Bradford	-	-	-	-	-	-	02-01-01
Bournemouth	v	Torquay	-	-	-	-	1-1	-	01-01-00
Bristol C	v	Oldham	-	1-1	2-2	3-0	2-0	0-2	03-03-02
Doncaster	v	Barnsley	-	-	-	-	-	-	00-00-00
Hartlepool	v	Brentford	0-1	-	-	-	-	1-2	01-00-03
Luton	v	Walsall	0-1	-	0-0	-	-	-	01-01-02
Milton K	v	Hull	-	-	-	-	-	-	00-00-00
Stockport	v	Chesterfield	-	-	-	-	2-1	0-0	04-01-01
Tranmere	v	Huddersfield	2-3	1-0	2-0	1-0	2-1	-	08-01-01
Wrexham	v	Colchester	2-4	1-0	1-0	1-1	-	0-1	04-02-02

COCA-COLA LEAGUE DIVISION TWO

Cambridge U	v	Cheltenham	-	-	-	-	-	2-1	01-00-00
Darlington	v	Swansea	2-2	1-1	-	0-0	2-2	1-2	02-05-01
Grimsby	v	Chester	-	-	-	-	-	-	01-00-00
Kidderminstr	v	Bristol R	-	-	-	2-0	1-1	1-0	02-01-00
Leyton O	v	Lincoln	-	2-3	1-0	5-0	1-1	0-2	05-01-03
Mansfield	v	Wycombe	-	-	-	-	0-0	-	01-01-00
Rochdale	v	Northampton	-	0-3	-	-	-	1-1	02-04-03
Rushden & D	v	Bury	-	-	-	-	0-1	-	00-00-01
Southend	v	Shrewsbury	2-1	3-2	0-0	0-2	2-3	-	03-01-02
Yeovil	v	Scunthorpe	-	-	-	-	-	2-1	01-00-00

WEDNESDAY 23 FEBRUARY 2005
COCA-COLA CHAMPIONSHIP

Coventry	v	Wigan	-	-	-	-	-	1-1	00-01-00
Derby	v	Burnley	-	-	-	-	1-2	2-0	02-00-01
Nottm F	v	Preston	-	-	3-1	1-1	2-2	0-1	01-02-01

COCA-COLA LEAGUE DIVISION ONE

Sheff Wed	v	Peterboro	-	-	-	-	-	2-0	01-00-00
Swindon	v	Port Vale	1-1	2-1	0-1	3-0	1-2	0-0	06-03-03

COCA-COLA LEAGUE DIVISION TWO

Boston	v	Notts Co	-	-	-	-	-	-	00-00-00
Oxford Utd	v	Macclesfield	-	-	-	0-2	0-1	3-1	01-00-02

SATURDAY 26 FEBRUARY 2005
FA BARCLAYCARD PREMIER LEAGUE

Aston Villa	v	Everton	3-0	3-0	2-1	0-0	3-2	0-0	10-06-00
Chelsea	v	WBA	-	-	-	-	2-0	-	01-01-00
Crystal Pal	v	Birmingham	1-1	0-2	1-2	0-0	-	-	03-02-03
Liverpool	v	Blackburn	2-0	-	-	4-3	1-1	4-0	06-03-01
Man Utd	v	Portsmouth	-	-	-	-	-	3-0	01-00-00
Middlesbro	v	Charlton	2-0	-	0-0	0-0	1-1	0-0	05-05-01
Newcastle	v	Bolton	-	-	-	3-2	1-0	0-0	04-01-00
Norwich	v	Man City	-	1-0	-	2-0	-	-	03-05-02
Southampton	v	Arsenal	0-0	0-1	3-2	0-2	3-2	0-1	05-03-08
Tottenham	v	Fulham	-	-	-	4-0	1-1	0-3	01-01-01

COCA-COLA CHAMPIONSHIP

Brighton	v	Millwall	-	-	-	-	1-0	-	01-01-01
Coventry	v	Stoke	-	-	-	-	0-1	4-2	01-00-01
Gillingham	v	Wigan	2-0	2-1	-	-	-	0-3	04-02-02
Ipswich	v	QPR	3-1	1-4	-	-	-	-	02-02-03
Leeds	v	West Ham	4-0	1-0	0-1	3-0	1-0	-	09-02-01
Nottm F	v	Derby	2-2	-	-	-	3-0	1-1	03-05-00
Plymouth	v	Crewe	-	-	-	-	1-3	-	02-00-01
Preston	v	Burnley	4-1	0-0	2-1	2-3	3-1	5-3	05-02-02
Reading	v	Leicester	-	-	-	-	1-3	-	00-01-01
Sheff Utd	v	Rotherham	-	-	-	2-2	1-0	5-0	02-01-00
Sunderland	v	Cardiff	-	-	-	-	-	0-0	00-01-00
Wolves	v	Watford	0-0	-	2-2	1-0	0-0	-	04-07-00

COCA-COLA LEAGUE DIVISION ONE

Barnsley	v	Torquay	-	-	-	-	-	-	00-00-00
Bournemouth	v	Tranmere	-	-	-	0-2	-	1-5	01-00-02
Brentford	v	Sheff Wed	-	-	-	-	-	0-3	00-00-01
Bristol C	v	Blackpool	-	5-2	-	2-1	2-0	2-1	06-01-02
Chesterfield	v	Peterboro	-	-	-	0-1	0-0	2-1	02-04-01
Doncaster	v	Swindon	-	-	-	-	-	-	00-00-00
Huddersfield	v	Oldham	-	-	-	0-0	1-1	-	01-03-00
Hull	v	Colchester	-	-	-	-	-	-	01-00-01
Port Vale	v	Luton	-	-	3-0	-	1-2	1-0	03-00-02
Stockport	v	Hartlepool	-	-	-	-	-	1-2	04-00-03
Walsall	v	Bradford	-	-	-	2-2	0-1	1-0	02-01-02
Wrexham	v	Milton K	-	-	-	-	-	-	00-00-00

COCA-COLA LEAGUE DIVISION TWO

Boston	v	Northampton	-	-	-	-	-	1-1	00-01-00
Cambridge U	v	Oxford Utd	-	2-0	1-0	-	1-1	1-1	02-04-01
Cheltenham	v	Lincoln	-	0-2	2-1	2-1	-	3-2	03-00-01
Grimsby	v	Yeovil	-	-	-	-	-	-	00-00-00

Leyton O	v	Darlington	3-2	2-1	1-0	0-0	2-1	1-0	08-03-00
Macclesfield	v	Bristol R	3-4	-	-	2-1	2-1	2-1	03-00-01
Rochdale	v	Kidderminstr	-	-	0-0	2-0	0-1	0-1	01-01-02
Rushden & D	v	Mansfield	-	-	-	3-1	-	-	01-00-00
Shrewsbury	v	Chester	2-0	0-1	-	-	-	0-0	05-03-01
Southend	v	Bury	-	-	-	-	1-2	1-0	02-01-01
Swansea	v	Scunthorpe	1-2	-	-	2-2	1-1	4-2	02-03-01
Wycombe	v	Notts Co	1-1	2-0	3-1	3-0	3-1	1-1	05-03-00

BELL'S SCOTTISH SECOND DIVISION

Alloa	v	Forfar	1-2/3-1	-	-	1-2/2-1	-	1-1/4-0	03-03-08
Arbroath	v	Dumbarton	-	-	-	-	-	2-1/0-3	05-02-03
Ayr	v	Berwick	-	-	-	-	-	-	03-00-01
Brechin	v	Stirling	-	-	-	3-1/2-1	-	-	05-00-04
Morton	v	Stranraer	3-0/1-0	-	-	1-1/2-2	-	-	02-02-00

BELL'S SCOTTISH THIRD DIVISION

Albion	v	East Fife	-	1-3/3-1	0-1/1-2	3-0/2-1	1-5/0-0	-	06-02-08
C'denbeath	v	Stenhsmuir	0-2/0-2	-	-	1-1/2-4	1-0/3-3	-	04-05-05
E Stirling	v	Gretna	-	-	-	-	0-4/1-2	0-1/2-4	00-00-04
Elgin	v	Queens P	-	-	-	2-0/0-1	2-2/0-0	2-2/1-3	01-03-02
Montrose	v	Peterhead	-	-	0-2/2-2	0-3/2-1	0-3/1-2	0-1/2-1	02-01-05

NATIONWIDE CONFERENCE

Barnet	v	Aldershot	-	-	-	-	-	2-1	01-00-00
Canvey Islnd	v	Accrington	-	-	-	-	-	-	00-00-00
Carlisle	v	York	-	0-1	1-1	2-1	1-1	1-2	04-04-04
Exeter	v	Burton	-	-	-	-	-	2-0	01-00-00
Farnborough	v	Leigh RMI	-	-	-	3-0	1-0	1-1	02-01-00
Forest G	v	Stevenage	1-2	3-2	2-3	0-0	0-3	3-1	02-01-03
Halifax	v	Northwich	-	-	-	-	0-5	5-3	03-01-03
Morecambe	v	Dagenham	-	-	2-3	1-1	2-1	3-2	02-02-01
Scarborough	v	Crawley	-	-	-	-	-	-	00-00-00
Tamworth	v	Hereford	-	-	-	-	-	1-3	00-00-01
Woking	v	Gravesend	-	-	-	-	2-3	3-2	01-00-01

TUESDAY 1 MARCH 2005
BANK OF SCOTLAND SCOTTISH PREMIER LEAGUE

Dundee Utd	v	Aberdeen	1-0/3-0	3-1/1-1	3-5/1-1	1-1	1-1/0-2	3-2	10-12-06

WEDNESDAY 2 MARCH 2005
BANK OF SCOTLAND SCOTTISH PREMIER LEAGUE

Celtic	v	Dundee	6-1/5-0	6-2/2-2	1-0/2-1/0-2	3-1	2-0/6-2	3-2	14-03-02
Dunfermline	v	Motherwell	1-1/1-2	-	1-2/1-2	5-2/3-1	1-0/3-0	1-0/3-0	09-05-06
Hearts	v	Rangers	2-1/2-3	0-4/1-2	0-1/1-4	2-2/0-2	0-4/0-2	0-4/1-1	06-06-20
Inv CT	v	Hibernian	-	-	-	-	-	-	00-00-00
Livingston	v	Kilmarnock	-	-	-	0-1	0-1/0-4	1-2/1-1	02-03-08

SATURDAY 5 MARCH 2005
FA BARCLAYCARD PREMIER LEAGUE

Arsenal	v	Portsmouth	-	-	-	-	-	1-1	00-01-00
Aston Villa	v	Middlesbro	3-1	1-0	1-1	0-0	1-0	0-2	05-04-01
Crystal Pal	v	Man Utd	-	-	-	-	-	-	01-02-03
Everton	v	Blackburn	0-0	-	-	1-2	2-1	0-1	04-01-05
Fulham	v	Charlton	-	2-1	-	0-0	1-0	2-0	03-01-00
Man City	v	Bolton	-	2-0	-	-	2-0	6-2	04-00-01
Newcastle	v	Liverpool	1-4	2-2	2-1	0-2	1-0	1-1	04-05-03
Norwich	v	Chelsea	-	-	-	-	-	-	03-01-02
Southampton	v	Tottenham	1-1	0-1	2-0	1-0	1-0	1-0	08-04-04
WBA	v	Birmingham	1-3	0-3	1-1	1-0	1-1	-	04-03-04

COCA-COLA CHAMPIONSHIP

Home		Away							Record
Burnley	v	Sunderland	-	-	-	-	-	1-2	00-01-01
Cardiff	v	Sheff Utd	-	-	-	-	-	2-1	01-01-00
Crewe	v	Wolves	0-0	1-0	2-0	1-4	-	-	02-01-02
Derby	v	Plymouth	-	-	-	-	-	-	01-00-00
Leicester	v	Nottm F	3-1	-	-	-	1-0	-	03-01-01
Millwall	v	Leeds	-	-	-	-	-	-	00-00-00
QPR	v	Reading	-	-	-	0-0	-	-	00-02-01
Rotherham	v	Gillingham	-	-	-	3-2	1-1	1-1	01-03-01
Stoke	v	Brighton	-	-	-	3-1	1-0	-	03-02-00
Watford	v	Coventry	-	1-0	-	3-0	5-2	1-1	03-01-00
West Ham	v	Preston	-	-	-	-	-	1-2	00-00-01
Wigan	v	Ipswich	-	-	-	-	-	1-0	01-00-00

COCA-COLA LEAGUE DIVISION ONE

Home		Away							Record
Blackpool	v	Walsall	0-2	-	-	-	-	-	04-00-03
Bradford	v	Huddersfield	2-3	-	-	-	-	-	01-04-03
Colchester	v	Brentford	-	0-3	3-1	1-1	0-1	1-1	01-02-02
Hartlepool	v	Wrexham	-	-	-	-	4-3	2-0	04-00-02
Luton	v	Bristol C	-	1-2	0-3	-	2-2	3-2	01-03-05
Milton K	v	Stockport	-	-	2-0	3-1	-	-	02-00-00
Oldham	v	Port Vale	-	-	4-1	2-0	1-1	2-1	07-02-00
Peterboro	v	Barnsley	-	-	-	-	1-3	2-3	01-01-02
Swindon	v	Bournemouth	-	-	1-1	0-0	-	2-1	02-03-01
Torquay	v	Chesterfield	-	-	0-0	-	-	-	03-03-00
Tranmere	v	Hull	-	-	-	-	-	-	00-00-00

COCA-COLA LEAGUE DIVISION TWO

Home		Away							Record
Bristol R	v	Rochdale	-	-	-	0-2	1-2	0-0	00-01-02
Bury	v	Cambridge U	-	0-2	0-1	2-2	0-1	1-0	02-01-04
Chester	v	Southend	1-1	0-0	-	-	-	-	01-02-01
Darlington	v	Boston	-	-	-	-	2-3	3-0	02-00-01
Kidderminstr	v	Cheltenham	0-1	-	1-1	0-0	-	0-0	03-03-03
Lincoln	v	Wycombe	0-1	-	-	-	-	-	00-00-00
Mansfield	v	Shrewsbury	1-0	4-0	1-0	2-1	-	-	07-01-00
Northampton	v	Macclesfield	0-2	2-0	-	-	-	0-0	01-01-01
Notts Co	v	Swansea	-	-	0-1	-	-	-	04-00-00
Oxford Utd	v	Grimsby	0-0	-	-	-	-	-	01-02-02
Scunthorpe	v	Rushden & D	-	-	-	1-1	0-0	-	00-02-00
Yeovil	v	Leyton O	-	-	-	-	-	1-2	00-00-01

BANK OF SCOTLAND SCOTTISH PREMIER LEAGUE

Home		Away							Record
Dundee	v	Livingston	-	-	-	1-0/2-0	2-1/0-0	2-1/1-0/2-0	09-01-01
Dunfermline	v	Hearts	1-1/0-0	-	1-0	0-1/1-1	3-1/0-1	2-1/0-0	07-04-08
Hibernian	v	Celtic	-	0-2/2-1	0-0/2-5	1-4/1-1	0-1	1-2/0-4	05-07-17
Kilmarnock	v	Aberdeen	4-0/4-2	2-0/1-0	1-0/0-0	3-1	2-2/2-0	1-3/3-1/4-0	14-05-03
Motherwell	v	Dundee Utd	1-0/2-0	2-2/1-3	2-1	0-0/2-0	1-2/2-2	3-1/0-1	12-06-11
Rangers	v	Inv CT	-	-	-	-	-	-	00-00-00

BELL'S SCOTTISH FIRST DIVISION

Home		Away							Record
Falkirk	v	Partick	-	-	-	1-1/1-4	-	-	05-03-08
Queen Sth	v	Airdrie Utd	-	-	-	-	-	-	00-00-01
Ross C	v	Raith	-	-	0-0/4-0	1-0/4-2	-	3-2/1-1	04-02-00
St Johnstone	v	Hamilton	-	-	-	-	-	-	04-01-00
St Mirren	v	Clyde	-	-	-	4-1/2-2	1-4/1-2	2-1/2-3	03-02-03

BELL'S SCOTTISH SECOND DIVISION

Home		Away							Record
Arbroath	v	Morton	-	-	-	-	-	0-4/2-2	00-01-01
Ayr	v	Alloa	-	-	3-1/4-1	-	3-1/0-1	-	04-00-01
Brechin	v	Stranraer	-	-	-	-	3-1/3-1	-	04-05-03
Dumbarton	v	Berwick	0-0/1-1	2-1/0-2	-	-	1-2/2-2	1-1/4-1	06-08-06
Stirling	v	Forfar	3-1/2-2	-	3-3/1-0	-	-	-	05-02-01

BELL'S SCOTTISH THIRD DIVISION

Albion	v	Montrose	4-1/0-0	1-3/0-2	3-2/2-1	0-0/0-0	1-1/3-0	0-1/3-0	09-06-09
C'denbeath	v	Gretna	-	-	-	-	-	0-1/1-2	00-00-02
East Fife	v	Peterhead	-	-	1-1/2-1	0-1/2-3	3-3/0-2	-	01-02-03
Elgin	v	E Stirling	-	-	1-2/4-2	2-1/2-2	3-1/3-0	3-1/3-0	06-01-01
Queens P	v	Stenhsmuir	0-0/4-1	-	2-0/1-2	-	-	-	05-05-03

NATIONWIDE CONFERENCE

Accrington	v	Forest G	-	-	-	-	-	4-1	01-00-00
Aldershot	v	Farnborough	-	1-0	1-1	-	-	2-0	02-01-00
Burton	v	Canvey Islnd	-	-	-	-	-	-	00-00-00
Crawley	v	Halifax	-	-	-	-	-	-	00-00-00
Dagenham	v	Tamworth	-	-	-	-	-	0-0	00-01-00
Gravesend	v	Scarborough	-	-	-	-	5-2	1-1	01-01-00
Hereford	v	Morecambe	2-0	1-1	2-2	0-2	1-2	3-0	03-02-02
Leigh RMI	v	Barnet	-	-	-	3-3	4-2	1-4	01-01-01
Northwich	v	Woking	0-3	3-1	4-0	0-3	1-3	1-4	04-02-06
Stevenage	v	Carlisle	-	-	-	-	-	-	00-00-00
York	v	Exeter	-	0-0	0-3	2-3	0-2	-	03-01-03

SUNDAY 6 MARCH 2005
COCA-COLA LEAGUE DIVISION ONE

Sheff Wed	v	Doncaster	-	-	-	-	-	-	00-00-00

SATURDAY 12 MARCH 2005
COCA-COLA CHAMPIONSHIP

Burnley	v	Rotherham	-	-	-	3-0	2-6	1-1	03-04-02
Coventry	v	Cardiff	-	-	-	-	-	1-3	00-00-01
Crewe	v	Sunderland	1-4	-	-	-	-	3-0	01-00-02
Ipswich	v	Nottm F	-	3-1	-	-	3-4	1-2	02-00-04
Leeds	v	Gillingham	-	-	-	-	-	-	00-00-00
Leicester	v	Derby	1-2	0-1	2-1	0-3	3-1	-	04-02-05
Plymouth	v	Brighton	1-2	3-3	0-2	-	-	3-3	04-04-03
Preston	v	Wolves	-	-	2-0	1-2	0-2	-	01-01-02
QPR	v	Watford	1-2	-	1-1	-	-	-	00-01-01
Reading	v	West Ham	-	-	-	-	-	2-0	01-00-00
Stoke	v	Sheff Utd	-	-	-	-	0-0	2-2	00-05-02
Wigan	v	Millwall	0-1	1-1	1-0	-	-	0-0	01-03-01

COCA-COLA LEAGUE DIVISION ONE

Bristol C	v	Barnsley	1-1	-	-	-	2-0	2-1	05-01-02
Chesterfield	v	Huddersfield	-	-	-	1-1	1-0	-	01-02-00
Doncaster	v	Brentford	-	-	-	-	-	-	00-00-00
Hartlepool	v	Tranmere	-	-	-	-	-	0-0	00-02-00
Hull	v	Torquay	1-0	0-0	1-2	1-0	1-1	0-1	04-03-02
Luton	v	Swindon	-	-	2-3	-	3-0	0-3	02-01-02
Milton K	v	Port Vale	-	-	-	-	-	-	00-00-00
Peterboro	v	Bradford	-	-	-	-	-	-	02-01-00
Sheff Wed	v	Blackpool	-	-	-	-	-	0-1	00-00-01
Stockport	v	Colchester	-	-	-	-	1-1	1-3	01-02-01
Walsall	v	Bournemouth	1-0	-	1-1	-	-	-	03-03-00
Wrexham	v	Oldham	1-2	0-3	3-1	3-3	-	4-0	03-01-02

COCA-COLA LEAGUE DIVISION TWO

Boston	v	Grimsby	-	-	-	-	-	-	00-00-00
Bury	v	Bristol R	-	0-0	1-0	-	0-1	0-0	02-04-01
Darlington	v	Yeovil	-	-	-	-	-	3-2	02-00-00
Leyton O	v	Cambridge U	2-0	-	-	-	1-1	0-1	03-04-03
Mansfield	v	Oxford Utd	-	-	-	2-1	-	3-1	02-00-00
Notts Co	v	Kidderminstr	-	-	-	-	-	-	00-00-00
Rushden & D	v	Northampton	-	-	-	-	-	-	00-00-00

Sponsored by Stan James

Scunthorpe	v	Cheltenham	-	-	1-1	1-2	-	5-2	01-01-01
Shrewsbury	v	Macclesfield	-	0-1	2-2	1-1	2-3	-	01-02-02
Southend	v	Lincoln	-	2-2	1-0	1-1	0-1	0-2	02-02-02
Swansea	v	Rochdale	1-1	1-0	-	0-1	1-1	1-1	03-03-01
Wycombe	v	Chester	-	-	-	-	-	-	02-00-00

BANK OF SCOTLAND SCOTTISH PREMIER LEAGUE

Aberdeen	v	Hibernian	-	2-2/4-0	0-2/1-0	2-0	0-1	3-1/0-1	14-06-08
Celtic	v	Dunfermline	5-0/5-0	-	3-1	3-1/5-0/5-0	2-1/1-0	5-0/1-2	17-00-04
Dundee	v	Rangers	0-4/1-1	2-3/1-7	1-1/0-1/0-3	0-0	0-3/2-2	0-2	01-08-10
Hearts	v	Inv CT	-	-	-	-	-	-	00-00-00
Kilmarnock	v	Dundee Utd	2-0/2-0	1-1/1-0	1-0/0-0	2-0/2-2	1-2	0-2	07-05-06
Livingston	v	Motherwell	-	-	-	3-1	3-2/1-0	1-0/3-1	05-00-00

BELL'S SCOTTISH FIRST DIVISION

Airdrie Utd	v	Falkirk	0-3/1-2	0-0/0-2	1-2/1-2	2-1/1-0	-	-	06-07-10
Clyde	v	Queen Sth	2-0/2-1	3-0/3-1	-	-	2-1/2-2	3-1/2-0	14-04-03
Hamilton	v	St Mirren	0-0/0-0	-	-	-	-	-	04-09-01
Partick	v	Ross C	-	0-2/4-2	-	0-0/1-1	-	-	01-02-01
Raith	v	St Johnstone	-	-	-	-	-	1-4/1-1	01-05-03

BELL'S SCOTTISH SECOND DIVISION

Alloa	v	Brechin	-	-	-	-	-	-	04-01-01
Berwick	v	Stirling	-	-	2-2/4-1	-	-	-	03-07-01
Forfar	v	Dumbarton	-	5-0/4-3	-	-	2-0/0-1	3-1/1-0	05-00-01
Morton	v	Ayr	1-2/1-4	0-0/1-2	1-1/0-6	-	-	-	05-04-09
Stranraer	v	Arbroath	-	2-2/0-1	2-1/0-1	-	-	-	08-01-04

BELL'S SCOTTISH THIRD DIVISION

E Stirling	v	C'denbeath	1-1/0-0	0-1/0-4	0-2/0-2	-	-	1-1/0-1	08-07-09
Gretna	v	Queens P	-	-	-	-	2-2/0-1	1-1/0-1	00-02-02
Montrose	v	Elgin	-	-	0-0/2-1	0-2/1-0	1-0/2-0	3-3/4-3	05-02-01
Peterhead	v	Albion	-	-	1-2/1-1	0-0/0-2	2-0/0-0	2-1/5-0	03-03-02
Stenhsmuir	v	East Fife	-	-	-	-	-	3-0/0-1	05-06-06

NATIONWIDE CONFERENCE

Barnet	v	Crawley	-	-	-	-	-	-	00-00-00
Canvey Islnd	v	Aldershot	-	2-1	1-1	1-3	0-1	-	01-01-02
Carlisle	v	Accrington	-	-	-	-	-	-	00-00-00
Exeter	v	Dagenham	-	-	-	-	-	1-1	00-01-00
Farnborough	v	Gravesend	-	3-2	1-0	-	1-1	1-2	03-01-01
Forest G	v	Hereford	2-1	0-1	1-1	1-1	1-3	1-7	01-02-03
Halifax	v	York	-	0-2	1-3	1-1	-	-	01-04-03
Morecambe	v	Burton	-	-	-	-	5-0	2-1	02-00-00
Scarborough	v	Leigh RMI	-	-	1-1	2-5	2-0	4-1	02-01-01
Tamworth	v	Northwich	-	-	-	-	-	2-1	01-00-00
Woking	v	Stevenage	1-2	0-2	1-1	1-1	1-5	1-1	04-03-03

TUESDAY 15 MARCH 2005
COCA-COLA CHAMPIONSHIP

Brighton	v	Wigan	-	-	-	2-1	-	-	03-00-00
Cardiff	v	Ipswich	-	-	-	-	-	2-3	00-00-01
Gillingham	v	Stoke	4-0	3-0	-	-	1-1	3-1	03-01-00
Millwall	v	Coventry	-	-	-	3-2	2-0	2-1	05-00-00
Rotherham	v	Reading	-	-	1-3	-	0-0	5-1	02-03-02
Sheff Utd	v	Preston	-	-	3-2	2-2	1-0	2-0	04-01-00
Sunderland	v	Plymouth	-	-	-	-	-	-	02-00-01
Watford	v	Leicester	-	1-1	-	-	1-2	-	03-02-04
West Ham	v	Crewe	-	-	-	-	-	4-2	01-00-00
Wolves	v	Burnley	-	-	1-0	3-0	3-0	-	04-00-00

WEDNESDAY 16 MARCH 2005
COCA-COLA CHAMPIONSHIP

Derby	v	QPR	-	-	-	-	-	01-01-01
Nottm F	v	Leeds	1-1	-	-	-	-	03-04-00

FRIDAY 18 MARCH 2005
COCA-COLA LEAGUE DIVISION ONE

Tranmere	v	Peterboro	-	-	-	1-0	1-1	0-0	03-03-00

SATURDAY 19 MARCH 2005
FA BARCLAYCARD PREMIER LEAGUE

Birmingham	v	Aston Villa	-	-	-	-	3-0	0-0	01-01-00
Blackburn	v	Arsenal	1-2	-	-	2-3	2-0	0-2	03-02-05
Bolton	v	Norwich	2-0	1-0	1-0	-	-	-	04-00-00
Charlton	v	WBA	-	0-0	-	-	1-0	-	05-03-00
Chelsea	v	Crystal Pal	-	-	-	-	-	-	05-02-00
Liverpool	v	Everton	3-2	0-1	3-1	1-1	0-0	0-0	07-07-02
Man Utd	v	Fulham	-	-	-	3-2	3-0	1-3	02-00-01
Middlesbro	v	Southampton	3-0	3-2	0-1	1-3	2-2	3-1	04-03-03
Portsmouth	v	Newcastle	-	-	-	-	-	1-1	02-02-01
Tottenham	v	Man City	-	-	0-0	-	0-2	1-1	05-03-02

COCA-COLA CHAMPIONSHIP

Brighton	v	Reading	-	-	-	3-1	0-1	-	01-00-03
Cardiff	v	Crewe	-	-	-	-	2-1	3-0	02-03-01
Derby	v	Leeds	2-2	0-1	1-1	0-1	-	-	00-03-04
Gillingham	v	Ipswich	-	-	-	-	1-3	1-2	00-00-02
Millwall	v	Plymouth	-	-	-	-	-	-	02-02-00
Nottm F	v	Wigan	-	-	-	-	-	1-0	01-00-00
Rotherham	v	QPR	-	-	-	-	-	-	00-00-00
Sheff Utd	v	Burnley	-	-	2-0	3-0	4-2	1-0	05-00-00
Sunderland	v	Coventry	-	1-1	1-0	-	-	0-0	02-03-00
Watford	v	Preston	-	-	2-3	1-1	0-1	2-0	03-01-02
West Ham	v	Leicester	3-2	2-1	0-1	1-0	-	-	09-00-01
Wolves	v	Stoke	-	-	-	-	0-0	-	02-04-01

COCA-COLA LEAGUE DIVISION ONE

Barnsley	v	Milton K	-	-	0-1	1-1	-	-	01-01-01
Blackpool	v	Doncaster	-	-	-	-	-	-	02-00-00
Bournemouth	v	Hull	-	-	-	-	0-0	-	03-03-02
Bradford	v	Hartlepool	-	-	-	-	-	-	01-01-01
Brentford	v	Chesterfield	-	1-1	-	0-0	2-1	1-1	03-04-01
Colchester	v	Sheff Wed	-	-	-	-	-	3-1	01-00-00
Huddersfield	v	Stockport	3-0	0-2	0-0	-	2-1	-	05-02-02
Oldham	v	Luton	1-1	2-1	2-0	-	1-2	3-0	06-02-01
Port Vale	v	Walsall	-	1-2	0-2	-	-	-	00-00-00
Swindon	v	Wrexham	-	-	2-2	3-1	-	1-0	02-02-00
Torquay	v	Bristol C	-	-	-	-	-	-	00-00-00

COCA-COLA LEAGUE DIVISION TWO

Bristol R	v	Mansfield	-	-	-	0-1	-	1-3	00-02-02
Cambridge U	v	Wycombe	-	1-2	1-0	2-0	-	-	02-01-01
Cheltenham	v	Southend	-	2-1	2-1	1-1	-	1-1	02-02-00
Chester	v	Notts Co	-	-	-	-	-	-	01-01-01
Grimsby	v	Darlington	-	-	-	-	-	-	00-01-00
Kidderminstr	v	Rushden & D	0-0	2-0	-	3-0	0-2	-	03-01-02
Lincoln	v	Shrewsbury	-	1-2	2-2	1-2	1-1	-	01-02-04
Macclesfield	v	Leyton O	-	1-0	0-2	2-1	3-1	1-0	05-00-01
Northampton	v	Swansea	-	2-1	2-1	-	-	2-1	04-01-01
Oxford Utd	v	Boston	-	-	-	-	2-1	0-0	01-01-00
Rochdale	v	Scunthorpe	2-2	-	3-2	2-2	1-2	2-0	08-03-04

Sponsored by Stan James

Yeovil	v	Bury	-	-	-	-	-	2-1	01-00-00

BANK OF SCOTLAND SCOTTISH PREMIER LEAGUE

Aberdeen	v	Dundee	2-2/1-2	0-2/0-1	0-2/0-2	0-0	0-0/3-3	2-2/1-2	06-07-06
Dundee Utd	v	Celtic	1-1/1-2	2-1/0-1	1-2/0-4	0-4	0-2	1-5	08-05-14
Dunfermline	v	Hibernian	-	-	1-1/2-1	1-0	1-1	0-0/1-1	04-11-01
Hearts	v	Livingston	-	-	-	1-3/2-3	2-1	3-1/1-1	02-01-02
Inv CT	v	Motherwell	-	-	-	-	-	-	00-00-00
Rangers	v	Kilmarnock	1-0/1-1	2-1/1-0	0-3/5-1	3-1/5-0	6-1/4-0	4-0/2-0	17-01-04

BELL'S SCOTTISH FIRST DIVISION

Airdrie Utd	v	Clyde	-	-	1-3/1-0	1-2/2-2	-	-	04-05-02
Hamilton	v	Queen Sth	-	0-3/1-1	-	1-1/3-1	-	-	02-03-01
Partick	v	St Mirren	-	-	-	3-3/1-0	-	-	01-04-01
Raith	v	Falkirk	1-1/2-1	2-1/0-1	0-2/0-0	5-2/5-1	-	0-1/2-0	09-03-06
St Johnstone	v	Ross C	-	-	-	-	1-1/2-0	1-1/1-1	01-03-00

BELL'S SCOTTISH SECOND DIVISION

Alloa	v	Berwick	-	-	-	2-2/1-1	-	2-3/4-2	07-03-03
Arbroath	v	Brechin	-	-	-	-	-	-	02-02-04
Forfar	v	Ayr	-	-	-	-	-	-	04-02-03
Morton	v	Stirling	-	-	-	-	5-1/2-2	-	05-06-03
Stranraer	v	Dumbarton	-	-	-	-	1-0/1-2	-	05-03-02

BELL'S SCOTTISH THIRD DIVISION

E Stirling	v	East Fife	-	0-2/1-0	2-5/1-0	2-1/1-2	1-4/0-4	-	08-01-08
Elgin	v	C'denbeath	-	-	2-3/0-2	-	-	0-4/0-0	00-01-03
Gretna	v	Peterhead	-	-	-	-	1-4/1-1	3-2/3-2	02-01-01
Montrose	v	Queens P	1-0/3-0	2-1/0-2	-	3-1/3-1	1-0/1-1	0-0/1-1	11-07-05
Stenhsmuir	v	Albion	4-1/1-2	-	-	-	-	-	05-02-03

NATIONWIDE CONFERENCE

Accrington	v	Morecambe	-	-	-	-	-	1-0	03-01-01
Aldershot	v	Stevenage	-	-	-	-	-	2-0	01-00-00
Barnet	v	Farnborough	-	-	-	0-3	1-2	0-2	01-00-03
Carlisle	v	Northwich	-	-	-	-	-	-	00-00-00
Dagenham	v	Forest G	-	-	3-1	1-1	3-1	5-2	03-01-00
Exeter	v	Woking	-	-	-	-	-	1-2	00-00-01
Gravesend	v	Canvey Islnd	-	0-1	1-2	0-1	-	-	00-00-03
Hereford	v	Crawley	-	-	-	-	-	-	00-00-00
Leigh RMI	v	Burton	-	-	-	-	4-2	0-1	01-00-01
Scarborough	v	Halifax	1-0	-	-	-	0-1	1-0	06-00-02
Tamworth	v	York	-	-	-	-	-	-	00-00-00

FRIDAY 25 MARCH 2005
COCA-COLA LEAGUE DIVISION TWO

Bury	v	Grimsby	1-0	-	-	-	-	-	02-00-00
Southend	v	Rochdale	1-1	3-3	3-0	0-0	1-0	4-0	04-03-00
Swansea	v	Macclesfield	-	1-0	-	0-1	1-0	3-0	03-01-01

NATIONWIDE CONFERENCE

Burton	v	Accrington	-	-	-	3-1	-	1-1	01-01-00
Canvey Islnd	v	Carlisle	-	-	-	-	-	-	00-00-00
Crawley	v	Leigh RMI	-	-	-	-	-	-	00-00-00
Farnborough	v	Hereford	0-4	-	-	4-2	2-2	0-5	01-01-03
Forest G	v	Barnet	-	-	-	2-2	4-4	1-1	00-03-00
Halifax	v	Tamworth	-	-	-	-	-	1-2	00-00-01
Morecambe	v	Exeter	-	-	-	-	-	0-3	00-00-01
Northwich	v	Gravesend	-	-	-	-	1-2	0-0	00-01-01
Stevenage	v	Dagenham	-	-	0-2	1-3	2-0	0-2	03-00-03
Woking	v	Scarborough	-	0-2	1-1	1-2	2-1	2-1	02-01-02
York	v	Aldershot	-	-	-	-	-	-	00-00-00

COCA-COLA LEAGUE DIVISION ONE

Home		Away							Record
Bristol C	v	Bournemouth	-	3-1	3-3	1-0	-	2-0	04-02-01
Chesterfield	v	Tranmere	-	-	-	0-2	1-0	2-2	01-01-01
Doncaster	v	Bradford	-	-	-	-	-	-	00-00-00
Hartlepool	v	Huddersfield	-	-	-	-	-	-	01-01-01
Hull	v	Port Vale	-	-	-	-	-	-	02-01-01
Luton	v	Barnsley	-	-	-	-	2-3	0-1	01-01-04
Milton K	v	Swindon	-	-	-	-	-	-	01-00-00
Peterboro	v	Colchester	-	-	3-1	3-1	0-1	1-2	05-00-02
Sheff Wed	v	Torquay	-	-	-	-	-	-	00-00-00
Stockport	v	Blackpool	-	-	-	-	2-2	1-3	03-04-01
Walsall	v	Oldham	3-1	-	3-2	-	-	-	02-02-00
Wrexham	v	Brentford	-	0-1	2-1	0-3	-	1-0	02-03-04

COCA-COLA LEAGUE DIVISION TWO

Home		Away							Record
Boston	v	Yeovil	-	-	4-1	4-0	-	3-2	05-01-02
Darlington	v	Kidderminstr	-	-	1-2	2-0	2-1	0-2	03-00-02
Leyton O	v	Cheltenham	-	1-0	0-0	0-2	-	1-4	01-01-02
Mansfield	v	Chester	3-0	2-1	-	-	-	-	07-00-03
Notts Co	v	Bristol R	1-1	0-2	1-1	-	-	-	05-03-01
Rushden & D	v	Lincoln	-	-	-	0-0	1-0	-	01-01-00
Scunthorpe	v	Oxford Utd	-	1-0	-	1-0	2-0	1-1	03-01-00
Shrewsbury	v	Cambridge U	1-1	-	-	-	3-1	-	01-03-01
Wycombe	v	Northampton	1-2	-	1-0	2-1	1-1	-	03-02-01

COCA-COLA LEAGUE DIVISION ONE

Home		Away							Record
Barnsley	v	Walsall	-	3-2	-	4-1	-	-	03-00-00
Blackpool	v	Hartlepool	-	-	1-2	-	-	4-0	03-01-01
Bournemouth	v	Milton K	-	-	-	-	-	-	00-00-00
Bradford	v	Stockport	1-2	-	-	2-4	-	-	02-00-06
Brentford	v	Peterboro	3-0	-	1-0	2-1	1-1	0-3	05-01-04
Colchester	v	Chesterfield	1-0	1-0	-	1-2	2-0	1-0	06-00-03
Oldham	v	Hull	-	-	-	-	-	-	01-01-01
Swindon	v	Bristol C	3-2	-	1-1	1-2	1-1	1-1	04-03-03
Torquay	v	Luton	-	-	-	0-1	-	-	00-00-01
Tranmere	v	Doncaster	-	-	-	-	-	-	00-01-00

COCA-COLA LEAGUE DIVISION TWO

Home		Away							Record
Bristol R	v	Darlington	-	-	-	1-0	2-1	0-3	02-00-01
Cambridge U	v	Southend	3-0	-	-	-	1-1	0-1	03-01-03
Cheltenham	v	Swansea	-	0-0	-	2-2	-	3-4	00-02-01
Chester	v	Bury	-	-	-	-	-	-	04-01-01
Grimsby	v	Rushden & D	-	-	-	-	-	1-0	01-00-00
Kidderminstr	v	Mansfield	-	-	1-0	1-1	-	2-1	02-01-00
Lincoln	v	Scunthorpe	-	-	1-1	3-2	1-0	1-1	08-05-01
Macclesfield	v	Boston	-	-	-	-	2-0	0-0	03-02-02
Northampton	v	Shrewsbury	-	3-0	-	-	-	-	02-01-01
Oxford Utd	v	Leyton O	-	-	-	1-1	0-2	2-1	02-01-01
Rochdale	v	Wycombe	-	-	-	-	-	-	00-01-00

NATIONWIDE CONFERENCE

Home		Away							Record
Accrington	v	York	-	-	-	-	-	-	00-00-00
Aldershot	v	Woking	-	-	-	-	-	2-1	01-00-00
Barnet	v	Canvey Islnd	-	-	-	-	-	-	00-00-00
Carlisle	v	Halifax	0-1	1-1	2-2	0-0	-	-	01-06-02
Dagenham	v	Crawley	-	-	-	-	-	-	00-00-00
Exeter	v	Farnborough	-	-	-	-	-	1-1	00-01-00
Gravesend	v	Forest G	-	-	-	-	1-1	1-1	00-02-00
Hereford	v	Northwich	2-2	3-0	0-0	1-0	1-2	1-0	03-03-01
Leigh RMI	v	Morecambe	-	-	1-0	0-1	1-0	3-1	03-00-01

Scarborough	v	Burton	-	-	-	-	4-1	1-2	01-00-01
Tamworth	v	Stevenage	-	-	-	-	-	1-2	00-00-01

TUESDAY 29 MARCH 2005
COCA-COLA LEAGUE DIVISION ONE

Huddersfield	v	Sheff Wed	-	-	0-0	-	-	-	00-01-00
Port Vale	v	Wrexham	-	-	1-1	1-3	-	1-0	02-01-01

COCA-COLA LEAGUE DIVISION TWO

Yeovil	v	Notts Co	-	-	-	-	-	-	00-00-00

FRIDAY 1 APRIL 2005
COCA-COLA LEAGUE DIVISION ONE

Doncaster	v	Colchester	-	-	-	-	-	-	05-01-02

COCA-COLA LEAGUE DIVISION TWO

Southend	v	Bristol R	-	-	-	2-1	2-2	0-1	03-03-01

SATURDAY 2 APRIL 2005
FA BARCLAYCARD PREMIER LEAGUE

Arsenal	v	Norwich	-	-	-	-	-	-	04-02-01
Birmingham	v	Tottenham	-	-	-	-	1-1	1-0	01-01-00
Charlton	v	Man City	-	0-1	4-0	-	2-2	0-3	02-03-02
Crystal Pal	v	Middlesbro	-	-	-	-	-	-	01-00-01
Fulham	v	Portsmouth	-	1-0	3-1	-	-	2-0	03-00-00
Liverpool	v	Bolton	-	-	-	1-1	2-0	3-1	04-01-00
Man Utd	v	Blackburn	3-2	-	-	2-1	3-1	2-1	08-02-00
Newcastle	v	Aston Villa	2-1	0-1	3-0	3-0	1-1	1-1	08-02-02
Southampton	v	Chelsea	0-2	1-2	3-2	0-2	1-1	0-1	05-03-07
WBA	v	Everton	-	-	-	-	1-2	-	00-00-01

COCA-COLA CHAMPIONSHIP

Burnley	v	Watford	-	-	2-0	1-0	4-7	2-3	04-01-02
Coventry	v	Brighton	-	-	-	-	0-0	-	00-01-00
Crewe	v	Nottm F	-	0-3	1-0	0-3	-	3-1	02-00-03
Ipswich	v	Derby	-	-	0-1	3-1	0-1	2-1	04-00-02
Leeds	v	Wolves	-	-	-	-	-	4-1	02-00-00
Leicester	v	Millwall	-	-	-	-	4-1	-	04-01-01
Plymouth	v	Cardiff	1-1	-	2-1	-	2-2	-	01-04-01
Preston	v	Gillingham	1-1	0-2	0-0	0-2	3-0	0-0	03-06-03
QPR	v	Sunderland	2-2	-	-	-	-	-	01-01-01
Reading	v	Sheff Utd	-	-	-	-	0-2	2-1	03-00-04
Stoke	v	Rotherham	-	-	1-1	-	2-0	0-2	03-01-01
Wigan	v	West Ham	-	-	-	-	-	1-1	00-01-00

COCA-COLA LEAGUE DIVISION ONE

Bristol C	v	Port Vale	2-0	-	1-1	1-1	2-0	0-1	03-04-02
Chesterfield	v	Bradford	-	-	-	-	-	-	01-00-00
Hartlepool	v	Swindon	-	-	-	-	-	2-0	01-00-00
Hull	v	Barnsley	-	-	-	-	-	-	00-01-02
Luton	v	Blackpool	1-0	3-2	-	-	1-3	3-2	05-00-01
Milton K	v	Oldham	-	-	-	-	-	-	03-00-00
Peterboro	v	Huddersfield	-	-	-	1-2	0-1	-	01-01-02
Sheff Wed	v	Tranmere	-	-	1-0	-	-	2-0	02-00-00
Stockport	v	Brentford	-	-	-	-	2-3	1-1	02-02-03
Walsall	v	Torquay	-	-	-	-	-	-	01-02-01
Wrexham	v	Bournemouth	0-1	1-0	2-2	2-1	3-2	0-1	08-01-02

COCA-COLA LEAGUE DIVISION TWO

Boston	v	Cheltenham	-	-	-	-	-	3-1	03-02-00
Bury	v	Rochdale	-	-	-	-	1-1	1-2	00-03-03

Darlington	v	Chester	1-2	3-1	-	-	-	-	03-02-02
Leyton O	v	Northampton	-	0-0	-	-	-	1-1	02-03-00
Mansfield	v	Grimsby	-	-	-	-	-	-	00-01-00
Notts Co	v	Lincoln	2-3	-	-	-	-	-	00-00-02
Rushden & D	v	Yeovil	1-2	1-1	1-2	-	-	-	00-02-02
Scunthorpe	v	Macclesfield	-	-	2-2	1-1	1-1	1-0	02-03-00
Shrewsbury	v	Oxford Utd	-	-	-	1-0	1-2	-	02-02-01
Swansea	v	Cambridge U	2-0	-	1-1	-	2-0	0-2	05-03-01
Wycombe	v	Kidderminstr	-	-	-	-	-	-	02-02-01

BANK OF SCOTLAND SCOTTISH PREMIER LEAGUE

Celtic	v	Hearts	1-1/3-0	4-0/2-3	6-1/1-0	2-0/2-0	4-2/1-0	5-0/2-2	19-10-03
Dundee	v	Kilmarnock	1-1/2-1	0-0/1-2	0-0/2-2/2-1	1-2/2-0	2-1/2-2/0-1	1-2/2-0	08-07-04
Hibernian	v	Dundee Utd	-	3-2/1-0	3-0/1-0	0-1	2-1/1-1	2-2	15-06-05
Inv CT	v	Aberdeen	-	-	-	-	-	-	00-00-00
Livingston	v	Dunfermline	-	0-1/1-0	-	0-0/4-1	1-1	0-0/0-0	03-04-03
Motherwell	v	Rangers	1-0/1-5	1-5/2-0	0-1/1-2	2-2	1-0	1-1/0-1	09-05-16

BELL'S SCOTTISH FIRST DIVISION

Clyde	v	Hamilton	-	2-1/1-0	-	-	-	-	03-02-04
Falkirk	v	St Johnstone	-	-	-	-	1-0/1-1	0-3/0-1	05-04-04
Queen Sth	v	Partick	0-0/2-2	1-2/1-1	1-2/1-3	-	-	-	00-03-05
Ross C	v	Airdrie Utd	-	-	1-1/3-4	0-1/4-1	-	-	01-01-02
St Mirren	v	Raith	2-1/3-1	3-2/3-0	-	1-1/1-0	-	2-1/1-1	06-04-04

BELL'S SCOTTISH SECOND DIVISION

Ayr	v	Arbroath	-	-	-	0-1/0-0	1-0/4-0	-	02-01-01
Berwick	v	Forfar	-	2-2/2-0	1-1/1-0	1-1/0-2	2-1/0-0	0-4/3-1	07-05-03
Brechin	v	Morton	-	-	-	-	-	-	00-01-05
Dumbarton	v	Alloa	-	-	-	-	-	1-0/3-1	02-04-03
Stirling	v	Stranraer	-	1-1/2-5	2-0/0-1	-	-	1-0/2-2	06-03-03

BELL'S SCOTTISH THIRD DIVISION

Albion	v	Elgin	-	-	1-1/0-1	4-4/2-2	1-1/1-1	1-2/1-2	00-05-03
C'denbeath	v	Montrose	4-1/1-0	1-1/2-1	2-0/2-1	-	-	3-3/0-0	07-05-07
East Fife	v	Gretna	-	-	-	-	3-2/2-1	-	02-00-00
Peterhead	v	Stenhsmuir	-	-	-	-	-	-	00-00-00
Queens P	v	E Stirling	0-4/2-1	2-1/0-1	-	2-3/1-0	0-2/3-4	3-0/1-0	14-05-08

NATIONWIDE CONFERENCE

Burton	v	Aldershot	-	-	-	-	-	1-4	00-00-01
Canvey Islnd	v	Exeter	-	-	-	-	-	-	00-00-00
Crawley	v	Accrington	-	-	-	-	-	-	00-00-00
Farnborough	v	Carlisle	-	-	-	-	-	-	00-00-00
Forest G	v	Tamworth	-	-	-	-	-	2-1	02-00-00
Halifax	v	Leigh RMI	-	-	-	-	1-0	2-1	02-00-00
Morecambe	v	Scarborough	-	0-1	4-4	2-0	3-1	2-1	03-01-01
Northwich	v	Barnet	-	-	-	0-3	1-1	1-1	00-03-03
Stevenage	v	Hereford	0-3	0-3	2-1	3-1	0-2	0-2	03-00-04
Woking	v	Dagenham	-	-	4-4	0-2	0-0	0-0	00-05-03
York	v	Gravesend	-	-	-	-	-	-	00-00-00

TUESDAY 5 APRIL 2005
COCA-COLA CHAMPIONSHIP

Burnley	v	West Ham	-	-	-	-	-	1-1	00-01-00
Crewe	v	Derby	-	-	-	-	-	3-0	01-00-00
Ipswich	v	Rotherham	-	-	-	-	1-2	2-1	01-00-01
Leeds	v	Sheff Utd	-	-	-	-	-	-	05-00-00
Leicester	v	Wolves	-	-	-	-	1-0	0-0	04-04-00
Plymouth	v	Watford	-	-	-	-	-	-	01-03-02
Preston	v	Brighton	-	-	-	-	2-2	-	01-01-00
QPR	v	Gillingham	-	-	2-2	-	-	-	00-01-00

230   *Sponsored by Stan James*

Reading	v	Millwall	2-0	2-0	3-4	-	2-0	1-0	04-01-02
Stoke	v	Cardiff	-	2-1	-	1-1	-	2-3	01-01-01
Wigan	v	Sunderland	-	-	-	-	-	0-0	00-01-00

WEDNESDAY 6 APRIL 2005
COCA-COLA CHAMPIONSHIP

Coventry	v	Nottm F	4-0	-	-	0-0	0-1	1-3	01-05-06

FRIDAY 8 APRIL 2005
COCA-COLA LEAGUE DIVISION ONE

Tranmere	v	Stockport	1-1	0-0	2-1	-	1-0	3-2	05-02-00

COCA-COLA LEAGUE DIVISION TWO

Cheltenham	v	Shrewsbury	-	0-1	1-1	1-0	-	-	01-01-01

SATURDAY 9 APRIL 2005
FA BARCLAYCARD PREMIER LEAGUE

Aston Villa	v	WBA	-	-	-	-	2-1	-	01-00-00
Blackburn	v	Southampton	0-2	-	-	2-0	1-0	1-1	07-02-01
Bolton	v	Fulham	-	3-1	0-2	0-0	0-0	0-2	04-03-03
Chelsea	v	Birmingham	-	-	-	-	3-0	0-0	02-01-00
Everton	v	Crystal Pal	-	-	-	-	-	-	02-02-02
Man City	v	Liverpool	-	-	1-1	-	0-3	2-2	02-05-03
Middlesbro	v	Arsenal	1-6	2-1	0-1	0-4	0-2	0-4	02-00-08
Norwich	v	Man Utd	-	-	-	-	-	-	02-00-05
Portsmouth	v	Charlton	-	0-2	-	-	-	1-2	03-01-06
Tottenham	v	Newcastle	2-0	3-1	4-2	1-3	0-1	1-0	07-01-04

COCA-COLA CHAMPIONSHIP

Brighton	v	Leicester	-	-	-	-	0-1	-	02-01-02
Cardiff	v	Wigan	-	0-0	-	2-2	0-0	0-0	01-06-01
Derby	v	Stoke	-	-	-	-	2-0	0-3	04-00-01
Gillingham	v	Burnley	2-1	2-2	0-0	2-2	4-2	0-3	06-04-01
Millwall	v	Crewe	-	-	-	2-0	-	1-1	02-01-00
Nottm F	v	Plymouth	-	-	-	-	-	-	00-00-00
Rotherham	v	Preston	-	-	-	1-0	0-0	1-0	05-01-01
Sheff Utd	v	QPR	2-0	1-1	1-1	-	-	-	02-06-01
Sunderland	v	Reading	-	-	-	-	-	2-0	02-01-01
Watford	v	Leeds	-	1-2	-	-	-	-	01-01-01
West Ham	v	Coventry	2-0	5-0	1-1	-	-	2-0	06-03-02
Wolves	v	Ipswich	1-0	2-1	-	-	1-1	-	03-05-01

COCA-COLA LEAGUE DIVISION ONE

Barnsley	v	Wrexham	-	-	-	-	-	2-1	01-00-00
Blackpool	v	Peterboro	-	-	-	2-2	3-0	1-4	04-02-01
Bournemouth	v	Luton	1-0	1-0	3-2	-	-	6-3	05-01-00
Brentford	v	Bristol C	-	2-1	2-1	2-2	1-0	1-2	05-03-03
Colchester	v	Hartlepool	-	-	-	-	-	1-2	03-00-04
Huddersfield	v	Doncaster	-	-	-	-	-	3-1	01-00-00
Oldham	v	Sheff Wed	-	-	-	-	-	1-0	03-02-00
Port Vale	v	Chesterfield	-	-	-	4-1	5-2	1-1	03-01-00
Swindon	v	Walsall	-	1-1	1-4	-	-	-	01-02-01
Torquay	v	Milton K	-	-	-	-	-	-	00-00-00

COCA-COLA LEAGUE DIVISION TWO

Bristol R	v	Rushden & D	-	-	-	0-3	1-2	-	00-00-02
Cambridge U	v	Darlington	2-1	-	-	-	1-2	1-0	04-00-03
Chester	v	Boston	-	-	2-2	1-2	-	-	00-01-01
Grimsby	v	Wycombe	-	-	-	-	-	3-1	01-01-00
Kidderminstr	v	Bury	-	-	-	-	3-2	0-2	01-00-01
Lincoln	v	Swansea	-	0-1	-	3-0	1-0	2-1	04-01-01

Macclesfield v	Southend	-	1-2	1-0	0-0	2-1	1-2	02-01-02
Northampton v	Scunthorpe	-	-	-	-	-	1-1	04-01-03
Oxford Utd v	Notts Co	-	2-3	2-3	-	-	-	01-03-02
Rochdale v	Leyton O	2-1	1-4	3-1	3-0	1-0	3-0	07-00-03
Yeovil v	Mansfield	-	-	-	-	-	1-1	00-01-00

BANK OF SCOTLAND SCOTTISH PREMIER LEAGUE

Aberdeen v	Motherwell	1-1/1-1	1-1/2-1	3-3	4-2/1-0	1-1	0-3/0-2	14-11-05
Dundee v	Dunfermline	1-0/3-1	-	3-0/0-1	2-2	2-3/2-2	0-2/0-1	04-04-07
Hearts v	Hibernian	-	0-3/2-1	0-0/1-1	1-1	5-1/4-4	2-0	14-11-03
Kilmarnock v	Inv CT	-	-	-	-	-	-	00-00-00
Livingston v	Celtic	-	-	-	0-0/1-3	0-2	0-2	00-01-03
Rangers v	Dundee Utd	2-1/0-1	4-1/3-0	3-0/0-2	3-2	3-0	2-1	19-02-06

BELL'S SCOTTISH FIRST DIVISION

Falkirk v	Ross C	-	-	2-3/1-1	4-2/1-4	2-0/3-0	0-2/2-0	04-01-03
Hamilton v	Airdrie Utd	1-1/0-2	-	-	-	1-0/2-1	2-1/0-1	08-03-06
Raith v	Partick	-	-	-	1-2/2-0	-	-	06-05-04
St Johnstone v	Clyde	-	-	-	-	0-1/1-2	3-0/1-3	02-02-03
St Mirren v	Queen Sth	-	-	-	-	2-1/2-2	1-2/3-1	02-01-01

BELL'S SCOTTISH SECOND DIVISION

Alloa v	Arbroath	1-1/1-2	0-0/2-1	-	-	0-3/3-2	2-2/4-0	09-07-08
Ayr v	Stirling	-	-	-	-	-	-	05-02-03
Berwick v	Stranraer	-	-	1-1/0-2	2-2/4-1	3-4/1-0	-	10-03-06
Dumbarton v	Brechin	1-2/2-0	1-3/2-1	0-2/1-0	1-2/2-1	1-0/1-3	-	11-02-08
Forfar v	Morton	-	-	-	2-1/2-1	-	2-3/2-1	04-02-05

BELL'S SCOTTISH THIRD DIVISION

Albion v	C'denbeath	0-1/1-1	1-4/0-3	1-0/0-0	-	-	1-2/2-4	09-02-12
East Fife v	Elgin	-	-	1-1/1-1	3-0/0-1	4-0/5-0	-	03-02-01
Gretna v	Stenhsmuir	-	-	-	-	-	-	00-00-00
Montrose v	E Stirling	2-0/1-0	1-2/0-0	0-1/1-1	2-0/2-0	2-2/5-4	5-1/1-0	14-07-05
Peterhead v	Queens P	-	-	-	2-1/1-2	3-0/3-1	4-1/1-1	04-01-01

NATIONWIDE CONFERENCE

Accrington v	Stevenage	-	-	-	-	-	2-1	01-00-00
Aldershot v	Crawley	-	-	-	-	-	-	00-00-00
Barnet v	Halifax	2-2	0-1	1-0	-	0-0	4-1	03-03-01
Carlisle v	Forest G	-	-	-	-	-	-	00-00-00
Dagenham v	Burton	-	-	-	-	1-2	0-2	00-00-02
Exeter v	Northwich	-	-	-	-	-	2-0	01-00-00
Gravesend v	Morecambe	-	-	-	-	3-2	6-0	02-00-00
Hereford v	York	-	-	-	-	-	-	02-01-02
Leigh RMI v	Woking	-	-	2-0	3-1	1-0	0-1	03-00-01
Scarborough v	Farnborough	-	-	-	1-0	1-0	2-1	03-00-00
Tamworth v	Canvey Islnd	-	-	-	-	-	-	00-00-00

SUNDAY 10 APRIL 2005
COCA-COLA LEAGUE DIVISION ONE

Bradford v	Hull	-	-	-	-	-	-	02-03-02

FRIDAY 15 APRIL 2005
COCA-COLA LEAGUE DIVISION ONE

Hartlepool v	Sheff Wed	-	-	-	-	-	1-1	00-01-00

SATURDAY 16 APRIL 2005
FA BARCLAYCARD PREMIER LEAGUE

Arsenal v	Everton	1-0	4-1	4-1	4-3	2-1	2-1	14-01-01
Birmingham v	Portsmouth	4-1	1-0	0-0	1-1	-	2-0	05-03-03
Charlton v	Bolton	-	2-1	-	1-2	1-1	1-2	02-02-03

Home		Away							Date
Crystal Pal	v	Norwich	5-1	1-0	1-1	3-2	2-0	1-0	07-01-05
Fulham	v	Man City	3-0	0-0	-	-	0-1	2-2	01-02-01
Liverpool	v	Tottenham	3-2	2-0	3-1	1-0	2-1	0-0	11-04-01
Man Utd	v	Chelsea	1-1	3-2	3-3	0-3	2-1	1-1	03-08-04
Newcastle	v	Middlesbro	1-1	2-1	1-2	3-0	2-0	2-1	07-03-02
Southampton	v	Aston Villa	1-4	2-0	2-0	1-3	2-2	1-1	07-04-05
WBA	v	Blackburn	-	2-2	1-0	-	0-2	-	03-02-01

COCA-COLA CHAMPIONSHIP

Home		Away							Date
Burnley	v	Brighton	-	-	-	-	1-3	-	02-00-02
Coventry	v	Wolves	-	-	-	0-1	0-2	-	00-00-02
Gillingham	v	Crewe	-	-	0-1	1-0	-	2-0	03-00-04
Ipswich	v	Sunderland	0-2	-	1-0	5-0	-	1-0	06-01-02
Leicester	v	Wigan	-	-	-	-	-	-	00-00-00
Preston	v	Cardiff	-	0-0	-	-	-	2-2	02-03-00
QPR	v	Leeds	-	-	-	-	-	-	04-00-02
Reading	v	Nottm F	-	-	-	-	1-0	3-0	02-01-00
Rotherham	v	Watford	-	-	-	1-1	2-1	1-1	01-03-00
Sheff Utd	v	Derby	-	-	-	-	2-0	1-1	03-01-01
Stoke	v	Plymouth	-	-	-	-	-	-	01-02-00
West Ham	v	Millwall	-	-	-	-	-	1-1	02-02-00

COCA-COLA LEAGUE DIVISION ONE

Home		Away							Date
Barnsley	v	Oldham	-	-	-	-	2-2	1-1	04-03-01
Bradford	v	Brentford	-	-	-	-	-	-	03-00-02
Bristol C	v	Wrexham	-	4-0	2-1	1-0	-	1-0	06-01-00
Chesterfield	v	Bournemouth	3-1	0-1	-	2-1	-	1-1	03-03-01
Huddersfield	v	Colchester	-	-	-	2-1	1-1	-	01-01-00
Hull	v	Swindon	-	-	-	-	-	-	01-01-02
Luton	v	Milton K	-	-	-	-	-	-	01-02-01
Peterboro	v	Walsall	-	-	2-0	-	-	-	01-01-02
Stockport	v	Doncaster	-	-	-	-	-	-	02-01-00
Torquay	v	Port Vale	-	-	-	-	-	-	00-00-00
Tranmere	v	Blackpool	-	-	-	4-0	2-1	1-1	03-01-00

COCA-COLA LEAGUE DIVISION TWO

Home		Away							Date
Cheltenham	v	Northampton	-	2-1	-	-	1-1	4-3	02-01-00
Chester	v	Bristol R	-	-	-	-	-	-	00-02-01
Kidderminstr	v	Yeovil	0-1	4-0	-	-	-	0-1	04-04-03
Lincoln	v	Macclesfield	1-0	1-1	1-2	1-0	3-0	3-2	04-02-01
Mansfield	v	Darlington	0-1	1-2	3-2	4-2	-	3-1	05-01-04
Notts Co	v	Grimsby	-	-	-	-	-	3-1	03-00-01
Rochdale	v	Shrewsbury	1-0	2-1	1-7	1-0	1-1	-	05-01-02
Rushden & D	v	Boston	-	-	0-0	-	1-0	-	01-01-00
Scunthorpe	v	Cambridge U	3-2	0-3	-	-	1-2	4-0	04-02-03
Southend	v	Leyton O	2-2	1-1	0-1	1-2	1-0	1-2	01-03-03
Swansea	v	Oxford Utd	-	-	1-2	0-0	3-2	0-0	01-03-02
Wycombe	v	Bury	-	3-0	2-1	0-2	-	-	03-00-02

BANK OF SCOTLAND SCOTTISH PREMIER LEAGUE

Home		Away							Date
Celtic	v	Aberdeen	2-0/3-2	7-0/5-1	6-0	2-0/1-0	7-0	4-0/1-2	21-04-05
Dundee Utd	v	Hearts	0-0/1-3	0-2/0-1	0-4/1-1	0-2	0-3	2-1/0-2	08-10-10
Dunfermline	v	Rangers	0-2/0-3	-	0-0	1-4/2-4/1-1	0-6/1-3	2-0/2-3	01-04-15
Hibernian	v	Livingston	-	-	-	0-3	1-0/2-2	0-2/3-1	02-01-02
Inv CT	v	Dundee	-	-	-	-	-	-	00-00-00
Motherwell	v	Kilmarnock	0-0/1-2	0-4/2-0	1-2	2-2/2-0	0-1	2-1/1-0	10-04-06

BELL'S SCOTTISH FIRST DIVISION

Home		Away							Date
Airdrie Utd	v	St Mirren	1-0/0-3	0-2/0-1	-	0-0/2-3	-	-	05-05-08
Clyde	v	Falkirk	-	-	3-1/0-3	1-1/2-3	2-0/0-0	1-2/4-2	04-04-06
Partick	v	St Johnstone	-	-	-	-	-	-	03-02-04
Queen Sth	v	Raith	-	-	-	-	-	0-2/1-1	00-01-02
Ross C	v	Hamilton	-	2-1/0-1	-	-	-	-	01-00-01

BELL'S SCOTTISH SECOND DIVISION

Arbroath	v	Berwick	-	-	0-2/2-0	-	-	1-0/1-2	07-01-07
Brechin	v	Ayr	-	-	-	-	-	3-1/0-3	01-03-04
Morton	v	Alloa	-	-	2-0/1-1	1-1/0-0	-	2-2/2-1	04-04-00
Stirling	v	Dumbarton	-	-	-	4-5/2-1	-		06-03-04
Stranraer	v	Forfar	-	-	2-0/3-1	2-0/0-3	2-0/3-2	-	10-02-01

BELL'S SCOTTISH THIRD DIVISION

C'denbeath	v	Peterhead	-	-	2-0/4-0	-	-	2-0/0-3	03-00-01
E Stirling	v	Albion	0-1/4-1	4-3/3-1	1-1/1-0	1-2/1-2	0-3/0-4	3-4/1-8	10-04-14
Elgin	v	Gretna	-	-	-	-	0-2/2-2	3-3/1-1	00-03-01
Queens P	v	East Fife	-	0-1/1-0	-	1-2/2-0	0-0/1-2	-	07-02-06
Stenhsmuir	v	Montrose	4-0/3-1	-	-	-	-	-	07-00-05

NATIONWIDE CONFERENCE

Burton	v	Carlisle	-	-	-	-	-	-	00-00-00
Canvey Islnd	v	Scarborough	-	-	-	-	-		00-00-00
Crawley	v	Exeter	-	-	-	-	-		00-00-00
Farnborough	v	Tamworth	-	-	-	-		3-3	00-01-00
Forest G	v	Leigh RMI	-	-	3-1	1-2	4-1	2-2	02-01-01
Halifax	v	Hereford	-	-	-		1-0	1-2	02-02-04
Morecambe	v	Barnet	-	-	-	1-0	1-1	1-3	01-01-01
Northwich	v	Aldershot	-	-	-	-		1-1	00-00-00
Stevenage	v	Gravesend	-	-	-		1-0	2-2	01-01-00
Woking	v	Accrington	-	-	-	-		2-2	00-01-00
York	v	Dagenham	-	-	-	-	-		00-00-00

TUESDAY 19 APRIL 2005
FA BARCLAYCARD PREMIER LEAGUE

Bolton	v	Southampton	-	-	-	0-1	1-1	0-0	00-03-02
Middlesbro	v	Fulham	-	-	-	2-1	2-2	2-1	02-01-00
Norwich	v	Newcastle	-	-	-	-	-	-	01-00-02
Portsmouth	v	Liverpool	-	-	-	-	-	1-0	01-00-00

WEDNESDAY 20 APRIL 2005
FA BARCLAYCARD PREMIER LEAGUE

Aston Villa	v	Charlton	3-4	-	2-1	1-0	2-0	2-1	04-01-02
Blackburn	v	Crystal Pal	-	1-1	2-0	-	-	-	03-02-01
Chelsea	v	Arsenal	0-0	2-3	2-2	1-1	1-1	1-2	04-06-05
Everton	v	Man Utd	1-4	1-1	1-3	0-2	1-2	3-4	02-03-11
Man City	v	Birmingham	-	1-0	-	3-0	1-0	0-0	04-02-01
Tottenham	v	WBA	-	-	-	-	3-1	-	01-00-00

SATURDAY 23 APRIL 2005
FA BARCLAYCARD PREMIER LEAGUE

Arsenal	v	Tottenham	0-0	2-1	2-0	2-1	3-0	2-1	09-06-01
Aston Villa	v	Bolton	-	-	-	3-2	2-0	1-1	03-01-01
Blackburn	v	Man City	-	1-4	-	-	1-0	2-3	05-00-03
Chelsea	v	Fulham	-	-	-	3-2	1-1	2-1	02-01-00
Crystal Pal	v	Liverpool	-	-	-	-	-	-	02-01-03
Everton	v	Birmingham	-	-	-	-	1-1	1-0	01-01-00
Man Utd	v	Newcastle	0-0	5-1	2-0	3-1	5-3	0-0	07-05-00
Middlesbro	v	WBA	-	-	-	-	3-0	-	05-01-00
Norwich	v	Charlton	-	0-3	-	-	-	-	00-01-05
Portsmouth	v	Southampton	-	-	-	-	-	1-0	01-00-00

COCA-COLA CHAMPIONSHIP

Brighton	v	West Ham	-	-	-	-	-	-	02-00-00
Cardiff	v	Reading	-	1-0	-	2-2	-	2-3	03-01-02
Crewe	v	Stoke	-	-	-	-	-	2-0	02-00-01
Derby	v	Gillingham	-	-	-	-	1-1	2-1	01-01-00
Leeds	v	Ipswich	-	-	1-2	2-0	-	-	03-02-02

Sponsored by Stan James

Millwall	v	Preston	2-2	0-2	-	2-1	2-1	0-1	03-01-03
Nottm F	v	Burnley	-	-	5-0	1-0	2-0	1-1	03-01-00
Plymouth	v	Coventry	-	-	-	-	-	-	00-00-00
Sunderland	v	Leicester	-	2-0	0-0	2-1	-	-	03-04-03
Watford	v	Sheff Utd	1-1	-	4-1	0-3	2-0	0-2	03-02-03
Wigan	v	QPR	-	-	-	1-2	1-1	-	00-01-01
Wolves	v	Rotherham	-	-	-	2-1	0-0	-	01-01-00

COCA-COLA LEAGUE DIVISION ONE

Blackpool	v	Chesterfield	1-1	2-2	1-3	1-0	1-1	1-0	05-04-03
Bournemouth	v	Peterboro	-	-	2-1	0-2	-	1-2	02-00-05
Brentford	v	Huddersfield	-	-	-	3-0	1-0	-	05-01-02
Colchester	v	Bradford	-	-	-	-	-	-	00-00-00
Doncaster	v	Hartlepool	-	-	-	-	-	-	04-03-00
Milton K	v	Bristol C	-	-	-	-	-	-	00-00-00
Oldham	v	Torquay	-	-	-	-	-	-	00-00-00
Port Vale	v	Barnsley	1-0	2-2	-	-	0-0	3-1	05-03-02
Sheff Wed	v	Stockport	-	-	2-4	5-0	-	2-2	01-01-01
Swindon	v	Tranmere	2-3	3-1	-	2-2	1-1	2-0	06-03-01
Walsall	v	Hull	-	-	-	-	-	-	01-01-00
Wrexham	v	Luton	1-1	1-0	3-1	-	-	2-1	05-01-00

COCA-COLA LEAGUE DIVISION TWO

Boston	v	Kidderminstr	-	-	-	-	3-0	2-2	02-01-04
Bristol R	v	Swansea	-	-	1-0	4-1	3-1	2-1	06-02-01
Bury	v	Cheltenham	-	-	-	-	-	1-1	00-01-00
Cambridge U	v	Rochdale	1-1	-	-	-	2-2	0-0	02-05-01
Darlington	v	Rushden & D	-	-	-	0-0	2-2	-	00-02-00
Grimsby	v	Scunthorpe	-	-	-	-	-	-	01-01-00
Leyton O	v	Chester	2-2	1-2	-	-	-	-	05-02-03
Macclesfield	v	Mansfield	-	5-2	0-1	0-1	-	1-1	02-01-02
Northampton	v	Lincoln	0-0	1-0	-	-	-	1-1	03-06-01
Oxford Utd	v	Southend	-	-	-	2-0	0-1	2-0	04-00-03
Shrewsbury	v	Notts Co	-	-	-	-	-	-	01-01-02
Yeovil	v	Wycombe	-	-	-	-	-	-	03-02-00

BELL'S SCOTTISH FIRST DIVISION

Falkirk	v	St Mirren	1-1/1-0	3-1/2-0	-	3-2/0-0	2-0/3-1	0-0/1-0	12-06-00
Partick	v	Clyde	0-2/0-1	0-0/1-2	-	3-0/2-1	-	-	03-03-04
Raith	v	Hamilton	0-2/1-1	-	-	-	1-1/1-1	-	06-06-03
Ross C	v	Queen Sth	-	1-1/2-0	-	-	2-0/0-3	1-0/1-2	03-01-02
St Johnstone	v	Airdrie Utd	-	-	-	-	-	-	08-04-01

BELL'S SCOTTISH SECOND DIVISION

Alloa	v	Stirling	7-0/2-2	4-4/1-0	-	-	-	-	04-02-01
Arbroath	v	Forfar	2-1/2-2	-	3-4/1-1	-	-	0-0/0-1	01-08-04
Ayr	v	Stranraer	7-1/4-0	-	-	-	-	-	06-02-00
Brechin	v	Berwick	1-1/0-3	0-3/1-2	-	-	2-4/2-2	-	06-04-06
Morton	v	Dumbarton	-	-	-	-	-	2-2/3-2	06-02-02

BELL'S SCOTTISH THIRD DIVISION

Albion	v	Queens P	2-1/1-0	2-4/0-3	-	2-1/2-0	0-2/2-1	3-1/3-1	13-05-07
C'denbeath	v	East Fife	-	4-0/1-0	1-0/3-2	-	-	-	06-03-03
E Stirling	v	Stenhsmuir	1-1/1-1	-	-	-	-	-	02-04-05
Elgin	v	Peterhead	-	-	1-3/0-1	4-1/0-3	3-0/0-4	2-3/1-0	03-00-05
Montrose	v	Gretna	-	-	-	-	0-2/0-1	2-0/1-4	01-00-03

NATIONWIDE CONFERENCE

Aldershot	v	Scarborough	-	-	-	-	-	1-2	00-00-01
Carlisle	v	Exeter	1-3	0-0	0-1	1-0	0-2	-	05-01-03
Dagenham	v	Barnet	-	-	-	1-1	5-1	5-2	02-01-00
Forest G	v	Canvey Islnd	-	-	-	-	-	-	00-00-00
Gravesend	v	Burton	-	-	-	-	3-2	1-2	02-01-05

Halifax	v	Woking	-	-	-	-	1-1	2-2	02-03-02
Hereford	v	Accrington	-	-	-	-	-	1-0	01-00-00
Northwich	v	Crawley	-	-	-	-	-	-	00-00-00
Stevenage	v	Leigh RMI	-	-	3-0	0-1	3-1	4-0	03-00-01
Tamworth	v	Morecambe	-	-	-	-	-	2-3	00-00-01
York	v	Farnborough	-	-	-	-	-	-	00-00-00

FRIDAY 29 APRIL 2005
COCA-COLA LEAGUE DIVISION ONE

| Tranmere | v | Port Vale | 1-1 | 2-1 | - | 3-1 | 1-0 | 1-0 | 07-02-01 |

SATURDAY 30 APRIL 2005
FA BARCLAYCARD PREMIER LEAGUE

Birmingham	v	Blackburn	-	1-0	0-2	-	0-1	0-4	02-00-03
Bolton	v	Chelsea	-	-	-	2-2	1-1	0-2	02-02-01
Charlton	v	Man Utd	0-1	-	3-3	0-2	1-3	0-2	02-01-04
Fulham	v	Everton	-	-	-	2-0	2-0	2-1	03-00-00
Liverpool	v	Middlesbro	3-1	0-0	0-0	2-0	1-1	2-0	07-03-00
Man City	v	Portsmouth	-	4-2	-	3-1	-	1-1	03-03-00
Newcastle	v	Crystal Pal	-	-	-	-	-	-	01-00-01
Southampton	v	Norwich	-	-	-	-	-	-	03-03-01
Tottenham	v	Aston Villa	1-0	2-4	0-0	0-0	1-0	2-1	07-04-05
WBA	v	Arsenal	-	-	-	-	1-2	-	00-00-01

COCA-COLA CHAMPIONSHIP

Burnley	v	Plymouth	-	-	-	-	-	-	03-01-00
Coventry	v	Derby	1-1	2-0	2-0	-	3-0	2-0	07-01-02
Gillingham	v	Cardiff	-	4-1	-	-	-	1-2	03-01-03
Ipswich	v	Crewe	1-2	2-1	-	-	-	6-4	03-00-01
Leicester	v	Leeds	1-2	2-1	3-1	0-2	-	4-0	06-00-04
Preston	v	Wigan	2-2	1-4	-	-	-	2-4	05-05-02
QPR	v	Nottm F	-	1-1	1-0	-	-	-	03-03-04
Reading	v	Wolves	-	-	-	-	0-1	-	03-01-02
Rotherham	v	Brighton	2-1	1-3	-	-	1-0	-	05-01-02
Sheff Utd	v	Millwall	-	-	-	3-2	3-1	2-1	04-01-00
Stoke	v	Watford	-	-	-	-	1-2	3-1	05-01-01
West Ham	v	Sunderland	-	1-1	0-2	3-0	2-0	3-2	06-01-01

COCA-COLA LEAGUE DIVISION ONE

Barnsley	v	Colchester	-	-	-	-	1-1	1-0	01-01-00
Bradford	v	Bournemouth	-	-	-	-	-	-	04-01-03
Bristol C	v	Doncaster	-	-	-	-	-	-	00-00-00
Chesterfield	v	Oldham	1-3	0-1	-	4-2	0-1	1-1	02-01-03
Hartlepool	v	Walsall	-	-	-	-	-	-	01-01-00
Huddersfield	v	Swindon	1-2	4-0	-	2-0	2-3	-	02-02-02
Hull	v	Sheff Wed	-	-	-	-	-	-	00-00-01
Luton	v	Brentford	-	1-2	3-1	-	0-1	4-1	04-01-02
Peterboro	v	Milton K	-	-	-	-	-	-	00-00-00
Stockport	v	Wrexham	-	-	-	-	-	0-1	02-02-04
Torquay	v	Blackpool	-	-	3-2	-	-	-	02-00-00

COCA-COLA LEAGUE DIVISION TWO

Cheltenham	v	Macclesfield	-	1-1	1-1	4-1	-	3-2	03-03-02
Chester	v	Northampton	-	0-2	-	-	-	-	04-00-02
Kidderminstr	v	Grimsby	-	-	-	-	-	-	00-00-00
Lincoln	v	Darlington	-	1-0	2-2	1-1	1-1	1-1	06-05-02
Mansfield	v	Boston	-	-	-	-	-	2-1	01-00-00
Notts Co	v	Bury	-	2-2	1-0	1-2	-	-	02-01-03
Rochdale	v	Oxford Utd	-	-	-	1-1	2-1	1-2	01-01-01
Rushden & D	v	Cambridge U	-	-	-	-	4-1	-	01-00-00
Scunthorpe	v	Bristol R	-	0-2	-	1-2	2-2	1-2	00-01-03
Southend	v	Yeovil	-	-	-	-	-	0-2	00-00-01
Swansea	v	Shrewsbury	1-1	1-1	-	3-3	2-0	-	02-04-04

Sponsored by Stan James

| Wycombe | v | Leyton O | - | - | - | - | - | - | 01-00-00 |

BELL'S SCOTTISH FIRST DIVISION

Airdrie Utd	v	Partick	-	-	-	1-0/1-1	-	-	04-08-00
Clyde	v	Raith	-	-	0-0/3-1	3-2/1-2	-	0-0/4-1	04-03-03
Hamilton	v	Falkirk	2-1/0-2	-	-	-	-	-	02-04-03
Queen Sth	v	St Johnstone	-	-	-	-	0-0/1-2	1-1/1-1	00-04-01
St Mirren	v	Ross C	-	-	-	1-0/1-1	1-1/1-0	1-1/2-0	03-03-00

BELL'S SCOTTISH SECOND DIVISION

Berwick	v	Ayr	-	-	-	-	-	-	01-01-02
Dumbarton	v	Arbroath	-	-	-	-	-	1-1/1-0	03-04-03
Forfar	v	Alloa	1-2/3-1	-	-	0-1/4-1	-	1-1/2-0	07-05-03
Stirling	v	Brechin	-	-	-	1-3/1-3	-	-	04-02-03
Stranraer	v	Morton	2-3/0-1	-	-	1-4/0-0	-	-	00-01-03

BELL'S SCOTTISH THIRD DIVISION

East Fife	v	Albion	-	1-4/2-1	0-0/2-1	0-0/2-3	0-4/1-1	-	06-05-04
Gretna	v	E Stirling	-	-	-	-	2-2/3-1	2-1/5-1	03-01-00
Peterhead	v	Montrose	-	-	2-0/1-1	4-0/3-1	4-2/3-0	0-0/1-2	05-02-01
Queens P	v	Elgin	-	-	-	0-0/3-0	1-2/3-2	5-2/4-0	04-01-01
Stenhsmuir	v	C'denbeath	1-2/4-1	-	-	0-3/0-1	4-1/1-1	-	04-04-05

NATIONWIDE CONFERENCE

Accrington	v	Aldershot	-	-	-	-	-	4-2	01-00-00
Barnet	v	Carlisle	1-0	3-0	0-1	-	-	-	04-01-02
Burton	v	Northwich	-	-	-	-	1-1	0-1	00-01-01
Canvey Islnd	v	York	-	-	-	-	-	-	00-00-00
Crawley	v	Stevenage	-	-	-	-	-	-	00-00-00
Exeter	v	Gravesend	-	-	-	-	-	0-1	00-00-01
Farnborough	v	Halifax	-	-	-	-	3-0	1-0	04-01-01
Leigh RMI	v	Dagenham	-	-	1-2	2-0	1-3	2-1	02-00-02
Morecambe	v	Forest G	3-1	1-1	0-2	2-0	4-0	4-0	04-01-01
Scarborough	v	Tamworth	-	-	-	-	-	0-1	00-00-01
Woking	v	Hereford	0-1	0-2	0-3	1-0	1-2	0-1	02-00-05

SATURDAY 7 MAY 2005
FA BARCLAYCARD PREMIER LEAGUE

Arsenal	v	Liverpool	0-0	0-1	2-0	1-1	1-1	4-2	05-06-05
Aston Villa	v	Man City	-	-	2-2	-	1-0	1-1	03-04-03
Blackburn	v	Fulham	-	2-0	1-2	3-0	2-1	0-2	03-00-02
Chelsea	v	Charlton	2-1	-	0-1	0-1	4-1	1-0	04-00-02
Crystal Pal	v	Southampton	-	-	-	-	-	-	03-02-01
Everton	v	Newcastle	1-0	0-2	1-1	1-3	2-1	2-2	05-03-04
Man Utd	v	WBA	-	-	-	-	1-0	-	01-00-00
Middlesbro	v	Tottenham	0-0	2-1	1-1	1-1	5-1	1-0	04-04-02
Norwich	v	Birmingham	2-0	0-1	1-0	0-1	-	-	02-02-03
Portsmouth	v	Bolton	0-2	0-0	1-2	-	-	4-0	01-03-03

COCA-COLA LEAGUE DIVISION ONE

Blackpool	v	Barnsley	-	-	-	-	1-2	0-2	00-00-02
Bournemouth	v	Hartlepool	-	-	-	-	2-1	2-2	02-02-01
Brentford	v	Hull	0-2	-	-	-	-	-	02-00-03
Colchester	v	Torquay	-	-	-	-	-	-	04-01-03
Doncaster	v	Luton	-	-	-	-	-	-	00-00-00
Milton K	v	Tranmere	-	-	0-0	-	-	-	00-01-00
Oldham	v	Bradford	-	-	-	-	-	-	00-02-01
Port Vale	v	Peterboro	-	-	5-0	4-1	1-0	3-0	04-00-00
Sheff Wed	v	Bristol C	-	-	-	-	-	1-0	02-00-00
Swindon	v	Chesterfield	-	-	-	2-1	3-0	2-0	03-01-00
Walsall	v	Stockport	-	1-2	-	1-0	-	-	01-01-03
Wrexham	v	Huddersfield	-	-	-	1-1	-	-	01-01-01

COCA-COLA LEAGUE DIVISION TWO

Boston	v	Rochdale	-	-	-	-	3-1	2-0	02-00-00
Bristol R	v	Wycombe	0-2	1-0	1-2	-	-	-	04-00-03
Bury	v	Swansea	-	-	3-0	-	3-2	2-0	07-00-00
Cambridge U	v	Notts Co	-	1-1	2-2	0-2	-	-	01-03-01
Darlington	v	Cheltenham	-	1-0	1-0	0-2	-	2-1	04-00-01
Grimsby	v	Southend	-	-	-	-	-	-	08-01-00
Leyton O	v	Mansfield	1-1	1-3	2-1	2-0	-	3-1	08-02-01
Macclesfield	v	Rushden & D	-	-	-	0-0	0-1	-	01-01-01
Northampton	v	Kidderminstr	-	-	-	-	-	0-1	00-00-01
Oxford Utd	v	Chester	-	-	-	-	-	-	01-00-00
Shrewsbury	v	Scunthorpe	2-1	-	0-2	2-2	1-2	-	02-02-03
Yeovil	v	Lincoln	-	-	-	-	-	3-1	01-00-00

BELL'S SCOTTISH FIRST DIVISION

Falkirk	v	Queen Sth	-	-	-	-	3-0/5-0	0-0/0-2	04-01-01
Partick	v	Hamilton	-	0-1/2-2	-	-	-	-	02-05-02
Raith	v	Airdrie Utd	1-3/0-1	1-1/2-0	1-1/5-0	2-2/2-1	0-0/1-0	-	05-08-06
Ross C	v	Clyde	-	2-0/2-2	0-2/2-0	4-0/2-1	1-1/1-1	0-1/0-0	04-04-02
St Johnstone	v	St Mirren	-	-	2-0/2-2	-	2-0/1-1	1-0/1-3	09-04-03

BELL'S SCOTTISH SECOND DIVISION

Alloa	v	Stranraer	-	1-1/4-0	-	2-2/0-0	-	-	03-06-02
Arbroath	v	Stirling	0-3/1-0	2-1/3-2	3-2/1-1	-	-	-	05-01-05
Ayr	v	Dumbarton	-	-	-	-	-	-	01-03-02
Brechin	v	Forfar	-	0-2/1-0	-	-	1-0/3-4	-	04-01-04
Morton	v	Berwick	-	-	-	1-2/3-2	-	1-3/2-1	03-01-02

BELL'S SCOTTISH THIRD DIVISION

Albion	v	Gretna	-	-	-	-	2-1/1-1	1-3/1-2	01-01-02
C'denbeath	v	Queens P	0-3/0-0	0-2/2-3	-	-	-	0-1/5-1	05-06-11
E Stirling	v	Peterhead	-	-	1-3/1-0	2-3/1-0	1-4/1-1	1-3/0-3	02-01-05
Elgin	v	Stenhsmuir	-	-	-	-	-	-	00-00-00
Montrose	v	East Fife	-	1-2/1-1	0-1/1-1	2-1/0-1	0-5/0-2	-	02-04-11

SUNDAY 8 MAY 2005
COCA-COLA CHAMPIONSHIP

Brighton	v	Ipswich	-	-	-	-	1-1	-	02-02-01
Cardiff	v	QPR	-	-	-	1-1	1-2	-	00-01-01
Crewe	v	Coventry	-	-	-	1-6	-	3-1	01-00-01
Derby	v	Preston	-	-	-	-	0-2	5-1	01-00-01
Leeds	v	Rotherham	-	-	-	-	-	-	00-00-00
Millwall	v	Burnley	1-2	1-1	-	0-2	1-1	2-0	03-02-03
Nottm F	v	Gillingham	-	-	0-1	2-2	4-1	0-0	01-02-01
Plymouth	v	Leicester	-	-	-	-	-	-	02-02-00
Sunderland	v	Stoke	-	-	-	-	-	1-1	03-03-01
Watford	v	West Ham	-	1-2	-	-	-	0-0	00-01-04
Wigan	v	Reading	4-1	1-0	1-1	0-2	-	0-2	05-03-02
Wolves	v	Sheff Utd	2-1	1-0	0-0	1-0	1-3	-	04-04-03

SATURDAY 14 MAY 2005
FA BARCLAYCARD PREMIER LEAGUE

Birmingham	v	Arsenal	-	-	-	-	0-4	0-3	00-00-02
Bolton	v	Everton	-	-	-	2-2	1-2	2-0	01-03-01
Charlton	v	Crystal Pal	-	2-1	-	-	-	-	02-02-01
Fulham	v	Norwich	-	1-1	2-0	-	-	-	01-01-00
Liverpool	v	Aston Villa	0-1	0-0	3-1	1-3	1-1	1-0	09-04-03
Man City	v	Middlesbro	-	-	1-1	-	0-0	0-1	01-02-03
Newcastle	v	Chelsea	0-1	0-1	0-0	1-2	2-1	2-1	06-02-08
Southampton	v	Man Utd	0-3	1-3	2-1	1-3	0-2	1-0	06-02-08
Tottenham	v	Blackburn	2-1	-	-	1-0	0-4	1-0	05-01-04
WBA	v	Portsmouth	2-2	3-2	2-0	5-0	-	-	06-03-03

SPECIAL OFFERS FROM HIGHDOWN

SUPERMAC: MY AUTOBIOGRAPHY
Malcolm Macdonald • Paperback
Special price: £7.99
Save £1 off RRP of £8.99
plus FREE post and packing

DALGLISH: THE BIOGRAPHY
Stephen Kelly • Paperback
Special price: £7.99
Save £1 off RRP of £8.99
plus FREE post and packing

GOAL: THE ART OF SCORING
Jason Thomas • Hardback
Special price: £16.99
Save £2 off RRP of £18.99
plus FREE post and packing
Published in August

JOCK STEIN:
THE DEFINITIVE BIOGRAPHY
Archie Macpherson • Hardback
Special price: £16.99
Save £2 off RRP of £18.99
plus FREE post and packing
Published in September

CLOWN PRINCE OF SOCCER?
THE LEN SHACKLETON STORY
Colin Malam • Hardback
Special price: £16.99
Save £2 off RRP of £18.99
plus FREE post and packing
Published in September

TO ORDER BOOKS TELEPHONE 01635 578080
OR SEND A CHEQUE PAYABLE TO HIGHDOWN TO RFM HOUSE,
COMPTON, NEWBURY, BERKSHIRE, RG20 6NL